Clare Hall is a Graduate College in the University of Cambridge. Its foundation by Clare College in 1966 was inspired by the concept of a centre for advanced study which would bring together research scholars of different nationalities and academic disciplines, from graduate students studying for higher degrees to senior professors. It is unique amongst Cambridge Colleges in the importance it attaches to bringing fully into the fabric of college life senior academic visitors who come to the University on study leave, many of whom live in family accommodation within the college.

The first part of the book outlines some of the history of Clare College and places this in the context of changes in the University and in the national scene. The second part gives an account of how Clare College came to found Clare Hall, including the changing social environment that made such a foundation desirable and the financial developments that made it possible. The final chapters describe Clare Hall since its foundation in February 1966, including the grant of a Royal Charter in 1984 and the development of the new West Court beginning in 1997. The final section of the last chapter outlines of some of the highlights in Clare College since 1966 which include the admission of women undergraduates in 1972.

Richard Eden, Emeritus Professor of Energy Studies, was first elected to a Fellowship at Clare College in 1951, also becoming Director of Studies in Mathematics . He was closely involved in the founding of Clare Hall in 1966 and in that year he became a Fellow of Clare Hall, where after retirement he is now an Honorary Fellow.

The Founder's Seal given to Clare Hall (now Clare College) by Elizabeth of Clare in 1359. On the left of the seal is the shield of the arms of Edward I, and on the right are the quartered arms of Castille and Leon. These two shields are those of Lady Elizabeth's grandparents. Below is the shield adopted as her own in 1353. The legend is *aula clare pia rege semper virgo maria*. The size is 6cm × 4cm.

CLARE COLLEGE
AND THE
FOUNDING OF CLARE HALL

RICHARD EDEN

Foreword by the President of Clare Hall
Professor Gillian Beer, Litt.D., FBA

CLARE HALL IN THE UNIVERSITY OF CAMBRIDGE

Published by the President and Fellows of Clare Hall in the University of Cambridge,
Herschel Road, Cambridge CB3 9AL, United Kingdom

© The President and Fellows of Clare Hall
in the University of Cambridge, 1998

ISBN 0 9532717 0 6

British Library Cataloguing in Publication data

Eden, Richard John
Clare College and the Founding of Clare Hall.
1. Clare College – Clare Hall – History

Library of Congress cataloguing in publication data

Clare College and the Founding of Clare Hall.

Contents: Recent history of Clare College and the founding of
Clare Hall in 1966 / Richard John Eden

Printed at Cambridge University Press, Cambridge CB2 2BS United Kingdom

CONTENTS

List of illustrations	page xi
Foreword by Professor Gillian Beer, Litt.D., FBA, President of Clare Hall	xv
Preface	xix
Chronology	xxiii

1 ORIGINS — 1
Introduction	1
The university and the colleges	3
The medieval university	5
The early colleges	7
Fifteenth to eighteenth centuries	11
State intervention and university expansion	14
The second world war	17
A climate for change	18
The new colleges	19

2 CLARE COLLEGE 1815 to 1951 — 22
Henry Thirkill	22
Clare 1815 to 1914	25
Clare in the first world war	29
The inter-war years	31
The second world war	34
The post-war period 1945 to 1951	36

3 UNIVERSITY GROWTH AND COLLEGIATE VALUES — 38
Post-war Cambridge	38
Higher education: the national scene	40
Seeking to hold back the tide	42

Unrest amongst the faculty	44
The Bridges Syndicate	45
Bridges and the 1922 Royal Commission	46
The Bridges scheme in outline	49
Graduate students	52
A University Centre	55
Regent House discussions of the Bridges proposals	56
Responses and outcomes	58

4 CLARE COLLEGE: NEEDS AND OPTIONS — 60

Investment policy	60
College needs	64
The size and composition of the governing body	67
The Mastership election 1957–58	70
Ashby as Master – early days	72
A modest increase in the number of fellows	75
Visiting fellows	76
Discovering new needs	78
Clare considers the Bridges Report	79
Options for increasing the number of fellows	80
Women as guests in Clare College	84

5 PROPOSALS FOR A GRADUATE COLONY — 86

Ideas for an extension to Clare	86
Clare land in West Cambridge	89
First proposal from the extension committee	90
A hostile response	93
Heine consults fellows	95
Ashby consults graduate students	97
Northam returns from sabbatical leave	99
A site in Herschel Road	101
A revised proposal: paper A	102
Northam's alternative : paper B	104
Deadlock	105
After the meeting	107

Contents vii

6	WHICH FENCE TO JUMP?	109
	A working lunch	109
	Conflicting views	112
	Which fence to jump?	114
	A visit to Harwell	116
	A new proposal	118
	Princeton, theoretical physics and visiting scholars	121
7	A CENTRE FOR ADVANCED STUDY	125
	Ashby's introduction	125
	Presenting the proposal	126
	Northam gives support	128
	Most fellows agree	131
	Godwin suggests the name "Clare Hall"	132
	The governing body approves	133
8	COMMITTEE OF THREE	135
	Meetings	135
	Paper no. 2: aims and needs	135
	Ashby's draft of a possible appeal to foundations	138
	Amendments by Northam and Eden	140
	The first lunchtime meeting	141
	Management and links with Clare College	141
	The name "Clare Hall"	142
	First draft of the report	142
	Report to the governing body	143
	The governing body approves	145
	Other work in progress	147
9	GETTING STARTED	149
	Clare Hall working committee	149
	Selection of an architect	150
	Choosing the first fellows	152
	The first five fellows-designate	154
	Report to the governing body	156
	Announcement	158
	Provisional council	159
	More fellows	162

Choosing a President	166
A functioning society	171
An Approved Foundation	173

10 THE CONSTITUTION — 175
Introduction	175
Early ideas	176
Interim arrangements	178
The bye-fellowships problem	181
An Approved Foundation	188
Trust Deed, 1966	190
Governing body and committees	192
Royal Charter, 1984	193

11 LAND, BUILDINGS AND FINANCE — 196
Clare land in West Cambridge	196
Buildings required: first ideas	198
Properties to be acquired	200
Schedule of requirements	202
Choice of architect: Ralph Erskine	205
Erskine's plans	207
Problems getting started	208
Completion 1969	210
Clare College income and expenditure	212
Explaining the proposal	213
Initial endowments	216

12 WHILE BUILDING CLARE HALL 1966 to 1969 — 217
The start of the presidency of Brian Pippard	217
Meals	221
Administration	222
Buildings	223
Fellows and associates	226
Graduate students	230

13 CLARE HALL 1969 to 1980 — 232
Setting up house	232
Meals	237
Management and the college staff	240

Governing body		242
The presidency of Robert Honeycombe 1973 to 1980		244
Fellows		248
Visiting fellows, associates, and life members		251
Graduate students		253
Clare Hall talks, concerts and exhibitions		256
The Tanner lectures		259

14 CLARE HALL 1980 to 1998 — 261

The presidency of Michael Stoker 1980 to 1987		261
New buildings		267
The presidency of Anthony Low 1987 to 1994		270
Books, lectures, study groups, concerts, and art		276
The Longair review		278
The presidency of Gillian Beer 1994–		282
Meanwhile in Clare College 1966 to 1998		295
Appendix 1	Ashby's talk on the founding of Clare Hall	299
Appendix 2	Proposal for a Clare Institute for Advanced Study	311
Appendix 3	Fellows of Clare College, January 1964	315
Appendix 4	The Committee of Three	317
Appendix 5	Clare Hall Working Committee, and the Provisional Council	319
Appendix 6	Presidents of Clare Hall	321
Appendix 7	Clare Hall numbers in selected years	323
Appendix 8	The Tanner Lectures	326
Appendix 9	Clare Hall Funds	328
Appendix 10	Plans of Clare Hall Main College and West Court	331
Bibliographical References		334
Index		337

LIST OF ILLUSTRATIONS

The Founder's Seal given to Clare Hall (now Clare College) by Elizabeth of Clare in 1359, *frontispiece* photograph courtesy of the Master, Fellows and Scholars of Clare College

1. Drawing of Clare Hall (now Clare College) by Edmund Prideaux (photograph by Keith Papworth), courtesy of the Master, Fellows and Scholars of Clare College — *page* 13
2. Loggan's View of the 'New' Buildings of Clare Hall (now Clare College), courtesy of the Master, Fellows and Scholars of Clare College — 14
3. Sir Henry Thirkill, Master of Clare College 1939–58 (painting by Frank Eastman), courtesy of the Master, Fellows and Scholars of Clare College — 23
4. Ackermann's view of Clare Hall (now Clare College) and barges on the river, courtesy of Prof Bob Hepple, Master of Clare College — 27
5. Clare College, opening of the Memorial Court, Armistice Day 1924, courtesy of the Master, Fellows and Scholars of Clare College — 32
6. *Conversation Piece* Discussions in the Combination Room, Clare College: H. Thirkill (Master, standing), W. Telfer (Dean, centre), W. J. Harrison (Bursar, left), (painting by Terence Cuneo, 1949), courtesy of the Master, Fellows and Scholars of Clare College — 35
7. Brian Cooper with Gerda Cooper, Mayor and Mayoress of Cambridge 1970–71, Bursar of Clare College 1949–1978, Fellow 1943– (photograph courtesy of Cambridge Evening News) — 61

List of illustrations

8. Brian Reddaway, Fellow of Clare College 1938– , Professor of Political Economy 1969–80, Emeritus 1980 (photograph by Edward Leigh) — 63
9. Eric Ashby, Master of Clare College 1958–75, courtesy of Prof. Bob Hepple, Master of Clare College — 73
10. John Northam, Fellow of Clare College 1950–72, 1987– , Senior Tutor 1957–66 — 99
11. Richard Eden, 1962 — 120
12. Richard and Elsie Eden, 1984 — 122
13. Fellows of Clare College on the Clare Hall Working Committee: — 151
    (a) Harry Godwin, (b) Bill Kingsford, (c) Don Holister, (d) Colin Turpin (advisor). (photographs by Tim Hunt, Clare College)
14. Fellows-designate of Clare Hall, 1964: — 155
    (a) Will Taylor, (b) Dick David, (c) Terence Armstrong, (d) Peter Dronke (photographs by Edward Leigh)
15. Fellows-designate of Clare Hall, 1964–66: — 164
    (a) John Coales, (b) Carmen Blacker, (c) Patrick Echlin, (d) Keith Cameron (photographs by Edward Leigh)
16. Ralph Erskine, Architect of Clare Hall 1964–69, 1983–85, Honorary Fellow 1997 — 206
17. Paul Mellon, KBE, D.Litt. Benefactor and Honorary Fellow of Clare College and Clare Hall — 215
18. Foundations for the Clare Hall buildings, 1967 — 223
19. *Elmside* from the garden (photograph by Nigel Bush, Reeve Photography) — 224
20. Clare Hall Topping Out by the President, Brian Pippard, 1969 (photograph courtesy of Cambridge Newspapers Limited) — 226
21. Opening of the Clare Hall new buildings by the University Vice-Chancellor, Sir Eric Ashby, with the President of Clare Hall, Professor Brian Pippard, 30 September 1969 (architect Ralph Erskine, photograph courtesy of Cambridge Evening News). — 233
22. Viewing the Clare Hall apartments, after the opening of the new buildings 30 September 1969, the University Chancellor, Lord — 234

	Adrian, the Vice-Chancellor, Sir Eric Ashby, and the President of Clare Hall, Professor Brian Pippard (architect Ralph Erskine, photograph courtesy of Cambridge Evening News)	
23.	Children in Clare Hall Family Walk	235
24.	Entrance stairs to the Common Room in Clare Hall (photograph by Nigel Bush, Reeve Photography)	236
25.	Clare Hall dining room, from Elmside garden (photograph by the author)	238
26.	Clare Hall dining room, interior view (photograph by Nigel Bush, Reeve Photography)	239
27.	Daryl Pool, Chef-Manager (photograph 1997 by the author)	240
28.	Robert Honeycombe, President 1973–80, with June Honeycombe	245
29.	*Keyneside*, renamed *Leslie Barnett House* in 1996	255
30.	Signing the Trust Deed for the Tanner Lectures Foundation: (a) Obert Tanner and (b) Eric Ashby, with Audrey Glauert JP supervising	258
31.	Michael Stoker, President 1980–87, with Veronica Stoker	262
32.	The Royal Charter for Clare Hall, 1984	265
33.	*Conversation Piece* in Clare Hall: Brian Pippard, Richard Eden, and Eric Ashby (Drawing by Bob Tulloch, 1984)	267
34.	The *Michael Stoker Building* and the Clare Hall Apartments (architect, Ralph Erskine)	269
35.	Anthony Low, President 1987–94, with Belle Low	271
36.	(a) Leslie Barnett, Senior Tutor 1972–88, Emeritus Fellow 1988 (b) Marjorie Chibnall, Fellow 1971–83, Emeritus Fellow 1983 (photographs (a) and (b) by Edward Leigh) (c) Geoffrey Bailey, Senior Tutor, 1989–96 (d) Hugh Whittaker, Senior Tutor 1996–	273
37.	The Gamelin Band in Clare Hall dining room, May 1995	277
38.	(a) Malcolm Longair, Fellow 1967–80, 1991– , Vice-President 1994– (b) Nick Shackleton, Fellow 1974–	279
39.	Gillian Beer, President 1994– (photograph by Jason Bell, courtesy of CAM, Cambridge University)	283
40.	Clare Hall Novice Crew of the Gillian Beer Boat at Clare College Boat House, 1997 (photograph by Priscilla Green)	284

xiv *List of illustrations*

41. (a) Geoffrey Cass, Fellow 1979– (photograph by Dave Parfitt, courtesy of Cambridge Newspapers Ltd.) (b) Edward Jarron, Fellow and Bursar 1996– (photograph by the author).	286
42. Gathering at Clare Hall on 26 September 1997 (a) Charlotte and Brian Pippard with Michael Stoker (centre), Tony Harding is on the right of the picture (photograph by the author) (b) John Northam with Elsie Eden (photograph by the author)	289
43. The *Libby Gardner Memorial Fountain:* David Gardner (left), Gillian Beer, and Nathan David (sculptor, right) (photograph by the author)	290
44. Brian and Charlotte Pippard with the Pro-Vice-Chancellor David Harrison, at the opening of the *Brian Pippard Building*, September 1997 (architects, Nicholas Ray Associates, photograph by Nigel Bush, Reeve Photography)	291
45. Clare Hall West Court from the garden (photograph by Nigel Bush, Reeve Photography)	292
46. The Terrace at Clare Hall West Court, 26 September 1997 (photograph by Nigel Bush, Reeve Photography)	293
47. The *Richard Eden Rooms* in Clare Hall West Court (photograph by Nigel Bush, Reeve Photography)	294
48. Plan of Clare Hall, Main Buildings	332
49. Plan of Clare Hall, West Court	333

FOREWORD

By Professor Gillian Beer, Litt.D., FBA
President Of Clare Hall

Richard Eden's account of Clare College and the Founding of Clare Hall is a heartening record of generosity and innovation. The Fellows of Clare effected more than even they perhaps foresaw when in 1964 they began to envisage the founding of a 'Clare Institute' for advanced research. As this volume makes clear in all its detail the original plan for a centre within Clare College expanded over the years into an entirely independent institution which yet retains ties of history and gratitude with Clare. Though many things have changed from the original concept, the fundamental ideas have been retained, and grown. Clare Hall is, as was originally intended, a place that welcomes scholarly visitors and their families from all over the world. It is a centre where interaction is valued, rather than hierarchy. It encourages contact between graduate students (also from all over the world) with Fellows, who may be short-term visitors or permanent Cambridge residents. As President of Clare Hall from 1994 I have been fortunate to join a community whose traditions of openness, international conversation, and intellectual distinction are already well established (a community that denies any interest in conventional traditions while creatively fostering its own ways!).

Any community is always in the process of change. When I arrived at the college I realised that the most pressing need was more housing for our graduate students. This was not a new idea, but the situation had become more urgent since we were by then able to house only a third of our graduate students – insufficient even for all of our first-year students. Three and a half years later we are currently housing eighty per cent of our graduate population and are now able to offer some housing for graduates with children. This change has been brought about by the commitment and hard work of many people, not least my predecessor, Anthony Low, who helped to organise the university fund for graduate housing, from which we have received grants. After some months of serious discussion the Governing Body decided to commit major college funds to transforming the housing situation of our students and we have bought four houses in the vicinity, rented others and built a fine building – the Brian Pippard Building, designed by Nicholas Ray Associates – within the college grounds. The implementation of such a major programme would not have been possible without the skill of our Bursar, Ed Jarron, and of our Domestic Bursar, Diana Smith. It demanded a great deal of our college staff, too, who rose to the occasion with good will. We also needed some luck, which we had in the form of a rise in the stock market during the crucial time of planning, buying, and building!

The building programme for graduates gives support to a group of hardworking and in the main underfunded people who are the future of many countries. We have seen the good effects for the college of gathering the GSB more closely in, visible through the increased presence and involvement of graduates in college life. Housing and computer facilities, together with tutorial support, underpin the college welfare of our graduates. Participation in a lively and open community is something they help to make, and share. As I write, the future of the college fee system is under review. Whatever the outcome, Clare Hall will continue to provide intellectual and social space for a graduate community.

Bricks and mortar bring with them fresh challenges, intellectual and social. We were fortunate indeed to acquire 11 Herschel Road – now named West Court – the former family home of Lord and Lady Rothschild. This large house with its fine garden, three minutes walk from the main building, has already provided the college with nine new apartments for visiting fellows and spacious public rooms, suitable for meetings, concerts, and parties. For the first time it is now easy to have more than two events happening at the same time and we need no longer fear that the proximity of concerts and parties with drown each other out! The second phase, now with the city planners, will mix the college in new and old ways. New Visiting Fellow apartments and a number of student study-bedrooms will be provided round a courtyard alongside the house. There is a swimming pool, at present being refurbished, and other communal social facilities are included in the plan.

One of the special resources of Clare Hall is our lecture programmes. We benefit enormously both from the input of college members, particularly Visiting Fellows, through talks and evening seminars, and from the internationally known Tanner Lectures and the Ashby Lecture with its attached period of residence for the speaker. The Tanner lectures, generously endowed by the Tanner Foundation of the late Obert Tanner, have been given on an extraordinary array of topics in the last few years: for example, the organisation of the universe, the history of jazz, the thought processes of monkeys. What makes the Tanner lectures peculiarly valuable is the opportunity to close with a day seminar to which a number of respondents are invited. Last year's event, around the work of the primatologist Dorothy Cheney, brought together distinguished speakers from various departments in Cambridge who found themselves engaging in interdisciplinary work with colleagues not previously known to them, colleagues whose own fields ranged from human autism to linguistics to archaeology and animal behaviour. Such an occasion is an object lesson in the 'human values' that the Tanner lectures specifically seek to enhance.

These special events give zest to college life but the experience of daily living as a community is what people will most remember. Almost all of our Fellows have busy university teaching and research careers alongside their college fellowships and the sheer weight of commitment needed to keep abreast of fast-moving subjects makes it difficult for all of them to be seen in college as often as they would like. At some point in the future we hope to be able to give more study space to Fellows. Being a graduate institution, very little teaching directly for our particular students goes on within the college; nevertheless, it would be to the benefit of the college and fellows if it were possible for more fellows to make the college their daily base for teaching, whether undergraduates or graduates. There is also a need for quiet research rooms for scholars. Given the other pressures on their time, many of the fellows are remarkably present at Clare Hall.

One of the most productive ideas in the formation of the college was that of transforming Visiting Fellows into Life Members once their initial visit was completed. As a result we have the advantage of many former Visiting Fellows returning for short, and sometimes longer, stays. They bring with them a deep knowledge of Clare Hall and Cambridge which benefits us all. Indeed, some of the effervescent atmosphere of life in Clare Hall must be attributed to the fact that our forty Visiting Fellows are on leave from their own institutions, released for a while from administrative burdens, with time to think, talk, and range further through the fields of knowledge! The discoveries and accords that spring up between people working in apparently disparate areas of knowledge is one of the great benefits that an advanced research community can bring. The presence of such a range of distinguished workers is a benefit to the university at large. Without Clare Hall as a base many people would be less willing to come for a relatively short time to visit a university department. The presence of a college whose function is to accommodate single people and families alike in a 'village' community is a quite distinctive gain to Cambridge life.

In writing this Foreword I was invited to concentrate on Clare Hall, its present and its future. That I have done, but in doing so it is again borne in on me that without the creativity and foresight of a group of Clare Fellows in the 1960s none of this would have been possible. So I end with renewed thanks to Clare and its Master, and to those Fellows. Among them was Richard Eden, who in this volume has provided a lively and learned account of the two colleges, Clare and Clare Hall.

Gillian Beer
January 1998

PREFACE

The Governing Body of Clare College began to discuss the possibility of a substantial expansion in the fellowship in 1957, partly to meet tutorial and teaching needs in the college and partly to help provide college fellowships for more teaching and research staff in the University. After a pause for the election of Sir Eric Ashby as Master in succession to Sir Henry Thirkill, there was a modest increase in the number of fellows but the need for more was reinforced by the report in 1962 of a University Syndicate on the relationship between the University and the Colleges, chaired by Lord Bridges with Ashby as deputy chairman. At the same time there was concern about the lack of facilities, especially housing, for the increasing numbers of graduate students associated with the University's expanding and successful research programme. During 1962–63 the fellows of Clare College considered setting up a new institution for graduate students, to be part of the college but with some degree of autonomy. However, the proposal did not attract enthusiasm from graduate students and it was opposed by some fellows for whom the main concern was still the need for a substantial expansion in the fellowship.

The dilemma was resolved when Ashby received a new proposal in January 1964 for an Institute for Advanced Study having special relations with Clare College. The aim of the Clare Institute was to create a community of men and women engaged in advanced study or research, with a membership that would include visiting fellows, research fellows, graduate students and permanent fellows, and with family housing in college that would include a substantial number of the visiting fellows. The word 'Institute' did not find favour and the suggestion was made that the new community be called Clare Hall, the ancient name by which Clare College itself had been known for over five hundred years. The proposal was then unanimously approved in principle by the Governing Body, which appointed a committee of three – Ashby, Eden and Northam – to work out the details. At the same time, it was agreed to make separate arrangements to provide housing for Clare College's graduate students. There was an exceptional warmth about the governing body's discussion on that day, the fellows knew that they were making a landmark decision and most had no doubts about their support for it, though few could have been aware of the remarkable success that would eventually be achieved. Although there were subsequent changes from the proposed institutional relationship between Clare Hall and Clare College, the ideas for the new community that were approved in January 1964 remain the essential features of Clare Hall, now an independent college in the University.

The first part of the book outlines some of the history of Clare College and places this in the context of changes in the University and in the national scene. The second part gives an account of how Clare College came to found Clare Hall. This part describes the changing educational and social environment that made such a foundation desirable and the financial developments that made it possible. The final chapters are about the history of Clare Hall since it became an Approved Foundation in the University in February 1966. These cover the initial period to 1969 when Clare Hall was still based in Clare College, the establishment of the college in its new buildings, the granting of the Royal Charter, and more recently the expansion that included the addition of Clare Hall West Court nearby in Herschel Road. I conclude the final chapter by sketching some of the highlights in Clare College since 1966 which included the admission of women undergraduates in 1972.

The book is also about the many participants in the foundation of Clare Hall. As the Master of Clare College, Ashby played a crucial role, always persuasive but also ready to adopt new ideas and to work for their success. In particular it was his willingness to adapt to circumstances that allowed the transition of the idea of Clare Hall as part of Clare College to a more independent 'Approved Foundation' with the same objectives – and eventually to an independent College with its own Royal Charter. The book is a tribute to Eric Ashby, and to John Northam whose intervention in the Autumn of 1963 gave time for new ideas to develop and whose guidance was so valuably decisive, to Brian Cooper and Brian Reddaway whose financial expertise and practical support made the foundation possible, and to the fellows of Clare College in the 1950's and 1960's whose diversity led to many ideas and whose cohesion enabled them to make a remarkable decision. It is a tribute to Harry Godwin who suggested the name Clare Hall, to the architect Ralph Erskine for his design, and to the presidents, fellows and graduate students in Clare Hall who have contributed to the successful development since its foundation.

In 1976, after writing the edited version of his talk on the founding of Clare Hall, Eric Ashby gave me his own files on the founding dating from January 1964. Later, I obtained John Northam's files on Clare Hall, which he had left in Clare College when he moved to a professorship in Bristol. Using those files and my own, I prepared a draft of the middle part of the book after my retirement in 1989 and a visit to Princeton. This was read early in 1992 by Eric Ashby and John Northam. By then, I had confirmed from annotations on the filed records that the story of our collaboration in the autumn of 1963 described in Eric's talk in 1976 had made use of some poetic license. It was no surprise that Eric cheerfully accepted this when we discussed the draft at his home in Newnham a few months before his death in October 1992.

Encouraged by the comments from Ashby and Northam, I began to prepare this account of Clare College and the founding of Clare Hall in more detail, but was diverted into the fascinating history of Clare College in the newly re-organised College Archives – and readers will observe this interest in the early chapters of the present book, though there remains a need for a more detailed history, particularly for the 19th and 20th centuries. I am grateful to Suzy Thompson, the assistant archivist in Clare, for her help at this stage of my study.

By December 1995, it seemed desirable to have the book read by a professional historian and I am indebted to my cousin-in-law Christopher Brooke, emeritus professor of ecclesiastical history, for his helpful and detailed comments that led *inter alia* to substantial restructuring. John Northam also made valuable comments on the new version. Some further changes and the addition of a chronology followed from comments by Carmen Blacker and Michael Loewe, emeritus fellows of Clare Hall, who read a later version in 1997. This near-final version was read by Brian Pippard, the first President of Clare Hall and formerly a Fellow of Clare College, and by Brian Cooper who was the Bursar of Clare College when Clare Hall was founded, and I am indebted to them for their detailed comments, corrections and suggestions. I thank the other former

Presidents of Clare Hall: Robert Honeycombe, Michael Stoker, and Anthony Low, for reading several chapters of the typescript and for their valuable recollections. I am grateful also to the Master of Clare College, Bob Hepple, for reading the typescript in some detail and for his suggestions and comments, and to the President of Clare Hall, Gillian Beer, for reading the typescript, for her comments, and for writing the *Foreword* to the book.

I am greatly indebted to the Master, Fellows and Scholars of Clare College and the President, Fellows and Graduate Students of Clare Hall for allowing me to use material from the college archives, and I wish to thank members of both colleges for providing or advising on illustrations, and Keith Papworth in the Cavendish Laboratory for his help in their preparation. I also wish to thank Edward Jarron, Bursar of Clare Hall for his help on arrangements for publication, and the staff at the Printing House of the Cambridge University Press for their help and advice in relation to the printing.

My special thanks go to my wife Elsie for her contribution to our joint involvement with Clare College and Clare Hall, for encouraging a degree of priority in my work on this history, and for her detailed help in reading drafts.

Richard Eden
Clare Hall
February 1998

CHRONOLOGY

1209	Beginnings of the University of Cambridge.
1326	University Hall founded by Richard de Badew.
1338	University Hall renamed *Clare Hall* by Lady Clare.
1359	Statutes for Clare Hall approved.
1570	New statutes for the University and the Colleges.
1840	Clare Hall undergraduates number about 40.
1856	Clare Hall renamed as Clare College.
1869, 1871	Women's Colleges founded – Girton and Newnham.
1874	Cavendish Laboratory for Physics opened.
1882	Government Commission imposes new Statutes on the University. Colleges are required to contribute to the University's income.
1910	Clare College undergraduates number about 200.
1914–18	First World War.
1919	Government grants emergency financial aid to the University.
1922	Royal Commission appointed for Oxford and Cambridge Universities.
1926	New Statutes for Cambridge University and the Colleges.
1939	Thirkill becomes Master of Clare.
1939–45	Second World War.
1953	Clare Investments sub-committee begins to invest in equities.
1955	Clare forms a Needs Committee to consider improvements and developments.
1955	General Board report seeks to limit growth of the University.
1956	Regent House rejects General Board's recommendations.
1957	Clare Tutorial Committee reports on the needs to expand the college fellowship.
1958	Ashby becomes Master of Clare College.
1959	Nearly half of the senior members of the University are not Fellows of a College.
1960	Bridges Syndicate set up to examine the relations between the University and the Colleges, Ashby is Vice-Chairman.
1962	Clare Committee reports on the consequences of increasing the fellowship.
1962	Clare Extension Committee formed.

1963 May	Clare Extension Committee recommends new centre (colony) for Graduate Students in Chesterton Lane – the Governing Body raises objections.
1963 Jul	Ashby finds that Graduate Students are not keen on a graduate colony.
1963 Jul	Women guests will be allowed to dine in Clare one night each week.
1963 Sep	Northam rejoins Extension Committee after sabbatical leave, and criticises the proposal for a graduate colony.
1963 Oct	Clare exchanges its land in Grange Road for properties in Herschel Road in a triangular deal with the University and St. John's.
1963 Oct	Extension Committee now recommends graduate colony should be on the Herschel Road site. Other changes do not remove opposition.
1963 Nov	Eden joins Ashby and Northam for working lunch to seek a compromise on conflicting views about an extension to the College.
1963 Dec	Ashby circulates new papers with the reports by the Extension Committee and by Northam for Governing Body to reach a decision on 11 January 1964.
1964 Jan 7	Eden writes proposal for Clare Institute for Advanced Study to include men and women, with visiting fellowships and family accommodation.
1964 Jan 9	Ashby circulates Eden's proposal to the Governing Body.
1964 Jan 11	Clare Governing Body gives unanimous approval in principle for the proposal, Godwin suggests the name *Clare Hall*
1964 Jan 11	Ashby, Eden and Northam (the 'Committee of Three') are asked to work on details and to make recommendations. The Needs Committee is asked to consider separate provision for Clare College Graduate Students' accommodation.
1964 Mar	Governing Body approves steps for immediate action on Clare Hall suggested by Committee of Three but with earlier admission of Graduate Students.
1964 Apr	Ashby on leave in the USA (April to June) – visits Paul Mellon, who suggests that he approaches the Old Dominion Foundation about Clare Hall. Ashby also has discussions with the Ford Foundation in New York.
1964 Apr/Jun	Clare Hall Working Committee, chaired by Godwin, identifies short-list of candidates for first five Fellows-designate, prepares brief for architect for new buildings in Herschel Road and a short-list for the choice of an architect.

Chronology

1964 Jun	Ashby returns from USA and Governing Body approves the first five Fellows-designate of Clare Hall: Taylor, David, Armstrong, Hesse, and Dronke.
1964 Jul	Press release by Clare College announces intentions for Clare Hall – ' a new graduate society for resident and visiting scholars within the college'. Ralph Erskine visits Clare and is appointed as architect for Clare Hall.
	The Old Dominion (Mellon) Foundation provides a substantial endowment and the Ford Foundation makes five year grant for visiting fellowships.
	Ashby chairs the first meeting of the Provisional Council of Clare Hall.
1964 Jul/Nov	Ideas about Clare Hall make a transition from a centre that is part of Clare College to a separate Approved Foundation with Clare College as Trustee.
1964 Oct	Clare Hall dinners commence weekly on Tuesdays for members of the Provisional Council and guests in the Master's Lodge of Clare College.
1964 Nov	Eden, Coales and Blacker are elected Fellows-designate of Clare Hall.
	The first elections of Visiting Fellows are made.
1964 Dec	Draft plans by Erskine for Clare Hall resemble the eventual layout.
1965 Feb	Provisional Council collects suggestions of candidates for President.
1965 Jun	Outline planning application made for Clare Hall buildings.
1965 Jul	Brian Pippard is elected as President-designate of Clare Hall and becomes a member of the Provisional Council.
1966 Jan	Building licence for Clare Hall granted provided construction begins by October.
1966 Feb	Clare Hall becomes an Approved Foundation on 8 February 1966 with Clare College as sole Trustee and Pippard as the first President.
	Clare College makes grant to Clare Hall for buildings and an initial endowment.
	Clare Hall has 18 Fellows: 10 Official, 5 Research, and 3 Visiting.
1966 Oct	Cameron appointed secretary/bursar for Clare Hall, but the main administration and finance continues until 1969 with Clare College Office under the bursar (Cooper).
	First stage of the buildings is started (foundations and basement).
1966 Nov	Echlin becomes first Praelector.
1967 Jan	Armstrong becomes first Tutor for Clare Hall Graduate Students.

1967 Feb	Clare Hall Governing Body meets in Elmside 11 February. First special dinner 16 February, held in Trinity Old Kitchen. Clare Hall College Council is set up.
1967 Apr	Longair becomes a Research Fellow in the first competitive election.
1967 May	Clare Hall has 37 Fellows: 13 Official, 12 Research, and 12 Visiting.
1967 May	Economies on building costs cause cancellation of upper floor of 10 studies. Second stage of building starts.
1967–69	Ashby is Vice-Chancellor of the University.
1967 Oct	4 Graduate Students admitted and resident in Elmside.
1967 Oct	Clare Hall Tuesday dinners are relocated to the University Centre.
1968 Apr	Associates to form a new class of membership of Clare Hall.
1968 Oct	18 Graduate Students in Clare Hall. Magic Room in Elmside to be renovated for use as a studio.
1969 Mar	Fellowship Committee is formed.
1969 May	New buildings completed, furnished during May and June.
1969 Jun	Francoise Mattock appointed manageress, in post 1969–77. First meals served at lunch on 20 June. Lunch daily, dinners on Tuesdays only.
1969 Aug	Pippard family take up residence in President's House. Visiting Fellows' families and two Research Fellows take up residence.
1969 Sep	Formal opening of Clare Hall buildings by Sir Eric Ashby.
1969 Oct	Clare Hall now has 45 Fellows: 17 Official, 17 Research, 11 Visiting; 16 Associates, and 33 Graduate Students.
1969 Oct	Weekly dinner night is changed to Wednesdays, supper on other weekdays. Clare Hall evening talks begin.
1970 Mar	Brian Routledge appointed College Clerk, and is in post 1970–95.
1972	Women undergraduates are admitted to Clare College
1972	Anthony Low is a Visiting Fellow in Clare Hall
1972 Mar	Daryl Pool appointed Chef and later Chef-Manager in Clare Hall.
1972 Sep	Leslie Barnett becomes Clare Hall Tutor for graduate students.
1972 Oct	Clare Hall graduate students now number 59, about half from overseas.
1973 Jan	Avril Yeo appointed Bursar following resignation of Cameron.
1973	Ivor Giaever, Visiting Fellow 1969, receives Nobel Prize for Physics.
1973 Oct	Robert Honeycombe becomes President of Clare Hall. Brian Pippard becomes a Professorial Fellow of Clare Hall.

Chronology

1973–80	High inflation and economic recession lead to reduced (real) endowment income: an establishment charge is introduced for visiting fellows, stipendiary research fellowships are postponed, and other grants to fellows and students are reduced.
1975 Jan	Lord Ashby is elected as the first Honorary Fellow.
1975	Brian Pippard receives a Knighthood.
1976 Jan	Derek Adams appointed Bursar of Clare Hall following the death of Avril Yeo.
1976 Feb	Tenth anniversary dinner: Lord Ashby lectures on The Founding of Clare Hall.
1978	Tanner Lecture series begins.
1980	Michael Stoker receives a Knighthood and becomes President of Clare Hall.
	Robert Honeycombe becomes a Professorial Fellow.
	Tony Harding becomes Bursar of Clare Hall.
	No. 3 Herschel Road is purchased, providing rooms for 9 graduate students.
1983	Ashby Lecture series begins.
1984	The Royal Charter for Clare Hall is approved and sealed on 22 October.
	Sir Robert Megarry, Vice-Chancellor of the Supreme Court of England becomes The Visitor to Clare Hall.
	A Coat of Arms for Clare Hall is approved by the Heralds of the College of Arms.
1984	The Magic Room Studio is converted to the Ashby Library.
1984/94	Clare Hall receives grants towards its endowment from the Colleges' Fund.
1985	John Garrod becomes Bursar of Clare Hall on retirement of Harding.
1986	Former Fellows and Associates are retitled as Life Members.
	Former Research Students (the Alumni) are retitled Graduate Members.
1987	The Michael Stoker Building is completed (architect Ralph Erskine) providing accommodation for 16 graduate students.
	Joseph Brodsky, visiting fellow and poet-in-residence 1977–78 is awarded the Nobel Prize for Literature.
	Anthony Low becomes President of Clare Hall.
1989	Sir Nicholas Browne-Wilkinson, becomes The Visitor to Clare Hall, in succession to Sir Robert Megarry.
1990	Robert Honeycombe receives a Knighthood.
1991	Geoffrey Cass receives a Knighthood.
1987–94	Graduate Student numbers approach 100.
1992	Sir Donald Nichols becomes The Visitor to Clare Hall.

1992	Longair Report on the Future of Clare Hall.
1993	Clare Hall rents 12 apartments in Benian's Court for Visiting Fellows.
1993/94	McLean Studies (architects Nicholas Ray Associates) are built on the site of Elmside's old coach house.
1994	Gillian Beer becomes President of Clare Hall.
	Anthony Low becomes an Emeritus Fellow of Clare Hall.
1995	Nick Shackleton, Professorial Fellow, is awarded the Crafoord Prize.
	Two houses are bought in Newnham for use by Graduate Students of Clare Hall.
1996	Edward Jarron becomes Bursar of Clare Hall in January 1996, following the death of John Garrod.
	Two houses are bought in Barton Road for use by Graduate Students.
	The Clare College – Clare Hall investment portfolios are separated.
	Sir Richard Scott becomes the Visitor to Clare Hall.
1997	Clare Hall purchases the large house at no.11 Herschel Road, and it is renamed Clare Hall West Court. The Longair Committee on the future of Clare Hall is reconvened to consider new options, leading to the conversion of Clare Hall West Court (architects Nicholas Ray Associates) to provide apartments for Visiting Fellows, and addtional public rooms for seminars, meetings, concerts or meals. The public rooms are named the Richard Eden Rooms.
	The Brian Pippard Building (architect Nicholas Ray) is completed and provides more accommodation for graduate students, including family apartments. The Libby Gardner memorial fountain is dedicated by David Gardner.
1998	Plans are prepared for building more accommodation for visiting fellows and graduate students in the grounds of Clare Hall West Court, and for a swimming pool, fitness centre, and a tennis court on adjacent land.

Plans of the main Clare Hall buildings and of West Court are illustrated in Appendix 10.

An outline of developments in Clare College after the founding of Clare Hall in February 1966 is given at the end of chapter 14.

Chapter 1

ORIGINS

INTRODUCTION

Clare Hall is a college for advanced study. Its members include graduate students studying for a higher degree in the university, research fellows working at post-doctoral level, permanent fellows holding faculty or research posts in the university, and visiting fellows who are on leave from their faculty positions in universities around the world. It is in the importance attached to the visiting fellowship programme that Clare Hall is differentiated from other graduate colleges in the university, and it was this concept that attracted the exceptional support from its founders.

The founding of Clare Hall in February 1966 was an act of remarkable generosity and foresight by the Master and Fellows of Clare College. In addition to the gift of land and buildings and an initial endowment, Clare College made a gift of the ancient name 'Clare Hall' by which the college itself had been known for more than five hundred years until its modern title was adopted in the mid 19th century. In 1984 Clare Hall became a fully independent graduate college in Cambridge University with its own Royal Charter and Statutes.

In this account of the founding of Clare Hall, I shall explore the origins of this remarkable initiative by the governing body of Clare College. Dominating the scene were the changing relations between the university and the colleges and the changing character of these institutions themselves. Within the university the 19th century had seen the beginnings of the modern structure of teaching and research in the sciences, aided by external pressure from the government. The 20th century saw growth and change in all faculties, made possible by the increasing level of financial support from central government, which was accompanied by diversification of subjects studied and taught.

In parallel with these changes in the size and character of the institutions in the university, there were changes in the social character of the academic scene. This was transformed firstly by the growth of the colleges in the 19th and early 20th century, and then by the changes in society fashioned by the impact of the second world war. Within Clare College it was these latter changes that prepared the way for the decision to found Clare Hall. However, they built on changes that had begun more than 100 years earlier, through increased wealth from the agricultural gains from enclosures, and through growth in the number of students from only 40 in 1840, mostly planning to become clergymen, to more than 200 by the turn of the century, with much more diverse careers in mind. It was after the second world war that the fellowship itself began to grow rapidly, and in response to perceived societal needs the admission of students was increasingly determined by academic merit.

A changing approach by colleges to the admission of undergraduates was accompanied by pressure in the university for increased graduate admissions and the provision of new facilities for them. These included the development of new research groups, particularly in the science departments, where external funding from government or industry allowed the appointment of new academic staff, wholly or primarily engaged in research. This conflicted with the needs of colleges, where the increased concern for academic standards led to an increased desire for 'in house' supervision by fellows of the college. The new research staff in the university and increasing numbers of the lecturers were often in subject areas with few undergraduates, so they did not meet the teaching needs of colleges. By 1960 this had caused such an imbalance between those academic staff with a college fellowship and those without, that there was concern that the collegiate character of the university was under threat. It was this concern that eventually set the scene for the discussions in Clare College that led to the founding of Clare Hall, though – as we shall see – the exploration of ideas for changing or developing the college had begun much earlier.

The second part of this account of the founding of Clare Hall describes the evolution from an initial agreement in principle, to found 'a centre for advanced study having close association with the college', to the practical steps of setting up an 'Approved Foundation' as a preliminary to the creation of a full college. The third part follows developments during the early years of Clare Hall from the Approved Foundation in 1966 to the Royal Charter in 1984 and beyond.

THE UNIVERSITY AND THE COLLEGES

The university and the colleges are interdependent – most fellows of colleges other than research fellows hold university posts and most university lecturers and professors are fellows of colleges, though (excluding research fellows) in almost all cases the university is their principal employer. Undergraduates are admitted to the university through a selection process in each college, their lectures and examinations are arranged by the university, but their colleges arrange tutorials. Graduate students are admitted by the university but this is subject to their acceptance also by a college. Thus, most academics in Cambridge have a joint responsibility to the university and to a college and a desire to maintain the collegiate character of the university. However, the colleges and the university are also independent institutions, each with its own endowment, royal charter and statutes. Together, they form a federation with interdependence ensured by interlocking statutes, by shared committees and through mutual support. The university is the federation itself, as well as being a constituent member.

There are 31 colleges in the university, of which two (Clare Hall and Darwin) admit only graduates and several other of the more recent foundations cater primarily for graduates or for mature students as undergraduates. The colleges vary in size from less than 200 students to over 600, and three admit women only. For undergraduates, each college takes responsibility for providing accommodation for the students it has admitted. All colleges are willing to accept students in any of the full range of subjects that can be studied in the university, though some have a marginally stronger reputation in some subjects. A college will also, through tutors and directors of studies, advise undergraduates on their academic options and arrange supervisions of students in small groups or individually. For many undergraduates the social, cultural and intellectual environment that is provided by their college will prove to be the most lasting benefit that will be recalled in later years. However, it is the university that provides undergraduates with all the formal lectures, laboratory classes and examinations that lead to degrees. These are managed by departments, which sometimes also arrange departmental supervisions on behalf of colleges. The teaching in related subjects is coordinated by faculties within which the departments are grouped.

Research students are admitted to the university, formally by the Board of Graduate Studies, though each such student is also required to be accepted by a college. In practice, it is the faculties or departments that make the initial decision to admit a student, and often in science subjects this decision is delegated to the research group, or the relevant member of the faculty, with whom the student is likely to working for a research degree. There is a close relation between teaching and research in the university, and most university lecturers and professors are active in both. In some subjects this is also true for research fellows, who are likely to be helping their college by giving supervisions. In some cases also, research students may do some teaching through helping in examples classes, seminars, or in college supervisions.

The dual involvement of most teaching staff in college and in university activities does not extend to all groups of graduate employees. Research staff in university departments or institutes and full-time administrative staff in the university central offices or departments may be members of a college but they only rarely hold fellowships. In addition the technical, clerical and service staff are almost always fully employed by a single institution – a department or a college. However, much of the administration in the university departments and in the colleges is carried out by members of the various faculties on a part-time basis, and policy choices mainly derive from the academic staff.

There is a continuously changing relationship between the pattern of teaching, research and administration, and between the role of university or college, not only within the system as a whole, but also for an individual don (a teaching member of a faculty or fellow of a college), as his or her career develops. It was the coincidence between stresses from over-rapid change in the college – university balance and the improving economic environment in the early 1960s that led to the foundation of Clare Hall and other new colleges.

THE MEDIEVAL UNIVERSITY

The University of Cambridge probably dates from 1209 when a group of masters and scholars from Oxford settled in the town[1]. In that year there were riots in Oxford, clerks were hanged by the secular authorities, and the schools were closed for a period of five years. Cambridge was not an obvious choice for a new university, but it was a thriving community, acting both as a local market town and as a trading centre for commerce all over the fenlands. It came within the diocese of Ely, only 15 miles away, and had received charters from King John in 1201 and 1207 consolidating it as a corporation.

Ely itself being only a small village with no suitable accommodation, it is likely that the scholars from Oxford and a group of clerks in the service of the Bishop of Ely (in the absence abroad of the Bishop who had deemed it prudent to remove himself from the jurisdiction of King John) decided to open schools in the county town of Cambridge[2]. Their choice was probably also influenced by the family connections in the area of several of the leading masters in the group[3]. John Grim, doctor of theology, who was master of the schools of Oxford in 1201 (the chief official before the appointment of a chancellor) was from an important Cambridge family and may have been born in the town. The suitability of Cambridge as a location for a university was enhanced by the existence in the twelfth century of several religious houses[4] in or near the town[5], so it was presumably already a place of learning, known as such by the clerks of Ely, though secular instruction had been limited to elementary schools of grammar. The Augustinian Priory of Barnwell was founded in 1112 following an earlier foundation in 1091 at St. Giles in Cambridge; the Benedictine nunnery of St. Rhadegund before about 1145 where Jesus College now stands; and the Hospital of St. John about 1195 on the present site of St. John's College.

---

[1] Leader, *A History of the University of Cambridge, vol.I, the University to 1546*, pp. 18–19 (Cambridge 1988). See also Leedham-Green, *A Concise History of the University of Cambridge* (Cambridge 1996).
[2] Brooke, Highfield and Swaan, *Oxford and Cambridge*, pp. 55–56 (Cambridge 1988).
[3] Hackett, *The Original Statutes of Cambridge University: the Text and its History*, pp. 46–47 (Cambridge 1970).
[4] Brooke, *The churches of medieval Cambridge*, in *History, Society and the Churches: Essays in Honour of Owen Chadwick*, ed. Beales and Best (Cambridge 1985) pp. 49–76 at pp. 72–74.
[5] Willis and Clark, *The Architectural History of the University of Cambridge, vol.I*, chapter I (Cambridge 1988, first published 1886)

The early medieval university consisted of its members acting as a corporation. It was a guild of masters who taught their trade to their apprentices – the scholars. The common property of the masters and scholars who fled Oxford for Cambridge in 1209 would probably have fitted into a single chest: some account books, a little cash, and perhaps a few books, vestments, or vessels bequeathed to it by recently deceased masters[6]. The masters rented their lodgings and classrooms, and when they assembled they used nearby churches.

The university then was a corporation of learned men, associated for the purpose of teaching, and possessing the privilege that no-one should be allowed to teach within their domain without their sanction, which would only be granted on evidence of ability. A new scholar was required to work under the supervision of a master of arts, whom he paid. The master placed his name on the matricula (class list) which made him a legal undergraduate. He attended lectures and scholastic disputations, and if progress was satisfactory he was allowed to present himself for testing in a public disputation. Success in this made him a bachelor of arts, which allowed him to assist the masters in teaching. After three more years of satisfactory progress, with support from the masters in his faculty he was able to graduate as a master. The graduation ceremony included taking an oath to continue teaching in the university for one or two years, a period known as his 'regency'. The 'regent masters' ensured a continuing supply of teachers in the university faculty of arts. The newly qualified master of arts could then become a member of one of the superior faculties, such as theology or law, and after passing through similar stages of study for a bachelor's degree and beyond, he could become a master of one of these faculties also.

Early in the 13th century the mendicant orders of the friars began to establish themselves in Cambridge – the Franciscans about 1226, initially near the site of the present Guildhall before moving to the present site of Sidney Sussex; then the Dominicans, the Carmelites and the White Friars. Their presence in the town was a major influence on the development of instruction in the university. However, by the end of the century there was open conflict between the secular scholars and the friars, with the latter using the independence of their religious houses to cut corners in their

---

[6] Leader, loc. cit. p. 17

studies and complete their degrees more quickly than was possible for the scholars, constrained as they were by university requirements. In 1303, the university passed statutes concentrating power in the hands of the masters of the faculty of arts, setting aside the friars – the leading authorities on theology, and making restrictions on where the friars could preach[7]. After three years of further strife a compromise was agreed before a papal judges delegate in Bordeaux, and in 1318 the Pope himself confirmed the university's basic status by declaring its faculties a 'studium generale' and the community of masters and scholars a university, whose degrees carried a licence to teach throughout Christendom. However, for at least another century the friars continued to dominate the teaching of theology. Subsequently, as the religious houses declined or were closed, the colleges were able to acquire their precincts, and provide a basis for future college development.

THE EARLY COLLEGES

The university as a body concerned itself with the physical and moral welfare of students through the supervision exercised by the masters responsible for the hostels in which many of the students were housed, which was reinforced by the superintending powers granted in 1265–6 by King Henry III, over rents and regulations in the lodging houses. An inquiry in 1270, presided over by Edward, the future king, upheld the university's privileges, including the fixing of rents of students' lodgings in the town of Cambridge.

However, with the growth of student numbers in the thirteenth century, the lodgings were supplemented or replaced by academical halls, often owned by ecclesiastical landlords[8]. The earliest colleges with their own endowments were in Paris and Oxford, and Merton College in Oxford provided the model for subsequent foundations there and in Cambridge.

The first Cambridge college, Peterhouse, was founded towards the end of the thirteenth century by the tenth Bishop of Ely, Hugh de Balsham, a Benedictine monk and sub-prior in the cathedral priory[9]. His election in 1257, following the death of his predecessor whilst overseas on the king's

[7] Walker, *Peterhouse*, chapter I (Heffer 1935).
[8] Brooke, Highfield and Swaan, loc. cit. pp. 59 and 92.
[9] Walker, loc. cit.

business, was recommended by the monks of Ely but opposed by the king. Henry III, who had his own candidate, sought to reinforce his views by wreaking havoc on the lands, woods and fisheries in the Bishopric. Meanwhile, the cloistered monk, of whom the king had spoken in contemptuous terms, went directly to Rome, secured the desired confirmation, and was consecrated by Pope Alexander IV on 14 October 1257. His subsequent responsibilities included oversight of the religious houses, the churches and the fledgling university in Cambridge. The student hostels had no endowments and disputes over rents were frequent; they would have lived in considerable poverty.

In 1280, by Royal Letters from King Edward I, Bishop Hugh obtained a licence to introduce into the Hospital of St. John the Evangelist in Cambridge, *'studious scholars who should in everything live together as students in the University of Cambridge according to the rule of the scholars at Oxford who are called Merton'*. The foundation of Merton had been endowed for the education of secular clerks. Although it was a religious community, its purpose was learning, not religious contemplation, though endowments usually required regular prayers for the benefactors. A college was a corporation with common stock through which students of small means could live and pray in a community and take advantage of the teaching that was available in the university.

The bishop's idea of grafting a Merton 'look alike' on to the Hospital of St. John was not a success. The Hospital was an Augustinian institution, staffed by canons of the Order, with the twin objectives of religious service and care for the aged and the poor. It had been founded in about 1195 by a group of burgesses of the town who would then have obtained an Episcopal licence from the Bishop of Ely[10]. Evidently the canons, the old people and the scholars did not mix well, and this soon led the canons and scholars to combine in a petition to the bishop for a separation.

In March 1284, the bishop ordered the scholars to remove to two hostels near the Church of St. Peter, outside the Trumpington Gate just beyond the King's Ditch, which bounded medieval Cambridge on the south and the east. He assigned for their separate use and support the Church of St. Peter – later renamed St. Mary the Less, with its altar dues and the tithes

---

[10] Rubin, *Charity and Community in Medieval Cambridge* (Cambridge 1987).

The early colleges

of two mills in its possession, later adding the rectory of Thriplow to the endowment. The two hostels and the church had been the property of the canons of St. John, and they were compensated for their lost income through the rents of certain houses in the neighbourhood of their hospital. The removal of the scholars to the hostels by St. Peter's church was confirmed by King Edward I at Westminster on 28 May 1284, thus establishing Peterhouse, Domus Sancti Petri, sive Aula scholarium Episcopi Eliensis[11], the first Cambridge college.

Hugh de Balsham died in 1286, and his bequest of 300 marks to the college enabled them to purchase land to the south of the church of St. Peter on which they built a 'grand hall'. Later, in 1307 on the demise of the Order of the Sack, the buildings and land of its Cambridge friary near to Peterhouse was released to the 'scholars of the Bishop of Ely'. Between 1317 and 1352 seven new colleges were founded. The first two, King's Hall (1317) and Michaelhouse (1324) were later absorbed into the foundation by Henry VIII of Trinity College in 1546.

In 1326, Richard de Badew, Chancellor of the University obtained a royal licence to establish the college of University Hall for graduate members of the university. The college was located in two houses in Milne Street, near to the present site of the old court of Clare College, which had been purchased by the university in 1298. The endowment was small and for a few years Richard de Badew provided supplementary aid[12]. The problems were compounded by a fire which heavily damaged the buildings. Help came from Lady Elizabeth de Clare, a grand-daughter of King Edward I and three times the widow of wealthy husbands[13]. In 1336 she gave the fledgling college of ten fellows a benefice worth £20 per year, and in 1338 Richard de Badew transferred all the rights and titles that had

---

[11] The House of St.Peter, or the Hall of the Scholars of the Bishop of Ely.
[12] Chibnall, *Richard de Badew and the University of Cambridge 1315–1340* (Cambridge 1963), see also ref.1 (Leader) p. 82.
[13] The Lady Clare was Elizabeth de Burgh, youngest daughter of Gilbert of Clare, Earl of Gloucester, who inherited the Clare lands as her share of the family estates after the death of her brother Gilbert at the battle of Bannockburn. She was three times married, and was barely twenty seven when she was widowed for the third time. Married in 1308 (at the age of thirteen) to John de Burgh, who died in 1313, she was abducted and married without the king's licence, and probably against her will, by Theobald Verdun. Within five months he too was dead; and she took as her third husband Roger Damory, who supported the losing side at the battle of Boroughbridge and paid the penalty on the scaffold in 1322. Elizabeth survived him for forty years without remarrying (note by Dr M. M. Chibnall).

been obtained for University Hall to Lady Clare. The college was renamed Clare House (Domus de Clare), though as early as 1346 it was being styled Clare Hall, and in that year she provided the college with three more benefices.

In 1359 Lady Clare promulgated a set of statutes which were to serve the college for nearly two hundred years. The statutes make clear that the foundation was to advance Divine learning and to benefit the State. Ten years earlier, in the Spring of 1349, the Black Death – bubonic plague – had struck East Anglia causing the death of one third of the inhabitants. This disaster was witnessed by Elizabeth de Clare and her response is evident in the preamble to the statutes: She wrote[14],

Seeing that a large number of men have been carried off by the plague, knowledge is now beginning to be lamentably lacking among men. Hence we have turned the eyes of our mind to the University of Cambridge ... and to the Hall therein ... which we would have to be called Clare Hall (Domus de Clare), and nothing else, for all time ...

The original Seal of Clare Hall also dates from 1359 and is illustrated in the frontispiece of this book. The name Clare Hall was retained until 1856, when it was changed to Clare College by a resolution of the Master and Fellows – a decision taken, presumably, to give the college a more modern image at a time when there was competition between colleges to increase the number of students.

Pembroke Hall was founded in 1347 by Mary de Valence, Countess of Pembroke, and a close friend of Lady Clare. Gonville Hall was founded in 1348 by Edmund Gonville, who died in 1351. His plans were fulfilled by his executor, Bishop William Bateman of Norwich, who was also in the process of founding a college himself, Trinity Hall (1350). The last of the 14th century colleges was the college of Corpus Christi and the Blessed Virgin Mary, founded in 1352, three years after the first wave of the Black Death. It was founded by a corporation made up of the amalgamated guilds of Corpus Christi and the Blessed Virgin Mary, which were made up of townsmen though under the patronage of the Duke of Lancaster. It was to be eighty years before the next college was founded.

---

[14] Quoted by Ashby in his sermon for the Commemoration of Benefactors in Clare College in 1981, printed in *Clare Association Annual, 1980–81*, p. 7.

FIFTEENTH TO EIGHTEENTH CENTURIES

At the end of the 14th century all the colleges, except King's Hall with 40 fellows and royal patronage, were small communities of scholars – mainly graduates working for higher degrees. Most of the younger scholars, the undergraduates – about 700 in number, were distributed amongst some 20 hostels or lodging houses. Even though the university had no buildings of its own until the north side of the Schools Quadrangle was completed in 1400, the colleges had no substantial role in university affairs. However, this was to change in the 15th century, when it proved more easy to find benefactors to found colleges than to endow the university. In general the endowment of a college consisted of land and land charges. These could not be sold until new statutes were provided in the reign of Elizabeth I and even then the proceeds could only be used for the acquisition of new endowments, later collectively known as corporate capital. There would have been a need for a more flexible income stream, and with increasing numbers of students the colleges evidently began to appreciate that resident scholars could provide a useful source of revenue, or at least a contribution towards overheads, so the provision of rooms for paying scholars and the ownership of hostels began to pass to the colleges.

Growth in numbers of scholars was accompanied by the founding of four more colleges between 1441 and 1496, King's, Queens', St. Catharine's and Jesus. In the next century six more were founded, including the two largest: St. John's in 1511 and Trinity in 1546. Trinity was formed through an amalgamation imposed by King Henry VIII of two existing colleges, King's Hall and Michaelhouse, and a hostel, Physwick Hall taken from Gonville Hall. The colleges found also that it was convenient, probably in line with a sense of duty, and presumably profitable, for them to provide tuition and lectures for their resident scholars. This proved so successful that the university lectures by the regent masters became redundant as their audiences faded away. The balance was partly restored by the endowment by Henry VIII of five regius professorships to provide university lectures at a more senior and distinguished level than those previously given by the regents.

The rise in prosperity and influence of the colleges was reflected in the additional political and religious hazards met by their Masters[15]. This

---

[15] Leedham-Green, *A Concise History of the University of Cambridge* (Cambridge 1996).

apart, an oligarchy of Masters of colleges increasingly dominated the government of the university, in part through their informal meetings following the university sermons in Great St. Mary's Church, held weekly in term time[16]. Their influence was formalised by the new statutes for the university in 1570, drafted by John Whitgift and Andrew Perne and approved by Cecil and Elizabeth I. Notably, the Caput – a small committee chaired by the Vice-Chancellor, was given a major say in all university appointments, and any member had the power to veto any Grace put before the university.

Overall numbers of students in Cambridge increased from about 1,600 in 1570 to about 3,000 in the 1620s and 1630s[17], growth that was probably due partly to a broadening of the social range now seeking a university education. It was during this period, in 1638–42, that the Clare bridge was built and the rebuilding of Clare College Old Court began, though it was nearly a century before it was completed[18]. The Elizabethan statutes required celibacy of the fellows, but from an early date were interpreted as allowing the Masters of most colleges to marry. Thus the age and experience of the Masters gave them common cause as well as an entrenched reluctance to permit change. Their conservatism did not help them to cope with the decline by nearly two-thirds in the number of students between the 1630s and the 1760s. The 18th century saw a corresponding decline in both scholarship and academic responsibility amongst the dons and students, with fellows drawing college dividends whilst non-resident, professors who did not lecture and students who would not attend such lectures as were given, and Masters who sometimes held multiple appointments and preferred life in their country rectories to life in Cambridge[19]. Even in the 19th century, the colleges rarely provided

---

[16] Brooke, Highfield and Swaan, loc. cit. p. 163.
[17] See: *The Historical Register of the University of Cambridge 1910* (ed. J. R. Tanner) (Cambridge 1917, reprinted 1984), for a good account of the University's constitution, privileges, degrees, and class lists to 1910, taken from the *Cambridge University Calendar* (which was published from 1796 to 1913). Matriculations rose from about 300 per annum to about 500 in the same period. Presumably the total of students included a substantial fraction who had not matriculated, particularly bearing in mind that by no means all students would proceed to a degree.
[18] See chapter 1 of *Life in Clare Hall, Cambridge 1658–1713* by Harrison (Heffers, 1958).
[19] See, for example, Winstanley, *The University of Cambridge in the Eighteenth Century* (Cambridge 1922, 1935). See also Leedham-Green, loc. cit.

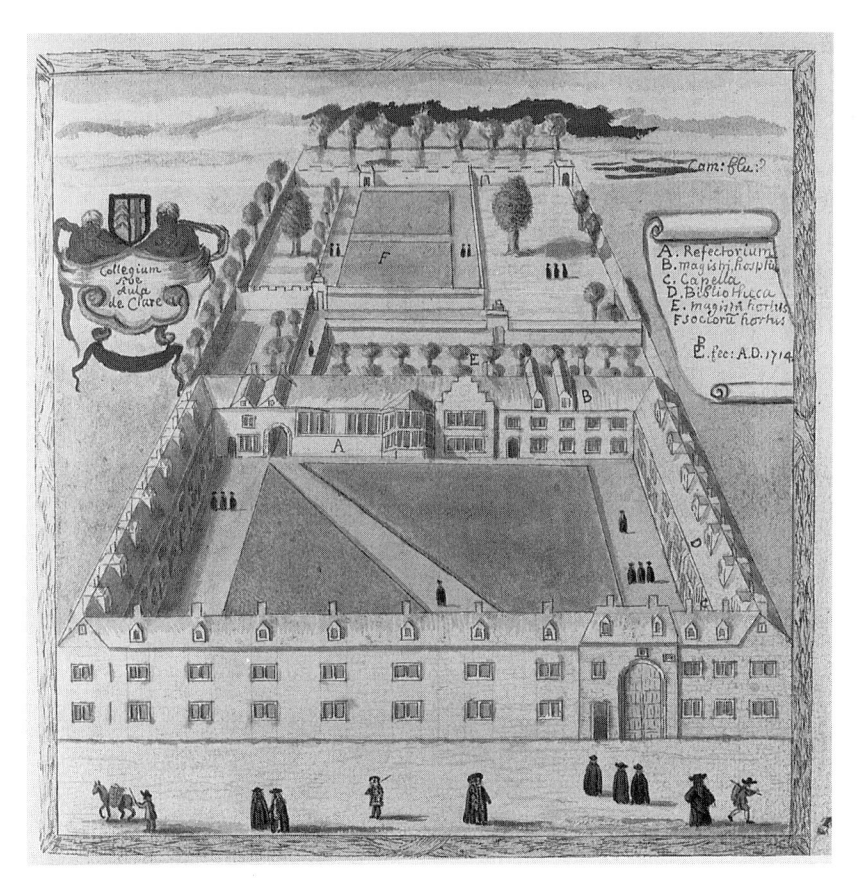

1. Drawing of Clare Hall (now Clare College) by Edmund Prideaux, fellow-commoner. The drawing is dated 1714, but it shows the college as it was before the rebuilding in 1638–42, so it is evidently based on an earlier drawing.

undergraduate teaching appropriate to an honours degree. Most students took ordinary degrees, many no degrees at all, and the few who wanted high honours had to pay for private coaching, and until 1851 even an aspiring classicist was required first to obtain honours in the mathematics tripos.

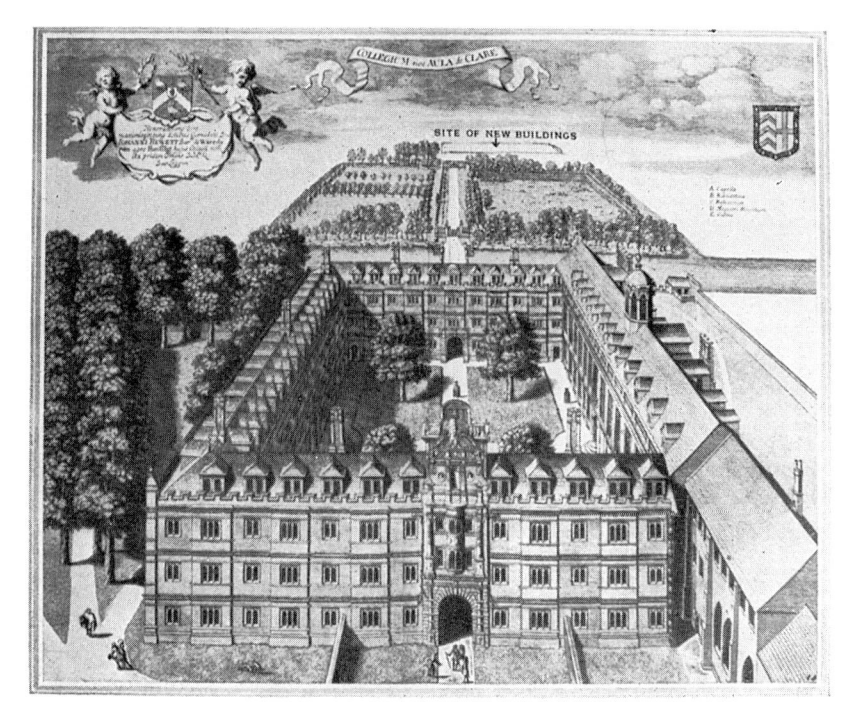

2. Loggan's View of the 'New' Buildings of Clare Hall The drawing was made circa 1688 when building of the north range was in progress. Loggan anticipated also the completion of the new Master's Lodge to the west by 27 years. The words NEW BUILDING at the top of the picture refer to the proposed site of the Memorial Court and were evidently added circa 1920.

STATE INTERVENTION AND UNIVERSITY EXPANSION

There were many proposals for reform early in the 19th century, but few succeeded until changes were imposed by the government. There had been some changes in the examination system – tentative at first in the 18th century, when a written paper was introduced to supplement the oral disputations, then more substantial as the tripos system became established in mathematics, and later in the 19th century in other subjects. The Royal Commission in 1852 recommended the creation of a large staff of university lecturers, independent of college fellowships. These recommendations were not implemented, but the Cambridge University Act of 1856 set up an institutional structure that would in the future allow such implementation[20]. The Act defined the authority of the University Senate, and particularly of its members resident in Cambridge; it set up the Council of the Senate to provide for broader membership than the Caput and Heads of Colleges, and also created the Financial Board. A second Royal Commission was set up by Gladstone in 1872 which led to new Statutes in 1882. A newly created General Board of Studies provided a focus for the introduction of new courses and examinations in the university and for the introduction of university lecturers or demonstrators. Such changes were needed particularly for the teaching of experimental sciences, which required common facilities in the university that could not be provided in each college. In 1870 in response to a teaching need in experimental physics, the Chancellor of the University, the Duke of Devonshire, made a gift to the university to cover the cost of setting up a physics laboratory – the Cavendish Laboratory.

In 1871 an Act of Parliament abolished the requirement that all fellowships should be open only to Anglicans[21]. Two colleges for women were established, Girton (initially in Hitchin) in 1869 and Newnham in 1871, but although their students were allowed to take university examinations, their results were not formally recognised for degrees in the university until 1948. In 1895 the university began to accept affiliated students with degrees from other universities, either to take conventional tripos courses or to achieve a degree through writing a dissertation involving some experimental studies. Those choosing the latter option became known as research students, and the first batch in 1895 included Rutherford, soon to obtain a Nobel prize in chemistry and, later to obtain the evidence that most of the mass of an atom is found in its small central nucleus. Rutherford became the Cavendish Professor in 1919 and presided over the golden years of nuclear physics in the laboratory.

The discussions of reform early in the 19th century were a reflection of the new-found enthusiasm for education in the schools and amongst the prospering middle classes. The numbers of undergraduates began to

---

[20] Searby, *History of the University of Cambridge, vol.III, 1750–1870* (Cambridge, 1997).
[21] Until 1856, the Anglican requirement had also applied to all degrees.

increase after the end of the Napoleonic wars, though St. John's and Trinity continued to dominate by taking half the new students until the mid-19th century. Then there was a general expansion with the other colleges growing much faster than either of the two largest. Almost all undergraduates were admitted by colleges, but the university began to admit small numbers of non-collegiate students in 1859–60 and more after the creation of the board for non-collegiate students in 1869 which led to the founding of Fitzwilliam College in the mid-twentieth century[22].

In 1870 there were 2,000 undergraduates – 45% at St. John's and Trinity, and by 1920 there were over 4,500, with less than 25% at St. John's and Trinity. The competition to attract new students led to the provision of boat houses[23] and sports fields in all colleges – evidently most schoolboys or their fathers judged colleges by their successes in rowing or rugby, rather than through more remote academic achievements. It should be noted that, early in the 20th century, it was not uncommon for a member of the Cambridge team in some sport, also to achieve success at a national or international level. Cambridge runners won gold at the Olympics and Cambridge tennis players won championships at Wimbledon.

The 1914–18 war had a devastating effect on the Cambridge colleges, both through the numbers of casualties and through the fall in numbers of students[24]. Over 2,000 Cambridge men were killed and nearly 3,000 wounded. In 1909–10 there were about 3,700 male undergraduates in residence in the university; in the Michaelmas term of 1914, only weeks after the outbreak of war, there were less than 1,700, in the Easter term 1916 there were only 575. Within three months of the armistice, by January 1919 numbers had risen to more than 2,600, and by October they exceeded 4,500.

The loss of income from student's fees during the war and the two-fold inflation of costs caused a crisis in the finances of the university, and help was sought from government. The colleges had their own financial problems and were already helping the university through a 'colleges tax' imposed by an Act of Parliament in 1881 giving a transfer of about

---

[22] Grave, *Fitzwilliam College, 1869–1969* (Cambridge 1983).
[23] Boat Houses were normally owned by the undergraduates collectively in each college.
[24] Brooke, *A History of the University of Cambridge, vol IV, 1870–1990*, p. 331 (Cambridge 1993).

£30,000 p.a. to the university in 1910–25. The government provided a similar amount of emergency aid in 1919, and set up a Royal Commission, which reported in 1922. By 1926, the universities of Oxford and Cambridge had new constitutions, and the statutes of both universities and all colleges had been revised. The independence of colleges was preserved, and arrangements were made in Cambridge for university lecturers to receive a primary salary from the university, which might be supplemented by a college if the lecturer held a fellowship. The university would receive an annual grant from the government. This provided a stable income, allowing the university to use new endowments for buildings rather than salaries for members of staff. Endowments in the 1930s allowed a new building for the University Library[25] and an extension to the Cavendish Laboratory[26].

THE SECOND WORLD WAR

Although the immediate impact of the second world war on Cambridge was much less than that of the first war, in the longer term it heralded and accelerated revolutionary changes in academic standards for the admission of students and in attitudes to research. There were fewer casualties amongst Cambridge men and women in 1939–45 than in 1914–18, but most war-time students would have had friends or relatives who were killed in the armed forces or in air-raids. The university and the colleges continued to function though at a somewhat reduced level. In arts subjects, government policy allowed study for one year in Cambridge, and in the sciences two years study was normal – at least for those of adequate academic standards.

During the war, many students postponed coming to Cambridge, choosing to join the armed forces directly from school, and of those who came to the university most stayed for only one year and few stayed for more than two years. There was some preference given to scholars, particularly in science, who usually stayed for two years, sometimes completing the usual three-year course in that time, before being directed to work in which their education was likely to be useful. Most science

---

[25] Half the cost of the new library in the 1930s was met by a grant of £250,000 from the Rockefeller Foundation
[26] The Austin Wing of the Laboratory.

students were interviewed by the former academic and author C.P.Snow who was the principal recruitment advisor in Cambridge, or by his colleague Major Walters[27], and there was a significant element of choice – at least for the scientists who were also scholars.

A CLIMATE FOR CHANGE

In the years around 1960, within the university there was a sense of optimism reflecting a national expectation of increasing prosperity coupled with an unprecedented public and political enthusiasm for the expansion of higher education – this is discussed in chapter 3. For the first time in the history of the university it was possible – even easy – for junior members of the faculties to make significant changes, sometimes in the face of initial opposition from the university barons. In the university there was no 'peasants revolt' – more a change of direction – and some of the older more established dons were in the vanguard of the new movement[28]. But, as in the years following the first world war, the 1950s saw a notable transition of influence from older dons, whose fondest memories included life in the pre-war colleges, to a younger generation whose memories of student days were masked by up to seven years experience of national service. Many of the scientists had returned to Cambridge with extensive experience of research, others had used or gained technical knowledge in the application of technology at the leading edge of development. Others had used their knowledge of languages or mathematics for code-breaking in the still secret ultra programme at Bletchley Park.

Notably also, many of the students destined to become Cambridge dons, had returned in 1945–46 to resume their studies as graduate research students – not as undergraduates, since most had qualified for their first degrees during the various wartime dispensations that allowed fast-track or shortened courses to lead to graduation. They had benefited too from the new national enthusiasm for higher education, stimulated in part by

---

[27] Sir Henry Thirkill, Master of Clare College, also helped with the wartime interviewing of scientists (note from Brian Cooper).

[28] But not in some colleges; see Brooke, *A History of Gonville and Caius College* (Woodbridge 1985) pp. 272–4. But even in the Peasants Revolt in Caius, the division was not simply old v. young – Fisher and Needham were in sympathy with the Peasants.

the contribution of science and scientists to the conclusion of the war, that provided grants to all returning students needing further studies to complete their first degrees, and research grants to qualified students which could lead to a Ph.D[29].

In the 1950s, as a result of government grants to universities and students, there was considerable expansion in university facilities for teaching and research. The increasing diversity of subjects studied in the humanities and the growth of research teams in the sciences, led to a substantial body of graduate staff of the university who were not fellows or members of any college. It was feared that the collegiate character of the university, with its shared responsibilities, would not survive the stresses of this new dichotomy amongst senior members. The older dons, who still dominated the university hierarchy, were too astute to allow a revolt in the faculty, though they were surprised at the indignation about their bland policies of minimal future expansion – keeping Cambridge as nearly unchanged as possible – partly to avoid exacerbating the problem of non-fellows. New perspectives began to take hold around 1960, and many were welcomed by those older dons still holding some of the reins of influence. However, few dons, young or old, anticipated the student demonstrations that came later in the 1960s – activities that were more strident elsewhere than in Cambridge, which brought to an end the golden period of national approval and political enthusiasm for expansion of the universities.

THE NEW COLLEGES

It was only in 1948 that women were recognised as full members of the University of Cambridge. Although they had been allowed to take the university examinations and be classified in the honours degrees, and to give lectures and act as examiners, they had not been full members of the faculties, nor were they previously members of the Regent House – the statutory authority in the university. This belated recognition made another anomaly more visible: There were only two women's colleges

---

[29] Although research students had been first admitted in 1895, it was not until the 1920s that the Ph.D. had been established as a higher degree normally requiring three years of research and residence in Cambridge.

(Newnham and Girton), both relatively poorly endowed, so very few women academics held college fellowships – statutes prevented them from being fellows of any of the men's colleges. Thus was formed in the 1950s a dining club – the Society for women members of the Regent House who are not fellows of any college. The views of this society on the development of new colleges, particularly towards providing places for members of the faculties, proved to be important and far-sighted, not only for the founding of two new women's colleges but also for the founding of graduate colleges in the 1960s. Following a change in university statutes that had previously required all colleges to be single sex, the new graduate colleges set an example by admitting both men and women that was later followed by all the men's colleges and by Girton college.

New Hall was founded in 1954 to provide more places for women in Cambridge, at a time when they formed a small minority of the student body. It was founded, initially on a modest scale, by a proposal from a committee of supportive academics, which was formed following an initiative from Dame Myra Curtis, the Principal of Newnham. Its first President was Dame Rosemary Murray, formerly Tutor of Girton, and from its foundation the college has admitted both graduates and undergraduates.

The second new women's college, Lucy Cavendish, originated from the dining club formed in the 1950s for the Society for women members of the Regent House who are not fellows of any college. Key members of the founding club included Margaret Braithwaite, philosopher, Dr Anna Bidder, zoologist, who became the first President of the college, and Dr Kathleen Wood-Legh, a remarkable medieval historian who had been blind since childhood[30]. In 1963 the members of the dining club formed a trust, which with the aid of initially modest endowments became Lucy Cavendish College in 1966, initially for graduates only, but extending to undergraduates in 1971 and specialising in the education of women as mature students.

Churchill College was founded in 1960 in a traditional manner derived from a large initial endowment, though by a somewhat indirect route. The project was started by Sir Winston Churchill himself, who wanted to see in Britain a great Institute of Technology like MIT in the United States.

---

[30] See Brooke, *A History of the University of Cambridge, vol IV*, loc. cit. p. 571.

His advisers, intent on the new foundation having access to students of the highest quality, concluded that it had to be located in Cambridge University. With this constraint, the concept would best be met by founding a Cambridge college with a high proportion of undergraduates and research students studying engineering and science, thus contributing in a major way to the group of departments in the university that now form the school of technology. When the proposal was brought to the university by the distinguished scientists Lord Todd and Sir John Cockcroft, who was to be the first Master of Churchill, they were backed not only by the prestige of Churchill, but also by substantial promises of financial support from industry and from other benefactors in the UK, in the British Commonwealth and in the United States. This formidable backing was both fortunate and necessary for success of the proposal, as it flew in the face of the recent policy proposals of the university's central committees designed to resist further expansion in the numbers of undergraduates. The foundation of Churchill was not the result of the new involvement of the post-war academics; it was a victory for some university barons over their peers on the central committees.

However, the post-war generation was to have a more important role in the later developments with which this story is concerned – developments which led to the founding of three graduate colleges in the 1960s: Darwin College, University College (later renamed as Wolfson College), and Clare Hall.

Chapter 2

CLARE COLLEGE 1815 to 1951

HENRY THIRKILL

It was in the 1950s, when Sir Henry Thirkill was the Master of Clare College, that the governing body began to examine the possibility of extending the college in some way so as to bring into the society more members of the university faculties who were not at that time fellows of any college. These considerations were taken up again by Clare in the 1960s under the new Master, Sir Eric Ashby. Subsequently, following a change of direction through new influences and ideas, they led to the founding of Clare Hall.

However, the influence of Thirkill on Clare began long before the 1950s, and continued up to his retirement in 1958. His influence on the selection of the fellows who were to elect Ashby as Master, and were later to found Clare Hall can hardly be over-stated. In his recollections of Cambridge and Clare[1], Harry Godwin wrote

... from 1920, when he first became tutor, to his death in 1971, Henry Thirkill played a role of overwhelming importance in the evolution of Clare. He was a great and modest man whose whole life was inspired by affection for the college and those many generations of its inhabitants with whom he dealt ... He continued to lecture in physics until 1933, but although he had effectively closed his scientific career, he kept a close friendship with former colleagues and ... Lord Rutherford was one of Henry's regular companions in afternoon walks. It was hard to realise how far his modesty cloaked Henry's ability, and unwary university thrusters too often discounted him. It is 'a propos' to recall how Brian Pippard brought to dinner in Clare, during Henry's mastership, that pre-eminent physicist, Heisenberg[2]. They conversed amicably in the combination room and Heisenberg later confided that he had begun by regarding the Master as a

---

[1] Godwin, *Cambridge and Clare*, pp. 134–136, (Cambridge 1985).
[2] Heisenberg certainly stayed in Clare College during one of his visits, but on this occasion, Brian Pippard believes the guest was Fritz London, also a distinguished physicist.

3. Sir Henry Thirkill, Master of Clare College 1939–58 (painting by Frank Eastman).

conventional lightweight, until it was suddenly borne in upon him that the course of the conversation had been entirely controlled and his own attitudes quietly elicited by his seemingly ineffective host ...

Henry Thirkill came to Clare College as an undergraduate in 1905 and was elected into a fellowship in 1910. He was appointed as a demonstrator in the Cavendish Laboratory in 1912, where his research was on the conduction of electricity in gases. After war service he became the tutor of Clare College in 1920 and was the Master from 1939 to 1958. He was the Vice-Chancellor of the University in 1945–47 during the most critical post-war period when new appointments and strategic decisions were made that would affect the university far into the future. He was a member of one or more of the three central committees of the university for 30 years from the mid 1920s until his retirement in 1958, and yet he was so self-effacing that his enormous influence in the university from the 1920s to the 1950s seems almost invisible.

I knew Thirkill from 1951, when I first became a fellow of Clare and director of studies in mathematics, and observed at first hand his skill in chairing college and inter-college committees in seeming impartiality. Within a college meeting, after a discussion of an issue requiring a decision, he would bring from his pocket a typed minute and, before reading it, would say with an expression of total innocence, "I wonder whether something like this would be suitable." I do not recall the typed version ever being challenged or changed, though we were always uncertain whether Sir Henry had different versions in different pockets. For an inter-college committee his methods were less obvious, except to those close colleagues with whom he held discussions before the meetings. As with all those of influence in Cambridge affairs, Thirkill benefited from the large number of dons with whom he had worked closely in the past and who had admired and respected his judgement. In his later years in the 1950s, although still influential, like Whewell a century earlier he had become conservative, seeking to protect those values that he had helped to enhance from the ravages of change created by the new enthusiasms of the post-war generation of young dons.

The Revd. W. Telfer was a contemporary of Thirkill as a freshman in 1905; he was a wrangler[3] in 1908, and later became Dean of Clare and assistant tutor, and then Master of Selwyn. In an 80th birthday tribute[4], Telfer wrote about the time when he and Thirkill were undergraduates,

The intake then consisted of two rather distinct elements, most easily described as those that occupied the attics and the rest. The majority of the college consisted of pensioners who were comfortably well off. But some of those who won entrance scholarships and exhibitions, even given help from their schools or public authorities, came into residence knowing they would have to be extremely careful of

---

[3] A wrangler is a student with first class honours in part II of the mathematical tripos. Until 1910, the term related to part I of the same tripos, in which candidates were arranged in order of merit, the senior wrangler being top of the first class.

[4] *Henry Thirkill 80,* booklet printed for Clare College, 8 August 1966.

their expenditure. College and university corporate life was fully open to the poor scholar, so long as he chose the outlets to social activity that could be afforded ... Against this background and amongst the crowd of brash young men of every sort who made up the college intake in 1905, Thirkill appeared modest to a degree ...

CLARE 1815 to 1914

In 1905, when Henry Thirkill was a freshman at Clare College, the university reforms of 1850–70 were beginning to bear fruit and there were an increasing number of courses and examination options available to undergraduates. Fellows of colleges were allowed to marry and a knowledge of Greek was no longer a requirement for all students. Advanced students were making an appearance in the university to obtain degrees through research projects in science laboratories and in libraries. The reforms had also led to changes in college teaching, though the slowly changing fellowship meant that supervision in the new subjects was often done by a new breed of private tutors outside the colleges, successors to the great mathematical coaches of the previous century.

But many features of college life were unchanged and in 1905 when Thirkill came to Clare Dr Edward Atkinson, at the age of 85, was in his 49th year as Master. He had been Vice-Chancellor of the university in 1870 when the Duke of Devonshire, the Chancellor, had written to him offering a gift of £6,300 to meet the cost of providing a building and apparatus for the proposed professor of experimental physics, which led to the appointment of Clerk Maxwell as the first Cavendish Professor. It was in the Cavendish Laboratory that Thirkill became an Assistant Demonstrator in 1912, working alongside the redoubtable Dr G. F. C. Searle. Searle had first become a Demonstrator with J. J. Thomson in 1891, and he continued to teach in the undergraduate class in experimental physics for more than 50 years, finally retiring (for the second time) after the second world war.

Atkinson had been admitted to Clare as a sizar[5] in 1838, graduating in 1842 as 3rd in the merit order in classics, having been classed as a senior optime in mathematics earlier in the same year[6]. Dr William Webb was

---

[5] Sizar: an undergraduate in receipt of a room and meals or a grant towards living costs.
[6] Until 1851, candidates for honours in classics (excepting the sons of Peers) were required to have obtained honours in mathematics. Senior optime denotes 2nd class honours.

the Master, having been elected in 1815. Webb had graduated in 1797 with an aegrotat, but he was listed amongst the wranglers (first class in mathematics). Although Webb had a reputation as a conservative in university affairs who opposed reforms, the early years of his Mastership were a period of great activity in the college, in sharp contrast to the inactivity since completion of the new chapel nearly 50 years earlier. The day following his election, orders were passed by the governing body for the reorganisation of the Master's Lodge and for improvements to the west front of the college[7], and three years later rooms for undergraduates were constructed above the hall[8].

Dr Webb also achieved a resolution of a long running dispute[9] with King's College, which had begun nearly two centuries earlier when Clare decided to rebuild the old court and needed a bridge across the river[10] and causeway across the meadow beyond – then called Butts Close belonging to King's. A petition by Clare to King Charles had led to a renewable lease for the land worth £5 per annum, whilst King's received a similar lease for a small plot of land near their chapel at 12 pence per annum. Webb succeeded in negotiating an Act of Parliament in 1823 allowing the Clare land between the Old Court and King's Chapel together with the White Horse Inn to be exchanged for Butts Close, the land between the river and Queen's Road which now forms the Clare avenue and fellows' garden.

In an important contribution to the future rise of Clare, Dr Webb carried through a major reform in the system of letting the college farms, by which the revenues of the college were substantially increased[11]. As Master and bursar, he inherited a system in which the college estates were usually let for periods of 21 years, and the leases renewed every 7 years, the tenant paying a fine for such renewal. The fine would provide an

---

[7] Wardale, *Clare College*, p. 202 (Robinson, London, 1899).
[8] Willis and Clark, *Architectural History of the University of Cambridge* vol.I, p. 114 (Cambridge 1886, reprinted 1988).
[9] See Willis and Clark, loc. cit. pp. 88–92 and appendix I; see also Wardale, loc. cit. pp. 202–204.
[10] The bridge was useful also for getting out of Cambridge without going through the town during times of plague.
[11] See Wardale, loc. cit. p. 204, and the chapter by Harrison on Clare College in the *Victoria History of Cambridge* vol.III, p. 340. Dr Webb was a farmer with a particular enthusiasm for pigs – which led to many humorous stories. He had become wealthy by marriage, no doubt a factor in his awareness of the need for reform of the college's system of fixing farm rents.

4. Ackermann's view of Clare Hall (now Clare College) and barges on the river, dated circa 1810.

immediate payment that could be distributed to the fellows, thus there was a great temptation to maximise it at the expense of maintaining a low rent. To meet the losses for the existing holders of fellowships resulting from the abolition of fines and the transition to market-based rack rents considerable sums were borrowed and repaid as the college finances permitted. The passing of the Enclosures Act also increased the college revenues, and from 1841 onwards the college records show frequent orders for the increase of the stipends of the Master and fellows.

During the Mastership of Dr Webb there was some increase in the number of undergraduates in Clare, though in 1840 the total in residence was only 40. It seems that he did not want the number of students to exceed the number that could be conveniently accommodated in the Old Court, which, of course, also provided rooms for the fellows. Dr Atkinson became senior tutor in 1850 and Master in 1856, initiating a remarkable period of growth in student numbers at Clare, which increased to 70 in

1870 and 123 in 1880, reaching 210 by 1910. During this period the fivefold increase in numbers in Clare may be compared with a doubling of the total numbers of undergraduates in the university.

The growth of Clare in the period from 1840 to 1910 was achieved in a competitive environment, with each college seeking to attract more students by enhancing its reputation in the public (fee-paying) schools by the provision of good sporting facilities and by their success in the competitive games between the college teams. A college order dated May 11, 1865 records 'That a further portion of the land mentioned in the preceding order be laid out for the use of members of the college as a cricket ground at an expense not exceeding £150.' In 1876 it was agreed to enlarge the cricket ground, and level it at the expense of the college; negotiations were also opened with King's College for the formation of a joint ground. The Clare–King's playing field was in West Cambridge where the university library now stands – the subsequent history of part of this land was to be relevant to the founding of Clare Hall on its present site nearly a century later.

The importance attached to success in sports is illustrated in the monumental and eccentric *History of Clare College 1326–1926* produced by Mansfield Forbes[12] in the 1920s, in which there is no mention of the dramatically changing academic scene after 1870, but much enthusiasm and description of the achievements of Clare men in rugby and other sports. However, it may not have been Forbes' intention to ignore academic activity in the college – it seems that the history was originally intended as a collective project by the fellows, but after adopting it at his own and as the project grew – one volume becoming two – there seemed little prospect for its completion in a finite time, so it was terminated in procrustean style through an imposed collaboration with the college Dean, Revd. H. W. (Fluffy) Fulford and the junior fellow, Harry Godwin[13].

William Mollison (Master from 1915 to 1929) came to Clare in 1872 after studying in Scotland and became 2nd wrangler in 1876 and 2nd Smith's

---

[12] Mansfield Forbes, *History of Clare College 1326–1926* (two volumes, published by Clare College 1926).
[13] Godwin, loc. cit. p. 100. See also *Mansfield Forbes and his Cambridge,* by Hugh Carey (Cambridge 1984).

prizeman[14]. He was immediately elected to a fellowship and was a tutor from 1880–94 and senior tutor from 1894–1913, ably maintaining the expansion that had been started by Atkinson. From 1904 to 1915, Dr Mollison was secretary of the General Board of Studies, which was responsible for all teaching arrangements in the university (there were no Faculty Boards until the 1920s). In Alumni Cantabrigienses[15], Mollison is described as 'a distinguished mathematician and a sound mathematical scholar ... remarkable for his alertness, energy and perseverance.' Amongst Mollison's students were: G. H. A. Wilson, who was 5th wrangler in 1895 and Master of Clare from 1929–39, W. J. Harrison, who was 3rd wrangler in 1907 and a Smith's prizeman in 1908, becoming a fellow of Clare in 1907 and bursar from 1929 to 1948, and Henry Thirkill (Master from 1939–58) who obtained first class honours in the natural sciences tripos (taking physics) in 1908 and became a fellow in 1910.

At the beginning of the 20th century, only about one quarter of the Clare undergraduates took honours degrees, the remainder ('poll men') taking an ordinary degree or leaving without completing the required three and a half years residence. The academic quality of the honours men appears to have been good, particularly in mathematics and science – perhaps reflecting Mollison's influence as senior tutor responsible for college admissions and as the principal college teacher in mathematics. In the ten year period to 1910, half of the 60 Clare candidates in the mathematical tripos obtained first class degrees. In the same period in the natural sciences tripos, more than two fifths of the candidates were in the first class, significantly above the university average. In contrast, in the arts subjects the fraction of Clare men obtaining first class degrees was below the university average[16].

CLARE IN THE FIRST WORLD WAR

Amongst the fellows of Clare during the war, Harrison's mathematics was put to use on the ballistics of gunnery, and Thirkill's expertise in physics

---

[14] Beginning in 1769, Smith's prizes were awarded each year to two junior graduates most proficient in a mathematics examination. After 1883, the prizes were awarded for the two best essays by a B.A. on a subject in mathematics or natural philosophy.
[15] *Alumni Cantabrigienses*, part 2, 1752–1900, edited by J. and J. A. Venn (Cambridge).
[16] *Cambridge Historical Register 1910*, (Cambridge 1917).

took him to be head of wireless for the army in East Africa, where he was awarded the Military Cross. A notable contribution to the war effort came from Gilbert West[17], a Clare scholar in 1916, who was working with a fellow physicist in the following year on radio direction-finding on the East coast. He picked up a radio message by the German Naval Command giving in clear an order for the German fleet to proceed at once to sea. Within a few hours by bicycle and village telephone he conveyed this message to the appropriate section of the British Admiralty and set in progress the opening steps towards the Battle of Jutland.

In his reminiscences written in 1985, Harry Godwin recalled,

> During 1914–18 the tremendous flow of war casualties had been met in the Cambridge region by the discharge of hospital trains at a large sidings next to the Long Road at the south side of the town. Thence the wounded suffered the uncomfortable transportation to the large temporary 'Eastern General' hospital that had been built on the Clare-King's playing field, ... The cessation of the war was followed by such acute housing shortages that throughout the country 'squatters' took possession of any premises temporarily left vacant, and this is what happened to the wooden huts of the Eastern General hospital, which indeed suffered such occupation until the building of the University Library offered a reason for repossessing the site so strong that it could not reasonably be refused.

The increase in numbers of students at Clare in the second half of the 19th century had created great pressure on accommodation for students, and already in 1911 the college building committee was reporting on the options for new buildings encouraged by a gift of £5,000 later supplemented by another gift of £10,000. Initially, there was support for building just across the river in the near garden, though there was also significant opposition. However, after exploratory drilling it was found to be too costly on this site and the committee recommended that the new buildings should be in the far (fellows') garden on the west side of Queen's Road between the road and the King's & Clare cricket ground. The intention was to build a new Master's Lodge on this site, but prior to 1911 the college statutes required the Master to reside in the buildings on the west front of the old court and north of the archway so in that year the relevant statute was changed to The college shall provide a residence for

---

[17] See Godwin, loc. cit. Gilbert West's son Richard studied at Clare and became a Professorial Fellow – on several occasions he was regularly in Clare Hall whilst on sabbatical leave from Clare College.

the Master. By May 1915, the governing body was able to agree 'in general principle' that: (i) a new Lodge be built in the fellows' garden, and (ii) the old Lodge be converted into college rooms. The constraints of wartime and the desire of the new Master, Dr Mollison, to live in college led to a change of mind, and in May 1916 the governing body decided that, subject to the approval by the college council of the estimates, the Lodge be put into a suitable condition for occupation by the Master'. This change of mind may also have been affected by the fact that, at the time of the decision, five of the fellows (Wilson, Crick, Thirkill, Roberts and Harrison) were on leave of absence for military service.

THE INTER-WAR YEARS

The returning service-men in 1919 sought to recreate the pre-war social environment, whilst the fellows sought to improve the college facilities for the undergraduates, most substantially through the building of the Memorial Court across Queen's Road from the old Court of Clare. In 1924 the first phase of the Memorial Court was opened by the Chancellor, Lord Balfour. The cost was met from the two pre-war endowments and from gifts in memory of those members of the college who had lost their lives in the war. The court was built on the old fellows' garden, set back from Queen's Road on the gravel ridge that bounded the flood plain of the river Cam.

The college finances had been adversely affected by the fall in student numbers during the war, only partly offset by the residence in the college of army officers on staff courses, but there was a high priority given to the provision of rooms for undergraduates, both in the Memorial Court and through new accommodation on the college site in Chesterton Lane, now called the 'Colony'. This priority, coupled with the preference by benefactors for endowing buildings rather than fellowships, limited the number of fellows during the inter-war years. College investments were mainly in land, and the allowed types of reinvestment were limited and required the approval of the Ministry of Agriculture. Wilson was the college bursar until 1927, when he became the University Treasurer under the new statutes of 1925–26, a position he held until he was elected as Master of Clare in 1929. He was succeeded as bursar by Harrison, who continued the policy for increasing college income by moving investments

5. Clare College, opening of the Memorial Court by the University Chancellor, Lord Balfour on Armistice Day 1924, with Sir Giles Gilbert Scott (architect), the Master (Dr Mollison) and Fellows.

from land to commercial property. Godwin attributes the ability of Clare to complete the Memorial Court during the 1930s to the skill with which Harrison managed the financial affairs of the college, though the margin of income available for the new building was also helped by delaying maintenance on the Old Court and keeping a strict limit on the number of fellows, so there were later costs for repairs and also academic penalties through the need to use external supervisors for Clare students. Some of the cost of the new buildings was met by using part of the college's endowments for which there was a statutory requirement to repay the capital through a 'sinking fund' over a period of years lasting until the 1950s.

During the inter-war years, continuing the pre-war practices, colleges did not aim to provide undergraduate supervision for all parts of undergraduates' courses. However, in 1920 there was an important reorganisation of the educational arrangements in the college – the first sign of the influence of Henry Thirkill, recently returned from hospital in Bristol following war service in East Africa. The pre-war system had involved two tutors, one of whom was the senior tutor. Mollison had become a tutor in 1880 and he was senior tutor from 1894 until he became Master in 1915. Wardale was a tutor from 1894 until 1915, and senior tutor from then until 1919 when the system was changed. The new system was headed by a single tutor, initially Wardale, but in 1920, due to his ill-health, he was replaced by Thirkill. The tutor was supported by an assistant tutor for finance, looking after all the financial duties previously carried out by the tutors, and by one or more assistant tutors who were also directors of studies in specified subjects. Each student was assigned by the tutor to an assistant tutor, who would be responsible for advising him and for arranging supervisions, unless the tutor took this responsibility himself.

At the first meeting of the Clare governing body in 1926, when the new college statutes came into effect, Dr Mollison was the Master and there were eleven fellows: the Revd. H. W. Fulford, senior fellow first elected in 1877, who had been Dean before the war; Prof H. M. Chadwick, the distinguished professor of Anglo-Saxon; Wilson, about to become University Treasurer and soon to be Master; Thirkill, then a lecturer in physics and the tutor; Harrison, mathematics fellow and about to become bursar; W. J. Landon, 'Secretary' (chief administrator) of the faculty of engineering; the Revd. W. Telfer, formerly a mathematician, who was the Dean and later became the Master of Selwyn; Raymond Priestley, a geologist and distinguished explorer who had been with both Scott and Shackleton in the Antarctic – he was secretary of the newly formed Board of Research Studies and later became the Secretary-General of the Faculties before leaving Cambridge to become a Vice-Chancellor briefly in Australia then at Birmingham University; A. D. Nock, a young classic, but already developing an international reputation, who later in the decade became a professor at Harvard and was, I believe, a founder-member of the Society of Fellows; and Harry Godwin, at that time a young research fellow in botany; one fellow, was absent from the meeting – Mansfield Forbes, English.

Of these twelve fellows, five were involved in college teaching, typically doing twelve hours supervision each week in term time. Thirkill was director of studies in natural sciences, medicine and agriculture, but he would have supervised only in natural sciences. Harrison directed studies in mathematics and mechanical sciences, and supervised in mathematics. Landon supervised in mechanical sciences, Nock in classics and Forbes in English. Godwin also was doing an considerable amount of teaching in botany but mainly in other colleges and in the laboratory. With an average of about 200 undergraduates in Clare in this period, much of their supervision was done by members of the university (often not fellows of any college) who supported themselves by providing this teaching service to a number of colleges. It would have been the responsibility of directors of studies, then as now, to find suitable supervisors for their students.

Harrison became bursar in 1927 when Wilson was appointed University Treasurer, and most of the supervision in mathematics then came from outside the college until 1933. In that year Harold Taylor, a New Zealander who had come to Clare after a first degree in Dunedin, was elected to a research fellowship after winning a Smith's prize in mathematics; subsequently in 1936 he became an official fellow when he was appointed to a university lectureship in mathematics. In 1929 Dr E. T. C. (Tenney) Spooner, a university lecturer in pathology, became a fellow. The following year, after Nock had left Clare for a professorship at Harvard, Nicholas Hammond from Caius College was appointed a research fellow in classics – he found himself having to look after the supervision of 25 students, many of rather modest academic ability.

THE SECOND WORLD WAR

During the second world war many of the younger members of staff in the university and colleges were given leave of absence for military or government service. In Clare, Hammond was away during 1939–45 and had a distinguished role working with the resistance movement in Greece and in Crete and Syria, concluding the war as a Lt. Colonel having been mentioned twice in despatches and awarded the DSO. Taylor was away from the college during 1939–45, becoming a Lt. Colonel and a senior instructor at the school of artillery. In 1938 Brian Reddaway had become a fellow in economics and university lecturer, but was on leave during 1940–47 in the division of statistics at the Board of Trade, where he became chief statistician.

Henry Thirkill was elected Master of Clare in 1939, succeeding Wilson who had become Burgess (Member of Parliament) for the university. For a period before this Thirkill had the title of President in Clare so that he could preside at college meetings and at high table when Wilson was away on parliamentary duties. After becoming Master, Thirkill continued to take responsibility for admissions to the college, not only during the war but also until the mid 1950s, almost until he retired. Spooner was tutor of Clare from 1939 until 1947 when he moved to a professorship in London and Hammond became tutor. Harrison continued as bursar until 1949, but Telfer, who had been Dean since 1921, left in 1944 to become the Master of Selwyn College, being succeeded as Dean by the Revd. C. F. D. (Charlie) Moule, who later was the Lady Margaret Professor of Divinity during 1951–76.

6. *Conversation Piece* Discussions in the Combination Room, Clare College. H. Thirkill (Master, standing), W. Telfer (Dean, centre), W. J. Harrison (Bursar, left).

THE POST-WAR PERIOD 1945 to 1951

In 1939 there were only 12 fellows in Clare, but the number had increased to 22 by 1951 and to 32 by 1958, including two (Wilson and Harrison) who had been elected under the old statutes (pre 1926). After 1945, in the post-war environment of a new national enthusiasm for academic study and research and the resulting government money to fund students Clare began to recruit more fellows as directors of studies and supervisors. There was a shortage of supervisors, partly induced by the rapid growth of student numbers and partly because returning fellows were having difficulty in re-learning their earlier expertise following their war service which had usually been quite different in character from their academic work. In Clare, the mathematics fellow, Harold Taylor, returned in 1945 and had been regarded as the likely successor to Harrison as bursar, but he ceased to be available when he was immediately appointed as university treasurer, a post that had been held in the 1920s by a previous Clare mathematician, G. H. A. Wilson. Taylor was succeeded as mathematics fellow by Robert Rankin, who had been elected to a fellowship in 1939, but was away during 1940–45 when he became a leading authority on the mathematics of the ballistic trajectories of rockets – some way removed from his own research areas in pure mathematics.

It was at the invitation of Robert Rankin that I began to supervise Clare students in applied mathematics in 1949. At that time I held a fellowship at Peterhouse but in 1951 when Rankin became a professor in Birmingham University I became a fellow of Clare and director of studies in mathematics and in mathematics for natural sciences. My early students in Clare included Tim Smiley and Donald Lynden-Bell, both of whom later became fellows of the college and subsequently Cambridge professors, in philosophy and in astronomy respectively. Another was Walter Bodmer (later to become Sir Walter Bodmer), who used his mathematics for research in genetics, and became a professor in Oxford and later Director of Research of the Imperial Cancer Research Fund. I also recall an American graduate called Jim Watson who had rooms near mine in the Memorial Court in 1951–52. Two years later Crick and Watson provided the basis for the genetic code with their discovery of the double helix structure of DNA. They shared with Maurice Wilkins the Nobel Prize for Medicine in 1962.

Several of the post-war arrivals in Clare had an important role in developments that led to the founding of Clare Hall. Brian Cooper, who became a fellow in 1944 and directed studies in engineering, succeeded Harrison as bursar in 1949. Brian Pippard (later Sir Brian) was the physics fellow in 1947 and later became the first President of Clare Hall and the Cavendish Professor. Michael Stoker (later Sir Michael), who had been in the Royal Army Medical Corps during 1942–46, succeeded Spooner as the medical fellow in 1949 and was also an assistant tutor until 1958 when he became a professor in Glasgow before preceding Bodmer as Director of Research of the Imperial Cancer Research Fund, still later returning to Cambridge and becoming the third President of Clare Hall. Tony Harding was also an assistant tutor and fellow of Clare in the post-war period, much later becoming fellow and bursar of Clare Hall after intermitting with a distinguished career in the chemical industry. John Northam, elected as a fellow in 1950 after war service in the Royal Air Force, later became senior tutor and, as we shall see, was a major influence in the founding of Clare Hall.

Chapter 3

UNIVERSITY GROWTH AND COLLEGIATE VALUES

POST-WAR CAMBRIDGE

In the period after the end of the second world war, amongst returning ex-service men there was an unprecedented dedication to study and scholarship. This educational environment was different from that experienced after the first war when many returning ex-service men were allowed to take ordinary degrees and the students and dons generally sought to restore the pre-war atmosphere of the university. Release from the armed services came slowly after August 1945 despite the new-found political enthusiasm for education that followed the 1944 Education Act and the consequent priority that was given to the release of students whose studies had been interrupted. My own release benefited in this way, aided by the airlift that brought troops home from India in seats installed in the bomb-bays of aircraft, though delayed by the belief by the War-Office that I was still in Germany, and like most returning students I did not reach Cambridge until 1946. Those students not planning an academic career returned only briefly to satisfy residence requirements for a degree, taking advantage of the allowances that permitted a degree to be taken with only five terms residence instead of the normal nine terms. However, there was an accumulation of many of the best scholars over a seven-year period who returned with a determination to regain and surpass the academic distinction that they had achieved before their war service.

Never before – so the tutors told us – had Cambridge students collectively shown such enthusiasm for their studies. Their dedication extended to research – we had been surprised to discover not only that the government was prepared to pay our fees[1] and maintenance costs without

---

[1] Fees were paid for war veterans (including those directed to civilian national service), not (until 1960) for those students coming to Cambridge directly from school (except those with state scholarships).

the means tests on parents' income that had impoverished so many pre-war scholars but also that this seemingly inexplicable generosity apparently extended to research degrees provided one could find a suitable supervisor. It was helpful to have obtained first class honours, though this was not a necessary requirement because the results of many students had been affected by their interrupted studies and shortened courses. No students with less than three years national service were allowed priority release, and some had been away for seven years. Few had any opportunity for academic work during war-service, though some scientists, engineers and mathematicians, had their future careers fashioned from their war-time experiences, for example on aircraft design, on radar and on atomic energy.

The sudden accumulation of talent in the new Cambridge Ph.Ds in the post-war years was not initially matched by academic opportunities either in Cambridge or elsewhere, though some colleges took the opportunity to increase the numbers of research fellowships using funds that had remained dormant during the war. Competition was severe – in my own college (Peterhouse) three bye-fellows were appointed in 1949, of whom two later became Cambridge professors and one became a judge. The facilities for research students were also limited in most cases to the space available before the war. Except for those studying experimental subjects, few research students had any study facilities provided either by their colleges or by the university, though some libraries were sufficiently uncrowded to provide a work-place for some students. As most of the regular licensed lodgings were required for the increased numbers of undergraduates, most research students had to find their own lodgings in the town – usually also being their normal place of study.

In my own area of theoretical physics, the absence of academic posts in the UK encouraged many of my contemporaries to obtain post-doctoral appointments in the United States. When some of us later returned to faculty positions in Cambridge, our connections in North America led to a regular interchange and our own graduate students with their new Ph.Ds commonly went to America for a year or two – some stayed or returned later to academic posts there. More senior members of university faculties in America came to Cambridge for one or two semesters. This experience of academic interchange was later an important factor in the founding of Clare Hall.

HIGHER EDUCATION: THE NATIONAL SCENE[2]

In 1937 there were 50,000 students in 21 universities in the UK (including five just emerging from the dependent status of university college). About one quarter of the students were at London University, one quarter shared between Oxford and Cambridge, and one quarter at Scottish universities, the remaining 12,500 being shared between 14 institutions. Studies at Oxford and Cambridge were then dominated by the arts subjects (80 per cent of students and 70 per cent, respectively). From 1919 onwards, the direct contribution from the State came from the Treasury and was distributed through the University Grants Committee (UGC), thus providing a degree of insulation of the universities from interference by government. In 1937, the grants made up only one third of total university income in the UK, the remainder coming from fees, endowments, and local authorities. From 1946 onwards, the UGC grant was indispensable to all universities and formed the major part of their income. The initial grant to Cambridge in 1919 had been £30,000, during the second world war it was just under £120,000, but it increased post-war to £545,000 in 1947–48.[3]

Between 1935 and 1961 the number of university students in the UK more than doubled – from about 50,000 to 113,000 – with undertakings that it would go very much higher. During the period from 1953 to 1963, when Sir Keith Murray (later Lord Murray) was chairman of the UGC, approval was given for seven new universities, and the capital programme increased from £3.8 million in 1956 to £30 million in 1963. In 1959 the previous aim of a maximum of 135,000 students by the mid-sixties had been raised to 175,000, and later it was raised again. In parallel with this expansion, the Ministry of Education had initiated reforms in the local authorities' technical colleges and ten of the largest had been designated in 1957 as institutions to be supported by a direct grant from the Ministry, with the title of colleges of advanced technology.

In the same period of expansion, the procedures for the direct financial support of students were reformed by a committee under Sir Colin

---

[2] This section is largely based on Carswell, *Government and the Universities in Britain, 1960–1980* (Cambridge 1985).

[3] Vice-Chancellor's report by Sir Henry Thirkill, C.U. Reporter 1947–48 p. 161.

Higher education: the national scene

Anderson, whose report 'Grants to Students' was presented in 1960[4]. Their recommendation that all students who achieved at least two passes at the A level examination and were accepted by a university would receive a grant was immediately accepted by the government, though the maintenance element of the grant remained subject to a means test based on parental income. This entitlement was complemented by the report of the Robbins committee on higher education, which recommended an expansion of universities so that a place would be available for every qualified student[5].

In keeping with the spirit of the times, the Ministry of Education was renamed as the Department of Education and Science, to whom the University Grants Committee would report instead of to the Treasury. There was dual expansion of the universities and the parallel group of technical colleges and colleges for higher education which remained outside the protective umbrella of the UGC. New government funding for research and research studentships in universities was to be managed by research councils – for science, medicine, agriculture, and the natural environment, later to be joined by studentships in the arts subjects now administered by the British Academy.

The system of educational grants brought to the university a new group of undergraduates of high ability. Grants from the government enabled the university to increase the number of faculty appointments, not only in major teaching subjects but also in 'rarer subjects' and new disciplines, where there were fewer undergraduates. More time could be devoted to research, and there were major increases in the numbers of research students and other graduate students. Better facilities were provided for lecture rooms, laboratories and libraries.

However, these developments also gave rise to the discontents and strains that eventually led to the appointment in Cambridge of the Bridges Syndicate on the relations between the university and the colleges. Outstanding amongst these discontents was the large number of university teaching officers (UTOs) without college fellowships or close college connections – a clear consequence of the university outgrowing its

---

[4] Command 1051, HMSO, 1960.
[5] Report of the Committee on Higher Education (chaired by Lord Robbins), Cmnd 2154 (HMSO 1963).

traditional relationship with the colleges. Coupled with this problem was the failure of the university to provide satisfactory facilities for those members of its staff who had no college connections – many were not provided with offices and few had access to the kind of social facilities that so benefited academic life for college fellows.

SEEKING TO HOLD BACK THE TIDE

It was in this environment of national political and public enthusiasm for higher education and research that Cambridge University began to look again at its future development, particularly in view of the risks to its collegiate character through continuing expansion. The responsibility for a major review in the mid-1950s was given to the General Board, whose secretary (and principal scribe for their deliberations) was Dr Harold Taylor, fellow of Clare. Members of the Board also included Sir Henry Thirkill, Master of Clare (its longest serving member) and Dr Godwin (senior official fellow of Clare).

The General Board Report 1955–56 began by citing earlier concerns: In 1946, in a statement to the University Grants Committee, the Council of the Senate had observed[6]: "At present the number of university teaching officers (UTOs), other than professors, who are not fellows of colleges is nearly one-third of the total number, and it is undesirable that so large a proportion should be without fellowships." By April 1955 the position was worse and amongst UTOs there were 301 with and 370 without fellowships (excluding professors, for whom college fellowships were assured through a quota system). There were more than 100 graduates holding posts in the university who were not members of any college.

The unease at this imbalance of UTOs between university and the colleges was mirrored by unease about the increasing number of graduate students. Already in 1944 the Vice-Chancellor Dr Hele, Master of Emmanuel, had urged the university to consider founding a new college for graduate students so as to avoid an excessive proportion of graduates in the existing colleges. He was concerned that a conspicuous presence of graduate students whose concern was with research would provide a

---

[6] Cited in General Board: Report on the development of the university (C. U. Reporter 1955–6, p. 411 et seq.).

misleading example to the undergraduates, and might lead them away from the benefits (to themselves and to the nation) of a career outside the academic profession. He returned to this theme a year later in his report on retiring as Vice-Chancellor[7], but other problems were more urgent and there was no general support for founding a graduate college at that time.

The views of the General Board in 1955 are summarised by their statement:

The Board see no prospect of any development that would result in it becoming possible to provide college fellowships for the great majority of the staff of the university at its present size, but they think it most desirable that all members of the teaching staff of the university should be members of colleges, and that as many as possible should have more than just a nominal connection with a college. Ill considered expansion of the staff of the university would clearly make this objective more difficult to achieve.

As a sweetener for the recommendations that would follow, the Board expressed their hope that progress will be made as quickly as possible with the establishment of a faculty club. They then analysed the pressures that had led to expansion of the university – since 1945, eleven new university departments had come into being. There had been pressure to increase staff to reduce the burden of formal teaching and to give time for research and for sabbatical leave, and to increase research staff in areas given special impetus by the war. They noted that Cambridge was particularly well qualified to help the country by developing research in certain fundamental scientific fields. However, their view was that teaching and related needs were now largely satisfied – since 1946–47, over a period of 8 years, 276 offices and posts had been approved, averaging 35 per year. Proposals for 1957–62 would (if approved) give expansion at the same rate.

The General Board's view was that such growth was not sustainable[8]. Although they accepted that there was a need for limited expansion for research, they considered that it was essential that such expansion should as far as possible be compensated by a contraction elsewhere (in the same

---

[7] Dr Hele, C. U. Reporter 1945–46 p. 136.
[8] They failed to mention that the growth during the post-war period was enhanced by catching up on the appointments postponed during the war. The average annual increase in UTOs was 20 in the period 1938–59. Subsequently the average was 28 in the period 1959–97.

faculty). They would therefore ask faculties and departments proposing expansion in one area to indicate other areas in which contraction could take place.

They gave their views on the proper size of graduate teaching and research staff: There should be adequate UTOs (university teaching officers) for undergraduate teaching. Research of outstanding merit should be encouraged – but not on a permanent basis. There should be only a limited range of optional subjects in lectures and examinations so as to avoid causing excessive teaching requirements. All activities not concerned with undergraduate teaching should be reviewed from time to time with a view to reducing them, for example on retirement of senior members.

UNREST AMONGST THE FACULTY

The General Board report in 1955–56 provided a focus for a university discussion about the development of teaching and research and led to a recognition of the need for expansion of staff and facilities. This was the opposite of what had been intended. However, unlike Whewell, a century earlier, Thirkill did not have the control provided to the oligarchy by the Elizabethan statutes. The discussion of the report attracted university barons as well as angry young men. Lord Todd expressed doubts about the assumption that the university population would not increase, and said that it was certainly wrong to assume that the present balance between subjects would persist. Gold, a collaborator of Hoyle, criticised the Board for placing research in second place to undergraduate teaching and for ignoring the speed of change induced by research. Wilkinson and others pointed to the importance and increasing need for formal teaching for graduate (research) students.

In response to the discussion the General Board produced a second report in 1956. Firstly, and defensively, they said that the discussion had not appreciated how much expansion had taken place since 1938: graduate staff had increased by 82%, research students by 164%, undergraduates by 32%. Major new buildings completed since 1945 included a main building and workshop for engineering, stage I of the new chemistry laboratory and the veterinary school. Others were being planned or had already begun construction. They then essentially negated their earlier recommendations, about expansion being balanced by contraction elsewhere, by stating that these would only be interpreted as guidelines when considering proposals put forward for the next quinquenium.

A significant contribution to the discussion of the second report came from F. G. Young[9], who welcomed the change of emphasis and the extension of teaching needs to include those for research students – the logic of such a change pointed also to the need for a graduate college, a need that had been stated in 1944 by the then Vice-Chancellor, Dr Hele, and a university combination room or faculty club would not meet this need. He also suggested that senior researchers would welcome membership of such a college, and it would be a suitable milieu for senior visiting scholars who could not be accommodated in the existing college system.

THE BRIDGES SYNDICATE

In June 1960 a Grace was approved to appoint a Syndicate to review the relations between the university and the colleges. This was a result of the stresses that the 1956 report of the General Board had sought to reverse – or at least restrain – by limiting expansion of the university. When it was apparent from the discussion of their report that their solution was both unacceptable and unrealistic, it became necessary to re-examine the problems. It was decided that radical changes might be required, possibly at a level that would normally require a Royal Commission to take effect. For this reason, the Syndicate was to be chaired by Lord Bridges, who had earlier been head of the civil service and a war-time secretary of the Cabinet. The deputy Chairman would be Sir Eric Ashby, recently appointed as Master of Clare College, formerly Vice-Chancellor of Queen's University Belfast and one of the most respected university administrators in the country.

The terms of reference of the Syndicate were to report on any ways in which they think that the relations between the university and the colleges could be improved, and to consider the following five matters in particular:

---

[9] Young subsequently became the first Master of Darwin College for graduates.

(a) the employment of university graduate staff for college teaching and administration, and the employment of college graduate staff for university duties;
(b) the possibility of better co-ordination of university and college appointments;
(c) the possibility of increasing the participation of the graduate staff of the university in college duties and privileges;
(d) the facilities to be provided by the university for its graduate staff;
(e) the financial relations between the university and the colleges.

The Syndicate was told that its members were free to include in their report suggestions for changes in college practice which they considered desirable, and also bearing in mind the provisions of the Universities of Oxford and Cambridge Act, 1923, to recommend amendments of both the statutes and the ordinances of the university.

The scale of the problem as seen in 1959 is illustrated by the following table[10]:

	Year		1928	1938	1951	1959
University teaching officers (UTOs)			372	446	690	866
UTOs without college fellowships			109	170	318	414
Percent without fellowships:		Science	31	42	50	54
		Arts	21	28	33	30
		Other	62	78	86	91
		Total	29	38	46	48

BRIDGES AND THE 1922 ROYAL COMMISSION

The influence of Ashby is particularly evident in the historical approach described in section one of the Bridges report. Their selection of extracts from the report of the Royal Commission of 1922 (Cmd. 1588) both establish their viewpoint and provide a sense of historical continuity. The original author of these extracts was probably G. M. Trevelyan, later to become Regius Professor of Modern History in 1927 and Master of Trinity College in 1940. Trevelyan and Sir Hugh Anderson, the Master of Caius College, had been responsible for assembling the final draft of the Royal

[10] Reporter 1961–62 (Bridges report pages 1073–1151, 13 March 1962) see appendix J, table 2, p.1141.

Commission's report (as it related to Cambridge) at Heacham during the summer of 1921[11]. In many respects, despite the occasional quaint references to the Empire, the extracts still remain relevant to the educational strategy of the university seventy years after they were written and thirty years after they were quoted in the Bridges Report:

The Commission stressed in several passages the importance of teaching and research going hand in hand:

... the best teacher is one who imparts to his pupils his own sense of the living interest in their common subject; the subject should be regarded not as a fixed body of knowledge, but as a territory increased day by day with the accretion of new discoveries and new speculations. The proper interaction of teaching and research is of the very essence of the highest education' (paragraph 38).

... A university can only flourish if it is a seat of learning as well as a school for undergraduates. Its teachers must be men of learning, absorbing and utilising, by steady research, the new material which constantly becomes available throughout the field of knowledge, and themselves contributing to the supply of such material, according to their abilities. In the absence of research, teaching itself must inevitably lose both solidity and freshness and must become fatally impoverished in all its branches' (paragraph 105).

The Commission used the term *research* in a wide sense to cover:

not only
(i) the actual study and collation of new material, or the working out of special scientific problems,

but also
(ii) the promotion of thought and learning in the widest sense, including (a) the self-education, study and thought necessary before a student can decide on the particular branch of a subject for original work suited to his powers, (b) a constantly renewed familiarity with the discoveries and views of others, both living and dead, and (c) travel for purposes of study (paragraph 104).

The Commission thought that of these two duties – teaching and research – the latter tended to be neglected because of the pressure of the former. From this they derived their recommendation for increasing the numbers of university staff, particularly professors and 'readers', who should be able to devote more of their time to research.

---

[11] Brooke, *A History of the University of Cambridge*, vol IV, 1870–1990, p. 368 (Cambridge 1993).

They recommended that more attention should be devoted in future to advanced students:

> The two senior Universities of the Empire have also now the chance of becoming to a much greater extent than formerly centres of research, and of graduate study for the whole Empire and for American and foreign guests (paragraph 33).

> ... there is at the present time an increasing pressure of advanced students from the Empire and abroad who desire to come to Oxford and Cambridge for intellectual life and teaching of the highest order, and it appears clear that owing to concurrent pressure of ordinary undergraduates on the resources and space of the university, the needs of the advanced students will not be adequately met in future if energetic steps are not taken to provide specially for them (paragraph 106).

The Commission expressed the greatest faith in the college system and held:

> ... strongly that, as the efficient maintenance of college teaching is of the greatest value to the student, nothing should be done to weaken this side of the existing educational system (paragraph 99).

> With all its characteristic difficulties, drawbacks, and exceptions, which are on the increase, the system of college instruction is largely accountable for the educational achievement of the two senior Universities. The teaching of the undergraduate, man to man, by his tutor or supervisor, who is very often resident in college alongside of his pupil, gives to the education at Oxford and Cambridge something scarcely to be got elsewhere in such full measure (paragraph 23).

The belief of the Commission in a fully collegiate university is implicit in their thinking and comes out clearly in certain passages, for example:

> (i) ... the college system offers, in our view, a valuable means of educational experiment and progress, which would be much reduced if the university were the one and only organ of teaching and the only body for choosing scholars and fellows. The colleges afford a number of centres of educational initiative, in matters of learning, instruction and the welfare of undergraduates (paragraph 12).
>
> 'Nevertheless, we recognise that there are certain respects in which the work done by the colleges needs to be supplemented to a greater extent than at present by university activity, and we therefore recommend certain changes in the existing financial and educational relations between college and university (paragraph 12).

(ii) Of all the problems which have engaged our attention, none has given rise to more discussion, because none has been of more fundamental importance, than that of the proper relation between the universities and the colleges in regard to teaching. In any institution, and above all in universities presenting the complexity of Oxford and Cambridge, efficiency and economy can only be secured by coordinating carefully the activities of the individuals and bodies concerned, and this can only be effected by some unifying and controlling power (paragraph 75).

(iii) At present most college teachers make themselves to some extent specialists and many of them have made valuable contributions to knowledge; but the university has hitherto only been able in a meagre way to offer them the stimulus and recognition of a special status together with such financial aid as might enable them to devote more time to their special studies and to publication. It is not desirable that these men should cease to be college teachers. Any sharp distinction between college teachers and university lecturers or university demonstrators and any divorce between teaching and research would, in our judgement, be detrimental to the highest interest of the university in its dual capacity (paragraph 91).

THE BRIDGES SCHEME IN OUTLINE

The Bridges Syndicate endorsed the view of the 1922 Royal Commission in placing a high value on a fully collegiate university and the efficient maintenance of college teaching. However, they observed that the difficulties of maintaining such a teaching system were markedly greater in 1962 than in 1922. This was due to the great increase in the number of subjects being taught and examined in the university, which made it harder for any college to provide teachers from amongst its own fellows in all, or even in most, subjects. Thus 'college teaching' for many undergraduates was provided by supervisors who were not fellows of any college.

The Syndicate concluded that it was necessary to make a number of changes to strengthen the collegiate character of the university. The proposed changes were intended to bring university and college teaching into a closer relationship that would not only improve teaching arrangements, but also would foster closer cooperation between members of faculties in related subject areas. Their proposals were also intended to provide college fellowships for the largest possible number of senior members of the university.

The proposed scheme was not concerned with professors and the most senior administrative officers for whom the university statutes already provided a quota system for college fellowships. It was however designed to cover nearly all other university teaching officers who had been appointed to the retiring age and, in addition, assistant directors of research who had completed at least five years' service. In describing the scheme, university officers in these classes were called 'qualified officers'. Nothing in the proposed scheme would preclude a college from electing to a fellowship any university officer, or indeed any other person whom it might wish to elect.

The essence of the proposed scheme was three-fold:

firstly, a schedule would be maintained of qualified officers who were not already fellows of colleges, who wished to be considered for election to a fellowship, and who had expressed willingness to fulfil the obligations of fellowship which a college might impose: such officers were described in the report as 'officers on the schedule';

secondly, each college would be expected to have among its fellows not fewer than a prescribed quota of qualified officers, and, if at any time its quota was not full, to fill it by electing qualified officers in accordance with the scheme (outlined in appendix B of the report);

thirdly, a college which was fulfilling its obligations under the scheme and was deemed eligible for financial assistance for this purpose would be entitled to receive such assistance from the university.

Since the scheme would have such important consequences for the colleges, the Syndicate recommended that it should be managed by a new body, the Board of Colleges, which would have a status comparable with the three main central committees of the university. For the purpose of drawing up the original schedule and keeping it up to date, every university officer who was not already a fellow of a college would, on his becoming a qualified officer, be asked by the Board of Colleges whether he wished to be included in the schedule as being a person who, if invited into a fellowship, would be prepared to undertake college duties. What the schedule would provide was an assurance to colleges seeking to elect fellows that all those on the schedule were willing in one way or another to take responsibilities in a college.

The Syndicate recommended that the college quotas should be determined by the Council of the Senate. It would be based on student numbers in each college, and periodically revised by the Council, in each case on the recommendation of the Board of Colleges. On the basis of 1962 data it appeared that the resulting increase in the total college fellowship would be less than 30 per cent. This would have sufficed to provide fellowships for all those qualified officers who were willing to undertake college duties. Such duties, the Syndicate suggested, might be: to undertake supervision of undergraduates (in rare subjects, perhaps for a group of colleges), to take part in college examinations, to assist in tutorial work, to look after research students, or to be responsible for some administrative duty. The Syndicate assumed that a college would be under no obligation to continue in his fellowship any fellow who had ceased to discharge the duties which the college had assigned to him. On the other hand, it would naturally be open to a college to elect an officer on the schedule to a fellowship without imposing special obligations, and equally to waive any obligations which might originally have been imposed. Although there would be no obligation on colleges to offer fellowships to qualified officers not on the schedule, nevertheless colleges which appoint such officers to fellowships should be allowed to count them against the quota and to claim from the university grants in respect of them.

The Syndicate commented that there would doubtless grow up in the university a class of university teaching officers who had not put their names down for fellowships, or had declined fellowships, and who looked for their amenities to a (proposed) university centre, or to a graduate college, if one should be founded; but the idea that this class was in any way underprivileged would, they hoped, disappear.

However, in addition to their proposal to increase the numbers of university staff holding college fellowships, the Syndicate considered it desirable to increase the involvement in university teaching of fellows who were not members of the university staff. This could be done by creating a new class of *Faculty Lecturers*, chosen from such fellows of colleges, who would give lectures or otherwise assist in university teaching on a part-time basis.

It was recognised that the increases in the numbers of fellowships which the scheme involved would result in financial difficulties for many colleges unless substantial help could be found. The Syndicate recommended that this difficulty should be met by the use for new purposes of the college contributions to the university. These contributions amounted in the year 1961–62 to £144,000, only about 3 per cent of the university's recurrent income. The Syndicate proposed that the college contributions should in future be used to promote purposes of common interest to the university and the colleges. These could include:

(a) payments to the poorer colleges to cover the costs of increasing the number of their fellows;
(b) payments to cover the cost of some (part-time) faculty lecturers;
(c) payments to colleges for buildings and other capital purposes, including the additions to buildings which might be necessary in colleges which were called on to add substantially to their fellowship.

GRADUATE STUDENTS

The Bridges Syndicate considered that if their proposals were adopted, a solution would have been found to the problem that so many existing university teaching officers on the university's permanent staff had previously been largely cut off from college life. But the balance of the scheme could easily be upset if close co-operation were not maintained between the university and the colleges. For example, if the number of UTOs was to continue the 3.8 per cent annual increase of the previous decade, it was clear that the colleges would not be able to elect the increased numbers into fellowships. It would be for the university itself to solve the problem of creating additional fellowships, for example by founding a graduate college.

The balance could also be affected by increases in student numbers, a matter in which there was room for more co-operation between the university and the colleges. One reason for the expansion of university teaching staff since the end of the war had been the growth of undergraduate numbers over which the university, as opposed to the colleges, has had no control. Uncertainty about the future number of undergraduates is embarrassing to the university, not only in connection with the appointment of teaching staff, but also in determining its requirements for laboratory, lecture-room, and library accommodation, requirements which, if they are to be met, have to be formulated one or two quinquennia ahead. Although the trend of thought among colleges in

1961 was against any increase in undergraduate numbers, the Syndicate did not think that this was a reliable basis on which to plan the university's building programme. They recommended that colleges should provide the university every five years with estimates of the numbers of undergraduates they propose to admit each year during the ensuing five year period and that colleges should agree not to depart significantly from these estimates without permission from the university.

The Syndicate observed that the position on the number of graduate students was different. First, the university has some measure of control since candidates for research degrees must be approved by the appropriate Degree Committee and the Board of Graduate Studies. Secondly, the Syndicate thought that an increase in numbers was probable and ought to be accepted. Nevertheless they regarded it as essential that the university should exercise control over the extent, quality, and timing of the increase. They considered this to be all the more necessary because the facilities provided for graduate students fell short of what is required, even for the existing numbers.

In their enquiries the Syndicate was repeatedly reminded that there was in Cambridge no single focus for the life of the university as distinct from its colleges. There were offices, libraries, laboratories, and a Combination Room; but the university could only offer hospitality through one or other of the colleges. They commented

But it is the university faculties and departments at least as much as the colleges which attract scholars to Cambridge. The colleges, though willing to help the university to entertain its visitors and to provide centres for the life of its staff, are themselves overcrowded and can no longer undertake as much responsibility as they have in the past for social cohesion in the university.

The report continued:

There is another function which some colleges cannot adequately fulfil for the university, namely to provide cohesion for the increasingly large numbers of graduate research students. Only a few colleges are able to offer them amenities appropriate to their needs, and for many research students there is no communal life outside the library or the laboratory. They live in flats or lodgings scattered over the city. Many of them are married; many come from overseas.

The situation of research students was not one of the five particular matters mentioned in the terms of reference of the Bridges Syndicate, but since it had a bearing on relations between the university and the colleges, it was appropriate that they should comment on it. The number of registered research students in residence had increased greatly in recent years:

Year	Research students[12]
1929	204
1938	231
1951	760
1959	916
1961	1,114

There was also a growing number of people engaged in post-graduate courses and research but who were not registered as research students.

The Syndicate's report included a section on a graduate college:

... The buildings required by such a college would include
(i) a communal room for graduate students;
(ii) if possible, a certain number of living rooms for graduate students;
(iii) some provision of rooms for fellows or senior members.

The report continued:

We are naturally attracted by a proposal on these lines, and we believe that a graduate college would provide a new and valuable element in the life of the university. It would also, of course, ease the problem of the incorporation of teaching officers into college life ... But we recognise that a single graduate college would provide for only a proportion of research students in Cambridge and that the immediate need (apart from the building of blocks of flats in which married students can live) is for a University Centre, where research students could have meals, read and relax, and hold meetings, and where married research students ... could bring their wives. The recommendation we make for this Centre is summarised below, and we feel obliged to give it higher priority than the proposal for a graduate college. We should, however, like to see a graduate college come into existence, and would be happy to see an endowment sufficient to bring its creation into the nearer future than may be possible if it has to compete for funds with other university building projects.

---

[12] By the year 1994–95, the number of full-time graduate students had increased to 4,562 as listed by colleges. However, this would include students taking Masters degrees, and students who had exceeded three years of study towards a Ph.D. and were no longer paying fees. The number of Ph.D. students listed by faculties as studying for a Ph.D. in 1994–95 was 2,633.

A UNIVERSITY CENTRE

The need for a faculty club that would provide a centre for graduate staff of the university who were not fellows of colleges had been recognised in a report by the Council of the Senate in 1947 (Reporter 1947–48, p349). A Syndicate appointed to make recommendations reported in 1949, and this resulted in the opening of the University Combination Room in the Regent House in 1950, with a decision also to reserve the Arts School and the Small Examination Hall for later use as a faculty club. This reservation was rescinded in 1957 as a result of further discussions, which led to two alternative options – one for a new building in Granta Place facing the river and one being an extension of the Combination Room to include the East Room in the Old Schools. The latter scheme was finally approved in June 1959, despite much criticism from members of the Regent House. However, the site in Granta Place remained available if a more extensive development proved to be necessary. This was the target of the recommendation by the Bridges Syndicate (paragraphs 140, 141):

These considerations bring us to the conclusion that the university – as distinct from the colleges – still offers no adequate provision for the life of two large sectors of its membership: its academic and administrative staff and its research students. Several committees have made estimates of the cost of providing adequate amenities. The most formidable financial difficulty is that catering and other services become uneconomic if too few people use the amenities. We think there is a way out of this financial difficulty, namely, to meet the needs of research students and those of members of the Regent House through common kitchens and other services, by building a University Centre.

We therefore recommend the creation of a University Centre on the lines set out below which would provide Cambridge with something which we think it needs but has never yet had, namely a focus for the life of the university. One part of it would be reserved for members of the Regent House and another part for research students; but these two parts would share common services: kitchens, central heating, administration and caretaking, and so on. We do not regard the proposed Centre merely as a club. It should be the place for formal and informal university receptions, meetings of conferences in which the university acts as host, a place where scholars and prominent visitors to the university can be adequately welcomed, and a place where members of the university may bring their wives and guests.

In their conclusions the Syndicate argued that their proposals formed a package which, taken as a whole, would restore equilibrium and strengthen the dual loyalty of staff to the university and the colleges:

> It has been our task to carry out such a comprehensive review, at the instance of the university. We cannot expect that all our recommendations will be welcomed in all quarters. But we are all of us convinced that the measures which we have outlined, taken together, constitute a policy which would remove the serious lack of balance which has grown up in recent years between the university and the colleges. We cannot see any other way in which equilibrium can be effectively restored. We believe that viewed in perspective the changes which we have in mind are small compared to the advantages to be gained.

REGENT HOUSE DISCUSSIONS OF THE BRIDGES PROPOSALS

The discussion of the Bridges Report by the Regent House took place in the Easter Term of 1962[13]. There was considerable criticism of the quota system for college fellowships, which had been designed to ensure that each fully established university teaching officer (UTO) would have an opportunity to become a fellow of a college. The Syndicate did not seem to appreciate that the newly appointed UTOs were traditionally the main source from which colleges chose their fellows, particularly in the main teaching subjects for which all colleges wished to provide supervision and to have a fellow as Director of Studies. Under the proposed quota system, which was limited to more senior UTOs and excluded some 300 more junior UTOs, these prime candidates would not count against a college's quota. This would place extra strains on college finances for the poorer colleges (about half the colleges appeared to regard themselves as belonging to this group), and extra pressure on physical accommodation for most colleges. Many speakers expressed the view, some formally on behalf of their colleges, that the Syndicate's proposed quota system addressed only half the problem and its choice of priorities was unsatisfactory. Moreover, with continuing growth in the university, the problem of UTOs, who were not fellows of any college, would increase.

The proposed quota system was to be associated with financial transfers from richer colleges to poorer ones. Whilst this was welcomed by the

---

[13] C. U. Reporter 1961–62, pp 1714–54 (memoranda & comments), and pp.1840–54 (discussion).

potential recipients and not ruled out by the richer ones, discussants thought this was irrelevant to the main issue that the quota system excluded the preferred pool for recruitment of new fellows. The quota system misunderstood the nature of college fellowships – major college duties were normally taken up by well-established fellows, it was inappropriate to suppose that they could be allocated to a new member of the fellowship having no previous connection with the college.

It was observed by several speakers representing their colleges that the Syndicate's proposals, which it sought to describe as a *single unified scheme* were numerous and diverse, and were certainly not indivisible. Surprisingly, some colleges welcomed the idea of a Board of Colleges, even though they opposed the quota system whose operation would be one of the main functions of this Board. Others opposed the Board on the basis that it encroached on existing inter-college committees which functioned well, and it would cause confusion in the university due to its overlap with each of the three existing administrative committees (the Council, the General Board, and the Financial Board).

There was widespread support for the founding by the university of one or more colleges for graduate students and for the development of a university centre. The latter had been given priority by the Bridges Syndicate apparently on the basis that funds available within the university would not permit both. They had, however, commended the founding of a graduate college if a suitable endowment could be found. The Society for Women Members of the Regent House who are not fellows of any college challenged the implied financial assumptions. They advocated financial support from the university or the colleges for low-cost informal *faculty groups* like their society that would provide a meeting place – perhaps including a dining room, common room and library – at much lower cost than the foundation of a graduate college along the lines that were being proposed. Such *Societies* would solve the whole problem of members of university faculties who were not fellows instead of only half the problem, as would follow from the Syndicate's proposals. In time such a society might obtain additional endowment and develop into a full college.

The ideas of the Society for Women Members were prescient, in that they soon obtained initial financial support at a modest level, and later a more substantial endowment that led to their transformation into Lucy

Cavendish College. In the discussion in the Regent House, their ideas were commended by Brian Cooper, the Bursar of Clare, who suggested that such collegiate groups could well be the solution that was being looked for.

RESPONSES AND OUTCOMES

The building of the University Centre in Granta Place was the only direct outcome from the proposals of the Bridges Syndicate, but in addition a *Colleges Committee* was formed that provided termly meetings for heads of colleges to discuss matters of common interest, though it had no executive authority. However, largely in response to the Regent House discussion, the university founded a graduate college, initially called University College, with the requirement that half of its fellows were to be taken from the list of *qualified officers* that had been devised by the Bridges Syndicate. The Wolfson Foundation provided the finance for building the University Centre, allowing the university a greater margin for meeting the initial costs of setting up University College. Subsequently, following a further substantial gift from the Wolfson Foundation, the name was changed from University College to Wolfson College, and the college was allowed to accept a limited number of undergraduates in addition to its graduate intake.

The main outcome of the Bridges Syndicate was indirect and came chiefly from individual initiatives by the colleges in response to the views reflected in the Senate House discussion of their report, which was in many respects more far-sighted than the report itself. Fellows of colleges did not like the Syndicate's recommendations, particularly where they impacted on college autonomy, but the report and its discussion focused concern on the two problems: of members of faculties without college fellowships, and the increasing numbers of graduate students. Most colleges responded by electing more fellows. Once this process was initiated, market forces began to operate and it began to accelerate as each governing body sought to make elections before the most suitable candidates were taken by other colleges. However, there was a large and growing pool to draw from[14] and it was to be many years before the

---

[14] The number of UTOs more than doubled between 1959 and 1997.

scarcity made it difficult in some subjects for colleges to recruit fellows for urgent college teaching from amongst university lecturers.

The Bridges report had included as appendix E a memorandum written by two of its members, Mr M. McCrum and Professor F. G. Young, outlining the form that a graduate college might take. The need for one or more graduate colleges had been widely supported in subsequent discussions, but before the university had moved decisively to found University College, others had begun to explore the idea. Corpus Christi College, where McCrum was the senior tutor, had already in 1962 set up a graduate centre in Leckhampton House where all Corpus graduate students would be provided with accommodation. Leckhampton would remain part of Corpus, but some senior members of the university – not fellows of any college – would also be attached to the centre. In 1966, Darwin College was founded by Trinity, St. John's and Caius Colleges, as a result of a proposal from the Bursars of these colleges that had been initiated by Dr Bradfield the Senior Bursar of Trinity. The Bursars, together with the Bursar of King's, had been working closely together in another connection – on the removal by Parliament of the severely restrictive powers of the Ministry of Agriculture in relation to college investments. Their work involved many discussions with officials in the Ministry and frequent train journeys to London, which allowed time for consideration of other university issues on the return journey[15]. Their final agreement to place the proposal before their governing bodies was reached in mid-1962, courtesy of British Rail, during a prolonged delay just outside Cambridge station. Initially, the proposal was for a college for fellows only, like All Souls in Oxford, but in transit through the governing bodies of their colleges, it was decided to include graduate students. The first Master of Darwin College was Professor F. G. Young, who had for some years been a leading advocate for the founding of a graduate college in the university.

[15] Bradfield, in the *Darwin College Magazine 1989*, p. 15.

Chapter 4

CLARE COLLEGE: NEEDS AND OPTIONS

INVESTMENT POLICY

The appointment of Brian Cooper as bursar of Clare in 1949, coupled with the return of Brian Reddaway to a fellowship and a lectureship in economics, proved to be of great importance to the financial development of Clare that made possible the founding of Clare Hall. At that time changes in college investments required approval from the Ministry of Agriculture – a relic of the time when they had been entirely in land and associated property, though there was an important distinction between 'corporate capital' derived from endowments and 'general capital' derived from the investment of unspent income. In 1884, for example, the 'external income' of Clare was £10,145, of which over half came from 'lands at rack-rent' and 'tithe rent charges' and most of the remainder came from houses on long leases or houses at rack-rent. Rack rent arises from land and buildings, as opposed to land let on building leases where the tenant puts up the buildings which will revert to college ownership on the termination of the lease – thereafter being let at rack-rent or on new building leases.

This pattern was little changed until after the first war, when Wilson and Harrison began to move investments from farm land to commercial property. Allowing for the effects of inflation – about fourfold between 1884 and 1947, there was little overall change in the real value of the college's investment income in that period, amounting to only £37,000 in 1947. However, the college had built extensively – in the Memorial Court, and in Chesterton Lane on the site now called 'the Colony', so its real wealth including the college buildings had grown significantly, partly through new endowments specifically for these buildings.

The bursar's management accounts show investment income increasing during 1947–52 from about £37,000 to about £44,000, of which about half

7. Brian Cooper with Gerda Cooper, Mayor and Mayoress of Cambridge 1970–71, Bursar of Clare College 1949–1978, Fellow 1943–.

came from large shops, offices and factories, and a quarter came from government securities. However, this increase was due almost entirely to re-investment of surplus income, which did not seem likely to continue unspent, because of the ongoing increases in salaries for college staff and the clear signs that money would soon have to be spent on repairs to the fabric of the college. There was also some concern about the cost of the extension of the Memorial Building, an extension which is now called Thirkill Court in the south-west corner of the site opposite the University Library. A tender from Sindalls for about £95,000 for the building work was accepted in March 1952, and it was hoped that most of the cost would be provided through an appeal to former members of the college, but there remained some uncertainty about how far this would succeed[1].

In 1949, when Cooper was appointed as bursar, a large part of the college's investments were in government securities ('gilts'). It would have been obvious to Cooper and Reddaway that wartime inflation had caused these to become a terrible investment. However, it should be remembered that for 200 years up to 1914 there had been little inflation, thus government securities had provided a means of maintaining an income stream from corporate capital that was awaiting investment in land. More came with tithe redemption which was paid for (to the college) by the Church Commissioners in the form of government securities. Then, during the second world war the government raised money by issuing bonds to 'patriots', and after the war the nationalisation of many industries was financed by similar securities. Reddaway was convinced that inflation was here to stay, and therefore the sooner the college got out of gilts – the better.

Cooper and Reddaway took the view that the existing Clare statutes allowed the investment of general capital in equities since it was not forbidden, and they urged an immediate switch of investments. The Master, Sir Henry Thirkill, was concerned at a potential ambiguity about whether this was allowable, so action was delayed by about two years whilst, together with most other colleges, Clare changed its statutes. The proposed amendment, agreed by the governing body on 28 July 1951, gave to the finance committee: power to purchase, sell or transfer property, real or personal and securities (including stocks, funds and shares) of any description on behalf of the college, and may also apply moneys to any purpose to which the capital moneys arising under the Universities and Colleges Estates Act, 1925, may be applied.

In February 1953, the finance committee formed a sub-committee on investment, consisting of the Master, Cooper (the bursar), Taylor (who was then the university treasurer), and Reddaway, with authority to invest up to £100,000 in equities, of which not more than £5,000 was to be

---

[1] The bare buildings in Thirkill Court were almost entirely funded by donations from former members of Clare College; however, the college had to provide the fitments and furnishings.

8. Brian Reddaway, Fellow of Clare College 1938–, Professor of Political Economy 1969–80, Emeritus 1980.

invested in any one company. The following month, they reported that they had invested in 49 Companies, with about £2,000 in each company. There had also been sales of fixed interest stock amounting to £83,000, mostly gilts sold below par, in the range 77 to 98 per £100 stock, – this cannot have been helped by the two-year delay.

There was concern by the finance committee that it would be difficult to meet the rising needs for increased expenditure, and in February 1953 they had therefore increased the student fees by £5 per term, yielding about £4,500, but still leaving Clare fees amongst the lowest in the university[2], and also recommended to the governing body that fellows should in future

---

[2] For some years the lowest fees were at Trinity, followed by Clare. Cooper argued that larger fees could not be justified against costs but residence charges (room rents) ought to be increased, though in practice the room rents remained relatively low.

be allowed only one guest, instead of two, at college feasts. The deliberations of the finance committee were considered (by its members) to be confidential from the other fellows, so no significant explanation was given for this recommendation. The proposal about fewer guests at feasts met a hostile reception, since it was obvious that its financial effect would be small, and during the ensuing discussion fellows began to ask for more information about the financial affairs of the college. One of the senior fellows suggested that such information should not be made available outside the finance committee – a remark that produced a heated reply – so the Master swiftly withdrew the recommendation. The prudent outcome was that subsequently the governing body received from the bursar a regular annual report on the financial state of the college.

In July 1953, encouraged by the rising equity market, the finance committee doubled the equity investment limit to £200,000, and by the summer of 1954 it was decided that holdings of gilt-edged securities should be 'much reduced'. The policy appeared to be paying off, income from dividends was nearly double the return that would have come from gilt edged securities, there had been substantial capital appreciation (though the policy did not aim to make money by trading on capital gains – investment was for the long term future), and the risk factor was reduced by a widely based spread of equity investments with approximately equal amounts in each company, each by then increased to about £5,000.

COLLEGE NEEDS

By October 1955, the finance committee was becoming more confident that their earlier expectations were being proved in practice. At the meeting of the governing body in that month 'the bursar referred to the financial position of the college and to discussions which had taken place at a meeting of the college finance committee on the previous day. It was agreed unanimously that a "needs committee" be set up[3] to make a broad survey of the needs of the college, and to consider the desirable improvements and developments in the Old Court and Memorial Court

---

[3] The needs committee consisted of the Master, Godwin, Taylor, Willmer, Cooper, McDonald, Northam and Walker,

and cognate matters, and to place them in an order of priority. It was agreed that members of the governing body should be invited at an early date to send suggestions to the committee.'

Within six months, the "needs committee" had identified a first priority for renovating the stonework of the Old Court, and in March 1956 they received approval from the governing body for acceptance of an estimate from Rattee and Kett of about £4,000 per year and a total cost of about £28,500. There were additional costs for replacing all the wooden-framed windows by unpainted teak, and for more than ten years some part of the Old Court was surrounded by scaffolding.

The needs committee reported to the governing body at a special meeting which was held on 22 November 1956, and in three further two-hour sessions during the following week. Minute 1 of the meeting lists recommendations that were accepted without discussion:

the improvement of undergraduate meals;
an addendum to the catalogue of college plate;
the provision of more newspapers and magazines in the combination room;
an increase in the number of exchange telephone lines from the Memorial Buildings;
the provision of a respectable bathroom for fellows in the Old Court;
the improvement of Amalgamated Clubs' property (including the Boat House);

the provision of a new bell in the Memorial Buildings;
the provision of hard tennis courts;
the eradication of smells from the ditches round the garden;
the renovation of pictures;
the repair of gates;
the provision of an automatic internal telephone system for fellows' sets;

(improved) facilities for members of the college with dining rights;
travel allowances for fellows and research students;
the provision of pictures in public rooms;
the provision of vestry accommodation in the ante-chapel;
the intercalation of the fellows' library into the general amenities of the combination room;
the planting of spare ground near Bentley Road, etc.;

the replacement of certain benches in the chapel;
the purchase of a large house as a research students' hostel;
the provision of a servery in the Memorial Buildings;
the institution of a book fund for fellows;

the redecoration of Castlebrae; the provision of an undergraduate laundry;
the institution of an exchange scheme with Oriel for fellows' children's education;
the provision of a new door from the court to the screens;
the cleaning and repair of stone-work in the Old Court[4].

The report by the needs committee to the governing body was extensive, running to 18 pages of single-spaced typing, and containing a great amount of detail about the needs in different parts of the college. This was hardly surprising, as it followed a period of inactivity on maintenance or renovation that dated from long before the 1939–45 war. In all, there were twenty minutes concerned almost entirely with physical facilities, maintenance and improvement. The report also included a list of suggestions that had been made by fellows, showing the number of fellows making each of the suggestions. One of these items: the future of the Master's Lodge and a provision for the new Master was postponed until more information was known about who would be appointed. However, many other lesser items were approved after further discussion.

In January 1957, Thirkill informed the governing body that he wished to use his entitlement under the old statutes (under which he was originally elected to a fellowship in 1910). He would continue to live in college[5] and as senior fellow he would have first choice of any set of rooms, – his choice would be rooms F4 and F5, which had been in his use during his period as tutor. It was agreed to renovate these rooms so that they would be suitable for his occupation.

In March 1957, the finance committee was authorised to proceed with building work on college-owned land in Chesterton Lane[6] (now called the Colony) to provide accommodation for 40 undergraduates. Further developments in the Old Court were approved, including the provision of a library annex, a fellows' parlour in E4, and a guest room and sick room in B1.

---

[4] The repair of stone-work proved to be one of the most important and expensive of the items approved without further discussion. Its urgency was apparent to all Fellows who knew the Old Court.

[5] He declined an offer by the fellows to build a house for him as near as possible to the college.

[6] In the large garden of Hillside, which had previously been leased to a community of nuns. Adjoining land fronting on Castle Hill had been leased for a garage and repair shop, which was replaced in the 1980s by an extension to the Colony to provide further student rooms.

THE SIZE AND COMPOSITION OF THE GOVERNING BODY

It was not surprising that these discussions of physical needs encouraged more radical suggestions that would affect the nature of the college itself as a society. The committee on tutorial arrangements (consisting of the Master and the tutors) reported to the governing body at a special meeting on 10 May 1957. The problem that they sought to address was the conflict between the tutorial and teaching need to elect more fellows and a desire to limit the size of the fellowship.

The Master and Fellows are the trustees who own the college and its endowments and they have a responsibility, both collectively and individually, for safeguarding the endowments and ensuring that the objectives of the college are maintained and developed. There was concern that a substantial increase in the number of fellows could lead to a dilution in the sense of personal responsibility of each of the fellows for the well-being of the college and for its future. There is only one minute for the special meeting in May 1957; it reads: 'The attached memorandum on the size and composition of the governing body was discussed at great length.' This minute can be interpreted as meaning that Thirkill did not intend any changes to be made until his successor was appointed and in office in the college, and that is what happened.

The memorandum did not make recommendations, but it set out the options for consideration, and the ideas put forward provided an important legacy from Thirkill to his successor – as yet unknown. Dated 27 April 1957, it began

A Memorandum concerning the size and composition of the governing body

The preamble noted that in 1937 there were 12 fellows, there were 20 in 1947 and 33 in 1957. The size of the fellowship was considered under the headings:

(a) Financial limitations, noting the cost of each category of fellow.
(b) Physical limitations, for example on the high table in the hall, where the existing seating was for a maximum of 35 diners, the fixed size of the fellows' combination room, and the number of fellow's rooms or sets in the college.
(c) Other limitations, such as the question of having too many fellows on the college council, since this includes all fellows in Class B (those holding one or more of the qualifying offices of dean, bursar, tutor, director of studies, etc.).

Part II of the report listed all the fellows, their year of election under the different categories, and their university posts, and their college posts, where relevant[7]. The total number of fellows was 33, of whom 2 (Wilson and Harrison) had been elected under the old Statutes, and 31 under the Statutes of 1926. A number of needs were noted: For college teaching, there were major deficiencies in modern languages, chemistry, engineering; For administration in the college, there was an immediate need for one assistant tutor and one praelector. It was also necessary to look forward to the need for one assistant tutor to replace Dr Stoker by October 1958.

In conclusion, the committee noted that they had tried to indicate some of the factors which, again and again, demanded consideration in discussions concerning the filling of college posts, and which it thought should be in the minds of the governing body also. Although the committee had not been asked to make any final recommendation regarding the size and composition of the governing body, it wished to make the following observations:

1. Throughout, the committee found that its prime assumption was the need to preserve the unity of the governing body as a society at once varied and harmonious, of which the members can fulfil all the functions of the college and achieve a reasonably intimate acquaintance with one another.
2. The committee considers that the prerequisite for unity is not necessarily the observance of any particular numerical limit, high or low, but rather the preservation within the governing body of the balance required to ensure the smooth functioning of college life in its main departments: research, teaching, administration.
3. The governing body may decide, on the other hand, that it does not wish to expand by more than a small number in the near future. If this is so, then the teaching and administrative needs noted above seem to have first claim. It would obviously relieve the pressure to expand if fellows appointed to fill

---

[7] The names listed were:
Under the old statutes:
Mr Wilson, formerly Master;
Mr Harrison, formerly bursar.
Under the new statutes:
Classes, D and E: O. T. Jones, Hutton, Chibnall, Kingsford, Gilmour; being retired fellows and others elected in the interest of the college;
Class C: Godwin, Taylor, Baker, Moule, Boyd; being professors, readers or similar status;
Class B: Willmer, Reddaway, Cooper, Pippard, Stoker, Northam, McDonald, Robinson, Walker, Wedderburn, Elton, Forbes, Lipstein, Bullard, Eden; being 'official fellows';
Class A: West, Parkin, Smiley, Vinen, Reese, Ogilvie; being research fellows.

teaching gaps were asked to agree to accept vacant college administrative posts on request, so that a reserve might be created of fellows who were able to share college duties. Such a reserve would seem to be essential for the future if fellows who are unable to accept protracted duties are to be enabled to accept administrative posts of limited tenure.

If the current administrative requirements were met, and if by the same appointments certain major gaps in director of studies and teaching were closed, the total number of fellows might rise to about 36 or 37, an increase which might not entail any radical change in the society.

One consequence of a desire not to expand by more than a small number would be a tendency to give a strong preference to appointments in class B[8] to persons who were able to contribute in more than one of the fields: research, teaching and administration.

4. The governing body may, on the other hand, be prepared to envisage a more substantial increase in the near future. If so, more appointments in class B could be made on grounds that did not include college teaching and administration. It seems from experience difficult sometimes to decide between the claims of men of distinction in different fields so that such appointments could become relatively numerous. It seems to the committee that the size of the governing body could rapidly rise to over 40 if this course was pursued.

5. The committee has not tried to reach agreement within itself, and does not wish to recommend to the governing body one or other of the alternatives set out in 3 or 4, nor has it tried to relate the cost of them to the cost of other college needs. Its aim has been to draw attention to the ramifications of a problem which the committee thinks will be aggravated if it is tackled piecemeal and without full regard to all the complications. It does believe, however, that the governing body should make a deliberate decision as to the course that it means to pursue over the next few years.

The governing body did not immediately respond to the questions and options raised by this report because the attention of fellows had turned to the question of electing a new Master. However, one year later in April 1958, Dr Gordon Wright was elected as a fellow and director of studies in medical science to take the place of Dr Stoker. A month later there was a long discussion of a related memorandum prepared by the tutor on the

---

[8] Class B were the 'official fellows', at that time including all the tutors, the bursars, and the directors of studies in major subjects, who collectively carried the main responsibilities for management and teaching in the college.

issues involved in making certain elections to fellowships, and in a further meeting in June, the last meeting where the minutes are signed by Henry Thirkill, it was decided:

That the finance committee be asked to study the material considerations which would be involved if it were decided to expand considerably the size of the body of fellows and to increase the facilities to be offered to other senior members of the college or of the university.

At the first meeting to be chaired by the new Master, Sir Eric Ashby, on 1 October 1958, the governing body elected the retiring Master, Sir Henry Thirkill, to a fellowship under the entitlement that followed from his original fellowship held under the old statutes of the college.

THE MASTERSHIP ELECTION 1957–58

I was on leave from my fellowship in Clare from January 1954 to August 1955 and held a senior lectureship in Manchester from October 1955 until March 1957, when I returned to Cambridge as a lecturer in mathematics and was re-elected to a fellowship at Clare[9]. The process of seeking a new Master had begun in the Lent term of 1957, and in April when I returned to the college, the extent of support for internal candidates was being assessed. Although there was no shortage of distinguished names amongst the fellows, it soon became apparent that most fellows wanted to look for suitable candidates from outside the college. Thirkill had been a superb Master and administrator, both in the college and in the university, but he had retained the strings of power for too long and at too detailed a level. Only in the past year or two had the tutor begun to take over the admission of students, though his policies had not yet led to significant changes. A clear majority of fellows wanted to choose a Master from outside the college in order to allow new policies to be developed which would be led by the new generation of post-war fellows. Amongst these was a sizeable group that wanted to choose a distinguished scholar, who could represent the highest academic standards but would not be involved in administration at all. There was a smaller group, mainly drawn from

---

[9] I was also re-appointed in Clare as director of studies in mathematics and in mathematics for scientists. This involved arranging supervisions in mathematics for about 50 undergraduates (RJE).

The Mastership election 1957–58

the more senior fellows, who were concerned to choose a candidate who could be relied on to continue the traditional policies of the college.

By the end of the Easter term 1957, the fellows had formed three groups, one was the 'scholars group' supporting a distinguished Cambridge professor, who was thought unlikely to be involved in administration. A second was the 'traditional group' who supported a former fellow of the college, who had moved to a professorship in London, and was well known to the more senior fellows. The third group supported Sir Eric Ashby, then the Vice-Chancellor of Queen's University Belfast, a distinguished administrator and previously a professor of botany. Only a minority of fellows was prepared to indicate a second choice – not all would indicate their first choice – and, since no candidate had majority support, there was an impasse which continued until early in the Michaelmas term.

At that stage Reddaway suggested that we adopt a procedure that was commonly used when seeking agreement in international negotiations[10]. He suggested that we should agree to set a target date for a decision and, if no agreement had been reached by then, we should impose a penalty on ourselves – for example, to have no further discussions for a period of six months. The deadline and the penalty were agreed and this proved sufficient to concentrate our minds. Soon after this two fellows from the traditional group transferred to Ashby, and on my reckoning at that time it seemed that the scholars' group and the Ashby group had nearly equal support, both being larger than the traditional group. However, no-one in the latter group would indicate their second preference, so there was still a deadlock.

Early in November 1957, the senior fellow in the Ashby group received a request from the scholars' group that two members from each group should meet to discuss a proposal that they wished to make. The invitation was accepted and I was one of the two representatives from the Ashby group. We met in the law supervision room above the Porter's Lodge with two members from the scholars' group. They suggested that after an initial formal vote had been taken by the fellows we should agree to transfer all the votes from the scholars' group and the Ashby group to

---

[10] Based, pehaps, on his experience in the civil service during the war and on his subsequent role as an economic advisor to governments.

the candidate gaining the most votes, thus ensuring that this candidate be elected regardless of the views of those in the traditional group. We agreed to this proposal and suggested that in the event of equality the votes would all go to Ashby. This was accepted and I was given the unenviable task of reading out the agreement at the next meeting of the fellows, which – following a stunned silence – led to a request for an adjournment for a few days. At the next meeting, everyone in the traditional group transferred their support to Ashby giving him a substantial majority, and he was then immediately given unanimous support from all fellows. Although it had been a skilfully fought contest, there was remarkably little rancour – an indication of the good personal relations amongst the fellowship at that time, relations which it was feared by some would not survive any considerable increase in numbers.

Since the statutes required that the Master should have a Cambridge degree, it was necessary first to elect Sir Eric Ashby as a fellow, which we did on 13 March 1958, so that he could obtain an M.A. by incorporation. During the Easter term 1958, Sir Eric did not attend any GB meetings but he was able to come to a number of fellows' dinners, which were held on Wednesdays in term time, where he clearly enjoyed the traditional duty after dinner in hall, by which, as junior fellow, he was responsible for pouring the port for other fellows in the combination room. If any fellow had earlier entertained doubts about the election of Ashby, these doubts were soon set at rest.

ASHBY AS MASTER – EARLY DAYS

Sir Eric Ashby became the Master of Clare College on 1 October 1958, and he was the chairman of the governing body meeting held on that day. At that meeting, the former Master, Sir Henry Thirkill, was elected into a life fellowship and continued to live in college[11]. The governing body also gratefully received a gift of 40 quill pens for the use of fellows at college meetings, presented by Dr Michael Stoker on his retirement from his fellowship.

Following that meeting, Ashby returned to Belfast for two terms so as to

---

[11] Although he remained a member of the governing body, Thirkill did not attend the meetings.

9. Eric Ashby, Master of Clare College 1958–75.

complete his work there as Vice-Chancellor of Queen's University, and Dr Harry Godwin acted as Master *in locum tenens*. There was only one meeting of the governing body during this period, at which the finance committee reported on the costs of payments to fellows and of facilities for fellows. However, it was decided to take no action until after the Master had come into residence.

When Ashby took up residence in the Master's Lodge in Clare in April 1959, a major change of policy on admissions was already under way following the retirement of his predecessor, Sir Henry Thirkill. The senior tutor, John Northam was now responsible for all admissions of students to the college, and he was seeking to implement a policy of enlarging the range and variety of schools from which undergraduates would come to Clare. Previously, undergraduates in Clare had come primarily from fee-paying schools, (88 per cent in 1951, when I had first became a fellow of Clare). About one quarter of these had been admitted on the basis of their performance in the entrance scholarship examination and were of high academic quality. The rest were admitted on their schoolmasters' recommendation and interviews, with preference also for the sons of former Clare students. An understanding between Thirkill and many of these schools ensured that reasonable academic standards were maintained.

The new policy of recruiting from a much wider variety of schools was strongly supported within the governing body. Its implementation was a formidable task for Northam as senior tutor, who was supported by Ashby – particularly when former members of the college began to find that their sons could only gain admission to Clare if they met increasingly high academic standards.

At faculty level there was intense competition for university posts, and few of the post-war generation of fellows were ready to rest on their laurels, – academic status depended on quality in research and its recognition, and this made it difficult for fellows to achieve the level of dedication to college teaching and other duties that had been possible for the pre-war fellows. However, for all fellows at that time, the college still remained an important priority, and in the absence of the bureaucracy that developed in later years, it was possible to carry out duties in both college and university and still make progress in research. In college there were still contentious matters, such as the problem of the trees in the avenue leading from Queen's road to the Clare bridge, which we were told had been discussed intermittently since the 1920s. The avenue had originally been a causeway, walled on each side, so the roots of the trees were constricted and a number had died or were decayed. The present appearance was deceptive because, when the Memorial Court was built, the displaced clay from the foundations had been dumped along the north side of the causeway, thus concealing the retaining wall[12]. The modern fellows' garden had been laid out by one of the fellows, Nevill Willmer,

---

[12] Godwin 1985, loc. cit.

who was also a talented artist. On 27 May 1960, after a lengthy discussion about removing the trees and replanting, he was asked to make sketches to illustrate the appearance of the avenue, (i) if it was replanted with a double row of lime trees, and (ii) if it was replanted with a row of deciduous trees on the south side and a few trees on the north side so that the avenue is incorporated into the fellows' garden. At the time of writing, 35 years later, I believe that no decision on replanting has yet been taken.

The avenue was only one of the difficult issues raised by the needs committee which had been reconstituted in November 1959, its members being the Master, the bursar, the tutor, Willmer, and Reese, with a remit to review the 1955 report of the committee, to revise its findings if necessary, and to report to the governing body. A bicycle store in the Old Court provided another difficult issue when combined with a desire for the creation of a students' bar – these were both competing for space in the crypt under the college chapel. In November 1960, a large number of physical improvements were approved, including redecoration of the small hall, extension of the student bar, improvements in the college kitchens, and so forth.

A MODEST INCREASE IN THE NUMBER OF FELLOWS

By far the most contentious issue was the size of the fellowship, as it had been in the last years of the previous Master. In December 1959, when approving the election of Richard West (later professor of botany) to an official fellowship, the governing body noted that 'such an election should in no way prejudice adversely the future policy of the college with regard to the recruitment of fellows.'

Such concerns did not apply to honorary fellowships, though the numbers were small, and on 18 April 1960 the noted American philanthropist and scholar, Paul Mellon, was elected into an honorary fellowship. Mellon had been an affiliated student at Clare during 1929–31, and was a considerable benefactor to the college; later he was to make further gifts, including some of great importance in the founding of Clare Hall.

The fellows had many informal opportunities to comment on the work of the Bridges Syndicate through the Master and his guests, who often included some of the external members of the committee. There was only one formal discussion by the governing body on the "relations between the colleges and the university" (on 28 April 1961) and none of the comments were recorded in the minutes of the meeting. It was, however, decided 'that the governing body is in favour of a continuing modest increase in the number of fellows, primarily to meet the needs in the college'. A standing committee (subsequently called the fellowship committee) was set up to keep in review these needs, and to 'secure and recommend suitable candidates for fellowships'. The committee from April 1961 to 25 May 1962 included: the Master, the tutor (Northam), Moule, McDonald and Eden.

As a result of this new policy several new fellows were elected during the next two years. Part of the need for new fellows came from the increasing involvement of existing fellows in supervising research students. In 1958/9, Pippard, who had been elected to a fellowship in 1947 which involved a commitment to supervise undergraduates in physics for six hours a week, advised the governing body that his research commitments would prevent him continuing to provide college teaching at this level. Four years later, also because of commitments to research and the supervision of graduate students, I took similar action with regard to my teaching in mathematics, having previously persuaded the governing body to elect a second teaching fellow in mathematics.

There was also a need for additional fellows to help reduce the considerable range of responsibilities of Cooper, who had been both bursar and director of studies in engineering since 1949, and also held a university lectureship in engineering. In economics, Reddaway had been the director of the department of applied economics since 1955, and by 1961 there was an urgent need to find another teaching fellow in economics. The new fellows elected in the period from the election of Ashby as Master until 1961 included: Volker Heine (physics, later professor), Charles Feinstein (economics, senior tutor 1969–78, later professor in Oxford), Kenneth Riley (physics, senior tutor 1978–97). As a result of the review, the college would seek an additional teaching fellow in engineering, and also a fellow to fill a new post of domestic bursar.

VISITING FELLOWS

In the light of the new flexibility over the election of fellows, during discussions at a meeting of the fellowship committee, I suggested that Clare might elect occasional visiting fellows for periods from three months to one year. In my theoretical physics research group, I had already made use of the visiting fellowship programme at Churchill College with a visit during the previous year by Sam Treiman, a research colleague from Princeton University, who had become the first visiting fellow at Churchill. The governing body of Clare agreed in principle to my suggestion in February 1962, and in March they confirmed it, with an 'experiment' to invite a resident guest of the Master and fellows for a period not exceeding one academical year. The college statutes did not include any category of visiting fellow but in July it was agreed to change them so that the governing body should have the power to elect visiting fellows; the change would include the provision that neither honorary fellows nor visiting fellows shall have a voice in the government of the college.

The idea of visiting fellows was extended in May 1962 to include one schoolmaster visiting fellow for one term each academical year, as a means of strengthening the new policy on admissions, which sought to widen the range of schools who would wish to send students to the college.

In the same month, on the nomination of the fellowship committee, the governing body agreed to invite two such resident guests: on my nomination, John Wheeler from Princeton University, who was the world's leading authority on general relativity and had made important contributions to many other areas of theoretical physics; and on the Master's nomination, Mr A. H. M. Kirk-Greene, who was in Clare in 1947 and had become an administrator in Nigeria and author of books on Nigerian history. In November, it was agreed to invite Heisenberg[13], the founder of modern quantum mechanics, to a visiting fellowship for a term "even if this meant having two visiting fellows at one time. Such a double appointment was not to be taken as a precedent". Heisenberg was unable to come, but both Wheeler and Kirk-Greene accepted the invitations and made useful visits that benefited both the college and the university. However, although this visiting fellowship scheme continued at a modest level, it was to be overtaken quite soon by the more extensive visiting fellowship programme that resulted from the founding of Clare Hall.

---

[13] Both Pippard and Eden had independently worked with Heisenberg in 1948 when he had been a visiting lecturer in the Cavendish Laboratory for three months.

DISCOVERING NEW NEEDS

Meanwhile, other ideas were arising from the increasing numbers of fellows, notably the needs of young married fellows were impinging on the needs committee. On 26 May 1961 the committee was asked to "consider the erection of accommodation suitable for married fellows, perhaps with a library and common room". They reported in November in some detail on work that was going on in the college during 1960–61, including renovation of the stonework, rewiring of electric cables, installing a new telephone system, decoration and re-lighting in the chapel, lighting in the hall. Other work was being considered, including: redesigning the small hall and screens, enlargement of the bar and refurbishing in the Memorial Court[14].

The third part of the needs committee report considered long-range needs; they had been asked to consider how to provide accommodation for married fellows together with certain public rooms and a music room. This would involve a major building programme. Even if the college decided not to do this at present but to include it in future plans, such a decision would preclude any other major projects that might interfere with this intention.

The committee was divided on one major question and sought guidance from the governing body. The major question was whether a new building should be on the Queen's Road site, where there was room in the north west corner, or on the Chesterton Lane site. The committee had assumed that the main purpose of a new building would be to accommodate married fellows, not undergraduates. This could be accomplished by a fellows' building on the Queen's Road site, or by decanting some undergraduates into a new building on Chesterton Lane, and converting rooms in Memorial Court into fellows' sets. The committee suggested that the governing body should create a climate of opinion by discussing this general point; after which the committee would draw up a schedule of accommodation required and ask an architect to suggest how the accommodation might be provided.

The second long-range need was for residential accommodation for research students, especially those who are married. The college had recently acquired some property in Newnham village, where a block of

---

[14] Some of these had been approved earlier but since work had not commenced on them they remained on the "being considered" list.

flats suitable for research students could be built. The cost of this would be high enough to require that some sort of priority must be decided between this and accommodation for married fellows.

A proposal to enlarge the bar, though modest and simple to carry out by itself, could not be separated from a proposal to build an underground bicycle store along the south wall of the chapel. The committee suggested that the governing body should try to reach agreement which of the two alternatives it wants, either (a) an underground bicycle store entered by a ramp from the road which would release the whole of the crypt for other purposes, or (b) no bicycle store, in which case the bar could still be enlarged and the bicycles put into the other end of the crypt. Alternative (b) would be relatively inexpensive and could be carried out quickly. Alternative (a) would be relatively expensive and would have to be planned in conjunction with options for improving the forecourt and the approach to the college. The committee asked for guidance from the governing body on the priorities for the various development options. We shall return to the outcome of this request for guidance in the next chapter.

CLARE CONSIDERS THE BRIDGES REPORT

The above report from the needs committee in November 1961 came before the publication of the Bridges report on the relation between the university and the colleges. Although there were some discussions of the Bridges report at governing body meetings, there is no record of such discussions as it was left to the Master to convey the views expressed by fellows to the Colleges Committee, which was considering a collective response. Generally the fellows were unenthusiastic about the Bridges proposals – for example, the choice of new fellows would be made on merit and on college needs and not in terms of the quota system suggested in the report. As he was the principal author of the report, it would have been invidious for the governing body to have asked the Master to prepare a written version of the critical comments. I do not think that Sir Eric sought to stifle discussion in any way, but it would already have been evident to him that – like other colleges – Clare would go its own way with regard to increasing the number of fellowships.

Brian Cooper, the bursar of Clare, was the only fellow of Clare to speak in the Regent House discussions of the Bridges report. After a typical understatement that the quota system was not likely to be acceptable, Cooper commended the proposal from the Society of Women Members for collegiate groups, which he suggested would be 'pure colleges with ideas of scholarship but not ideas of grandeur', and 'could well be the solution that is being looked for.' He noted the low cost of setting one up, and added also that the collegiate groups need not all be of one sex (a very 'avant garde' suggestion at that time). Finally he observed that Clare College had itself originally been set up as a small graduate college (in the 14th century) from which it had evolved into one taking young scholars to meet a national need.

OPTIONS FOR INCREASING THE NUMBER OF FELLOWS

The fellowship committee reported to the governing body on the role intended for the new post of domestic bursar, and they recommended that Mr F.D.Holister, a lecturer in architecture, be appointed to the post and elected as a fellow. They also discussed other possible needs in the college for new fellows. As a result they were asked to examine the consequences to the college of expanding the fellowship by a considerable number, for example, to 50, 60 or 70. This request is not recorded in the minutes of the meeting, but their report, which came to the governing body in October 1962 was a major development in the strategic thinking in the college that eventually led to the foundation of Clare Hall.

Minute (3) of the Clare College governing body meeting on 5 October 1962 reads:

That the attached paper from the fellowship committee be received and that the fellowship committee be empowered to co-opt and be asked to present a further report in the light of the discussions.

The fellowship committee, which was chaired by the Master (Ashby), included the following fellows of the college from May 1962: McDonald, Moule, Reddaway, Parkin and Black (acting senior tutor during 1962–63 in the absence on leave of Dr Northam). The paper ends with the Master's initials, E. A. 24 September 1962. Following a college meeting that required a report for the governing body, Ashby would normally be the draftsman responsible for bringing together the ideas that had been raised. He would allow considerable freedom in such discussions, encouraging new ideas and reinforcing some, though it was rarely evident to those present when or if he introduced radical new ideas himself. However, he always attached great importance to the presentation of a report, and although the ideas themselves would have come generally from members of the fellowship committee, he would have drafted the report himself. In this instance, probably because of the importance of the subject and the significance of his role in drawing conclusions from the discussions Ashby added his initials[15].

The main part of the report was titled:

A note on the fellowship and the consequences of increasing it

The report began with a short historical review:

The statutes of 1359 prescribe a Master and 19 fellows in the college, although it seems that this number was not attained. The statutes of 1861 provided for 18 fellowships in all. In 1882 the number was reduced to 15 in all. The statutes of 1926 do not prescribe the number of fellows the college should have, but they do define five classes into which fellows should be elected.

Then followed a table giving some detail about the manner in which the fellowship had increased from 12 in 1928 to 16 in 1938, reaching 24 in 1951, 33 in 1959, and 45 in 1962. In the same period the teaching fellows had increased from 8 in 1928 to 26 in 1962. The age distribution of fellows was fairly uniform, ranging from 7 to 10 in each ten-year age range.

The distribution amongst subjects of the 34 non-professorial teaching fellows showed that there was adequate coverage of college needs in most areas, but the tutors had indicated some actual or potential difficulties in: Fine Arts, Architecture, English, Modern Languages, Economics, Pure Mathematics, and Mechanical Sciences.

Next the committee had examined the physical and domestic problems from increasing the fellowship to 50, 60 or 70. They concluded that there would be difficulties in retaining the ancient tradition of dining together at high table if the numbers exceeded 50. At that level, it would no longer be

---

[15] Ashby did not always add his initials to a report that he drafted, though he was normally the scribe or draftsman for any report that was required following any college meeting that he chaired, except for meetings on routine college business involving the tutor or the bursar, for example.

possible for fellows to use the combination room for lunch, though there were alternatives available, such as the use of high table in the hall, with an extended dais and a second narrower table.

The report continued:

There must be accommodation for meetings of the whole governing body, for even though most college business remains delegated to the council, the whole concept of the college as a society would be gravely weakened if all fellows did not take part in its government. On the present pattern, the maximum seating accommodation in the combination room for a meeting is 37. By setting the room out with rows of chairs it could be made to hold 50 to 60; though fellows might be unwilling to accept this as a permanent arrangement for governing body meetings. The governing body could, of course, meet with dignity, if some discomfort, in the hall; in which case as many as 70 fellows could be accommodated easily.

In addition to its use for formal meetings, the fellows were accustomed to adjourning for coffee to the combination room after dinner. It was observed that, if the fellowship exceeded 50, it would be necessary to spill over into the fellows' library after dinner. Also, any increase in the fellowship over the present number would put an additional load on the Butler's staff and the kitchen staff and with 60 fellows there would have to be additions to both these staffs.

It was noted that Clare was already less generous than other colleges in providing rooms for fellows. Any increase in fellowship would presumably consist of men active in teaching, who would need rooms, and an increase of fellowship to 60 or 70 would certainly involve one of two alternatives: either fewer undergraduate rooms in college, or building new sets to be used either by undergraduates or fellows.

The final two sections of the paper discussed reasons for or against increasing the fellowship, and indicated the options that might be considered. Purely from the viewpoint of college needs, it would be sufficient to expand from 45 to 50 fellows, and such expansion could be accommodated without serious problems. However, an increase of only 5 fellows would be much less than Clare's proper contribution[16] to help solve the university's problem, highlighted by the Bridges' report, of too many senior members of the university without college fellowships. If the

---

[16] Ashby's paper seems to have ignored the fact that Clare had expanded its fellowship from 33 to 45 in the three years since he took up residence as Master, and was already comfortably attaining the quota suggested by the Bridges Syndicate.

college wished to go beyond its own needs and provide directly or indirectly fellowships for large numbers of university officers, then it would be useful for the sake of discussion to think of an eventual increase of 20 to 30 rather than of 5. This would confront the college with difficult problems, and unless these were solved, the expansion might well weaken and not strengthen the college.

If the governing body chose to help solve these university problems, it could either wait and participate in whatever plan may be agreed by the university and the colleges, arising from the Bridges report; or it could set about solving its share (or more) of the university's problem, either alone or in cooperation with one or two other colleges. Any solution would involve practical difficulties but the committee did not believe these would be insurmountable. They suggested three alternatives for consideration:

(a) The simplest solution is to buy the problem off by contributing substantially towards the cost of a new independent foundation in Cambridge; this is a vicarious way of increasing the fellowship (in any event the finance committee may wish to respond to the appeal for Fitzwilliam House).

(b) The most conventional solution is to accommodate an increased fellowship in the college. Apart from the possible effects of this upon the cohesion of the society (about which we have very diverse views) there would be practical difficulties to be overcome. The chief of these and the solutions to them are as follows:
 – pressure on high table: two high table sittings or some restriction of dining rights
 – pressure on combination room: use fellows' library with or without alteration
 – governing body meetings: if necessary use the hall
 – fellows' rooms: either put more undergraduates into lodgings or build more accommodation (in Memorial Court, or Grange Road, or Chesterton Lane)
 – strain on domestic staff: increase its size

Comments on the Bridges report make it clear that some colleges could not afford, even if they were to approve, these and other financial consequences of increasing the size of the fellowship. Clare could meet the financial consequences. The governing body may therefore wish to discuss this solution on its merits without taking into account its cost.

(c) The most interesting solution – in the committee's view – would be to create a fresh society, linked with ourselves and our society, but having its own autonomy. This could be done by setting up (even in existing buildings, on the

Chesterton Lane site) a Clare Graduate College. This college might initially consist of our BAs and research students together with some 20 fellows (some perhaps of the kind who at present would be in class E[17] and including some voluntary migrants from Clare) and who might include women as well as men if the relevant statute were changed. They would have their own high table and combination room, but an arrangement of reciprocal dining rights would keep them close to the mother society. There would be two councils, each running its own college (the graduate college council under a Vice-Master?) but for certain purposes – e.g. the election of fellows – the fellows from both places could meet together as one governing body. Fellows who transferred to class E because they wished to discontinue their teaching for the college would move to the high table of the graduate college. Research fellows might be attached to either high table. The function of such a graduate college would be to bring together into one society a group of research students and a group of fellows whose interests incline them more to association with research students than with undergraduates. It might (or might not) be desirable to select fellows for this society who have some interests in common (as at St Anthony's College in Oxford).

The undergraduates who would be displaced if the college were to start in Chesterton Lane would be accommodated partly in new lodging houses (which we are told could be found) and partly in rooms in college occupied by research students.

This solution has some resemblance to the experiment Corpus is carrying out at Leckhampton House, but goes much further. Particulars of the financial and administrative arrangements adopted at Leckhampton House will be available at the meeting.

WOMEN AS GUESTS IN CLARE COLLEGE

Until the summer of 1963, neither fellows nor students could bring female guests to dine in the college hall, nor could they be brought to the fellows' combination room. In June of that year, the Master received a formal request from the undergraduates that they be allowed to bring 'lady guests' to dine in the hall on one night each week, preferably on a Friday or a Saturday. Such a request would normally have gone to the college council, which dealt with issues concerning student conduct. However, the Master thought that any change to such an ancient custom as not

---

[17] Class E fellows of Clare College are non-stipendiary, and normally include fellows having no specific college duties, such as directing studies.

allowing women to dine in the college hall should first be discussed by the governing body.

We met on 9 July 1963. There was general agreement that any decision should apply equally to fellows and students and we should therefore take an initial decision about high table. The resulting discussion was quite vigorous: some fellows suggested that the concession be limited to academic lady guests, others thought wives of fellows should be excluded – but this would create a dilemma if a wife was also an academic – so perhaps there should simply be an unwritten rule about wives as guests. Two fellows (Eden and Pippard) made it clear that they would not abide by any unwritten rules about not bringing their wives to dine – this triggered a ruling by the Master that he would not allow any resolution that distinguished between the type of lady that might be brought in as a guest.

When eventually a vote was first taken, it appeared that there was a majority of 14 votes to 13 in favour of allowing a fellow to bring a lady guest on one Friday night each week during full term. One fellow, having voted in favour, declared that he wished to change his vote on the grounds that we should not impose such a radical change with such a small majority. Ashby informed him that if he did so, he (Ashby), who had not yet voted, would vote and then as chairman give a casting vote in favour of the motion. He added that it was transparently obvious that this type of change and more would be coming to Cambridge colleges and there was absolutely no benefit to be gained by delaying six months or a year before bowing to the inevitable. Minute 3 for the meeting records that the GB resolved:

By a majority of 15 votes to 13 that on Friday nights in full term, fellows and senior members with dining rights be permitted to bring lady guests to dine in hall.

The decision about the student's request was referred to the college council, which subsequently agreed similar guest rights for all junior members of the college.

It was to be another nine years before Clare was one of the first of the previously men's colleges to admit women as undergraduates. However, it was only 18 months after the meeting in 1963 allowing occasional women guests that Clare was hosting men and women fellows-designate of Clare Hall at meals on a daily basis. Perhaps this experience encouraged the later decision of Clare College to be amongst the first colleges to become co-residential.

Chapter 5

PROPOSALS FOR A GRADUATE COLONY

IDEAS FOR AN EXTENSION TO CLARE

The report of the Clare College fellowship committee, dated 24 September 1962 and outlined in chapter 4, was discussed by the governing body on 5 October. By the end of this meeting, the fellowship committee had been empowered to co-opt, and the minutes record that it was asked to present a further report in the light of the discussion. The paper was already being interpreted as a proposal for an extension to the college, with the college's land in Chesterton Lane as the front runner for the development. In the same spirit the committee adopted the role and title of extension committee, though this is not recorded as such in the minutes.

Together with issues raised by the needs committee, the idea of an extension was discussed again by the governing body on 12 November and on 20 November. Other fellows, not on the committee, were getting involved, notably Wedderburn and Heine. Wedderburn was one of the law fellows, and later became a professor at the London School of Economics; he was an advisor to the Labour Party and was made a Life Peer in 1977. In earlier discussions he had advocated a general expansion of the college through taking both more undergraduates and more graduates, in order to help meet the urgent national need to provide more university places and to train future university teachers to cope with the expanding numbers in universities. There was considerable opposition and little support for the idea of increasing the number of undergraduates, but there was support for taking more graduate students. The number of research students in the university was rising at 10 per cent per annum, and it was felt that Clare should contribute to the resulting need to provide more places for graduates in colleges. At the same time, many fellows took the view that Clare should provide better facilities for

Ideas for an extension to Clare

graduate students in college, and there was particular concern about the provision of accommodation for married graduate students.

Heine was amongst the fellows most conscious of the needs of graduate students, and he expressed his concerns in a substantial contribution to the discussions of the governing body at their meeting on 5 October 1962. He was a research fellow at the time, who had come from New Zealand, initially to Bristol University to study for a Ph.D. in theoretical physics with Professor Mott. He moved to Cambridge to complete his Ph.D. when Mott became the Cavendish Professor in 1954, and was appointed a demonstrator in the Cavendish in 1958, becoming a research fellow of Clare in 1960. Subsequently he was head of one of the research groups in the Cavendish Laboratory, and in 1976 he became a professor of theoretical physics.

Soon after the discussion on 5 October, Heine and Pippard[1] sent a memorandum to the extension committee, which is illustrative of some of the views current at that time, particularly those that Heine himself had put forward at the governing body. Its aim was to describe the kind of community that might exist on the Chesterton Lane site, but they argued against this being a separate graduate institution, beginning:

> The first point is that the community at Chesterton Lane should not be autonomous or semi-autonomous, but an integrated part of Clare College in every way. We did not start from this position. Indeed the idea of giving birth to an independent daughter institution has an obvious appeal, nor does it appear tidy to suggest one community existing in two semi-detached halves. We have even been accused of a neo-colonialist attitude! However, we have come to the conclusion that any scheme for an autonomous institution is either unworkable or undesirable or does not help to solve the present problem.

They considered that the endowment required for an independent institution to achieve eminence and prestige would far exceed the amount that Clare could raise alone. They argued that an independent graduate institution with no undergraduate teaching would attract fellows who were needed for supervising and directing studies in the undergraduate colleges, unless it was confined to peripheral subjects like veterinary sciences. They emphasised the importance of fellows being involved in

---

[1] Pippard has advised me that Heine was the author and moving spirit of this memorandum (RJE).

each of three areas: undergraduate teaching, graduate supervision and in research, and took the view that this would be lost in any independent graduate institution.

Their paper continued by describing how 40 of the fellows would remain 'centred on the Old Court and Memorial Court', and another 20 to 40 at Chesterton Lane. The latter site could be further developed to provide accommodation for up to 100 research students (including married ones). There would be separate dining and perhaps lunching facilities at Chesterton Lane for the fellows and research students, but the undergraduates would remain centred on the Old Court. They continued,

At the last governing body meeting, transfer to Chesterton was likened to banishment to Siberia. We do not envisage it that way at all. We see numerous and exciting possibilities for branching out to develop a new kind of community, making an important contribution to the life of Cambridge ...

We have in mind perhaps no high table at Chesterton Lane but a more casual mixing of dons and research students. The presence of married research students would add a new dimension. Perhaps there could be flats or even houses with a few married fellows living "on campus' and contributing to undergraduate life in a different way from the usual sherry party. Certainly the gathering of a large group of research students will lead to many informal activities. A welcome might also be extended to overseas academic visitors on a much more generous scale than at present.

Heine and Pippard concluded their paper by suggesting that funds be raised through an appeal to old Clare men, so that the scheme could be established at an early date by a complete building programme in single stage.

I was sympathetic to the needs of graduate students, having recently stopped supervising undergraduates in Clare because of pressures of research and from supervising research students, but I did not wish to support an attempt to solve the Bridges problem of UTOs not holding fellowships, by creating second class Clare fellows on the Chesterton Lane site. In addition, I had been convinced for some years that the future expansion of the university would be in West Cambridge. A site there for the Clare extension would be ideally placed, not only for the University Library and the newly developing Sidgwick Avenue site, but also for the science developments, which I was confident would eventually take place to the West of Grange Road.

The minutes of the governing body meeting of 12 November, under the heading "Extension of the Clare Foundation", record that the committee co-opted the bursar and Dr Heine for further discussions, and note that "All fellows are having an opportunity to put their views on paper". That meeting had been concerned as much with the report of the college needs committee as with the possibility of an extension to the college. The discussion proved so lively that the meeting was adjourned and resumed the following week on 20 November.

Topics under discussion included the possibility of replacing the diseased trees on the Clare avenue leading from the Clare bridge to Queen's Road and the visiting fellowship programme. Such ongoing references to visiting fellows, although only at a normal level of one at a time, helped to familiarise even the most parochial fellows with the idea that visiting academics were a useful addition to the Cambridge scene.

CLARE LAND IN WEST CAMBRIDGE

Another item on the agenda for the governing body at that time proved later to be of critical importance to the founding of Clare Hall. This concerned a piece of Clare land between the University Library and Grange Road, amounting to about three-quarters of an acre, and then in use as a tennis court[2]. The university had advised us about a year earlier that they wished to purchase this land in order to obtain planning permission for building an extension to the University Library.

By January 1963, it was evident that Clare might require building land reasonably close to the Memorial Court at some stage in the future. We were therefore unwilling to give up our Grange Road tennis courts without some nearby land in exchange, and the bursar was asked to take a tough line in his negotiations with the University authorities. It is interesting to note that, wearing different hats, both the bursar and the Master were on the relevant university committees.

The resolution of the problem was aided by the fortunate coincidence that the Vice-Chancellor at the time, the Revd. J. Boys-Smith, was the Master of St. John's College, and had previously been bursar of his

---

[2] Much later, in 1997, this land was converted to a car park and a further extension of the University Library.

college. He therefore saw practical advantages to all parties of a triangular exchange. Clare would sell the Grange Road land to the University, the University would sell the Divinity School (located directly opposite to the main gates of St. John's) to St. John's College, and the latter would sell to Clare the freehold of the land in Herschel Road on which Clare Hall now stands[3].

FIRST PROPOSAL FROM THE EXTENSION COMMITTEE

The governing body minutes for 26 January, 4 March and 11 March 1963, contain no reference to the possible extension of the college. This does not mean that there was no discussion – the minutes generally only recorded decisions, and even these were sometimes incomplete. There is a note on the meeting of 26 January that there was a discussion of the draft by the colleges' committee of a collective response to the Bridges Report. Also, the minutes of 4 February note that the draft report to the college's committee on the Bridges Report is to be amended in the light of the discussion by Reddaway, Elton and Wedderburn. Thus Clare was involved in other issues raised by the Bridges Report, formally through responses from the governing body, and informally through the involvement of individual fellows in other committees of the University, notably Ashby on the Council of the Senate and the General Board, and Cooper on the Financial Board.

The extension committee produced a substantial report for the Clare governing body in May 1963. The report was presumably based on discussions by the committee, made up of the fellowship committee: Ashby, McDonald, Moule, Reddaway, Parkin and Black (acting Senior Tutor during 1962–63 in the absence on leave of Northam), plus the bursar (Cooper) and Heine (co-opted on 12 November 1962). However, its opening paragraph stated: *This report has been prepared by three members of the governing body as a basis for discussion.*

It seems that some members of the committee were reserving their positions, but evidently Ashby did not wish to delay the presentation of the report to the governing body, perhaps realising that he would have

---

[3] The story of this land is described in more detail in chapter 11.

First Proposal from the extension committee 91

difficulty in obtaining prior approval from the committee as a whole. The report proposed that Clare should establish a *Collegiate society of fellows and graduate students*. The society would be based on new buildings on college land in Chesterton Lane, but it would be an integral part of Clare.

There is a great deal in common between the ideas in the proposal and those in the earlier memorandum from Heine and Pippard. Thus, Heine was certainly one of the three co-authors of the report, along with Ashby, who would have taken responsibility for putting together the final draft. The third would have been Holister, an architect recently appointed as a fellow and domestic bursar. Presumably, the Master's reason for not listing the names of the three authors was to allow him to retain a degree of impartiality as chairman of the subsequent discussions by the governing body. It is odd that we did not ask who they were at the time – indeed, at first, I had the impression (wrongly as I soon learnt) that although the report had been put together by three fellows it expressed the views of the extension committee as a whole.

Much later, in 1992, Heine recalled that, after he was co-opted on to the extension committee, Ashby had asked him to work out the details for a specification of the required accommodation, and by way of illustration of what was required he had given him a copy of a specification for a hall of residence that had recently been considered by the University Grants Committee. Holister also recalled preparing a scheme for the proposed site on Clare land in Chesterton Lane, so it seems that they shared responsibility for the specification for the proposed buildings that was presented in the report.

The report began by explaining that the purpose of the proposal was to provide an extension of Clare College that would provide a collegiate society for senior members of the faculties and for graduate students. It should be free from many of the formalities and disciplines attached to an undergraduate society, for example fellows and graduates should share the same table; the society would not need to be locked in at night; the society should not exclude from its activities either the wives of its members or women scholars. The point of cohesion in the society, and the criterion for both junior and senior membership should be a common interest in research and graduate education.

The authors put forward the curious argument that prestige for an independent society would require lavish buildings, a Master's Lodge, a stately hall, etc. and would be impossibly expensive, but that prestige would be automatically conferred if the society was part of Clare. They concluded that the graduate extension should be an integral part of Clare: the students would be the graduates of Clare together with newcomers from outside Cambridge; the fellows would be elected according to the present statutes, would teach Clare undergraduates if appropriate, and have reciprocal dining rights with fellows attached to the present college.

The report next discussed the pattern and needs of the proposed extension. Responsibility and authority over the internal affairs of the extension would be delegated to the fellows attached to it. To this end there should be a Warden, who should reside on the site of the extension, and a Tutor for advanced students, who would be responsible for graduate admissions to Clare. The finances would be managed from the college, but there would be a block allocation of money to the extension, which could be spent at the discretion of the Warden and the fellows attached to it.

There should be residential accommodation for the Warden, for several fellows and about half of the graduate students, both single and married. Other desirable amenities in the extension were suggested, including studies for some non-resident members, a common room to be shared by fellows and graduate students, a dining hall and kitchens, a snack-bar which could also be used by wives living in the extension, a committee room which could also be used as a general meeting room for societies, seminars etc., guest rooms, (modest) office accommodation for secretaries, one or two larger houses for visiting scholars and their families – and perhaps for a fellow, and a squash court.

Section IV of the report set out requirements for buildings. It was proposed that there should be a large official residence for the Warden[4], and 5 dwellings for married fellows with a child, 5 sets for bachelor fellows in residence, 25 study work-rooms for fellows, 10 dwellings for married students with one child, 20 sets for bachelor students in residence, and 10 study work-rooms for students not in residence. The college centre would have a dining hall for 100 persons, a smaller snack-bar, kitchen, a spacious common room, a committee room, and a squash court.

[4] It was suggested that the Warden's Lodge should be large enough to meet the demands of an official residence in addition to that of a private home, and should have a minimum area of 3,000 sq. ft.

The authors of the report took the view that the land soon to be acquired in Herschel Road should be reserved for undergraduates. They therefore recommended that the college extension be developed on the land in Chesterton Lane, retaining the two larger accommodation blocks on the site and replacing the others by new buildings over a 4 to 5 year period. The total cost was estimated to be less than £200,000. In addition, there would need to be a subsidy for running costs equivalent to the income from a capital sum of £150,000.

The use of the existing buildings in Chesterton Lane for the new extension would mean that accommodation would have to be found elsewhere for the 91 undergraduates already living there. It was proposed that there should be a phased withdrawal to new accommodation, which would be provided partly by converting the attics[5] of Memorial Court to student rooms and by a new building in Herschel Road.

A HOSTILE RESPONSE

There was a special meeting of the governing body on 20 May 1963 to discuss the Report on the proposed extension to Clare College. It received a hostile reception, with criticism from most groupings amongst the fellows – conservatives, progressives, scholars, administrators, and researchers. However, the minutes of that meeting record:

4. That, subject to the satisfactory resolution of the many points on which the governing body does not wish to be committed, the governing body approves in principle the proposal to establish an extension to Clare College with the functions as set out in the attached Report.
5. That the Report be reconsidered in the light of the discussion by a committee consisting of Dr Black, Mr Cooper, Dr Heine, Mr Holister, Dr Laurie, Mr Reddaway, Mr Tapp, Dr Wright, and the Master.

Freely translated, minute 4 can be interpreted as meaning that most of the comments from the governing body were critical, but the Master and some of the fellows did not want the idea of an extension to die through disagreement on details.

---

[5] An earlier proposal to convert the attics in Memorial Court had been rejected by the governing body.

One of the most evident reasons for the hostile reception was the cost of the Warden's Lodge, which was estimated to cost around £24,000, including some furnishing, but excluding the value of the land. This was between 4 and 5 times the price of a modern 4 bedroomed house in a good area of Cambridge at that time. Many of the fellows had come of age during the war, and had formed their own households during the long period of post-war austerity. The resulting puritan instincts reacted against this apparent extravagance over the Warden's Lodge. It is interesting to note that the next version of the proposal, discussed on 28 October, omitted both the Warden and the Warden's Lodge. The high profile of the hostility to the cost of the Lodge may have served to distract attention from more fundamental objections which were certainly raised at this meeting, but which had to await the return from leave of absence of the Senior Tutor, Dr Northam, before they were expressed again with greater effect.

Other criticisms concerned the ambiguities over the additional fellows. If they had the same rights and status as existing fellows, would they be associated mainly with the extension? If so, they would be second class fellows, when compared with those in the main college buildings. If not, then the main buildings would be overcrowded. Would the extension be the main centre for Clare graduate students? If so, they would be detached from the main body of Clare fellows and both groups would lose thereby. The assumption in the report that the new fellows and the graduate students would have common interests in research was false. The new fellows would come from minority subjects, such as Chinese or Scandinavian languages, or medical research, whereas most graduates were researching in the major subjects, such as the physical sciences or history or English literature. The proposed location in Chesterton Lane was in the wrong part of Cambridge, particularly for graduate students and for fellows whose primary concerns were with research, since current and future developments of university buildings and departments would be in West Cambridge.

I was amongst those who were critical of the proposal, and in discussions with the bursar (Brian Cooper) after the meeting I learnt that he was quite strongly opposed to it, although he had been a member of the committee. Essentially, his view was that the Chesterton Lane site was functioning very satisfactorily for undergraduates (for whom the site had been developed), and he was reluctant to abandon a successful enterprise for one that was untried. I learnt later that Brian Reddaway (the other financial heavyweight on the committee) was also not in favour of the proposal. Thus, in the discussions at the governing body meeting the Master was himself inhibited from being a prime advocate of the proposals because he was in the chair, but he also lacked the support of the most senior fellows on the extension committee. However, his skill as chairman preserved the idea that a project of some sort was 'approved in principle', though the meeting ended with no clear indication of what changes might lead to its acceptability in practice.

HEINE CONSULTS FELLOWS

As part of the 'calming procedure', that allowed a proposal that few fellows liked to be approved 'in principle' by the governing body on 19 May 1963, it had been agreed that members of the extension committee would consult further with other fellows. As in much of the preparation of the proposal, Volker Heine appears to have been the principal activist in the consultation process. Heine and I certainly had plenty of opportunity to talk further about the extension, since we were at that time working closely together on a major reorganisation of the Physics courses for Part II of the Natural Science Tripos, which would allow physics undergraduates the option of taking Part II in Theoretical Physics. In addition we both had offices on the top floor of the Austin Wing of the old Cavendish Laboratory, located in the centre of town on the New Museums site. Although I was then in the Faculty of Mathematics, my involvement with this new Tripos development had arisen partly from my earlier work in initiating a Tripos in Mathematics with Physics, which allowed mathematics undergraduates to take physics lectures instead of applied mathematics lectures, for either Part I or Part II of this Tripos. Heine and I had first had discussions about the proposed extension immediately after the possibility had first been raised at the earlier meeting of the governing body in October 1962. He recalls that I agreed with his concern about the provision of improved facilities for graduate students, but also commented that visiting scholars (faculty) were also in need of a college connection and this was an important element in encouraging them to come to Cambridge.

More significantly for the short-term evolution of the proposal for an extension to Clare, Volker Heine had a long meeting with two unmarried research fellows (Ian Laurie and Roger Tapp), who were not on the extension committee and both of whom were living in college rooms. Heine's handwritten notes of this meeting include an addendum "1 + 3", so they were typed, probably with the top copy going to the Master. They begin:

It was agreed that the *first priority* should be living accommodation for about 30 graduates (20 bachelors and 10 married) and five married fellows with at most a small baby. In general, one would prefer to see bachelor fellows continuing to live in the main college, though nothing would bar any of them moving to the extension if they wished.

The *second priority* should be provision of some communal facilities. The purpose would be (a) to integrate the group into a bit of a community and (b) to draw into it those graduates (about 50%) not living on the site. Especially if the accommodation is mostly in the form of self-contained flats, something is required to help people to bump into each other informally, though without pushing them into artificially created communal activities. As regards (a), it was agreed at Gov. Body that Chesterton Lane has a community atmosphere without communal activities: however, its seems that the breakfasts together, the landladies and dinner in Hall, serve as integrating factors, the last mentioned much more so with the undergraduates than with research students. As regards (b), it would be undesirable for a cleavage to develop between research students living in the extension and those not.

They gave a high priority to the provision of facilities for common meals, which they said could be provided by a 'snack-bar, generally informal and modest in scale, but they were doubtful whether there would be sufficient usage to cover the catering costs if they were to be cheap enough to encourage use by students.

They thought that additional fellows, not living in the extension but associated with it, might help to make the catering proposals economically viable. However, they were doubtful whether such non-resident fellows would wish to use studies in the extension, since most would prefer to do their academic work in their departments. They were uncertain whether the provision of common meals would be sufficient to provide cohesion amongst the fellows associated with the extension, though they noted that this seemed to be working with the Society of Women Non-fellows (now Lucy Cavendish College). It was hoped that there might be some interaction between fellows and graduate students, though this would not be obligatory. There would be a need for a Warden to be the head of the society using the extension only if it included fellows, but they thought he would not need an extravagant house – as had been suggested earlier. In addition to the two questions of whether there should be a 'snack-bar' and whether there should be a society of fellows in addition to the graduate students, they discussed two other possible options: the provision of two or three houses for married fellows with families, and the provision of a house (at commercial rent) for a senior visiting academic.

Finally, Heine's notes show that they discussed an issue that seems very odd thirty years later, but evidently seemed then to be akin to the admission of women to the priesthood, perhaps influenced by the fact that two of the discussants were bachelors at the time. They were concerned with the consequences of having married research students in the extension

After wives come fiancees, and then girl friends. Indeed we were almost persuaded that the snack-bar would have to have segregated sections for bachelors, for wives, and for mixed sexes, with separate entrances. Ditto the common rooms. Whilst it is recognised that some people want, as a matter of important principle, a greater freedom of mingling of the sexes, some fellows are unhappy that it should be in Clare and forced upon those bachelor research students etc. who do not wish it.

They concluded that there might be more acceptance amongst the fellows of Clare for founding an independent small mixed college rather than having both sexes in the extension. Their discussion took place on 7 June 1963, just over a month before a meeting of the governing body considered a request from Clare undergraduates that they be allowed to bring lady guests to dine in Clare on one night a week in full term[6].

ASHBY CONSULTS GRADUATE STUDENTS

In his talk in 1976 on the tenth anniversary of the founding of Clare Hall[7], Lord Ashby described his recollections of the meeting with graduate students in the following terms:

---

[6] See chapter 4.
[7] Reprinted in appendix 1.

We conceived the bright idea of a student village for married and single research students, with (perhaps) some additional fellows (who would be bye-fellows of the college – though we did not know what that meant). We had some land and some money which could be used for this village. It was to have married quarters, a crêche, a laundry, perhaps a shop, a café, and (one fellow suggested) a resident midwife. It was an attractive idea and we played with it – and variations of it – in ten committee meetings during that academic year 1962–63. Until on 14 June 1963, the idea fell sick and died.

On that day I held a wine and cheese party in the Lodge and asked all the Clare research students to come, to discuss how they would like to live. (We had at the back of our minds a variant of Leckhampton, which Corpus had built for research students). It was a surprising and decisive meeting. The student from Australia or America wanted to live in the austere 18th century environment of Old Court, innocent of plumbing and other amenities. The Clare graduate, after three years in the college, could not get away fast enough to a room or a flat in Panton Street where he could live in freedom unmolested by tutors and the like. It seemed pretty clear that the customers were not as keen on our village as we were.

Ashby's use of the term 'student village' is a short-hand for the proposal of the extension committee – the first version of paper "A", which was the only proposal in serious discussion in June 1963, at the time of his meeting with graduate students. The term *student village* was not in common usage then , though in his talk ten years later Ashby said that after meeting with the graduate students the notes in his engagement book changed from *village committee* to *satellite committee* [8].

The idea did not 'fall sick and die' in June because of the graduate students response. When he joined the committee in September 1963 following his year's leave of absence in Norway, the Senior Tutor, John Northam, found the proposal to be alive and well and still strongly supported by the Master.

---

[8] However, in private discussions, Cooper and I used the term graduate village as meaning basic housing accommodation in flats or houses without any associated institutional features (see later in this chapter). Lord Ashby read an early version of this book early in 1992, and in discussion with me he said he was very willing to accept contemporary documentary evidence where it differed from personal recollections, citing an earlier example in his own researches on educational development in Nigeria (RJE).

NORTHAM RETURNS FROM SABBATICAL LEAVE

On his return from his sabbatical leave in Norway, Northam resumed his position as Senior Tutor, and ex officio replaced Black as a member of the extension committee. He was just in time to attend their meeting on 21 September, when they had hoped to approve the main elements for the final draft of their revised report for the governing body. Northam was provided with the earlier draft, which had been discussed by the governing body on 21 May. His copy of that draft carries the following handwritten notes on the first page:

10. John Northam, Fellow of Clare College 1950–72, 1987– , Senior Tutor 1957–66.

1) There is a problem that already exists and which we have to face – fellowships. Yet this effort looks to hypothetical problems which are not pressing.

2) It assumes that Clare will be prepared to accept into its governing body, Council, combination room etc. a considerable extra number. Has this been agreed?

3) If so (and I believe there are alternatives) then I believe that we should concentrate all our efforts on increasing facilities on site i.e. by building more rooms (public and tailored-for-some-dons), more independence; (consider an independent wing for research students if need be); i.e. reshape the college to cope with many more dons (and research students).

Present proposal seems one simply to provide a suburb, which will give living accommodation but not solve our main problem.

All this falls through if the governing body ...

In the margin against various parts of paragraph 2 of part II of the report, which specified rather grand requirements for a new independent society to be prestigious, Northam wrote: '*non-sequitur*', ... '*not necessary*', ... and '*This makes loose assumptions*'. Against paragraph 5 of part II, which said that the new fellows would be elected according to the present statutes, he wrote: '*But this does not help our main difficulty – doesn't even begin to ...*'.

The following members of the extension committee were present at their meeting on 21 September 1963 : The Master, Black, Cooper, Heine, Holister, Northam, Reddaway. It is unlikely that Northam had much open support at that meeting from those members of the extension committee who had not been involved in the drafting of the report. However, the bursar (Cooper) was only lukewarm about the proposals, and he would have welcomed the intervention of Northam, though probably not overtly. The reader will recall that in the Regent House discussion on the Bridges Report, Cooper had spoken in favour of the proposal by the Society of Women Members for 'Collegiate Societies' for Senior Members – an idea that had some features in common with the one now being put forward by Northam. However, Cooper (and probably Reddaway also), although lukewarm to the main proposals, would not have wished to provide a focus of opposition to the ideas and wishes of the Master and the earlier agreement in principle by the governing body at the meeting on 21 May. By 21 September, it would have been inappropriate for them to switch allegiance and join Northam's opposition to these proposals. A chairman as experienced as Ashby would have been aware of the degree of support from each member of the committee, ranging from the enthusiasm of Heine to the acquiescence of Cooper and Reddaway, but he did not seek formal agreement – thus he had earlier presented the proposal to the governing body as being from 'three of its members', rather from the extension committee. The un-named three that he had in mind were, presumably, Ashby himself, Heine and Holister.

A SITE IN HERSCHEL ROAD

The committee considered a report by Holister, which was evidently prepared in response to an earlier decision by the committee to relocate the proposed extension in Herschel Road. The report began:

> The site we now recommend to the governing body is situated at No. 3 Herschel Road. The land is at present owned by St. John's College but it seems certain that it can be obtained by the college as part exchange for our land in Grange Road.
>
> The area of the site is approximately 32,400 sq. ft. (diagram No.1) and on it is a large dwelling house ... divided into five flats which are let on six month tenancies ... Informal discussions have been held with the City Architect and Planning Officer and his deputy, and it would appear that they would not object to the college developing the site for the purpose of providing residential accommodation for a college extension. Few formal restrictions would be expected regarding the development and any scheme we proposed would be considered on its own merits. The restrictions we would have to observe would be:
>
> 1. The scale and type of buildings must not be discordant with the neighbourhood.
> 2. The existing building line to Herschel Road must be accepted.
> 3. No trees to be removed without good cause.
> 4. Any design should consider the needs for expansion over the coming years and should not be incapable of extension.

Holister's report goes on to discuss alternative ways in which residential accommodation could be developed, depending on whether the objective was to maximise its use by graduate students or by fellows. From their subsequent proposal it is evident that the committee decided to give priority to accommodation for graduate students, but also to provide for residence by five married fellows. The committee agreed that they would recommend Herschel Road (the 'Grange Road site') for the proposed extension, and that the Master should rewrite the committee's Report for consideration at its next meeting.

The committee agreed further, that 'Dr Northam should, if he wished, draw up an alternative proposal, possibly to be included in the Report to the governing body.' It was also decided that Holister should prepare a report on extensions to Memorial Court. This latter proposal appears to be a consequence of the earlier intention to use some existing accommodation on the Chesterton Lane site for graduate students, thus displacing undergraduates who would require rooms elsewhere. Although there was now no intention to do this, it seems that the idea of increasing accommodation for undergraduates had developed a momentum of its own. This momentum provided an opportunity to re-open a proposal to build attic rooms in the Memorial Court that had been turned down earlier by the governing body. There was also a possibility of developing other parts of the Memorial Court for common rooms, perhaps including a library.

The date of the next meeting of the extension committee, scheduled in the minutes for 25 October, was subsequently changed to Monday 28 October in the fellows' combination room, the normal time and place for a meeting of the governing body. Subsequently also, all fellows were invited to attend this meeting and it proved to be another landmark in the progress that eventually led to the founding of Clare Hall. The papers circulated to all fellows for that meeting included the second report from the extension committee – this is called paper 'A'. There was also an appendix written by Northam, which is referred to as appendix 'B' or paper 'B', and expresses his fundamental disagreement with the approach of the committee.

A REVISED PROPOSAL: PAPER A

Paper A began with a review of developments since the resolution of 21 May 1963, when the governing body had approved in principle the concept of an extension then put forward " subject to the satisfactory resolution of many points …". The extension committee had met five

A revised proposal: paper A

times and now wished to put forward in paper 'A' specific proposals to illustrate how the governing body's intention at its meeting last May could be achieved. They noted that Paper B was a statement from Dr Northam inviting the governing body to reconsider its resolution of 21 May, and added: *Clearly (B) should be discussed before (A)*.

The committee's proposals, based on the resolution of 21 May, were as follows:

(i) the extension should be built on the Grange Road site.
(ii) the order of priorities in planning the extension should be:
  (a) residence for about 30 graduates (20 single and 10 married) and 5 married fellows.
  (b) some communal facilities adjoining the residence.
  (c) a provision which would bring about 10 more fellows into the new Community; the intention being to create an informal sub-society.

The committee now had in mind something more informal than was previously suggested, and there should be no Warden, or Warden's residence. They thought that the problems of administration of the "colony" would now be negligibly small and they would prefer to see some social structure emerge from the colony itself, rather than prescribe it in advance. The suggestions were based on the expectation that the number of graduate students would increase, and that members of the university would increasingly be involved in research.

The committee indicated several possibilities for action by the college, but expressed the view that the majority of fellows would support the creation of an informal society with some common amenities where fellows and research students would have an opportunity to mix. But if the governing body accepted the proposals, there would be an inevitable change in the pattern of the society. They envisaged an increase of some 15 in the total numbers of fellows of Clare. There would also need to be an understanding that some of the fellows, without of course surrendering their rights in the Old Court, would consent to take part in the creation and maintenance of a sub-society (however informal) on the new site.

These proposals were independent of proposals to improve the amenities for undergraduates in Memorial Court except in one respect – the provision of a refectory to provide informal meals . The committee hoped, therefore, that the governing body would – if it approved the proposals – authorise the next step, which was to remit the project to the finance committee to authorise the expenditure on an architect's sketch plans, so that work could proceed. It was hoped that the extension could be opened in the academic year 1965–66. The following paragraphs provided the data which (if approved) could form the basis of a brief to the architect.

NORTHAM'S ALTERNATIVE: PAPER B

Northam's dissenting paper argued that the proposals put forward by the committee attempted too many things – to house research students, to increase the number of fellows, to use a new piece of land – and confused the one essential issue that needs settling before use of the site is compromised. He observed that even if the Bridges Report[9] had failed, the problem of fellowships was one of the most important that the colleges and university were faced with. He believed that we should decide to create a considerable number of fellowships with the prospect of further grants and development in the future. He thought that 30 new fellows, rising during the first phase to 50, would restore to the college a flexibility and freedom for development that it lacked at that time.

Northam suggested that this could be done in one of two ways:

(1) by adding these new fellows (and the probable further growth) to the existing society of Clare, or
(2) by creating a radically new (not a formal or traditional) society.

Northam argued that a large increase of fellowships within Clare would radically weaken the college. For this reason he favoured option (2): to create a radically new society. His own preference was to create 30–50 fellowships in a new society, which should be a society of fellows only in the first instance. This would mean a minimum of administration; what there was might be carried out on behalf of the new society by Clare. There should be no paraphernalia of tutors, bursars, praelectors, college officers etc. In time the society might attract to itself research students in the subjects represented by the fellowship, but it should not, at the outset, be saddled with our existing body of research students whose subjects might bear no relationship to the subjects of the fellows elected.

---

[9] See chapter 3.

The relationship of the new society with Clare could be established in a number of relatively trivial ways – by dining rights, by shared feasts, by nomenclature; but in Northam's view there would be a genuine possibility of interchange between the two societies. He hoped it would be possible for any fellow of Clare who at any time felt the need, either permanently or for a few years, to drop out of college life and pursue research undisturbed, to transfer his fellowship to the new society: conversely, for Clare to feel free to invite a fellow from the new society to transfer to the Clare fellowship in suitable circumstances.

The facilities connected with the new society could include an allowance of meals for fellows, a dining room, common room, studies, some residential accommodation at economic rent for bachelors and occasional visiting scholars (though the demand for this, on the analogy of our own society, is not likely to be large). The buildings for the new society should be on the newly acquired Clare land in Herschel Road. If such a proposal was adopted, the college could consider separately the problem of housing for the existing body of Clare graduate students – his view was that there were plenty of options available.

DEADLOCK

When I discussed these events with Northam in 1992, he recalled the meeting of the extension committee on 23 September 1963, when he had indicated his fundamental disagreement with the proposals for the extension. Ashby had said that, since he (Northam) had not been present during the earlier discussions of the committee, he was not entitled to oppose the proposals. However, Ashby then added "Nevertheless, if you wish, you may write up your views as an appendix to our report". When Ashby read the resulting paper, he was sufficiently concerned that he asked Northam to meet him on Saturday morning 26 October, in advance of the crucial meeting of the committee with other fellows. Northam recalled that 'Eric was not pleased', so evidently they came to the subsequent meeting without reaching any form of accommodation between their opposing views.

Most members of the governing body attended the discussions with the extension committee on the afternoon of Monday 28 October 1963. The revised proposals of the committee (paper A) and Northam's appendix (paper B) had been circulated to all fellows before the meeting. No minutes were kept of the discussion, indeed generally the extension committee did not keep any minutes of its meetings. However, my own recollections are clear since the meeting was a turning point in my own involvement in the discussions – the changes that had been made in the proposals had not neutralised the opposition.

Most fellows took part in the discussion, but it was entirely directed towards the issues raised in Part A – the committee's draft report – and there was no discussion of Northam's alternative proposal. I do not recall how this came about, but it was this omission that caused me to talk about it with Northam after the meeting – a conversation that was to have significant consequences, as we shall see in the next chapter. My guess is that Sir Eric had decided that the earlier decision in principle in favour of the main proposal set the ground rules for the discussion unless it was challenged. He would have chosen the initial speakers with this in mind. The normal practice was for Sir Eric, as chairman of the meeting, to invite comments initially from several fellows, whose views he knew. This was followed by contributions in sequence round the semi-circle in which fellows had happened to sit. Thus Heine would have been an early speaker in favour of the proposals, and there would probably have been general support from the senior fellow, Harry Godwin. The bursar would have indicated that the finance committee regarded the proposals as feasible.

However, the committee had not succeeded in allaying the fears of many fellows that a further increase in their numbers would have serious adverse effects on the cohesion of the society. They were not convinced that the provision of amenities for the 'new' fellows on the site in Herschel Road would avoid these adverse effects, since it was proposed that they would be members of the governing body. Secondly, if the new fellows were to be primarily associated with the new site, they would be detached from the main body of fellows and would appear to be second-class fellows, not fully concerned with the main functions of the college. Thirdly, many fellows took the view that it was undesirable to associate all Clare graduate students with the 'new' fellows in Herschel Road – other fellows were involved with graduate students, probably more closely than the prospective new fellows. Fourthly, some fellows were doubtful whether the graduate students would welcome such a change.

Graduate students were primarily concerned with independent and convenient accommodation; the proposed arrangements were too institutional for this purpose.

The meeting adjourned after about two hours; no decisions had been taken and there do not seem to be any records or minutes of the meeting.

AFTER THE MEETING

After the meeting on 28 October, Northam and I stayed on for five or ten minutes in the fellows combination room. I was concerned that, although his critical comments on the extension committees report had been reinforced by the views of other fellows, no-one had spoken in favour of his imaginative proposals for a 'new society' for senior members of the university, which had been virtually ignored in the discussion. I suggested that his ideas might provide a way forward if they was combined with some of the practical suggestions from the committee's proposal. In particular, I welcomed his idea of including visiting fellows in the proposed new society. My own experience, both in Cambridge and in the United States, was that the potential number of visiting fellows was much larger than Northam had suggested, and they could form an important part of the new society. Although neither Northam nor I knew it at the time, his ideas had many similarities with those put forward by the Society of Women Members in the discussion on the Bridges Report, which had been so warmly applauded by the bursar of Clare, Brian Cooper, in his own contribution to the Regent House discussion.

Northam and I agreed that the issue of accommodation for Clare graduate students should be dealt with separately from the issue of electing more fellows. This separation of objectives was to prove crucial to the resolution of the deadlock over decision-making by the governing body. I was aware that the bursar agreed with this, even though in a spirit of cooperation he had gone along with the proposals of the extension committee. He and I had discussed alternative options for graduate accommodation on several occasions, including the possibility of building a 'graduate village' in West Cambridge, with low-cost housing along the lines that I had seen on the campuses of universities in the United States. I recall the bursar remarking that the college should also provide basic furnishings, preferably robust, he said (ever the cautious approach to the care of college property), such that it could be 'hosed down' between tenancies. The idea of a graduate village of this type – with no common rooms or other institutional features – received little attention at the time. However not long after the Clare Hall project had commenced, Brian Cooper in his capacity as bursar went a long way towards the objective of a graduate village by purchasing on behalf of the college the St. Regis apartments in Chesterton Road[10], eventually to provide low cost housing for over one hundred graduate students, though I do not believe the furnishings met his earlier criterion that they could be hosed down.

[10] As with an earlier purchase of flats in Queen Edith's Way, Cooper bought the St. Regis flats very cheaply – partly by keeping it secret that Clare was after them and handling the purchase himself rather than using an agent.

Chapter 6

WHICH FENCE TO JUMP?

A WORKING LUNCH

On 9 October 1963, Ashby sent to all fellows a preliminary notice about a meeting of the governing body that was scheduled for 11 November. He asked fellows to reserve the whole afternoon for the meeting in view of the large number of items to be discussed. The regular business would include the tutor's report on tripos performances, the bursar's report on college finances, the domestic bursar's report on the recommendations of the college needs committee, and a report from the fellowship committee on the tenure of research fellowships that were due to come to an end in the year 1963–64. In addition to this regular business, the governing body would be asked to discuss the admissions policy of the college in relation to the Master's analysis of the quality of recent candidates for admission, and in relation to Cambridge colleges joining the national 'clearing house' scheme for university admissions. Other items included the question of what, if anything, to do about the deterioration of the trees in the avenue from the college to Queen',s Road, and a suggestion that there should be a tutor solely concerned with graduate students in the college – as opposed to the existing system in which they were shared between all the tutors.

Most of these matters were of direct concern to the senior tutor, but in many the Master also wished to be involved – usually in a supportive role, for example in helping to placate former members of the college whose sons no longer received preferential admission, or to help with some of the wide variety of ongoing activities or new developments that were under way in the college. Both Ashby and Northam thought that a regular exchange of views was essential but they had great difficulty in scheduling a time because of their other commitments, so they met once a week for a sandwich lunch in the dining room of the Master's Lodge.

Apart from his college responsibilities, Ashby was engaged in historical and educational studies, writing about his experience in developing education in Africa; he was a member or chairman of several national bodies, including the Presidency of the British Association in 1963; and he was active in university affairs. The evolution of discussions on the extension to the college needs to be viewed in this context. For example, Ashby's role in the university is summarised by Christopher Brooke[1] in the following words:

> The 1960s were creative years for all British universities, and Cambridge had its share in labs and faculties as well as in the colleges. In this new world Sir Eric Ashby, the Master of Clare, played a leading role. He had been vice-chairman of the Bridges Syndicate, and its leading spokesman within the University. The panache of his advocacy and the example he set helped to inspire, or shame, other colleges to play their part in providing for the underprivileged and the dispossessed. The dining table in the Clare Lodge was a natural meeting place of groups and committees in the 1960s as the Caius Lodge had been in the 1920s ...

Northam was equally busy. As the senior tutor in Clare, he was responsible for coordinating all tutorial activities and for advising his own group of students. He was also admissions tutor, and in the autumn was responsible for arranging interviews for all candidates for Clare scholarships, who would be coming to the college for their examinations early in December, and more generally he was responsible for liaison with schools. He gave lectures in the Faculty of English and took his share of college supervisions in literature and drama.

In addition to their weekly lunches, Ashby and Northam also met more randomly to take long walks together – following hundreds of years of tradition in Cambridge colleges. Ashby's said later[2] that it was on 1 November 1963, during a walk on the Coton footpath, that he and Northam reviewed the problem of the extension to the college, that had resulted from the impasse created by the discussion on 28 October described in the last chapter. Since the impasse involved Northam's opposition to the main scheme for a graduate colony, it is unlikely that

---

[1] Brooke, *A History of the University of Cambridge*, vol IV, 1870–1990, pp. 579–80 (Cambridge 1993).
[2] See Appendix 1. However, when I discussed this with Eric Ashby in 1992, he said that he and John Northam often had walks together and he agreed that this and other simplifications involved some poetic licence.

A working lunch

they did more than agree that it was necessary to find a way to resolve the problem that would be acceptable to most members of the governing body. This led to a suggestion, probably from Northam because of our discussion two days before, that I should be asked to join them for one of their working lunches where the extension would be the sole topic for discussion.

Our working lunch was a week or so later, taking about one hour. We were seeking a compromise between the committee's proposal 'A' for an extension, based on graduate students, and Northam's proposal 'B' for a new society of fellows. I thought we should try to identify those aspects of the proposals that could be made acceptable in some modified form: To be acceptable to the different and conflicting viewpoints amongst members of the governing body of Clare, a new Society would have to include some graduate students, but not to the extent of removing all of them from the main part of the college; it would have to include a substantial number of new fellows, but in such a way that it would naturally be their social focus (and possibly the academic focus for some), so that it did not destroy the cohesion of the existing group of fellows by increasing their numbers significantly; it would have to be attractive to both senior members and to graduate students, and its membership should be limited so that both groups would regard membership as a privilege – the implication of second class fellows must be avoided. Finally, through some constitutional device it was essential that the fellows in the new society should not be on the governing body of Clare College.

Our discussion was concerned with criteria to be satisfied and with objectives and I thought that these could include a much larger role for visiting fellowships in the extension than had been suggested by Northam, which in some unspecified way might help provide a purpose for the new Society. I was rather taken aback at the end of our working lunch, when Ashby asked me to write a paper setting out my ideas – I did not think that our discussion had come remotely near identifying an acceptable solution. However, Ashby evidently thought that I might have found a possible third way forward, – an unwritten proposal 'C' that was a mixture between proposals 'A' and 'B', whose details had yet to be worked out. It was this proposal 'C' that Ashby asked me to write.

I had neither the specific ideas, nor at that stage of term the time, to respond to Ashby's request – so I took no action. Two weeks later, feeling rather guilty about this, I consulted Northam about the possibility of my joining them again at one of their working lunches (which I then supposed still had the extension as part of their agenda), so that we could seek a more detailed specification of what the Master wanted me to do. Northam surprised me by saying that their discussions were entirely about other college business and Ashby had not raised any further questions about the extension since our joint lunchtime meeting – and I did nothing about it until two months later – early in January 1964.

CONFLICTING VIEWS

Early in December, Ashby circulated to all fellows a set of papers for a special meeting of the governing body which would be held on Saturday 11 January 1964. It is probable that he prepared them early in November, possibly before our lunchtime meeting though there may have been some changes (and misprints) added after that meeting. The papers show clearly that he had decided that the time had come for the governing body to reach a decision – one way or another, and Ashby confirmed this twelve years later in a lecture on Clare Hall's tenth anniversary. The papers included:

* an introductory note from the Master (Ashby).
* Part I of a new paper from Ashby, which is outlined below.
* Part II of the new paper, which described the proposed procedures for the meeting of the governing body on 11 January 1964. This outlined the alternative options for change and indicated the decisions that Ashby would ask the governing body to consider.
* paper 'A', which was an amended version of the extension committee's paper 'A' which had been discussed on 28 October.
* paper 'B', which was an unchanged copy of Northam's minority report in appendix B of the paper of 28 October.
** there was no paper 'C' included in the papers distributed in December.

The papers began with a personal note from Ashby:

Note from the Master

This is going to be a difficult meeting and (I hope) a decisive one. The purpose of this note is to set out the issues which confront the governing body and to include some views of my own which – whether fellows agree with them or not – ought at least to be taken into account. Part I is emphatically not for discussion; part II sets out what I shall ask the governing body to adopt as the pattern for the meeting.

Next followed part I of Ashby's paper, which was partly concerned with arguing against Northam's approach and his emphasis that the primary need was the creation of more fellowships. Northam's annotations make it clear that he was not involved in the preparation of these papers. There are fifteen handwritten comments by Northam on his copy of Part I of Ashby's paper, all essentially maintaining the viewpoint that had been expressed in his dissenting paper B. Their importance lies in the fact that they show clearly that Part I of the paper represented Ashby's views and that Northam had not been persuaded to abandon his alternative approach. This conclusion is reinforced by Northam's prepared comments at the governing body meeting on 11 January, which is described in chapter 7, and by my own recollection that – on reading the papers early in January – I concluded that nothing of substance had changed since the conflict of views evident at the governing body meeting 28 October.

Part I of Ashby's paper began by reminding the governing body that it had agreed to take an initiative to set up a satellite society – still to be part of Clare College – which would include fellows and graduate research students. The extension committee had prepared a proposal (paper 'A') that could be used as a brief for an architect if the fellows decided to go ahead on this basis. After this paper had been completed, Northam had returned from his sabbatical leave and had raised some matters of principle that he wished to have discussed and were set out in paper 'B'.

Ashby evidently saw Northam's paper as an obstacle to his getting a decision from the governing body that had prevaricated for nearly a year. He argued that Northam was over-stating the importance of college fellowships and he sought to illustrate this by some "crystal gazing" – outlining a scenario for the future of the university and the colleges in Cambridge. Competition would drive the university towards even greater emphasis on academic quality and research, and the role of the colleges would be thereby diminished. There would be greatly increased graduate schools, nests of specialists and a constant stream of visiting scholars. Their social life would revolve around the university departments and the graduate centre but not the colleges, and members of the faculties would be increasingly reluctant to accept the responsibilities of college fellowships which would be in competition with their time for research.

Colleges would be very different places – no closing of gates at night, no exclusion of women from senior or junior membership[3], gathering at lunch but not much communal dining at night, admission of students on academic merit, and the executive fellowship of the college reduced to (say) a dozen people, paid full-time or part-time by the college.

On the brighter side, Ashby observed that opinion in the academic world outside Cambridge was almost unanimous about the benefits from splitting universities into the social cohesion of small societies where senior and junior members mix. The response by colleges to the threat from the development of departments or research groups as the main social units in Cambridge should be to seek a complementary role that matched their strengths. One of these was the traditional role of undergraduate supervision, which the college should seek to strengthen by an increase in the fellowship. In research the college could increase the numbers of graduate students and aim to provide facilities or fellowships for scholars, particularly in the humanities where other support is scarce – this could include support for visiting scholars. These objectives should be borne in mind in considering the buildings for an extension to the college on a new site.

WHICH FENCE TO JUMP?

In his introduction to the papers sent to the governing body (GB) in December 1963, Ashby wrote: ... *part II sets out what I shall ask the governing body to adopt as the pattern for the meeting.* The first part of Part II outlined four options for consideration:

May we start from the assumption that we wish to take some initiative with our money and our site, to anticipate the future needs of the college?

We could direct our initiative either to getting bigger or to changing our pattern without getting bigger. At present much of our discussion is hampered by the conviction that if our society gets bigger, it will deteriorate; in any case we have nearly reached physical limits to the size of the fellowship. We have no room to manoeuvre until we decide whether to provide physical room to expand our own fellowship on the site (e.g. by transferring the Forbes Library to Memorial Court or the Master to Grange Road) or to create a fresh fellowship on another site.

---

[3] In 1963 all Cambridge colleges were single sex – all but three for men only.

Paper B (Northam's paper) advocates a large expansion, but not on the "old" site and not involving an increase in the governing body.

Paper A (the extension committee's proposal) advocates a more modest expansion, also not on the "old" site, but in such a way that the governing body would be enlarged. (Both A & B envisage common membership of Clare and easy migration between old and new sites).

A third possibility is to expand on the "old" site by drastic changes in the Old Court.

A fourth possibility is to change pattern but to get no bigger at all.

(1) *The GB is asked to decide in principle which of these alternatives it prefers.*

The second part of Part II sought to refine the decisions required. It includes several crucial misprints and I have indicated in parentheses what Ashby probably intended to write:

If the GB favours expansion on a new site, there is a question of emphasis:

Paper B emphasises facilities for fellows.

Paper C [*should be "A"*] emphasis[*es*] facilities for a mixture of research students and fellows, with flexibility as to the balance between them, but with a smaller addition of fellows than would be possible under A [*should be "B"*].

A third possibility is to build with a bias towards research students and not, substantially, to enlarge the fellowship at all.

(2) *The GB is asked to decide in principle which of these alternatives it prefers.*

If the GB favours the views of Paper B (emphasis on facilities for fellows), the suggestions in this paper should be focused clearly enough by the GB to enable the domestic bursar to make rough calculations about buildings.

If it favours the views of Paper A (a mixture but one which could not provide for as many additional fellows as A [*should read "as B"*]), then the GB should comment on and modify the proposals in paper B [*should be "paper A"*]. with a view to its submission to an architect early in 1964.

The committee has given some thought to other proposals which are ancillary to these questions but might affect the GB's views. They are:

(a) to build a self-service café in Memorial Court which would make it possible to run only one hall a night and perhaps dispense with the small hall.
(b) to provide some common room facilities (and supervision rooms) in the Memorial Court.

(c) to increase accommodation in Memorial Court by dormer rooms in the attics.

These proposals could be carried out quite independently of the main proposals.

Part II of the paper was followed by the extension committee's paper 'A' containing the main proposals for a graduate extension that had been discussed in October, and Northam's paper 'B', the appendix to the October report of the extension committee[4].

These papers, designed to provide the basis for the GB meeting on 11 January 1964, were distributed to the fellows during the week beginning 9 December – the week when candidates for college scholarships came to Cambridge for their examinations and interviews. This heralded an intensely concentrated period of work for many fellows so as to complete the marking and inter-college examination meetings and send the results out before Christmas. I was helping Northam with interviewing the candidates in mathematics, and was examining in the Clare – Trinity group of five colleges. Our final examiners' meeting was on 18 December – the day on which the Master of Clare and Lady Ashby hosted a traditional Christmas dinner for fellows and their wives. At that time this was the only occasion in the year when wives dined in the college except – perhaps – in the Master's Lodge as guests of Lady Ashby and the Master.

A VISIT TO HARWELL

Early in January 1964, I was due to consult in the theoretical physics division of the UK AEA (the Atomic Energy Research Establishment) at Harwell. When I drove there from Cambridge, early on Monday 6 January, I took with me the papers provided by Ashby for the meeting of the governing body that was scheduled for 11 January, intending to read them before my return.

I had been consulting at the AEA for a few days each year since 1956, though my first visit to Harwell there had been nearly twenty years earlier in August 1944, when the local airfield was used for as a staging post for airborne forces[5]. The tented transit camp at Harwell in 1944 was about

---

[4] Papers A and B are described in chapter 5.
[5] Our tented camp was flooded the night before cancellation of our proposed airlanding in Belgium; perhaps for this reason Harwell was not used for subsequent airborne operations.

A visit to Harwell

half a mile from the more solidly built aircraft hangars that were later converted for use by the Atomic Energy Authority. In the 1950s and 1960s, the theoretical physics division occupied offices on three floors, built into one end of a large hangar, which was otherwise used for experimental work in nuclear physics, including some of the early work on the development of fusion energy, which was later moved to Culham, and evolved into the European JET Laboratory.

At the time of my visit in January 1964, some of the physicists in the division were still engaged mainly on fundamental research into the theory of the atomic nucleus (an area in which I had worked in the 1950s) and on the theory of condensed matter, though many were becoming involved, at least part-time, in the commercial work that was spreading through the AEA. The head of the division was Walter Marshall, who later became Chairman of the Atomic Energy Authority and Chief Scientist in the Department of Energy, before becoming Chairman of the Central Electricity Generating Board and changing title to Lord Marshall of Goring. My visits were more for liaison than conventional consulting, so that some of the theoretical physicists at Harwell could, if they wished, keep in touch with what we were working on in Cambridge.

On the next day (Tuesday 7 January), since my hotel in Abington did not serve dinner before 7.30 p.m., I was planning to work until about 7 p.m., though almost all the several thousand staff at Harwell left between 4.20 and 4.30 in the fleet of buses that I could see from the window of my office. By 4.30 my thoughts about research were not progressing particularly well. So, looking for some lighter reading, I picked up the papers for the next meeting of the Clare governing body. Typed on twelve pages of foolscap, including the attached papers 'A' and 'B', they amounted to about 8,000 words. I was amazed to find in the part concerned with actual proposals (papers A and B), nothing seemed to have changed since the previous meeting of fellows on 28 October. I did not read the papers in detail, nor did I notice in Part II the misprints[6] and the reference to the non-existent paper 'C'.

I was particularly alarmed at the implications of Ashby's forceful introduction, coupled with papers 'A' and 'B'. I would have welcomed paper 'B' by Northam, except that it was too unspecific to have any

---

[6] Northam noticed the misprints and corrected some but simply wrote (?) against the second lot.

chance of adoption by the governing body. It seemed that paper 'A', which was more fully worked out, would succeed by default, rather than through merit – and I started to write an attack on it, generally supporting Northam's more critical comments.

At about 5 p.m. I had second thoughts – to the effect that Ashby was evidently determined that the governing body should reach a final decision at the special meeting on 11 January – come what may! The wrong decision would not be stopped by repeating the criticisms that had been made at previous meetings. It was clearly necessary to be constructive and make an alternative proposal that would be both viable and sufficiently interesting to meet the criteria that had been welcomed by Ashby and Northam at our working lunch in November. I tore up the page and a half already drafted, and wrote a new proposal[7], which is outlined in the next section and printed in appendix 2.

A NEW PROPOSAL

The paper began:

Proposal for an Institute for Advanced Study having Special Relations with Clare College[8].

1. *Needs*

There is an increasing need in Cambridge for an expanded fellowship to include people in the following classes: (a) University Lecturers not in primary teaching subjects, (b) Visiting Scholars, (c) Research PhDs not financed by Colleges. There is an increasing need for means of bringing research students into a wider community of Scholars than in Departments.

2. *Purposes*

An Institute for Advanced Study should provide facilities for a Society of Fellows in the following main categories:-

(a) University Lecturers etc. to form a semi-permanent nucleus for the Society, since the other fellows are all temporary.

---

[7] The origin or background to this proposal requires a digression on my own experiences in research which are outlined in the final section of this chapter.

[8] The proposal is printed in full in appendix 2, see also another description in chapter 7.

(b) Visiting Fellows selected from scholars on study-leave from overseas and (in increasing numbers) from other Universities in the UK.
(c) Research Fellows selected from (i) post-doctoral research workers on temporary appointments in departments (e.g. Applied Economics, Medical Research Council, Engineering etc.) and (ii) Research Students holding DSIR or other awards.

In addition there should be

(d) Associate Fellows, who are Fellows of Colleges e.g. some members of Clare College.

All the above Fellows to be non-stipendiary. In addition there could be Research Students in the Society but this might well come as the second stage or stage 1B of the development. First the Society should be set up as a single class society.

The paper then indicated how these objectives could be achieved. In a first stage there could be: 15 permanent fellows (men and women) holding university appointments; 15 visiting fellows – to be provided with some family accommodation; about 10 graduate students also with some accommodation (to be called junior research fellows so as to ensure a one-class society); associate fellows – particularly including some fellows of Clare College.

I suggested that the Institute be governed by a 12 member Council made up of fellows from Clare College and from the Institute and chaired by the Master of Clare College. Buildings required would include 15 flats on the college site, a dining room, common room, reading room, and 10 studies. Costs were estimated at £120,000 for buildings and £8,000 for annual running costs. The paper concluded by mentioning options for further expansion in a second stage of development. These would depend on whether other more satisfactory arrangements had been made for Clare Research Students and would require additional finance and land.

Following my visit to Harwell, I returned to Cambridge during the evening of Wednesday 8 January 1964, and early on Thursday morning the proposal (unedited) was typed by my secretary in the Cavendish Laboratory, who made three carbon copies – photo-copiers had not reached the Cavendish at that time. I took the top copy to the Clare College Porter's Lodge, five minutes walk from the Cavendish Laboratory, which was then still located in Free School Lane, and asked the Porter to deliver it immediately to the Master – not simply to leave it, but to ring the bell and hand it to him personally.

On my way to lunch going through the Old Court of Clare College I was intercepted by Ashby coming from the Master's Lodge, who greeted me with evident enthusiasm, "I think this is it ! Come in for a talk". He had already been joined by the senior fellow, Harry Godwin, who had also read the paper and expressed similar enthusiasm. We did not discuss the content, but Ashby said that we needed to have enough copies for distribution to all the fellows, later that day if possible. He asked if I could have copies made in the Cavendish (50 were needed) because the equipment and logistics of the college office were too archaic for such rapid production – it would take at least a week!

11. Richard Eden, 1962.

We also agreed that we should talk immediately to several fellows who had been involved in earlier proposals. Ashby said he would talk with Cooper. I agreed to talk to Northam, and with Heine since he and I were working closely on a new option for theoretical physics in Part II of the natural sciences tripos[9]. Heine's main concern was with Clare's graduate students, so his support would be ensured by our proposal for separate action by the college to provide them with residential accommodation.

After lunch on Thursday 9 January, my secretary retyped the proposal on waxed stencils (the technology of the day) and printed 80 copies, from which I delivered 50 to the Master's Lodge in Clare by 4 p.m. It is reprinted as appendix 2.

PRINCETON, THEORETICAL PHYSICS AND VISITING SCHOLARS

Both the title for my proposal and the content were strongly influenced by my experiences in visiting the Institute for Advanced Study in Princeton, New Jersey. I had gone there firstly in January 1954 with my wife and three young children, having been granted generous leave of absence from my fellowship and teaching duties in Clare College. We were met at the dockside in New York by a driver with a station wagon from the Institute, and driven to our apartment in Princeton, 50 miles south of New York. The following academic year, I had a research post in the University of Indiana in Bloomington, but we returned to Princeton for a month in May 1955 before going to Ottawa. I made short visits to Princeton during most years in the decade or more after 1955, and was at the Institute with my family during the Fall Semester in 1959, before going to Berkeley, California, until the autumn of 1960.

My academic experience during my first visit to the United States had convinced me of the importance of interactive research in theoretical physics. In Cambridge, before 1957 there had been no encouragement for research students and staff to talk and discuss research on a daily basis. Most of us were in the mathematics faculty, but research students were

---

[9] This Tripos was agreed in the Easter Term of 1964 and the first examination took place in 1966. In the summer of 1964, on my appointment as a Reader, I transferred from the Mathematics Faculty to the Department of Physics, where I was involved in the teaching and examining in the new Theoretical Physics Tripos Part II.

12. Richard and Elsie Eden, 1984.

not provided with a work place either in college or in the faculty. A few like myself had acquired a desk in the Cavendish Laboratory, but I had been asked to relinquish this on becoming a research fellow with my own rooms in Peterhouse. Lecturers had rooms in college but not in the university, so we did not see our research colleagues or members of the faculty except at the weekly seminars, which had themselves only come into existence after the war because of an initiative by the research students during 1948. In contrast to this, the Institute at Princeton, and later the Physics Department in Bloomington, provided an environment where informal discussions of staff and post-doctoral visitors were frequent, where natural collaborations developed and where there was an excitement about research. All visitors were provided with desks, perhaps in a shared office, and office doors were always open.

This creative interaction in research benefited greatly from the social interaction provided by the housing project at the Princeton Institute. In 1954, there were about eighty apartments provided for visitors within a few hundred yards of the central buildings and offices. We were a multinational group, and most visitors at that time had young families so the school bus made a morning call and there was a community-run preschool group for children from 3 to 5 years old. The social environment provided a community for wives, who were rarely academics in those days, and for the development of friendships that reinforced or supplemented those arising from working together at the Institute. By 1959, when we visited Princeton again, the average age and seniority of the visitors had increased, and they included a number making second visits like ourselves.

Our experience in Princeton was the basis for my suggestion in January 1964 for an Institute for Advanced Study having Special Relations with Clare College. The need was evident in the poor provision for visiting academics in Cambridge. The Society for Visiting Scholars was a relatively recent invention, imposed in the 1950s on reluctant university committees by Greta Burkill, the enterprising and remarkable wife of my former tutor, Charles Burkill, who later became the Master of Peterhouse. However, it was rare for colleges to provide any facilities for visiting academics; visitors in the humanities rarely benefited from any social or academic provision other than the use of libraries and the occasional seminar. Scientists with an influential sponsor would usually be allocated a desk in a shared office or a laboratory. Some might be given limited dining rights in a college, but this served to emphasise the isolation of wives of visitors since women were very rarely allowed to dine in a men's college even as a guest. Churchill College was an honourable exception to the general rule, in that since the foundation in 1960 they had provided a number of apartments for visiting fellows and their families within the college grounds. With the help of Sir John Cockcroft, Master of Churchill College, my research group[10] had benefited from a series of distinguished visitors who were fellows of Churchill College and were provided with

---

[10] From 1957 to 1964, I was in the faculty of mathematics but my theoretical physics research group was housed in a number of offices in the Cavendish Laboratory (the physics department) on the new top floor that had been provided and built for this purpose by the Cavendish Professor, Nevill Mott.

college housing. However, at that time even in Churchill College (a men's college) there was a convention that wives of fellows should not be brought as guests to dinner in college.

The essential ingredients of the proposed Clare institute for advanced study would be provided by housing on a college site for visitors, together with offices for those who did not have provision in university departments. In addition to these visiting scholars, the community would include Cambridge academics to provide a semi-permanent nucleus, post-doctoral research fellows, and research students. The community would need to include both men and women scholars as fellows, and spouses of fellows should be accepted as valued members.

Chapter 7

A CENTRE FOR ADVANCED STUDY

ASHBY'S INTRODUCTION

Ashby had warned me at lunchtime on Friday 10 January that he would begin the meeting on the next day by asking me to introduce my paper proposing an Institute for Advanced Study within Clare College. On the basis that the paper had only reached fellows on the previous day he advised me to assume that many of them would not have read it.

The governing body met in the fellows' combination room at 9.30 a.m. on Saturday 11 January 1964. At that time all fellows were able to sit near one of the small tables, which were grouped round about two-thirds of a semi-circle. Ashby had asked me to sit on his right, Godwin (as senior fellow) and Northam (as senior tutor) were on his left and both had been asked in advance to speak about the proposal.

Ashby's introduction was brief – certainly less than ten minutes. He reminded fellows that there was strong support for some contribution from Clare to the problems identified in the Bridges Report, and observed that we had given general encouragement to the idea to set up a satellite – still to be part of Clare College – which would contain some fellows and some research students and would recognise the fact that both these categories would include men who are married. There had been two papers under discussion for some months, one from the extension committee, paper 'A', and one from Dr Northam, paper 'B'. Although both of these had attracted support, it was evident that neither proposal had been entirely satisfactory to the governing body. A third paper by Dr Eden had been circulated to all fellows on the previous day, which he thought most fellows would have read. This paper included many of the features of papers 'A' and 'B' that had attracted support from the fellows and it contained a number of new features, which the fellows would wish to consider. He would therefore like to begin the discussion by asking Dr Eden to introduce his paper.

PRESENTING THE PROPOSAL

Forewarned by Ashby, I had prepared an introductory statement which I would read (or talk from) before summarising the paper directly from the printed version which had been circulated. This began:

Our consideration of a Clare extension or colony has been based largely on two needs:- (i) to improve facilities for graduate students in the college and (ii) to provide for the election of a number of new fellows as a contribution to action on the Bridges report. A third need has been in the minds of some fellows, (iii) that is the provision of places and accommodation for visiting fellows.

The "hiving off" of most graduates into a colony separate from the main body of the college is thought to be undesirable. The proportion of graduate students in Cambridge will rise and the college should adapt to include this higher proportion in the main body of the college, for example by some re-designing or new building in the Memorial Court, – but this is another question. My main point here is that the Clare colony should not be designed to deprive the college of its graduate students as this would imply a weakening of the parent foundation that runs counter to expected development.

Many of the Bridges fellows[1] are in subjects where little undergraduate teaching is involved, and it is often thought that this implies that they are associated with numerous research students and therefore a Clare colony of Bridges fellows and research students would be naturally cohesive. I do not believe this is the case. Most research students are in the subjects associated with major teaching at undergraduate level, mathematics, physics, chemistry, engineering, history. Further the present plan put forward emphasises graduates at the expense of Bridges fellows, except for Dr Northam's dissenting opinion.

The provision of accommodation is a very economic way of encouraging distinguished scholars from overseas to associate with the college, and in many cases would encourage them to come to Cambridge rather than elsewhere. This would therefore be an important contribution to scholarship in Cambridge as well as to Clare.

Future development in the college should be centred round an increase in the proportion of graduate students and we should consider what additional facilities

---

[1] Senior members of the faculties not having college fellowships (see chapter 3).

should be provided as a separate problem from the question of a Clare colony although my proposal for the latter will have some bearing on Clare research students.

If we are going to develop a colony or institution on the Grange Road site, the form it is to take should be decided in a wider educational and social context than the college alone. For this we need to consider how Cambridge will develop and whether we can provide some impetus for special development that we consider desirable. We have already considered the increase expected in research students, in Bridges fellows, and visitors and I want to consider the latter in more detail.

Sabbatical leave or study leave from the expanding universities in Britain will bring with it an increase in academic visitors to Cambridge in view of library and other facilities that do not exist in their own universities. In addition there is the important point that lecturers on sabbatical leave should be encouraged to move to another university – for many Cambridge would be ideal. I believe also we can expect a substantial rise in the number of senior academic visitors to Cambridge from overseas universities. This expansion provides us with an opportunity to set up a new community that will at the same time not only enhance the position of some visitors to Cambridge but also can contribute to the problem of Bridges fellows and be of great value to selected research students, and could be closely associated with the college.

I will make specific proposals for a new institute to be founded by Clare College. These proposals are designed to satisfy the following criteria which are I believe essential criteria for it to be successful:-

The Institute must be a place where academic staff would be proud to be fellows, whether they are on the Cambridge staff or visitors. It must in no sense be inferior in status to the college. It must be capable of expansion and be flexible so that it can adapt perhaps more easily than a college to changing needs. It must be viable financially – this point is I believe closely tied in with its status and function. It must contribute to the Bridges fellows, to research students and to visitors. It must have close association with Clare College but be a sufficiently independent Institute to be able to grow by attracting funds and its visitors in its own right.[2]

I believe that these criteria can be met by an institute that provides facilities for a society of fellows in the following main categories:

University lecturers and other senior members of the faculties to form a semi-permanent nucleus for the Society, since the other fellows are all temporary.

---

[2] The manuscript of my statement to the Governing Body ends at this point. The remainder is a reconstruction of the part of my talk where I summarised parts of the tabled copy of the proposal (see appendix 2).

Visiting fellows selected from scholars on study-leave from overseas and (in increasing numbers) from other universities in the UK.

Research fellows selected from (i) post-doctoral research workers on temporary appointments in departments (e.g. Applied Economics, Medical Research Council, Engineering etc.) and (ii) research students holding DSIR or other awards.

In addition there should be: Associate fellows, who are fellows of colleges, for example some members of Clare College.

All the above fellows to be non-stipendiary. In addition there could be research students in the society, but this might well come as the second stage or stage 1B of the development. First the society should be set up as a single class society.

It is suggested that the Institute should be governed by a council, to be chaired by the Master of Clare College, and including some fellows of Clare, the Director of the Institute, and representatives of the different categories of fellows in the Institute.

The Institute's buildings would, in the first instance, be not dissimilar to those that were proposed (in paper 'A') for the Grange Road site, but with more emphasis on visitor's flats and on long term expansion, though for a major expansion, given sufficient money, a new and larger site might be desirable. In the shorter term fellows of the Institute might lunch in the small hall of Clare College.

It was clear to me that most fellows were reacting favourably – so I decided to stop talking whilst there was a mood of general approval, and concluded by making a formal proposal: *that Clare College should found an Institute for Advanced Study having close associations with the college.*

NORTHAM GIVES SUPPORT

Ashby next asked for comments from Harry Godwin, the senior fellow, who welcomed the proposal in his usual enthusiastic style. He was followed by John Northam, as senior tutor, and the author of paper 'B'. Fortunately for an archivist, Northam had written out his contribution in advance and it was retained in *the Northam file* found in the Clare College Bursar's Office in 1991. Northam's handwritten notes read:

When I re-read the papers initially sent out as paper A – committee's report – and paper B my own amendments to that report, I had the feeling of visiting some old battlefield. The barbed wire is still there, there are occasional muffled explosions from the booby-traps, but no-one is fighting this particular battle any more. To put it a little more exactly, in the several months that have elapsed since my paper was written, a good deal of thinking has gone on which, I think, has clarified the issues a good deal. So I want initially to ignore the pattern of argument set out in papers A and B and instead try to present a different approach to what the Master very correctly defined as a difficult subject.

As we all know, the college decided while I was away to follow up a suggestion that we might create some sort of extension to the existing college on a very valuable site in Herschel Road. The debate as it has been presented so far has concerned itself exclusively with fellows and research students. I should like to begin my analysis by bringing into the picture undergraduates too.

Northam then explained that the college's commitment to take more undergraduates to help meet the increase in demand resulting from the post-war bulge in the birth-rate would only have a small effect since universities had over-subscribed for the increase in numbers. However, he called attention to improvements that he would like to see in the amenities for undergraduates provided by the college, including for example a public room with catering facilities. This could be either in the Old Court or in the Memorial Court on the site of the garages and it need not impinge on decisions about other uses for the site in Herschel Road. Northam continued:

I now come to research students, and perhaps I should begin by saying what happens to them at present. There are basically two classes of research students – the Cambridge graduate and the non-Cambridge graduate, for whom we provide, roughly speaking, accommodation and cohesion. We do not provide accommodation for Cambridge graduates unless they apply as married men for a college flat; the non-Cambridge graduate in his first year we bring into college. This is, I think, a distinct advantage for them in some ways, but in other ways it has drawbacks, since these mature students live in an undergraduate atmosphere. We do not provide accommodation for them after the first year unless they are fortunate enough to obtain a college flat.

I understand that discussions were held with some research students during my leave of absence; I am not clear as to the conclusions. My guess is that not all research students would wish to have accommodation provided for them in the form of an institution, but I think it could only be counted a gain if we had more accommodation of a suitable kind available outside college which could be offered to newcomers in the first instance and then to such others as wanted it. We already have flats in Queen Edith's Way and in Newnham; it may well be that we shall shortly acquire another block of flats. For the more distant future, some of us had thoughts that during the further development of the Chesterton Lane site provision might be made there for graduate accommodation. I should also like to see us trying to buy one large house to serve as a graduate hostel.

It isn't easy to forecast the growth of numbers of research students – except to say that the colleges can't accept an open-ended commitment to take them all up if the numbers grow astronomically – if only because some colleges simply will not have the money to put them up. I haven't finished with research students yet, but so far as I can see, we could provide in the reasonable ways that I've just outlined an increase in the amount of accommodation, grouped in various properties, that we could offer – without using Herschel Road.

As for the second thing that we provide – cohesion. Not so very long ago, a research student was told to dine in one night a week, was invited to a research meeting once a fortnight, and that was all. We now have, as you know, a common room, their own supervision room, a table in hall (though this seems to have lapsed during the past year), lunches with the fellows, dinners and so on. Here are the facilities for building up a source of identity and of making contact with the fellows. The facilities are not overloaded, though reasonable use is made of them; no doubt we could improve them by providing a larger common room and better eating facilities. If we decided to provide catering arrangements in Memorial Court, it should be possible to attach to it a new common room for research students – without using Herschel Road. I repeat: I haven't finished with research students yet, but I would suggest that we could improve our capacity for dealing with research students quite reasonably in the ways I have outlined.

Now I need to justify this effort to keep Herschel Road unencumbered. It seems to me to be a piece of property that enables us to contemplate something of vital importance.

The Master misrepresents me when he states that I say in my paper that "the problem of fellowships will remain one of the most important that the colleges and university are faced with". It is, in my opinion, an urgent problem now, and I believe that it needs to be tackled now so that it will not remain a problem. In very simple terms, this university faces a period of change and development – an exciting but potentially dangerous period – without cohesion. I don't just mean social cohesion, but without a coherent idea about what Cambridge education means. We are split by many things, but basically, I believe, by the division into fellows and non-fellows. I don't need to elaborate the theme. I believe that we shall find it difficult to give the right sort of critical attention to the future until we show signs of moving towards greater cohesion, and that means providing more places within societies in Cambridge for people at present excluded. I believe that it would be not only a useful thing in itself, but a heartening example to other colleges, and a powerful gesture of good intention if this college could map out a radical approach to this problem.

I won't elaborate my reasons for thinking that our present fellowship has just about reached its limit of absorption. This I feel strongly, but it's up to other fellows to say what they think. If at a later stage we do discuss the implications of increasing the present fellowship, I shall want to say something more. For the present I can only say that I think the situation is critical, that the college stands for more than is implied by the Master's note I, and that it is our duty as fellows not to let the fellowship degenerate into meaninglessness. I won't go into that except to explain why I look elsewhere for a solution.

But it isn't in a mood of defensiveness that I propose that we should use Herschel Road to set up a new society. I propose it as a radical response to the new conditions that have developed here since the war – the problem, briefly, of those members of the university who are not, for one reason or another, involved in undergraduate teaching. By offering a sizeable contribution towards solving the problem of these academics, by offering a pattern that other colleges may be able to adopt, and above all by showing imagination and initiative, I think we shall be doing an invaluable thing.

At this point, I think I should say that my own outline scheme has been given, quite independently, body and substance by Dr Eden's paper, and I'd like to suggest that we adopt that as a tentative scheme on which further deliberation is based. But before I stop, may I return to the question of research students? Dr Eden's scheme envisages the provision of excellent facilities in stage I – some will become junior research fellows. I should like to suggest that once we have agreed on the setting up of a fellowship as the first stage, – and only then – we might contemplate the growth of a second body of research students around the new foundation. This is to say, we could take more, possibly, and develop a further set of facilities associated with the new foundation if space and money are forthcoming.

I am behind Dr Eden's scheme. There are many details that I should want to question and many suggestions I should like to have amplified, but my own hope is that, after full deliberation, the fellows will decide to accept the proposal in outline and press on to turn it, or something like it, into reality. If you decide simultaneously to pursue the notion of improving the lot of undergraduates and research students in this College, so much the better.

MOST FELLOWS AGREE

Next after Northam, the bursar, Brian Cooper, was asked to give his comments, which Ashby had previously ascertained would be favourable to the proposal. He was followed by Brian Reddaway, then the Director of the Institute for Applied Economics. Initially I thought that Reddaway was in favour of the proposal as he spoke warmly about it – so I listed him as a 'plus', but he then said he would speak later to question one part so I listed him under (?). Next there were two other notable contributions to the discussion before the Master adopted the 'round table mode', asking each fellow to speak in turn. These two were John Baker (Professor Sir John Baker, chairman of the Engineering Department and later to become Lord Baker), and Brian Pippard. On the basis of their initial remarks, my notes show them both as 'unclassified', – it was not clear to me which side either was on. They both spoke later, leading me to move both into the 'favourable' list. (Northam's own notes shows that he had no such initial doubts about their support). By the time Baker had spoken for the second time, there had been 18 fellows clearly in favour of the proposal and only two (moderately) against it.

Although Ashby as chairman was orchestrating the discussion mostly in a round-table sequence, it was also interactive with either Ashby or myself responding to each comment and occasionally Godwin would add a remark. Since most comments were favourable this was generally a matter of welcoming the new insights that the previous speaker had displayed – this was a genuine response rather than a marketing ploy though it was good marketing also; both Ashby and I remarked afterwards on the enthusiasm with which the fellows had received the proposal and carried it forward. There was an exceptional warmth about the discussion, the fellows knew that they were making a landmark decision and most had no doubts about their support for it, though few could have been aware of the remarkable success that would eventually be achieved by the proposed new community.

GODWIN SUGGESTS THE NAME "CLARE HALL"

It is odd that one of the best of the constructive suggestions came as a result of a quite fiercely expressed objection. The next speaker after Baker's second intervention was Reddaway, also speaking for the second time. He made it clear that he would support the proposal if and only if the title of 'Institute' did not form part of the name. As head of the Institute of Applied Economics, he took the view that an Institute was an organisation whose members did as they were told by the Director – they were all part of a well-defined programme. He rightly pointed out that my proposal was for a 'Society' in which members would be working with complete independence, and often in different disciplines, with complete freedom from 'direction'. I was already confident that the proposal would command the support of almost all fellows and initially I held my ground on the proposed name, pointing to the character of the Institute for Advanced Study in Princeton which had been an important influence on my proposal and where members were entirely free to pursue their own programmes.

At this stage, Ashby allowed the discussion to become informal with several conversations going on simultaneously. It became temporarily more focused when Godwin suggested that we go back to the original name of the college and give the proposed new Society the name 'Clare Hall'. This caused a valuable diversion, enthusiasm being tempered by the potential confusion. Would the Post Office confuse Clare Hall with Clare College? No – because Trinity Hall seems to manage, without being overwhelmed by its larger neighbour, Trinity College. The diversion gave Ashby an opportunity to have a side discussion with me, saying that he hoped to achieve unanimous approval for the proposal and with this in mind would I agree that the name could be considered at a later stage. The discussion became formal again as soon as I said that the name of the new Society was not an essential feature of the proposal and it could be left for later consideration. This was sufficient for to secure the support of Reddaway[3]. Meanwhile Godwin had prepared a sketch which he passed to me, contrasting two shields (coats of arms), one for Clare College – *Floreat Disciplina*, and one for Clare Hall – *Floreat Studium*.

THE GOVERNING BODY APPROVES

After the resolution of the problem of the name by deferring a decision until later, almost all the remaining fellows spoke in favour of the proposal. My list records 31 names of fellows speaking in favour of the proposal, 1 seemed unclear, 2 spoke against, and 1 is unrecorded. Northam's list records 33 speaking in favour and 2 against. Subsequently,

---

[3] Reddaway was subsequently one of the most valuable participants in the founding of Clare Hall, both as a member of the Provisional Council and as a member of the College's finance committee. Later still his role on the investments committee that managed the joint Clare College – Clare Hall portfolio continued until 1996 (see chapter 14).

there was a unanimous vote by the governing body in favour of the proposal. The minutes of the meeting on 11 January 1964 record:

that the Governing Body approved in principle the proposals set out in the attached paper by Dr Eden and appointed the following to work out the functions and purpose of the Body referred to in Dr Eden's paper, to recommend how the proposals might be implemented, and to report back to the Governing Body:- The Master, Dr Eden, Dr Northam, with power to co-opt.

The governing body also recognised the validity of the argument put by Northam and by other fellows that the issues concerning graduate students should be considered separately from the development of the extension to the College. They resolved

that the College Needs Committee should meet to consider the provision for Research Students in the College.

Chapter 8

COMMITTEE OF THREE

MEETINGS

After the meeting of the governing body on 11 January 1964, Ashby suggested to Northam and me that we should meet over a working lunch (sandwiches in the Master's Lodge) at least once a week. We reserved a series of dates in our diaries, of which Ashby noted the lunchtime meetings in a lecture on the Tenth Anniversary of the founding of Clare Hall as: the 3rd, 10th, 15th, 17th, and 22nd February. In addition, we arranged that Ashby and I would meet after dinner on Wednesday 22 January. Northam was not able to join us at that time, but he and I would meet for lunch on Monday 27 January. We also met subsequently in pairs, or more briefly as three, on a number of occasions additional to the lunchtime meetings. We agreed the final version of our report at our meeting on 22 February, and it was presented to the governing body on Monday 6 March 1964.

PAPER NO.2: AIMS AND NEEDS

Ahead of my meeting with Ashby, scheduled for after dinner on 22 January, I thought it would be useful to prepare a paper setting out my views on how the three of us might proceed. The paper was marked *Confidential* and it began:

The Clare Institute Paper No. 2: 21 January 1964.

1. *Aims*

(a) To provide some facilities for advanced study and residence, and to establish a society of fellows primarily engaged on advanced study in Cambridge.
(b) To bring together an international community of visiting scholars, of Cambridge university lecturers and professors, and members of the university engaged primarily on research.

(c) The need for such an Institute arises from the increasing number of university teachers of all nations and disciplines who have both a need and desire to travel to another academic centre during sabbatical leave from their own universities. This provides an exceptional opportunity for Clare College to encourage this international exchange, to benefit from it, and to contribute towards international understanding and learning.

2. *Membership*

A. Visiting fellows (mainly on sabbatical leave)
B. Permanent fellows (mainly Cambridge university teaching officers)
C. Research fellows (mainly post-doctoral research "associates" in the university)
D. Associate fellows[1] (who also hold fellowships of another college but who are associated with a particular research group at the Institute)

All the above are temporary except class B. There are no stipends but it is hoped that "grants-in-aid" could be paid to help Visiting Fellows with incidental expenses not covered by their sabbatical salary.

3. *Function*

The Institute must develop an intellectual life of its own. In addition to acting as a centre for a larger community there must be facilities for advanced study and discussion within its walls. It must be the primary place of study for a significant fraction of the fellows, although others will work in university laboratories, libraries and departments.

This can be achieved in a variety of ways. For example:-

(a) Selection of visiting fellows to form groups likely to have common interests. These groups could vary slightly from year to year and could be centred round the interests of one or more of the permanent or the associate fellows, e.g. Scandinavian literature; oriental studies; sociology; economics; one of the sciences or mathematics; history of science.
(b) Summer symposia in selected fields, or with particular study projects e.g. science in industry; mathematical logic; disarmament; theoretical physics.
(c) A centre where specific study projects can be undertaken for which external finance can be arranged but which do not naturally fall under a particular department e.g. research on university admissions; on the relation of university scientists and industry (why is it so much closer in the USA?); on the national needs for students in various fields (e.g. too many geologists).

---

[1] The concept of Associate Fellow survives as an entitlement to Fellows of Clare College on sabbatical leave.

Section 4 of the paper enlarged on the *facilities required*, which included:

20 studies, 2 administrative offices, a seminar room for 30, a reading room, a common room, and a parlour, totalling 8,100 sq. ft.
Dining rooms for families and for academics, totalling 2,100 sq. ft. and capable of expansion.
12 one, two and three-bedroomed flats, totalling 7,200 sq. ft.
The existing Herschel House could provide another 5 flats. An additional two or three houses should be bought in the neighbourhood to provide additional accommodation, leading to an overall total of about 25 flats.

Longer term plans would require additional finance beyond what might be expected in the first stage from Clare and from Foundations. I thought that there would be a need for: an extension of the kitchen and dining facilities, more studies, and more flats.

Section 5 on management and links with Clare College, did not differ very much from those of the original proposal, with the Institute managed by a council, having equal representation from the College and the Institute, and chaired by the Master of Clare College. At this stage we were all expecting that the Institute (with some other name) would be part of Clare College, though located in Herschel Road.

The paper continued with some comments on the procedure for the selection of fellows of the Institute, some headings relating to capital and annual costs[2], and a timetable for development, including some early approaches to Foundations for financial support. The timetable was optimistic about completion of the new buildings, where a target date of just under three years was suggested; in the event it took just under five years, being completed in September 1969. However, the development estimates were more accurate on numbers, suggesting a total of 25 fellows in all classes in 1965, and 50 in 1967. The actual numbers were 21 in October 1965 and 38 in October 1967.

The final section concerned '*Action Now for committee*', – my peremptory style says much for the tolerance and easy relationship that we had with Ashby as Master:

---

[2] My guess, excluding the capital costs of the buildings, suggested an annual subvention from Clare of £12,000, (equivalent to a capital endowment of about £250,000), but this was made in the context of asking the Bursar for his estimates.

(a) EA[3] to prepare draft memo setting out aims, needs etc. for possible approach to a Foundation.
(b) EA and RJE to talk after dinner Wed. 22 Jan.
(c) JRN and RJE to meet for lunch Mon. 27 Jan. Suggest discussion of section 5 which is very preliminary, and section 6.
(d) Ask Cooper and Holister for estimates on annual and capital costs respectively for buildings indicated in section 4 and for 40/50/70 fellows. When do we ask them, this week or next?
(e) EA to talk with M Wilson[4] about project, subsequently also JRN and RJE.
(f) EA, JRN and RJE to meet for lunch on 3 Feb. at 12.45 p.m.

R J Eden

ASHBY'S DRAFT OF A POSSIBLE APPEAL TO FOUNDATIONS

Ashby had his own views on priorities for the work by our 'committee of three', which we discussed when he and I met after dinner on 22 January. He suggested that we should first seek to clarify the aims and needs for a 'Clare Centre for Advanced Study' [Ashby's words – avoiding the use of 'Institute']. He had read my paper dated 21 January, and made some use of it in his first draft of a possible appeal to foundations, which he sent to Northam and me two days later:

First draft of possible appeal to foundations for funds for Clare Centre for Advanced Study

NB This draft has one purpose only: to test whether we are agreed upon the function of the place we are setting up. The decision to make an appeal to foundations comes later in our programme.

Over the next twenty years there will be a massive expansion of universities in Britain: if government intentions are fulfilled, there will be for the first time an integrated system of higher education. It is essential that the existing universities should define their place in this system.

The place of Cambridge University has been defined in a statement recently published by the Council of the Senate. Briefly, it is that undergraduate education, with its traditionally close and informal relation between teacher and pupil based

---

[3] EA – Eric Ashby, JRN – John Northam, RJE – Richard Eden.
[4] Meridith Wilson, President of the University of Minnesota, who was a visitor to Clare for the Lent term of 1964 as a College guest since the statutes did not provide for visiting fellowships at that time.

on the colleges, should be maintained with no loss of quality, but should not be expanded; while graduate education and schools of research and advanced study should be considerably expanded. Owing to its libraries and laboratories and the distinction of some of its academic staff, Cambridge already attracts research students and senior scholars from overseas. It is also a place which attracts research units which are not integral parts of the university, such as the MRC Unit on molecular biology and the ARC unit on animal physiology. It is in the national interest that Cambridge should continue to offer these attractions of research and advanced study, and it is the university's policy to do so.

This policy raises two problems. One is that visiting scholars who work in Cambridge need to be attached to one or other of the small societies which are important for the intellectual vigour of the university. Scientific workers have their laboratories, but even they need informal contact with workers in other disciplines. Workers in the humanities and the social sciences are less likely to find in libraries or faculty rooms the opportunities for exchange of ideas which they need. Therefore the policy of enlarging graduate study at Cambridge carries with it the need to create amenities for senior scholars.

The second problem is complementary to the first. Colleges are mainly concerned with undergraduates. Already they are unable to offer fellowships to many university lecturers, simply because these lecturers teach subjects for which there is very little undergraduate demand; nevertheless the subjects themselves are important (e.g. oriental languages, history of science, veterinary science) and ought to be encouraged. Still less are colleges able to cater adequately for scientists attached to research units in Cambridge outside the university, or for visiting professors from overseas. If colleges have to remain preoccupied with undergraduates and find themselves unable to meet these other needs, there is a risk that they may find themselves less and less at the growing point of Cambridge intellectual life.

The Clare Centre for Advanced Study is intended to contribute to the solution of both these problems. Its purpose is to have, attached to Clare so that the college can participate in the life of advanced study in Cambridge, a centre for a small society of senior scholars in four categories: (i) university teaching officers active in research in "rare" subjects; (ii) post-doctoral research workers located in Cambridge; (iii) visiting scholars, e.g. persons on sabbatical leave from overseas or from other British universities; and (iv) fellows of other colleges who may wish temporarily to be associated with the Centre while some particular research group is there.

The Centre will combine three functions. It will have a core of permanent members who may well share common interests, e.g. the history of science and subjects relevant to this, which could include a field as wide as mathematics,

Arabic, Sanskrit, philosophy, sociology and history. It will offer study accommodation, a limited amount of residence, and the cohesion of a small society, to scholars from overseas who come to Cambridge to use its libraries and laboratories. It will endeavour to select its visiting fellows so that they form groups likely to have common interests, and it can be used as a place for small summer symposia.

From its own resources the college is financing the first stage of this project (building of the order of £120,000 and annual subsidy of the order of £5,000), and the project is intended to be viable on this slender endowment. But this restricts the use of the Centre to those who have their own sources of maintenance while at Cambridge. The value of the Centre would be immensely increased if we were able to offer grants-in-aid to visiting fellows (both from overseas and from other parts of Britain). This would in particular enable us to invite to the Centre scholars in subjects relevant to its interests and to create groups in residence there with common interests (e.g. in one year a group in topology; in another year a group in history of science or industrial sociology). Another way in which the value of the Centre could be increased is by the provision of more residential accommodation (of the kind a visiting professor from overseas would need) than we can afford to build from our own resources.

AMENDMENTS BY NORTHAM AND EDEN

Northam and I received the foregoing draft before our meeting, which took place after lunch on 27 January. Northam's notes on our meeting read:

Clare Institute. Notes on the Meeting of JRN and RJE on 27 January 1964

(1) Some modifications of the draft by EA on purpose and function were suggested, and the modified draft is enclosed.
(2) Management and links with Clare College were discussed, but no substantial changes suggested from paper 2 (21 Jan.).
(3) It was thought that several Clare fellows should initially either transfer or become associate fellows of the Institute, and it was thought that the Director should be a temporary appointment for 3 years renewable to 6 (maximum).
(4) Programme:-
   (Required for governing body meeting in March)
   (a) Purpose and Function as in EA's draft (version 1) or enclosed modification (version 2).
   (b) Outline of facilities, buildings, feasibility and capital cost.
   (c) Number of fellows, rough composition and sources of new fellows.
   (d) Current annual cost.

(e) Management and links with Clare.
(f) Proposals for timetable of detailed plans on the buildings, the fellowship, the statutes, the internal (Clare) finance, the external (appeal) finance.
(g) The name of the Institute – give alternatives, make recommendation with reasons and ask for a (transferable) vote.
(h) Approval of a notice for publication if the governing body still wants to go ahead.

THE FIRST LUNCHTIME MEETING

When we met for lunch in the dining room of the Master's Lodge on 3 February, we were in general agreement on the aims and needs but we differed on how to proceed in developing our report for the governing body. Ashby took the view that we needed to produce something akin to draft Statutes, since an attempt at specifying a legal framework for the new institution would both clarify our ideas and reveal problems or points on which we might have different views. He suggested that this might form the framework for our report to the governing body, for which he would be happy to be the scribe, putting together drafts in line with our discussions. As a justification for this, he put forward the generous but unconvincing argument that he was probably less busy than either Northam or me. However, alternative views prevailed and it was decided that I should first put down some thoughts about how our draft report might be constructed, whilst Ashby would prepare a revised draft (version 3) of the appeal to Foundations. These two drafts would provide a basis for discussion at our next lunchtime meeting, which was to be the following week on 10 February.

MANAGEMENT AND LINKS WITH CLARE COLLEGE

We also needed to be more specific about how the Institute might be linked to Clare College. I wrote two papers, one on 7 February about the management of the Institute and its links with Clare College, and one on the next day to provide a framework for the report by the committee of three, for discussion at our next meeting. Both papers were hand-written using carbon papers as underlay and copies were sent to Ashby and Northam. The first paper on management and links with Clare was intended as a start on the formalisation of the existing proposals and did not introduce any new structures or concepts.

The second paper was dated 8 February and suggested a framework for our eventual report to the governing body, designed to provide a basis for discussion at our next meeting. In six handwritten pages it suggested some main headings, and although it was not intended as a draft report it gave some detail where this had already been agreed, or already discussed even if not finalised.

THE NAME "CLARE HALL"

At our meeting on 10 February 1964, there was general agreement on most of the points in the two foregoing documents. However, the most memorable outcome at that meeting was our decision to recommend to the governing body that the new institution (within Clare College) should be called *'Clare Hall'*. As with most of the other points discussed at our lunchtime meetings, this was readily agreed – I believe it took only a few minutes. The credit for the name should go to Harry Godwin, for his inspired suggestion made at the governing body meeting on 11 January 1964.

FIRST DRAFT OF THE REPORT

After our decision on 10 February, we used the name Clare Hall in all our subsequent drafts for discussion. The first of these was a draft for our report to the governing body, written by Ashby on 13 February, so Northam and I were able to read it before we met with Ashby for lunch on 15 February. The first section (A) on the function and aims was left to be written when the remaining sections (B – D) were agreed:

Section B was headed *The new society and its relation to Clare College.* It began:

1. The new society to be called Clare Hall: a centre for advanced study (students)
2. Clare Hall will be legally part of Clare College, governed by a set of Statutes: "Of Clare Hall".
3. Among the provision in the statutes will be ... Then followed details about
    (a) the different classes of fellow and their election,
    (b) the government of Clare Hall by a joint Council,
    (c) finance.

Section C would concern Buildings and accommodation, and section D would indicated the related capital expenditure. Both sections would be prepared from a brief to be requested from Holister (the domestic bursar and a lecturer in architecture). Similarly, the bursar would be asked to prepare a brief for section E, which would be on recurrent expenditure.

Section F, on relations with the university, noted several points that would need to be discussed, such as: the inclusion of women, which would be dependent on the revision of the university Statute H, currently (at that time in 1964) under consideration.

Section G would be based on the section on interim arrangements in my framework paper of 8 February, but renamed as 'immediate arrangements'. Section H on questions for decision by the governing body should also follow my framework paper.

REPORT TO THE GOVERNING BODY

The second draft of our proposed report was written by Ashby after the discussion at our lunchtime meeting on 15 February. It was discussed at our meeting on the 17th, leading to the final version, which we approved on 22nd, for subsequent distribution to the governing body in time for their next meeting on 6 March. In the style that was common in Clare College at the time, the final version of our report was unsigned, it was prepared by Ashby, Eden and Northam. It began:

Proposed extension to Clare College
Report to governing body, 6 March 1964

1. On 11 January, the governing body unanimously approved in principle the proposals for an extension to the college as set out in a paper prepared by Dr Eden and circulated beforehand.

We were appointed to work out the functions and purpose of the Body referred to in Dr Eden's paper, to recommend how the proposals might be implemented, and to report back to the governing body.

2. *Purpose.* The purpose of the extension is to enable Clare to make a contribution to university activities which are likely to become increasingly important in Cambridge. The contributions would take the form of a society primarily intended to bring together three classes of people, none of which is well provided for at present, namely:-

(i) Those holding appointments in the university or in research institutions in Cambridge, especially those whose subjects are not in great demand for undergraduate teaching.
(ii) Research workers on grants, holders of post-doctoral fellowships, and research students of the calibre of research fellows.
(iii) Visiting scholars from outside Cambridge who are on study leave.

We believe that a society composed of these ingredients and attached to Clare would be of value to its members and would benefit the college and the university. Its nucleus would comprise teachers and research workers at two levels of seniority and resident in Cambridge, who would act as hosts to a succession of visiting scholars. At a later stage (see paragraph 9 (iii)) we would hope that more research students might be added to the society. We regard the extension as a place which would bring into the collegiate system of the university in the first instance another forty people; also as a place where scholars can work, where seminars can be held, and where there can be sustained exchange of views on academic matters.

3. We recommend that the new society should be called *Clare Hall*. It should be legally part of Clare College, governed by statutes entitled "Of Clare Hall." The society should consist of fellows of Clare Hall who would be bye-fellows of the college. This would not entail membership of the governing body of the college, but it would be consistent with our intention if it entitled them to certain dining rights in the college.

Section 4 outlined the required changes in the statutes of the college. Section 5 recommended that Clare Hall receive an annual grant from the college and that its accounts should be kept by the college bursar's office. There was a recommendation (suggested by Ashby) that official and research fellows of Clare Hall should receive an annual allowance of 300 meals per year that could be also be used for guests. The recommendations for building needs followed those suggested in earlier proposals. Our suggestions for accommodation were similar to those of the earlier proposal for a centre for advanced study and the building costs were estimated at £132,000, with annual running costs estimated at £17,000, to be met by an annual grant.

Government of Clare Hall should be vested in a Council chaired by the Master and including 5 fellows of the College and 5 of the Hall plus the Warden of the hall.

We suggested that immediate arrangements should include the appointment of a working committee on Clare Hall. This should be authorised to have sketch-plan proposals prepared for buildings; to have draft Statutes prepared; to have the names of five persons in mind as the foundation fellows in Class F of Clare Hall; these names to be brought to the governing body and, if approved, to be co-opted on to the working committee in order to constitute a provisional council. This should take over responsibility for developing the society and bring forward names for a Warden and a few more fellows even before buildings are started. If this was done, it would be necessary for the new society to have temporary lunching rights in the college (e.g. in the Small Hall). It was proposed also that the new Society should dine once a week in the dining room in the Master's Lodge.

Our report concluded:

11. The governing body is asked:
(i) to approve the functions and general pattern of the society outlined in this paper;
(ii) to appoint the working committee which will constitute the Clare College members of the provisional council;
(iii) to empower the working committee to transform itself into a provisional council by co-opting five persons approved by the governing body as Class F fellows of Clare Hall and bye-fellows of the college, and to allow this provisional council to proceed with the establishment of the society and the provision of accommodation, and to remain in being until the customary meeting of the governing body in May 1965.

THE GOVERNING BODY APPROVES

The report was discussed at the meeting of the governing body on 6 March 1964, and it was welcomed, subject to some comments which were noted in the minutes. These related particularly to the timing of the admission of research students. Wedderburn was unable to be present at that meeting, but he had written a letter to the Master, which was circulated to fellows, asking that any decisions on the proposal be postponed because of the new issues that were raised about the expansion of higher education by the Robbins Report. In particular, he urged that the college seek to contribute towards an increase in the number of research students, so as to help provide staff for the new and growing universities.

There was no support for postponing a decision, but some fellows took the opportunity to ask that research students be included at an early stage of the new society and this suggestion was accepted. The relevant part of the minutes of the meeting read:

... The Bursar reported the following decision of the finance committee, dated 2 March 1964:- "That the governing body be advised that the provision of finance for the developments envisaged in the report to be submitted to that Body on Friday, 6 March, 1964, would not prejudice other developments considered worthy by the college".

4. The governing body:
(i) approved the functions and general pattern of the society outlined in the attached report on the proposed extension to Clare College which had been circulated, *subject to the comments made below.*
(ii) appointed as a working committee, which will constitute the Clare College membership of the provisional council, the following: Mr Kingsford (who consents to act as Secretary), Mr Reddaway, Dr Eden, the Senior Tutor, the Bursar, the Domestic Bursar, and the Master as Chairman.
(iii) empowered the working committee to transform itself into a provisional council by co-opting five persons approved by the governing body as Class F fellows of Clare Hall and bye-fellows of the college, and to allow this provisional council to proceed with the establishment of the society and the provision of accommodation, and to remain in being until the statutory annual meeting of the governing body in May 1965.
(iv) agreed that nominations for those who may become the five Class F fellows referred to in paragraph (iii) should be made to the governing body jointly by the fellowship committee and the working committee.

Comment on the report on the proposed extension to Clare College, 6 March, 1964

The governing body agreed that the following changes should be made:

1. *The Warden* (last paragraph under 'Government' on page 2). It was agreed that the first appointment should be for 10 years, not 5, and that before the end of 10 years the question of the tenure of the Wardenship should be reconsidered[5]; it was agreed also that it would be desirable but not essential that the Warden should live on the site.
2. *Research Students.* Throughout the report the committee assumed that research students would be added to the society once it was established (para 9 (ii)). This assumption was considered by the governing body to be too remote. It was agreed not to call for a redraft of the report but to approve the report provided:-
   (a) Under *paragraph 2,* it is made clear that the purpose of the society is to

---

[5] In January 1965, when the Provisional Council began to consider the choice of the first President, it was decided that the tenure should be for seven years only, subsequently it was agreed that this would not be renewable for a second term.

bring together four classes of people, not three; the fourth class being "(iv) Research students."
  (b) Under *paragraph 9(ii)* it was agreed (as stated already) that the society should not in the first instance accept research students; but the governing body expressed the view that some research students should be added within about three years of the establishment of the Hall, even if this were to entail a corresponding reduction in the number of fellows proposed for Classes G and H in paragraph 4.
  (c) The governing body also hope that some research students might be given dining or lunching rights in the Hall once it is established.
3. Class G fellows should be described simply as "post-doctoral research workers and senior pre-doctoral research students.

OTHER WORK IN PROGRESS

In addition to our preparation of the report to the governing body, Ashby, Northam and I had also been looking further ahead. Our work included:

1. The preparation of a draft appeal for funds for Clare Hall – in this we were considerably helped by Meredith Wilson. He had great experience both in fund-raising for his own university and as a member of the board of trustees of a number of foundations. In the latter capacity, he had been involved with both the Ford Foundation and with a foundation set up by the Mellon family[6].
2. Soon after our first meeting in January, Ashby had written about the project to Paul Mellon, a former student in Clare College and a distinguished benefactor of the college and of other major charities. A reply came by return post enclosing a substantial personal cheque and suggesting that Ashby should get in touch with him again when the proposals were at a more advanced stage. This suggestion was taken up by Ashby during his leave of absence in America in the Easter term of 1964, when he and Lady Ashby visited Mr and Mrs Paul Mellon in Virginia, and led to a formal proposal to the Old Dominion Foundation (now called the Andrew Mellon Foundation). This resulted in an initial grant of $200,000 towards the costs of visiting fellows in Clare Hall, and there was encouragement for the college to ask for more at a later stage in the development[7].
3. We had begun to think about the architectural specification for the buildings for Clare Hall. In this we were considerably helped by Holister, an architect and Domestic Bursar of Clare College. This is discussed further in the next chapter and in chapter 11.

---

[6] The Old Dominion Foundation, now renamed the Andrew Mellon Foundation.
[7] Further details are given in chapter 11.

4. I had also prepared a paper setting out a draft programme[8] for the development of Clare Hall. It was not a paper on which we needed to reach agreement. At the time, Ashby thought it was 'too ambitious'. In retrospect, I had under-estimated the lead times for building work (as did everyone in Britain at that time), and I was too optimistic about the development of special symposia – they needed more space and money than Clare Hall could provide, though the college usually includes visiting fellows who are taking part in mathematical symposia at the nearby Newton Institute. However, most of the expectations on growth were fulfilled within 15 years: for example, my forecast for 1975–80 was for 80 fellows and 40 research students. The actual number of fellows in 1975 was 62, and there were 59 research students. In addition, in 1975 there were 32 visiting associates[9] and 20 resident senior members[10].

---

[8] Perhaps more a scenario than a programme, since we were not aiming to agree on it.
[9] The Visiting Associate class was largely amalgamated with Visiting Fellows during the 1980's.
[10] Re-named as Life Members in Residence from 1986.

Chapter 9

GETTING STARTED

CLARE HALL WORKING COMMITTEE

At their meeting on 6 March 1964, the governing body had approved the functions and general pattern of the Society outlined in the report by Ashby, Eden and Northam, on the proposed extension to Clare College, subject to amendments that clarified the intention to include research students and more senior researchers who may not have doctoral degrees. They appointed a working committee consisting of: Kingsford[1] (who consented to act as secretary), Reddaway, Eden, the senior tutor (Northam), the bursar (Cooper), the domestic bursar (Holister), and the Master as Chairman.

The working committee was asked, jointly with the fellowship committee, to nominate to the governing body the names of five initial fellows-designate of Clare Hall. When these five were approved, they would join with the members of the working committee to form the provisional council of Clare Hall. The provisional council would be empowered to proceed with the establishment of the society (of Clare Hall) and the provision of accommodation, and to remain in being until the statutory annual meeting of the governing body in May 1965.

The working committee met seven times under the chairmanship of Professor Godwin (later Sir Harry Godwin), who was Acting Master of Clare College from 12 March to 8 June 1964 whilst Ashby was on study leave in the United States. It met three more times in June with Ashby as chairman following his return to Cambridge.

---

[1] Kingsford had recently retired from his post as Secretary to the Syndics of Cambridge University Press, which was the senior full-time post in the Press until the reorganisation in 1972.

The first meeting was held on 11 April 1964 in the dining room of the Master's Lodge in Clare College. The following six topics were listed for discussion, and formed the main structure for the work of the committee for the following nine meetings:

Selection of an architect
Statutes
Consideration of the foundation fellows
Acquisition of the Herschel Road Site
Compilation of the building requirements
Draft announcement

SELECTION OF AN ARCHITECT

Holister opened the discussion by stating that he did not wish to act as architect, and the committee agreed with his view that the interests of the college would be best served through the availability of his advice as a member of the committee. A number of names were discussed, including some suggested by the Professor of Architecture, Sir Leslie Martin, and others (including Ralph Erskine) suggested by Holister. It was agreed that Holister would obtain more information about five of the possible candidates.

We soon received photographs of works by some of the candidates, but none of us was happy with the style of unfaced concrete that had been fashionable in recent university buildings. By the fifth meeting on 19 May, although we had not seen photographs of his work, it was evident that Ralph Erskine, a British architect practising in Sweden, was likely to be the favoured candidate, but a final decision awaited photographs of his work. These photographs were considered at the eighth meeting held on 12 June 1964 and chaired by Ashby following his return from the United States. It was agreed to recommend to the College Finance committee that Ralph Erskine be invited to meet the committee.

By this stage, considerable progress had been made on what was desired for the buildings of Clare Hall. Holister had been involved from an early stage and by the beginning of June he had produced a draft specification for discussion by the working committee. The evolution of this specification and the subsequent designs are described in more detail in chapter 11.

Selection of an architect 151

13. Fellows of Clare College on the Clare Hall Working Committee, Easter Term 1964.
(a) (above left) Harry Godwin , (b) (above right) R. J. L. (Bill) Kingsford
(c) (below left) Don Holister , (d) (below right) Colin Turpin (advisor)
Members shown in other illustrations: Ashby, Cooper, Eden, Northam and Reddaway.

Erskine visited from 8 to 10 July and stayed in the Master's Lodge. Holister met his mid-morning train at Cambridge station, and Erskine then talked with Ashby until lunch, when they were joined by all members of the working committee. During the afternoon, he visited the site in Herschel

Road with Holister and the Bursar. The next morning he had a long informal discussion with the working committee, and on the 10th, the committee met alone and decided in principle to recommend Erskine as the architect of Clare Hall. Subsequently he was formally commissioned as the architect for Clare Hall by the Finance committee on behalf of Clare College.

I was Erskine's host for lunch on the 10th, and after lunch he had further informal discussions in the fellows' Parlour on E staircase with the working committee. In the evening, the discussions moved to the Master's Lodge and we were joined by the first five fellows-designate of Clare Hall. I recall Ralph Erskine instructing me not to intervene whilst he sought to obtain the views of the five newcomers on how they thought the new society would function. For them it was a tough question – our new colleagues knowledge of our intentions was limited to the outline briefing that had been given to them two weeks earlier when Ashby had visited them individually to ask if he could nominate them to become fellows-designate. It was evident that Ashby's briefing had not included any information about the proposed buildings – and rather little about the society itself. As Ashby remarked later, it was a testimony to their courage that they each had agreed to be nominated.

CHOOSING THE FIRST FELLOWS

One of he most important functions of the Clare Hall working committee was to select jointly with the Clare College fellowship committee and nominate to the governing body five names for election as the first fellows-designate of Clare Hall. It was assumed that these five would be chosen from amongst members of the Regent House who were not yet fellows of any college.

There was some overlap between members of the two committees, which had their first joint meeting on 12 May 1964, when the additional members from the fellowship committee were Professor Moule, Lady Margaret Professor of Divinity and formerly Dean of Clare College, Dr Lipstein (later Professor) a distinguished international lawyer, and Dr Black, who had been acting senior tutor during Dr Northam's leave of absence in 1963–64. It was agreed to invite members of the Clare governing body to suggest up to three names each for consideration as possible fellows of Clare Hall.

At the next joint meeting on 18 May, an impressive range of qualities was specified that would be desirable – combining the qualities of Newton and Sophocles with those of the Archangel Gabriel – distinction in scholarship, breadth of interest and intellectual enthusiasm, ability to judge the quality and personality of others, enthusiasm for the project and willingness to give service and to undertake committee work, wide contacts in the University. A list of about two hundred University teaching officers and of persons holding other posts in the University was examined, with particular reference to names suggested by members of the Clare governing body. A long short-list of 32 names was agreed, for some of whom additional information was to be obtained. There were only two women on the list – an indication of the small number holding academic posts in the University.

Before these names were reconsidered at the next meeting on 30 May, Godwin reminded the joint committee that it had to consider only the election of the first five foundation fellows[2] and suggested that it should not regard the election as a means of meeting teaching needs of the College or of discharging obligations of the College (e.g. of loyalty to members of the College) or of enhancing the importance of a particular field of study; that it should consider primarily persons with the qualities of vision, drive, judgement of others, and experience likely to act as the driving force in constituting a new organisation; and that women (preferably two rather than one in isolation) should be included. The committee concurred, while noting that if one woman only was elected in the first five, a second could be added in a subsequent election, and that the balance of subject representation would be assisted by the College representatives on the provisional Clare Hall Council and could be further adjusted by later elections.

The joint committee classified the 32 names into groups, from which it was intended to select the final choice of five names from the leading group at a later meeting. This was held on 15 June after the return of Sir Eric Ashby, so he was able to take the chair. Five names were selected as first choices:

---

[2] The term foundation fellow kept recurring, though later the Provisional Council argued that it was inappropriate since there were many fellows additional to the original five in February 1966 when Clare Hall attained a legal existence as an Approved Foundation.

T. E. Armstrong, R. W. David, E. P. M. Dronke, Miss M. A. Hesse, and W. H. Taylor.

In his talk on the Founding of Clare Hall in 1976, Lord Ashby described his subsequent actions:

We got authority to approach the people we wanted as the five foundation fellows. The decision to approach them was made at a meeting on 15 June. My engagement book for 16 June records that I got on my bike and made the following visits on that day: Armstrong 11.15, Hesse 12.45, David 3.30, Taylor 4.30, Dronke 6.00. I had to be very careful at these visits because we still did not know what the status of the satellite would be, nor the standing of its fellows; and we were still assuming that the umbilical cord would persist long after birth. So it is a testimony to the courage of these five people that they all consented to accept nomination.

THE FIRST FIVE FELLOWS-DESIGNATE

The nominations from the Clare Hall working committee for the first five fellows-designate of Clare Hall were agreed by the governing body of Clare College at a special meeting on 25 June 1964. They were placed in an order of seniority determined by age:

Will Taylor was Reader in Crystallography on the staff of the Cavendish Laboratory. He had earlier been a senior colleague of Professor Sir Lawrence Bragg in Manchester, who succeeded Lord Rutherford as the Cavendish Professor in 1939. At Bragg's invitation in 1945, Taylor accepted a post in Cambridge as head of the crystallography research group, but Bragg had been unable to deliver an implied promise of a college fellowship since Taylor was not willing to take on the task of college teaching additional to his university duties for teaching and research.

Dick David was Secretary of the Syndics of the University Press and University Publisher, posts in which he had succeeded Kingsford in 1963. Although the post of publisher was of ancient origin dating back to the foundation of the Press in the 16th century and was of professorial status, it did not qualify within the professorial quota system which was intended to ensure that all professors would receive an offer of a college fellowship. The college at which David was an undergraduate would normally have been expected to consider making him an offer of a fellowship, but no offer had been forthcoming, possibly because it was a small college and determined to remain so. David had served in the navy throughout the war, becoming Lt-Commander in 1945, and he was an enthusiastic part-time botanist, specialising in sedges. He succeeded Taylor as senior fellow of Clare Hall in 1972.

The first fellows-designate

14. Fellows-designate of Clare Hall, June 1964.
(a) (above left) Will Taylor, (b) (above right) Dick David,
(c) (below left) Terence Armstrong, (d) (below right) Peter Dronke.

Terence Armstrong was an Assistant Director of Research (ADR)[3], later to become a Reader and in 1982–83 the Acting Director at the Scott Polar Research Institute. He had extensive experience of Arctic and sub-Arctic exploration, including sailing the North-West Passage, and he was also a Russian scholar. During the war he had been in the intelligence service, and was with the airborne forces in the battle of Arnhem where he was wounded but was amongst those able to cross the river Rhine safely during the subsequent withdrawal. He later became the first tutor for the graduate students in Clare Hall, and he was the Vice-President from 1985–87 before retiring as an emeritus fellow.

Mary Hesse was a lecturer in the philosophy of science (later to become professor). This was a subject with a relatively small number of undergraduate students, insufficient in any one college to justify appointing a fellow to do college teaching in the subject. Subsequently, in 1965 before Clare Hall was recognised by the university as an 'approved foundation', Dr Hesse accepted an offer of a fellowship at University College (later renamed as Wolfson College), so she was an active member of Clare Hall and its provisional council only for one year.

Peter Dronke was a lecturer in medieval Latin with a formidable reputation for scholarship. He had taken his first degree in the Victoria University, New Zealand, and a second degree in Oxford University, where he was a research fellow of Merton College before coming to Cambridge as a university lecturer. He later became professor of medieval latin literature and a professorial fellow of Clare Hall.

REPORT TO THE GOVERNING BODY

During the Easter vacation of 1964, at the request of Ashby, Colin Turpin (a law fellow) had prepared a first draft of the modifications to the Clare College statutes that would be required so that Clare Hall could come into existence as a semi-autonomous academic centre within the college, along the lines that had been suggested by the committee of three. Although the suggested legal changes may have met these objectives because statutes tend to be 'enabling' rather than 'prescriptive', the draft by Turpin necessarily related more to the statutes of Clare College than to the needs of Clare Hall. Thus, it was not at all clear to the committee exactly how Clare Hall was intended to function in practice. At the first meeting of the working committee, Kingsford was therefore asked to prepare a suitable account in non-legal language that described the constitution and its operation.

---

[3] ADR is a research appointment equivalent to university lecturer.

Kingsford produced an account of how Clare Hall would function in three stages, each one being modified at meetings of the committee. The full version was considered at the meeting on 12 June after Ashby had returned from the United States, and – with further amendments made at that meeting – it was distributed to all fellows for the governing body meeting on 15 July. Although the agenda for that meeting includes a note about this paper, it is not mentioned in the recorded minutes of the meeting, which are wrong[4].

The paper from the working committee dated 12 June on the functioning of Clare Hall began with a section on the Constitution of the Society which would consist of a Warden and fellows of Clare Hall, the Warden also to be a fellow of Clare Hall and all to be bye-fellows of Clare College. The bye-fellows would not be members of the governing body of Clare College, thus seeming to avoid the difficulties of expansion of the Clare fellowship which had caused concern to many fellows. This suggestion itself proved to be unacceptable and eventually led, in February 1966, to a foundation that was much more independent of Clare College than had been expected during the discussions of the working committee. Still later it led to complete independence when Clare Hall received its own Royal Charter in 1984.

The second part of the report concerned the Government of Clare Hall, suggesting that most decisions would be made by a joint Council made up equally of 5 fellows of the College and 5 of the Hall, of which the Master of Clare College would be the Chairman, and the Warden of Clare Hall would be a member. Arrangements would be made for meetings of the other fellows of Clare Hall, and there should be a systematic rotation of membership of the joint Council. These concepts were abandoned within a few months following difficulties encountered over the status of bye-fellows.

The way in which the constitution of Clare Hall and its government developed is described in chapter 10.

---

[4] The minutes also ignore a second important paper from the Clare needs committee, which reported the purchase of St. Regis, a block of flats in Chesterton Road, to be used for Clare graduate students. This purchase was in response to the decision at the meeting of the governing body on 11 January 1964, where it had been agreed to take action on providing accommodation for the Clare College graduate students. Copies of these two papers have now been placed with the governing body minutes in the Clare College archives.

158   *Getting started*

The remainder of the report set out the procedures by which the finances of Clare Hall would be managed and how rooms would be allocated. It concluded by outlining the interim arrangements for government by the Clare Hall provisional council[5], for lunching and dining rights and for the filling of vacancies.

ANNOUNCEMENT

The draft announcement about the founding of Clare Hall, that had been prepared by the committee of three, was considered and revised. The final version was agreed on 22 June at the tenth meeting of the working committee, and approved by the governing body at the special meeting held to elect the five fellows-designate on 25 June. The announcement to the Press was made on Friday 3 July after the occupants of the flats in Herschel House and the two adjoining houses had been informed of the plans[6].

Clare Hall: a new development by Clare College

Clare College has decided to promote within the College a new development to be known as Clare Hall. The intention is that Clare Hall shall make a contribution to meeting current Cambridge needs by providing a new graduate society for resident and visiting scholars. Its fellowship is designed to bring together four categories: (i) scholars holding appointments in the university or in research institutions in Cambridge, whose subjects may not be in great demand for undergraduate teaching; (ii) post-doctoral and other senior research workers; (iii) visiting scholars in Cambridge on study-leave; (iv) research fellows elected from among more senior research students; When the new society has been established, a body of research students who are not fellows will be added.

It is intended that fellowships of Clare Hall shall be open to men and women on equal terms, subject to the approval of Queen in Council of the required changes in the statutes of the University and the colleges.

It is proposed that Clare Hall shall be legally part of Clare College, governed by statutes of the College. The Society will consist of about forty fellows of Clare Hall, who will also be bye-fellows of the College. It will be governed by a Council composed of five fellows of the Hall, five fellows of the College, the Warden of the Hall and the Master of the College as chairman.

---

[5] Consisting of the members of the Clare Hall working committee and the first five fellows-designate of Clare Hall.
[6] The problem of displacing tenants of the flats is described in chapter 11.

The buildings, which will include flats, studies, a seminar room, and dining rooms, will be on a site in Herschel Road. Here, within five minutes' walk of Clare College, Clare Hall will be able to develop an identity of its own and to maintain, socially and intellectually, a close relationship with the College.

The resulting press coverage was helped by the intention to elect women bye-fellows at Clare College which had been all-male since its foundation in 1326. There was a further press release on 9 July announcing the names of the first five fellows-designate and that an endowment of $200,000 had been received from the Old Dominion Foundation of New York to subsidise research fellowships and visiting fellowships at Clare Hall.

However, the University Registrary (R. M. Rattenbury)[7] had reservations about using the same announcement in the Cambridge University Reporter, and on his advice it was restricted to essentials: namely, that Clare College would be seeking to amend its Statutes to enable it to promote within the College a Society for Graduates to be known as Clare Hall, which would be open to men and women and of which the Fellows would be bye-Fellows of Clare College. Subject to consent for the change in Statutes the Governing Body recorded its intention to elect as Fellows ... (then followed the names of the first five fellows-designate).

PROVISIONAL COUNCIL

The Clare Hall working committee had been authorised to transform itself into the provisional council by co-opting the first five fellows-designate of Clare Hall when their names had been approved by the governing body of Clare College.

The agenda for the first meeting of the council was set out by Eric Ashby, who asked members to meet in the dining room of the Master's Lodge for an informal discussion on 22 July 1964. The headings for discussion were based on the issues that had been considered by the working committee, including such items as the constitution of Clare Hall and when to choose a Warden (head), how to deal with the plans for the proposed new buildings, whether there should be additional fellows-designate in any one of the three categories – permanent, visiting and

---

[7] The Registrary is (*inter alia*) the Secretary of the Council of the Senate and, was the senior full-time official in the University until the Vice-Chancellor became full-time in 1992.

research. The agenda also included a note that the Council should decide how the embryo society might function during 1964–65. Ashby suggested that members might dine in the Master's Lodge on one night a week, adding with characteristic courtesy that it would be convenient to avoid Wednesdays, Fridays and Saturdays. The governing body had already agreed that fellows-designate could lunch as guests with the fellows of Clare College, thus neatly overcoming the problem that both college and university statutes prevented women from becoming members of the college.

All the Clare College members of the council attended the meeting, namely: Ashby, (Master and chairman), Cooper (bursar), Eden, Holister, and Northam (senior tutor). The fellows-designate of Clare Hall attending were: Armstrong, Dronke, Hesse, and Taylor (David was unable to attend).

Kingsford, who had been secretary to the working committee, agreed to act as secretary of the provisional council until May 1965. The council decided that 'President' would be a better title than Warden, and that although the President should preside over the Society, he should not be personally responsible for its administration. The period of office of the first President should be 'up to ten years', and it was desirable to agree on a recommendation as President by May 1965. The Master's offer of the dining room in the Lodge for Clare Hall dinners was gratefully accepted with Tuesday as the designated day. Dining would begin on 13 October for all members of the provisional council and any further fellows-designate of Clare Hall up to a total of about twenty.

Clare College had already received an endowment to subsidise visiting fellowships at Clare Hall on the understanding that there could be an early but modest start to a visiting programme[8]. The provisional council agreed to recommend (to the governing body of Clare) that invitations be made to two academics known to be coming to Cambridge in the first half of 1965, Miss Jean Bannister, a physiologist from Somerville College, Oxford, and Professor Bernard Cohen, a historian of science from Harvard, both of whom subsequently accepted. Four others were considered, with decisions postponed for further details. It was also decided to proceed with the selection of five additional fellows-designate, and lists of all qualified members of the staff of the university not holding

---

[8] See the discussion of finance and endowments in chapter 11.

fellowships would be circulated, including a note of those names that had been selected earlier for the long short-list by the working committee additional to the five that had been approved as fellows-designate.

At this first meeting of the provisional council, there were no substantive comments on the proposed constitution that had been set out earlier by the working committee. However, shortly after the meeting, prompted by questions raised by Colin Turpin, fellow in law, Ashby began to have second thoughts about the constitution, because it appeared that if Clare Hall was to be an institution within Clare College, it would not be recognised by the University and its fellows would not be members of the Regent House[9]. He therefore sent a memorandum describing his concerns to all members of the provisional council on 28 July. His suggestions for resolving these concerns led to an immediate and opposing response from Northam, and an exchange of letters which is described in more detail in chapter 10, which discusses the evolution of ideas about the constitution.

The provisional council did not have an opportunity to respond formally to Ashby's memo until their second meeting on 21 September 1964. By that date a new option had come to light, namely that Clare Hall might, without severing its links with Clare College, become one of the Approved Societies under consideration by the Council of the Senate on behalf of the University, with Clare College as Trustee. This would have the consequence that a fellowship of Clare Hall would by itself qualify for membership of the Regent House, the crucial difference being that the fellows would be members of the governing body of an institution recognised by the University.

At this second meeting, the Council also agreed that as soon as possible fellows of Clare Hall should be made members of Clare College and that a change of Statutes to permit the admission of women fellows of Clare Hall as members of Clare College should be sought[10]. It was further agreed

---

[9] The Regent House is the ultimate legislative authority in Cambridge University, and its approval is required for any major development or institutional change.

[10] No action was taken on this suggestion, and all fellows of Clare Hall remained as guests of Clare College. The relevance of membership of Clare College ceased to be significant towards the end of 1964 when it was decided that Clare Hall should become an Approved Foundation. The temporary arrangement that all members of Clare Hall, men and women, would be guests in Clare College proved to be very satisfactory. It was not until 1972 that Clare College admitted women undergraduates, though women fellows were admitted one year earlier.

that, while formal recommendations on the following matters would remain with the provisional council, all fellows in Class F should be invited to attend meetings for their discussion: selection of fellows, nomination of the President, election of representatives (on University bodies); consideration of building plans; with the one reservation that invitations to visiting fellows may sometimes have to be made by the provisional council without reference to other fellows of Clare Hall. More generally, it was agreed that when the opinions of colleges were sought by the university on any matter relevant to the fellows of Clare Hall, the fellows-designate should be informed and invited to offer an opinion, and their independent opinion should be annexed to the opinion of Clare College when it is returned to the university.

The minute of the meeting of the provisional council on 21 September 1964 that all fellows-designate of Clare Hall should be involved in decisions and planning was put into effect subsequently by inviting all 'fellows-designate' of Clare Hall to attend the meetings of the provisional council, effectively as non-voting members.

MORE FELLOWS

On 21 September 1964 the provisional council decided that all its members, together with all members of the Clare College governing body[11], should be invited to submit names for additional fellows-designate by the end of October for consideration at the Council's meeting on 17 November. Soon after that meeting, I was approached by Will Taylor, who inquired whether I would be willing to be nominated as a fellow-designate for Clare Hall. He had evidently been prompted by Eric Ashby, since he explained that he understood that I had been responsible for suggesting many of the features of Clare Hall that were now beginning to be realised.

At the Council's meeting on 17 November, members first discussed a paper from Mary Hesse suggesting that Clare Hall should choose fellows from a limited range of subjects so that there would be several with

---

[11] In practice all subsequent nominations came from the fellows-designate of Clare Hall, a change of procedure that was suggested by Ashby, though he and others sometimes made suggestions that were taken up by one or more of the fellows-designate.

More fellows

common subject interests in the society, thus making it more of a research centre. However, this approach did not find favour[12] and it was agreed not to confine new elections to any limited group of subjects. It was then agreed to recommend three further names as fellows-designate to the governing body of Clare College. These were:

Dr Richard J. Eden, Reader in theoretical physics in the Cavendish Laboratory and a fellow of Clare College[13]. Dr Eden had previously been the Stokes Lecturer in Mathematics, and before joining Clare as Director of Studies in Mathematics in 1951 he had been awarded a Smith's Prize and had held research fellowships at Peterhouse and at Pembroke. He had also held visiting appointments in a number of universities and research centres in the United States and Europe. He was later, in 1982, appointed Professor of Energy Studies, an interdisciplinary subject that he had developed in the Cavendish Laboratory.

Mr John F. Coales, who was Reader in control engineering at the time but was appointed to a personal professorship in 1965, so when Clare Hall was officially established in February 1966, he was the first professorial fellow of the college. He had graduated at Sidney Sussex College, and then followed a distinguished scientific research career in the Admiralty until 1946. In that year he became research Director of Elliott Brothers (London), where he was responsible for a wide range of developments in computer instrumentation and control systems. He returned to Cambridge in 1953 to organise graduate courses on control engineering. He was the President of the International Federation of Automatic Control in 1963, he became the President of the Institution of Electrical Engineers in 1971, in 1975 he was Chairman of the Council of Engineering Institutions, and in 1976 he was a founder fellow of the fellowship of Engineering.

Dr. Carmen Blacker, lecturer in Japanese, who had a special interest in Japanese Religion, particularly Zen Buddhism. Her first degree was in Japanese at the School of Oriental Studies in London, after which she took Modern Greats in Oxford, and obtained a Ph.D. in London University. In 1950 she went to Harvard for a year, followed by two years in Japan at Keito University in Tokyo. She had already visited Japan five times when she came to Clare Hall and has been a regular visitor since then. Her distinguished scholarship has been recognised in her election to the British Academy, and overseas by visiting professorships in the United States and in Japan where, in 1989, she was awarded the Order of the Precious Crown.

---

[12] This idea had been considered much earlier, but it had been decided that it would limit the overall quality in the selection of candidates as fellows-designate.
[13] My fellowship in Clare College could continue until Clare Hall acquired an independent legal status – as it did in February 1966, when I became instead a Fellow of Clare Hall.

15. Fellows-designate of Clare Hall, 1964–66.
(a) (above left) John Coales, (b) (above right) Carmen Blacker,
(c) (below left) Patrick Echlin, (d) (below right) Keith Cameron, bursar 1966–72.

In addition to nominations for the permanent fellows, we had been seeking suggestions for research fellows and for visiting fellows, and the names of those nominated had been submitted to the Clare College governing body. At the meeting of the Council on 8 December, Ashby was able to announce that the governing body had endorsed the recommendations for ten additional fellows, including the three 'official' or permanent fellows listed above. The list included our first two research fellows:

Mr John G. Coates, who was a research student working for a Cambridge Ph.D. studying the language and literature of the Komi, a Finno-Ugrian people living in northern USSR-Europe. His supervisor was Terence Armstrong, a fellow-designate of Clare Hall, but his background was unusual for a research student. Coates had served with such distinction in the Commandos during the war that he had been awarded the DSO. He worked in the Foreign Office from 1947–62 and had a knowledge of Russian, Finnish and Hungarian. He was an Assistant Professor of Languages in the University of Idaho during 1962–63, before becoming a Cambridge research student during the following academic year. He then joined the Secretariat of the Royal Society with responsibility for Eastern European matters, but with support from Clare Hall he was able to return to full time academic work in Cambridge and complete his Ph.D. Subsequently, he became Dean of Students at the newly established University of East Anglia near Norwich.

Dr S. J. Tambiah, who was already an established scholar and a University Assistant lecturer in Archaeology and Anthropology. He later achieved great distinction as one of the leading anthropologists concerned with South East Asia, and he became a professor at Harvard University.

The endowment from the Old Dominion Foundation and a five-year grant from the Ford Foundation were to be used to subsidise visiting fellowships and had been given on the understanding that Clare Hall would make a modest but early start to the programme. By December 1964, six nominations for visiting fellowships had been approved:

Dr Sachin Chaudri, economics, from India, for April and May 1965.
Professor B. Cohen, history of science, from Harvard University, for six months from January 1965.
Dr J. W. Garland, solid state physics, from the University of California in Berkeley, from February to June 1965.
Dr J. B. Jones, crystallography, from Adelaide for the academic year 1965–66.
Miss Jean Bannister, a physiologist and a fellow of Somerville College, Oxford, from January 1965
Professor W. Sellers, philosophy of science, from the University of Minnesota for the academic year 1965–66.

There was no problem in finding suitable names for additional fellows-designate. By 15 February 1965, three more had been nominated and approved:

Dr Ronald Popperwell, a lecturer in Norwegian, specialising in Norwegian literature and in the pronunciation of the language. He was secretary of the faculty board of Modern and Medieval Languages. Later as a talented violinist he helped develop the musical traditions in Clare Hall.

Dr Stanley Evans, a physicist and an ADR in the British Antarctic Survey, working on radio sounding of ice sheets. He subsequently became a lecturer in the faculty of Engineering, and after eleven years as a fellow of Clare Hall, in 1976 he left to become a fellow and tutor in Jesus College.

Dr Patrick Echlin, a botanist and an SAR[14] in the Department of Botany, specialising in the use of electron microscopy techniques in studying the structure and morphology of microscopic plants. He later became a lecturer in the same department. In Clare Hall he subsequently became Steward and Praelector, and in 1993–94 he was the first University Proctor to come from Clare Hall.

Thus by the middle of February 1965, Clare Hall had eleven (permanent) fellows-designate, one research fellow, and three visiting fellows. Two more research fellows were elected during April and May, both joining Clare Hall in October:

Ms Polly Hill, an economist and sociologist [Dr Hill from 1967, but she was initially listed in Clare Hall records under her married name, Mrs M. E. Humphreys]. Dr Hill had been in the civil service from 1940 to 1951, and had then worked mainly in Ghana, subsequently carrying out fieldwork in villages in Northern Nigeria and in Southern India. During 1973–79 she was the University's Smuts Reader in Commonwealth Studies.

Dr Elliott Leader, a theoretical physicist, working on the theory of elementary particles. Initially from South Africa, he had been Dr Eden's research student from 1960–63 and was returning to work with him again after two years in the United States. Subsequently, Dr Leader moved directly from his research fellowship to become professor of applied mathematics at Westfield College in London University.

CHOOSING A PRESIDENT

During the Easter Term 1964, there were occasional discussions in the Clare Hall working committee about the appointment of a 'Warden' for Clare Hall. At that time the Warden was expected to be an amalgam of a

---

[14] Senior Assistant in Research, the research-equivalent post to university assistant lecturer

landlord, a general manager, a social focus and a chairman of the proposed new foundation[15], which was then seen as a residential and academic centre within Clare College to be managed by a joint council of six fellows of the College and six fellows of the Hall. The minutes of the ninth meeting of the committee, held on 15 June 1964, record that

(i) It was agreed to propose to the governing body at its July meeting that the nomination of the first Warden should be made jointly by the working committee and the fellowship committee unless the provisional Clare Hall Council shall have come into being.
(ii) It was agreed that at the same meeting members of the governing body should be asked to suggest the names of suitable persons, who might be drawn from fellows of the College, the first five fellows of Clare Hall, and professors who are already fellows of other colleges.

At the first meeting of the provisional council, held on 22 July, it was agreed that President would be a better title than Warden. It was evident that the Council was taking a more realistic approach than the earlier working committee to the problem of persuading an academic of distinction to take on the job of President. Thus, it was decided that, while (qua a Master of a College) he would be required to preside over the society and to co-ordinate and be responsible for the discharge of its activities, he would not personally undertake the administration; and that the qualities required would be intellectual distinction and width, with the capacity to identify himself with the development of the society; the area of choice would be regularly reviewed and it was thought desirable to make a recommendation by May 1965.

The status of the President became clearer at the meeting of the Council on 21 September (by implication though not explicitly), when the Council welcomed the possibility of Clare Hall becoming an Approved Society within the University, instead of an institution within Clare College. By December, this had evolved into the concept of an Approved Foundation with Clare College as Trustee, a status similar to that of Churchill College at that time. Thus it was by then clear that the President of Clare Hall would be a Head of House on a par with a Master of a College.

---

[15] The role of the Warden was codified in some detail in the report of the Working Committee dated 12 June 1964, which was received by the governing body of Clare College at their meeting on 15 July.

This change stimulated more serious thinking about the duties and qualities required for a President, and in January 1965, it was agreed:

(i) that a woman would be no less eligible than a man;
(ii) that the day-to-day running of the society would not fall on the President, but would be undertaken by a competent secretary/housekeeper responsible to him, and that the keeping of accounts and payment of wages and bills would be undertaken by the Bursar's office;
(iii) that it would be desirable that the first President should be appointed while the society is still in its formative period;
(iv) that the first period of office should be seven years[16];
(v) that, in the consideration of names, the following desiderata should be borne in mind: the nominee to hold an appointment in the University; to be of outstanding intellectual attainment and of wide intellectual interests and enthusiasm; to be likely to identify himself with, but not to dominate, the development of the society; to be likely to be a competent chairman and co-ordinator and executant of the society's affairs; and to be academically sociable. It is desirable, but not essential, that the nominee should be married and aged between 40 and 60.
(vi) that names, with specifications, should be submitted to the Master by 3 February, for consideration at the next meeting.

The agenda for the Council's meeting in February contained a list of thirteen Presidential 'possibles', ranging from casual suggestions to formal proposals[17]. The names included three Nobel prize winners and six fellows of the Royal Society. At the more humble end of the spectrum were four members of the provisional council including two fellows-designate of Clare Hall. It will be recalled that it had been earlier decided that all fellows-designate would attend the meetings of the Council, and at the February meeting in addition to the six who were members of the Council it was noted that Miss Blacker, Mr Coales, and Dr Tambiah were in attendance.

---

[16] The decision to appoint each President for a fixed period was based on the idea that it would encourage the election of a young President (i.e. aged circa 45) since it would avoid the risk of an unduly long tenure that might result from an appointment to retiring age. This theory worked only for the first President, who was aged 45 on election. Subsequently the age of election increased in line with the age of the more senior fellows of the college, finally stabilising at around 60 years.

[17] At this stage there was the utmost secrecy about the names, none were to be approached, though the four who were members of the provisional council had, of course, received copies of the list in the agenda.

By March 1965, the role of the President had been codified in part of a revised statement about how Clare Hall would function, which was intended to provide a guide to a legal draftsman for a possible pattern of government of Clare Hall to be specified in a Trust Deed establishing it as an Approved Foundation. This draft stated that the election of the President would be made by the governing body of Clare College on the recommendation of the provisional Clare Hall Council, for an initial period of seven years, which could be renewed. The clause allowing renewal was subsequently changed (on 15 June) at the request of the fellows-designate of Clare Hall to disallow the re-election of a President, unless in a particular and exceptional circumstance the regulations were amended to permit re-election.

Prior to the meeting of the provisional council on 15 June, at the suggestion of Ashby it had been agreed that the final selection of the first President from a short-list of candidates would be made by the fellows-designate of Clare Hall who were members of the Council. Earlier discussions and reduction to a short-list involved all members of the Council and (to some extent) fellows-designate who were not members of the Council.

At the meeting on 18 May the Council agreed that the fellows of Clare Hall should renew their discussions of the choice for President, and Taylor, the senior fellow-designate, undertook to convene them. No record was kept of these discussions, and I do not recall how the short-list was derived. However, I do remember the final meeting though I was present for only part of it. Taylor had invited only the five fellows-designate who were members of the provisional council, and the meeting took place in the Master's dining room after lunch, probably on Tuesday 8 June. At that stage the short-list included only three candidates – Armstrong, Eden and Pippard. Armstrong and I offered to withdraw from the meeting, and we did so after Taylor had ascertained that neither of us would have any objection to the election of Brian Pippard if that proved to be the recommendation of the remaining three fellows-designate. The remaining three evidently reached a decision quite quickly since Taylor telephoned me about half an hour later to say that they (Taylor, David and Dronke) had agreed on Pippard as the nominee. On 15 June 1965, on the recommendation of the fellows-designate of Clare Hall, the provisional council agreed unanimously :

that Professor A. B. Pippard be recommended to the governing body for election as the first President and that the Master should seek his acceptance in the meantime.

At that time, Brian Pippard was Plummer Professor of Physics and, for the previous 15 years he had been an outstanding leader of research in low temperature physics in the Cavendish Laboratory, an area that had attracted many of the best of the Cambridge graduates in physics in that period. Elected to the Royal Society in 1956, he was awarded the Society's Hughes Medal in 1959. He was an undergraduate at Clare College during 1938–41, and during his war-service in 1941–45 he worked at Malvern on the development of radar. He became a fellow of Clare College and Director of Studies in Physics in 1947, and as a talented pianist he was active in maintaining the Clare music tradition. As a member of the governing body he had contributed to the debates and discussions that led to the decision to found Clare Hall. When invited to become the first President of Clare Hall he was aged 44, married to Charlotte and with three daughters. They had lived in the United States during 1955–56 when Brian was visiting professor at the University of Chicago. In 1971, he became Cavendish Professor of Experimental Physics, a position he held for 11 years, and he was knighted in 1975.

The nomination of Pippard as President-designate of Clare Hall, by the provisional council on 15 June 1965, had been completed without consulting him, so (in principle at least) we were not aware whether he would accept the offer. We required his agreement before we could forward the nomination to the governing body of Clare College for their confirmation of the appointment. Lord Ashby recounted the next stage in his talk on the tenth anniversary of the founding of Clare Hall:

On 15 June [1965] the provisional council decided to ask Brian Pippard whether he would allow his name to go forward [as President]. I approached him armed with a battery of arguments as to why he should consent, and a battery of rejoinders to any objections he might be likely to raise against consenting. In the event none of these armaments was necessary. To our delight he accepted, with what I am sure was unfeigned pleasure, and with only one condition: that the President's drawing room should be large enough to hold a grand piano[18].

[18] Pippard also told Ashby that he would not want the President to have the possibility of a second term beyond seven years.

Having ascertained that Pippard was prepared to accept the nomination and agreed with his request that there would be adequate administrative support and that there would be some enlargement of the President's house[19], on 16 July the provisional council agreed to recommend to the governing body of Clare College that the necessary steps be taken for Professor Pippard' s election. Since it was still uncertain when the Trust Deed for the founding of Clare Hall would be approved, at their meeting on 23 July 1965 the governing body of Clare agreed to record their intention to elect Professor A. B. Pippard into the office of President of Clare Hall from a date in the academic year 1965-66 to be determined, until 30 September 1973. Pippard then became a member of the provisional council, though Sir Eric Ashby continued as chairman until February 1966, when Clare Hall became an Approved Foundation.

A FUNCTIONING SOCIETY

Eric Ashby's generous invitation for the fellows-designate of Clare Hall, together with other members of the provisional council, to dine in the Master's Lodge once a week was accepted at the meeting of the Council on 22 July, and it was agreed that these Clare Hall dinners would begin at 7.30 p.m. on Tuesday 13 October 1964 and continue until 1 December. Meanwhile the five fellows-designate of Clare Hall began to join the fellows of Clare College for lunch on a regular basis.

At the meeting of the provisional council on 27 October 1964 it was agreed that guests could be brought to the Tuesday dinners. Although it was implicit in all discussions that spouses would be part of the Society in Clare Hall, I was concerned to ensure that no "unwritten conventions" would develop to inhibit this development. It was important to begin these guest nights as we should wish them to continue, so the following week my wife came to the Clare Hall dinner as the first guest. She came again a week or two later, when Lady Ashby also joined us, and subsequently my wife, Elsie, and Helen Ashby came fairly frequently to the Tuesday dinners. The precedent at issue was not one of establishing that women were welcome in Clare Hall – we had elected Mary Hesse

---

[19] An additional bedroom, an enlarged dining room, and the drawing room enlarged sufficiently to provide room for a grand piano.

amongst the first five and Carmen Blacker was elected in November 1964, after which she came regularly to the Tuesday dinners. The need was to make wives welcome on all social occasions, since we believed this to be critical to the success of the visiting fellowships programme.

In addition to the dinners in the Master's Lodge on Tuesdays in term time, during the Summer my wife and I had held two parties for fellows-designate and their wives at our home, and subsequently Iris and Terence Armstrong invited all the Clare Hall community to their house in Harston. We had in mind the social environment at the Princeton Institute for Advanced Study, where we had been made equally welcome and provided with housing amongst some 80 other visiting academic families within walking distance from the Institute. This could be contrasted by the very limited welcome for wives of visiting academics to Cambridge at that time. The visiting academics – at least in the sciences – were usually given a desk in a shared room or laboratory (not so in the arts faculties). There were very few colleges with a visiting fellowship programme, and, except for Churchill College, those with visiting fellows limited their numbers to one or two in each college. Women could not have lunch or dinner in college, so for those fortunate enough to be visiting fellows, the husband might have the privilege of high table dinner and even go to some feasts, whilst his wife remained at home to sup on 'cheese and toast'. It was not an arrangement to encourage repeat visits to Cambridge.

Meanwhile, from April 1965 meetings of the provisional council were also attended by other fellows-designate of Clare Hall. Major concerns included revisions of the drafts for the Trust Deed and the Constitution, criteria for the choice of the first President, discussions of possible research or visiting fellows, and the design of the buildings. There were a number of meetings with Ralph Erskine, the architect of Clare Hall (see chapter 11).

In November 1965, the provisional council learnt with regret of the resignation of Dr Mary Hesse from her position as fellow-designate of Clare Hall. Her involvement in wider policy issues in the university had led to an invitation for her to become a fellow of the newly founded University College[20]. We were sorry to lose her contribution to our discussions on the development of Clare Hall.

---

[20] Later renamed as Wolfson College.

AN APPROVED FOUNDATION

There was no reference to Clare Hall in the minutes of the Clare governing body meeting of 26 October 1964, which was primarily concerned with discussion of a report from the General Board's committee on Teaching, to which the College wished to respond. At the next meeting, which was held on 23 November 1964, a report was received from the provisional council of Clare Hall, and the governing body: (i) declared its intention of electing J. F. Coales, Miss Carmen Blacker and R. J. Eden into fellowships of Clare Hall in Class F, when the necessary constitutional changes have been made; (ii) endorsed recommendations for 3 Clare Hall research fellows and for 6 Clare Hall visiting fellows. (iii) agreed that the Clare Hall Society should continue to have lunching rights in the College until their own buildings were ready; the arrangements were left to the Steward. (iv) agreed that Clare Hall should seek to become an Approved Foundation or Society, with Clare College as trustee exercising some continuing powers over Clare Hall but providing it with a large measure of autonomy in the management of its own affairs.

The factors leading to the proposal that Clare Hall become an Approved Foundation are described in chapter 10. The outcome was the legal foundation of Clare Hall on Monday 7 February 1966, when the governing body of Clare College sealed a Trust Deed establishing Clare Hall as a Society with the Master, Fellows and Scholars of Clare College as Trustees. On that day the Trustees appointed Professor A. B. Pippard as the President of Clare Hall until 30 September 1973. They also appointed 9 official fellows until such time as the governing body of Clare Hall shall determine, 1 professorial fellow, 5 research fellows, and 3 visiting fellows[21].

The provisional council with all the other fellows-designate met on Tuesday 8 February, when they were informed by Sir Eric Ashby, Chairman of the Council and Master of Clare College, of the sealing of the

---

[21] There were four additional visiting fellows-designate appointed by the Provisional Council whose tenure ended before the legal establishment of Clare Hall as an Approved Foundation: Jean Bannister, (physiology, UK), Bernard Cohen (history of science, United States), James Garland (theoretical physics, United States), and Sachin Chaudhuri (economics, India).

Trust Deed and the subsequent elections. He then formally dissolved the Council. Professor Brian Pippard, President of Clare Hall, thanked the Master and fellows of the College for their work on the provisional council during the previous 19 months, and on behalf of the governing body he invited Mr Cooper to attend its meetings during the discussion of matters of finance and Mr Holister similarly for buildings, and Mr Kingsford to continue to act as secretary; and he informed the Master that he or other representatives from the provisional council would be welcome whenever he thought their advice might be valuable.

On the following Saturday, 12 February 1966, the Regent House approved a Grace recognising Clare Hall as an Approved Foundation in the University, back-dated to take effect from the sealing of the Trust Deed on 7 February 1966.

Chapter 10

THE CONSTITUTION

INTRODUCTION

In formal terms the government of a Cambridge college is determined by its Statutes. These provide the legal basis for the corporate identity and any changes have to be approved by the Privy Council – usually taking about two years to achieve since it must first be established that neither other colleges nor the university has any objections to a proposed change. The Statutes of all Cambridge colleges were revised on a semi-uniform basis immediately following the 1923 Act of Parliament on the universities of Oxford and Cambridge[1]. Generally the Statutes aimed to be permissive rather than prescriptive, leaving considerable freedom in the manner by which any individual college is managed. In practice, there is a great deal of variation between colleges in the way that they are managed, depending on their size and wealth, and on whether they are for graduates only, as with Clare Hall. At a more detailed constitutional level, the mode of operation of each college is prescribed by Ordinances that are more prescriptive in character, and can be changed more readily by the governing body of the college. In general the governing body consists of all the fellows, though certain categories of fellow may be excluded, notably bye-fellows, honorary fellows and (usually) emeritus fellows, though in some colleges a fellow who has held office for a sufficiently long period may on retirement become a life fellow rather than an emeritus fellow.

The diversity between colleges is much more evident at the management level. Although the head of house, variously called Master, President, Principal, Warden, etc. is ex officio the chairman of the

---

[1] These common features of College Statutes are attributed by Brooke in *History of the University of Cambridge,* loc. cit. (vol IV p. 369) to their common authorship by the Trinity lawyer H. A. Holland, consequent on decisions by the Commissioners who put into effect the 1923 Act of Parliament.

governing body and of certain of a college's committees[2], his or her involvement in management varies widely between colleges. The degree and type of involvement of the head of house may be a matter of personal choice in a medium sized college. In a large and wealthy college with a strong team associated with the offices of the bursar and the tutor, and with strong professional management particularly in the bursar's office, the Master's involvement in financial management is likely to be small, though he or she would chair committees at which new projects are developed and approved. In a small college, the head of house is usually a key member of the management team, which would include also the bursar and the tutor, the latter – like the head of house – being part-time.

In Clare College, in the period 1959–66 leading up to the foundation of Clare Hall, the Master, Sir Eric Ashby, did not hold a paid university post, having come from his previous post as Vice-Chancellor of the Queen's University Belfast. However, he was not expected to be a full-time Master – it was correctly assumed that he would be much in demand on committees in the university and elsewhere as a government advisor in addition to his own academic work on the environment, on the development of universities and on the history of science and on the development of education. The bursar, Brian Cooper, was also a lecturer in the department of engineering; the senior tutor, John Northam, was a lecturer in the faculty of English; the newly appointed domestic bursar, Darnton Holister, was a lecturer in architecture; all three also directed studies in their own subjects. There was a small clerical and secretarial support staff for the bursar, the senior tutor and the Master.

With this background of part-time management in Clare College, it is not surprising that the management of the proposed extension of the college was not regarded as a significant problem, and it was given little attention during the discussions of the fellows.

EARLY IDEAS

Prior to the proposal for a Clare Institute for Advanced Study which was approved in principle by the governing body of Clare College on 11

---

[2] In some colleges these duties are shared between the Master and a President, or between the Master and a Vice-Master.

Early ideas

January 1964, the concept that was under discussion was an 'extension' to the college. The extension was intended to provide a centre for all of the Clare graduate students and accommodation for some of them. Some fellows would be attached to this centre, and they would assist in its 'internal management'. Thus it was clearly intended that the extension would be part of Clare College, though the later use of the term 'colony' to describe the proposed graduate centre, might have led to more independence in due course[3].

My proposal on 11 January 1964 included both a greater degree of independence for the new Society and a greater degree of interdependence with the college. The former would be achieved as a semi-autonomous institute within Clare, having its own director and eventually its own bursar, and having its own fund-raising capability – and, by implication, management of any funds that were raised. The interdependence would be achieved through a council for the institute, which would be chaired by the Master of Clare and would include the director of the institute and equal numbers of fellows of the institute and fellows of Clare College. By implication the fellows of the institute would not be fellows of Clare College, though this was not spelt out explicitly. However, I thought that it was essential that the fellows of the institute should have a common purpose – and this was to be achieved, in part, by their function in nominating the visiting fellows and research fellows and generally helping in the selection process. More importantly, they would provide an ongoing social and intellectual focus for the institute attractive enough to be welcoming to visiting fellows and their families.

Although the word 'institute' was dropped from the title of the new centre, the idea that Clare Hall would be a semi-autonomous society within Clare College, governed by a joint council, drawn equally from fellows of Clare and fellows of Clare Hall, survived the discussions of the committee of three in the Lent term 1964, and was included in our report to the governing body of Clare College on 6 March 1964. Our report confirmed the main categories of fellows – permanent, research and visiting, referring to their role as hosts to a succession of visiting scholars.

---

[3] The Clare College accommodation for undergraduates on the Chesterton Lane – Castle Hill site (the site initially proposed for the graduate extension) began to be called the 'Colony' during the 1960s – a name that is now firmly established.

This time, however, we were explicit about the status of the proposed new fellows in relation to Clare College, and we noted

> the fellows of Clare Hall would have to be called bye-fellows of the College; otherwise they would, under the statutes of 1926, have a place on the governing body.

INTERIM ARRANGEMENTS

When it approved the report of the committee of three at its meeting on 6 March 1964, the governing body acted on our proposals for interim arrangements by appointing the Clare Hall working committee. This committee was empowered to transform itself into the Clare Hall provisional council by co-opting five persons approved by the governing body as class F fellows of Clare Hall and bye-fellows of Clare College[4].

Before going on leave to the United States for the Easter term 1964, the Master had asked one of the law fellows, Colin Turpin, to prepare a draft of changes to the Statutes of Clare College that would be required if it was to include a partly autonomous Clare Hall within the society. Turpin wrote his report during the Easter vacation, completing it early in April 1964, just in time for the first meeting of the Clare Hall working committee, (see chapter 9). He found that the changes required to the college statutes were quite extensive because provision had to be made for a new class of fellows who would not be on the foundation of the college, and in some measure for the separate government of the new institution.

His memorandum went on to list about 50 amendments or additions to the Statutes that would be required for the incorporation of Clare Hall into Clare College. Although these amendments later ceased to be relevant to the establishment of Clare Hall, they included one feature which was to be important in leading to a change of direction during the summer of 1964. This feature arose from the first item listed in the Turpin memorandum:

---

[4] Classes A to E were the existing fellows of Clare College: A being research fellows, B teaching fellows and college officers, C professorial fellows, D fellows who had passed the retiring age but whose long service (20 years) entitled them to be life-fellows, and E non-stipendiary fellows. The proposed new classes of fellow relating to Clare Hall were: F official fellows, G research fellows, and H visiting fellows.

A new Statute should be introduced after the present Statute 8, to read as follows:

9. *Of Bye-Fellows*

(1) There shall be in the College such Classes of Bye-Fellowships as the governing body may from time to time determine.
(2) Bye-Fellows shall not be on the foundation of the College and shall not be members of the governing body.
    A Fellow who is elected to a Bye-Fellowship shall thereby cease to be a Fellow, and a Bye-Fellow who is elected to a Fellowship shall thereby cease to be a Bye-Fellow.
(3) Subject to the provision of these Statutes, the periods, conditions, and privileges of tenure of Bye-Fellowships of any Class may be determined or varied by the governing body at any time.

A large part of the time of the Clare Hall working committee was concerned with reviewing and revising a report prepared in three stages by Kingsford. The general description of the constitution of Clare Hall and its operation was set out in five sections under the headings: constitution, government, finance, rooms, and interim arrangements. The final version was agreed on 12 June at the eighth meeting of the committee and the Master undertook to circulate it to the governing body of the college for their meeting on 15 July 1964, which would also include an oral report about the site, the choice of architect, fellowships and endowment. The report has been outlined in chapter 9, and it would have been discussed at the meeting of the governing body in July though there is no mention of it in the minutes[5].

The proposed interim arrangements related mainly to the provisional council of Clare Hall and its role in further development. This council was to come into being upon the election of the first five fellows of Clare Hall and to remain in being until the annual meeting of the governing body of the college in May 1965, the month when normal changes and elections were made to committees, when it might be extended. It would consist of the Master (as Chairman), the Warden of Clare Hall, when chosen, the six

---

[5] In a separate item of the Agenda for the meeting of the GB on 15 July 1964, the needs committee reported on the provision for research students in Clare College (specifically, the purchase of the St. Regis block of apartments in Chesterton Road), this important item – complementary to the decision to found Clare Hall – was also omitted from the minutes of the meeting. Copies of these documents from my own records have now been added to the archives in Clare College.

members of the existing working committee with five initial fellows-designate of Clare Hall to be chosen by the governing body of the college; nominations for those who may become these five fellows to be made jointly by the working committee and the fellowship committee of the college.

The role of the provisional council would be subject to any changes that might be decided by the governing body. With this proviso, it would be empowered to recommend to the governing body the person to be designated as the (first) Warden. It would also be empowered to recommend to the finance committee the first stage of the building to be undertaken, and to propose to the governing body further names for election to fellowships (designate) of Clare Hall. Its members would have corporate lunching rights in the college (e.g. in the Small Hall) and dining rights once a week (in the Master's dining room, by his invitation).

In the longer term it was intended that the provisional council would become the council of Clare Hall. It would continue to include 6 fellows of Clare College and 6 fellows of Clare Hall (the latter being bye-fellows of Clare College). The council would be responsible for managing Clare Hall, partly through delegated authority and partly through recommendations to the governing body of the college. The Clare Hall representatives on the council would be elected annually by the whole of the fellowship of Clare Hall, who would otherwise have a relatively slight involvement in its management

There was an emergency meeting of the governing body on 25 June to elect the initial five fellows of Clare Hall (see chapter 9). Thus they had already been elected when the report of the Clare Hall working committee reached the governing body on 15 July 1964. An additional important point had meanwhile been made by the bursar, Brian Cooper, who observed that the women's colleges might be alarmed at a general change to the Statutes of Clare College to allow for the admission of women members, and he suggested that it would be both courteous and politic to consult them[6].

---

[6] The interdependence of the colleges and the university in Cambridge gives a group of members of the Regent House the legal power to delay, and sometimes prevent, any change in statute by the university or by another college.

THE BYE-FELLOWSHIPS PROBLEM

The transition of the concept of Clare Hall from a centre for advanced study within Clare College to an Approved Foundation did not begin to be considered until a few days after the first meeting of the provisional council which was held on 22 July 1964. This meeting was attended by members of the former working committee and by the five new fellows-designate of Clare Hall. The report of the working committee outlined in chapter 9 was discussed but only minor amendments were suggested including a recommendation that President would be a better title than Warden.

After the meeting the Master asked Colin Turpin to prepare a draft of the required changes to the Clare College Statutes – which were expected to be an update of his original draft prepared over the Easter vacation. However, it was only at this stage – in discussions with Turpin – that Ashby fully appreciated one of the consequences of the proposed arrangement that fellows of Clare Hall would be bye-fellows of Clare College and therefore not on the governing body. The problem was that bye-fellows of a college would not be recognised as fellows by the university and therefore such a college appointment would not lead to membership of the university's Regent House, unless they had qualified through some other appointment, for example through holding a university teaching post. The same lack of status was observed by Mary Hesse, a fellow-designate of Clare Hall, and she wrote about it to Ashby immediately after the meeting of 22 July. She also noted that the proposed constitution would result in a subsidiary role for fellows of Clare Hall in its government – this contrasted unfavourably with the status of fellows of all other Colleges who were *ex officio* members of their governing bodies.

As with many aspects of the founding of Clare Hall, Ashby's role was pivotal in the subsequent developments that allowed it eventually to become an independent college with its own Royal Charter. He had been on leave of absence during the Easter Term of 1964, so he had not been present during the discussions on the constitution in which the working committee considered ways to amend the Statutes of Clare College so that Clare Hall would be founded as a centre within the College. Thus it came as a surprise when he learnt that a bye-fellow would not have the same status in the University as a fellow. Moreover, simply calling them fellows of Clare Hall would not give them the desired status since Clare Hall itself, being part of Clare College, would not have separate recognition by the University

Ashby explained the dilemma – as he saw it – in a memorandum to members of the provisional council dated 28 July 1964, in which he took account of both the points raised by Hesse. Characteristically, having identified a problem he also suggested in the same memorandum some changes that he thought could provide a possible solution. After observing that there was a need for guidance before changes of Statutes could be drafted, Ashby's memorandum read as follows:

1. On one hand the college has always intended that fellowship in Classes F and G[7] should be recognised by the university as equivalent to any other college fellowship (e.g. for inclusion in the Roll of the Regent House under Statute A,III,(3)). We have been advised that to ensure this we should omit the title "bye-fellow of Clare College", and describe the fellows of Clare Hall simply as fellows in Classes F and G. On the other hand one of the purposes of the college in proposing the pattern for Clare Hall was to extend the society without increasing the size of the governing body. We have been advised that this is quite simple: fellows in Classes F and G would be entitled, according to the Act of 1923, to join the governing body if a change of statute is to be enacted, but they would not otherwise take part in the government of Clare College, nor be members of its governing body. Nor would this arrangement affect the division of lunching and dining rights between fellows in Classes A-E in Clare College and fellows in Classes F and G in Clare Hall. As for visiting fellows, they are already provided for in the college statutes (15) and they can be invited under this Statute either by Clare College or Clare Hall. We do not need, therefore, to incorporate in the statutes fellowships in Class H.

Accordingly I should like to know whether you would agree that wherever "bye-fellow" appears in the general statement it should be replaced by "fellows in Classes F and G". These will simply be two additional categories of fellowships of the college, tenable at Clare Hall, and known as fellows (Clare Hall), together with visiting fellows, who are not recognised as "actual" fellows under the Act.

2. The second point concerns the internal government of Clare Hall. According to the general statement the fellows in Classes F and G meet together only in order to elect representatives on the Clare Hall council. In making this suggestion the working committee assumed (I think) that Clare Hall would be a society of scholars not wishing to spend much of their time in college

---

[7] Official fellows and research fellows of Clare Hall.

administration; but it does now seem desirable that the *whole* body of fellows F and G should take part in (i) recommending the name of a President, (ii) recommending elections to fellowships in Classes F and G, (iii) inviting visiting fellows to Clare Hall, and (iv) electing representatives to any committees to which they may delegate responsibility.

A simple way to achieve this would be to include *all* fellows in classes F and G on the Clare Hall council and to regard this council as the governing body of Clare Hall. (There would be complications in calling it a "governing body" while it is still legally part of Clare College). There is precedent for having governing bodies with extraneous members, so the presence of six fellows elected by the governing body from classes B, C and E would be quite proper (i.e. six of the 'full' fellows of Clare College).

This body should reserve to itself the functions (i) to (iv) set out above. It would doubtless wish to delegate the day-to-day affairs of the Hall to an executive committee. The statutes should therefore entitle the Clare Hall council to delegate responsibility (except (i) to (iv) above and any other powers it wishes to retain) to an executive committee of a size and composition to be determined by the council.

If this suggestion is adopted, the governing body of Clare College would comprise fellows A-E with the addition of fellows F and G when a change of statute has to be enacted. The Clare Hall council would be the effective governing body of Clare Hall and would comprise fellows F and G with the addition of six fellows elected by the governing body from among fellows B, C and E (A-fellows are research fellows and D-fellows are retired). This council could in turn delegate all but four of its responsibilities to an executive committee elected by itself. The Master would be chairman of the council.

Ashby's memorandum concluded by asking members of the provisional council whether they would be willing to see draft statutes drawn up which embodied the suggested pattern of government.

It was an unusual misjudgement for Ashby to suppose that such radical changes could be decided by correspondence, and – more seriously – to suppose that they would be acceptable to the fellows of Clare College. His memorandum met with robust opposition from two of the fellows of Clare College on the Provisional Council (Northam and Cooper – see below). In contrast he had a favourable response from four of the fellows-designate of Clare Hall, each of whom wrote to Ashby welcoming his suggestions. Mary Hesse also welcomed the suggestion to abandon the bye-fellowships idea, but she rightly observed that the proposed new arrangements would imply a permanent subsidiary role for Clare Hall within Clare College, and she thought that the aim should be for a partnership, which could be achieved by greater symmetry between representation on the governing bodies of the college and the hall.

Northam responded to the Ashby memorandum by letter on 31 July, expressing his concern about the prospect at some stage in the future of the fellows of Clare Hall dominating the governing body of the college and outvoting the fellowship of the college on the enactment of statutes. He also criticised Ashby's second point concerning the government of Clare Hall, where the six fellows of the college would be a minority from an early date. He argued that the existing proposals were balanced and viable, whereas Ashby's new proposals promised all sorts of problems in the future. Surprisingly, Northam's letter did not make the obvious point that it was inconceivable that Ashby's new proposal would be acceptable to the governing body[8].

Ashby's reply to Northam on 1 August said that he would try to get in touch for a talk about these issues, but in the meantime in his letter he sought to allay Northam's concerns. He made it clear that he only recently became aware of the limitations on the status of bye-fellows when he came to read the Act, and he suggested that the Provisional Council had also been unaware of this[9]. In addition, he argued that Northam's fears were groundless since the number of Clare Hall fellows could be limited. He continued:

Since the one danger you mention has no substance, I feel I must say (to use a Reddawayism) that I am implacably opposed to anything which makes Clare Hall fellows even seem to be inferior in status, let alone really to be inferior in status, to other fellows in Clare or elsewhere. The device of calling them bye-fellows not only makes them seem inferior, but actually condemns them to be inferior. For instance, they have no status under Statute A,III,3 *(of the University)*, and this[10],

---

[8] I did not respond to Ashby's memorandum, except through discussion with Northam. I thought that Ashby's proposals were unlikely to be accepted by the fellows of Clare College, but I was content to observe developments without expressing any preferences of my own, because I thought the momentum behind the Clare Hall proposal was sufficient to ensure that the main objectives of the Society would be achieved whatever form of constitution was adopted.

[9] Ashby commented 'the working committee must have been nodding on this point'; evidently he did not wish to allow the possibility that we were aware of the point but considered it to be unimportant.

[10] This statute ensured that fellows on the governing bodies of colleges would be members of the university's Regent House.

to my mind, would be quite intolerable, and would irrevocably damage the status of the Society. You ask how many Cambridge fellows would depend on election to Clare Hall fellowships to get on to the Regent House Roll. The answer is that even if only one were to depend on this, the whole prestige of the society would collapse if we were unable to grant him this privilege.

In conclusion, Ashby suggested having a discussion (with Northam) as soon as possible, but said that rather than tolerate the device of bye-fellows he would prefer a complete split, with the recognition of Clare Hall as a separate society like Darwin – adding that he 'thought a complete split at this stage would be a tragic end to a fascinating experiment'[11]. He sought to reinforce his case by encouraging Turpin to write in support of his approach – though Turpin's subsequent letter to Northam was worded with his usual moderation and provided no new arguments. There is a contemporary note written by Northam in the margin of Ashby's letter to him, to the effect that the committee should have been aware of the limitations of the bye-fellowship status since he (Northam) had said this. This and other marginal notes show that he was unpersuaded by Ashby's arguments.

A few days after his second letter to Northam, Ashby received letters from four of the fellows-designate of Clare Hall welcoming the idea that they should be full fellows of Clare College, though Taylor had reservations about whether the other changes suggested by Ashby would be feasible in practice. The same issues of practical feasibility were noted by the bursar, Brian Cooper, in a letter dated 5 August. He also opposed Ashby's suggestion that fellows of Clare Hall should be full fellows of Clare College rather than bye-fellows. He received an immediate reply from Ashby giving the same arguments on status that had been unsuccessful in persuading Northam. However, on the more general issue of government of Clare Hall, Ashby said that he hoped that statutes could be devised that would allow a gradual evolution of Clare Hall to increasing independence, having in mind ultimate full independence

---

[11] At this stage (1 August 1964), Ashby may not have been fully aware of the option for Clare Hall to become an Approved Foundation – a constitutional subtlety of the Cambridge scene. An Approved Foundation is recognised by the University for most purposes in the same way as a college (though without a Royal Charter and not fully independent). Churchill College was initially an Approved Foundation for several years, and for University College and Darwin College this status was under consideration by the Council of the Senate in the Easter Term of 1964 when Ashby was on leave in the United States.

though he said he hoped this would be a long way off. He thought there should be further discussions on options before any decisions were taken.

Ashby's response defending his position was countered by an immediate and forthright letter from Cooper, to the effect that the bye-fellowship concept had been fully discussed and was crucial to the enlargement of the fellowship. He noted *inter alia* that Richard Eden had mentioned repeatedly the necessity of a departmental tie-up for fellows – a relationship with the university that should be sufficient. His view was that we wanted academic scholars as fellows – not status-seekers or academic politicians. Finally he observed that Ashby's proposals involved such a fundamental change that they would require a full review by the Clare College Council before proceeding further.

Most members of the working committee at their meetings in May and June would have been aware of the status (or lack of status) of bye-fellows in relation to the university, but they did not think it was important. The objective of Clare Hall was to provide an attractive college environment for members of the university faculties who did not have college fellowships. It would have been assumed that their status in the university was already ensured by their faculty appointments. This was true for all members of the working committee, and it applied to all five fellows-designate of Clare Hall. However, Ashby himself was an exception to this rule since he did not hold a post in the university, and his own membership of the Regent House was dependent on the university Statute A,III,3 which stated that the Roll of the Regent House should include Heads of colleges and fellows. Thus he could appreciate the importance of university recognition for fellows of Clare Hall, which he correctly argued would not be achieved by bye-fellowships of the college.

The exchange of letters between Ashby and others took place early in August 1964, and I went away on a family holiday soon afterwards, so did not meet with Ashby again until some time in September. Ashby's initial discovery of the bye-fellowships problem had come from Turpin and was confirmed by discussions with Trevor Thomas, the Bursar of St. John's who had been a colleague of Ashby on the Council of the Senate and was a considerable expert on the interpretation of Statutes and Ordinances. At some stage, probably during August, Ashby discovered that the institutional arrangements in the University for an Approved Foundation might provide an option for Clare Hall. It is clear from the minutes of the second meeting of the Provisional Council, held on 21 September, that Ashby had been exploring this concept as a means of resolving the conflict between the desires of the fellows-designate of Clare Hall for full fellowship status and the views of Clare College fellows on the need to limit the size of their governing body. It is likely that he had discovered this option as a result of further discussions with Trevor Thomas, whom he had often consulted in relation to archaic Cambridge rules and practices. In particular, he concluded that the relationship of Clare College with Clare Hall could be satisfactorily maintained if Clare Hall was to become an Approved Foundation with Clare College as the Trustee.

From his subsequent correspondence with the Registrary[12] of the University (Rattenbury) and others, it is evident that Ashby was initially expecting that the legal role of Trustee would provide a permanent formal relationship between Clare College and Clare Hall, within which other formal and informal arrangements could be established. Government by a joint council would be replaced by a two-level system involving fellows of the college as trustees and fellows of Clare Hall as its governing body. Apart from this governmental change, there was an expectation of a close and enduring relationship, which would retain all the essential features that had been planned for Clare Hall as a semi-autonomous institution within Clare College. Subsequent discussions with the Registrary show that, at this stage, Ashby was probably over-estimating the role of the Trustees in the government of an Approved Foundation. However, his enthusiasm for founding Clare Hall remained undiminished as he conducted a series of revisions of the draft trust deed to allow it a sufficient degree of independence to meet the requirements of the university for an Approved Foundation. Although most of the formal and informal arrangements proved to be less permanent than had been expected, they were very important during the formative years from 1964–69 when the success of Clare Hall certainly justified the change of view by Ashby between the beginning of August and mid-September 1964 and the subsequent decisions of the provisional council.

---

[12] The Registrary is (inter alia) the Secretary of the Council of the Senate.

AN APPROVED FOUNDATION

Ashby's memo of 28 July was only briefly considered when he chaired the second meeting of the provisional council on 21 September. Ashby asked the council to note that there was a new possibility that Clare Hall might, without severing its links with Clare College, become one of the proposed Approved Societies with Clare College as Trustee, with the consequence that a fellowship of Clare Hall would be fully recognised by the university. The fellows-designate of Clare Hall indicated that they would favour this possibility, and with this in mind it was agreed that the formulation of statutes be deferred. In view of the consequent delays in completing formalities relating to the government of Clare Hall, it was suggested that it might be desirable in the interim for the provisional council (not necessarily with the same members) to continue in being for some period beyond May 1965.

Immediately after this meeting Ashby wrote informally to the Registrary of the University asking for a discussion on the options for Clare Hall, and indicated that the preference appeared to be for an Approved Society that retained some formal links with Clare College. As an example, he suggested that the college might be the Trustee for the new foundation.

A month later, at the next meeting of the provisional council (on 27 October) Ashby reported that, following discussions with the Registrary, it appeared that recognition as an Approved Society would not be inconsistent with the preservation of a formal affiliation between Clare Hall and Clare College. This option was discussed at the Clare governing body meeting on 23 November 1964, and the minutes record that:

> (iv) Over the constitution of Clare Hall it was agreed that the following suggestion should be pursued: that Clare Hall should seek to become an Approved Foundation or Society, with Clare College as trustee exercising some continuing powers over Clare Hall but providing it with a large measure of autonomy in the management of its own affairs.

Ashby reported this decision to the provisional council on 8 December. The finance committee would draw up a draft Trust Deed, which would be submitted for comment to the provisional council, and when agreed would be submitted to the governing body for approval. After approval, the Trust Deed would go to the Council of the Senate, with the application for recognition of Clare Hall as an Approved Foundation.

One consequence of this change of direction towards greater independence of Clare Hall was that the provisional council would remain in existence for a longer period. At the same time, the consideration of candidates for President of Clare Hall became a lower priority. I assumed then that the Master wanted to be more certain of the form of Clare Hall and its relationship with the college before encouraging the choice of a President. The delay (until June 1965) also provided an opportunity for the fellows-designate of Clare Hall to get to know each other and to develop closer relations with the fellows of the college.

Meanwhile, Ashby in consultation with the bursar and the finance committee began work on the preparation of a draft Trust Deed for the establishment of Clare Hall as an Approved Foundation. The early drafts show a proposed level of financial control that was quite detailed and would never have survived scrutiny by the Registrary of the university. However, many of these details were acquired from the earlier proposed arrangement in which Clare Hall would be a centre for advanced study within Clare College and, in addition to the land and a capital allowance for buildings in Herschel Road, the finance committee had planned to make an annual subvention for running costs. Clearly they would not have been able to give any open-ended commitment with such arrangements.

However, after the concept of Clare Hall as an Approved Foundation became clearer, the finance committee decided that they would set aside £450,000 from the funds of the college, to be earmarked as a Trust Fund for Clare Hall, part to cover the cost of the buildings and the balance to be used as capital to provide an endowment income which would be at the disposal of the governing body of Clare Hall. Under these circumstances the Trust Deed would not need to protect the college so carefully against open-ended commitments for annual expenditure, and it was therefore possible to reduce the detailed control. Some of these changes towards a greater degree of financial independence for Clare Hall were made prior to submission of a draft Deed to the Council of the Senate; some were made following suggestions from a committee of the Council. The latter changes were offered in a letter from Ashby to the Registrary on 4 November 1965, in which he also suggested that he and Pippard (the President-designate of Clare Hall) should appear before the committee to explain the intention of the Trust Deed and discuss the proposed amendments. In the event, they went to talk to the Registrary, rather than the committee itself.

The concerns of the Council of the Senate related in part to the fact that Clare College would be the sole Trustee for Clare Hall. These concerns were met by including in the Trust Deed a clause that allowed for the lifting of financial controls at the request of the governing body of Clare Hall after a period of fourteen years, or by mutual consent after a period of between seven and fourteen years. After the same period, if so requested by Clare Hall, the power to make changes in the Regulations and Ordinances governing the conduct of the Society would pass from Clare College to Clare Hall.

Clare Hall was constitutionally established as an Approved Foundation in the university on Monday 7 February 1966. This was achieved through a Grace recognising Clare Hall which was approved in the Regent House on Saturday 12 February, with the recognition backdated to the day when the governing body of Clare College sealed a Trust Deed establishing the Hall as a Society with the Master, Fellows and Scholars of Clare College as Trustees. The Trust Deed had been sealed on 7 February, and on the same day the Trustees elected the first President, Professor A. B. Pippard, and the first eighteen fellows.

TRUST DEED, 1966

The Trust Deed was made on 7 February 1966 by the Master, Fellows and Scholars of Clare College in the University of Cambridge. The preamble states that it has been decided by the said Master, Fellows and Scholars to found a new Society in the said University to be named Clare Hall, hereinafter referred to as "the Society"; that one hundred pounds has already been paid into a Trust Fund and it is apprehended that further moneys investments and properties will be transferred to the Trustees from divers sources; that the deed is executed in order to declare the trusts upon which these (endowments) are to be held.

The objects of the Trust were to found a new Society in Cambridge for the advancement of education learning and research among advanced scholars and graduate and research students in the university and to maintain carry on administer and endow that Society; and to make such provision for the status of the Society within the university as the Trustees may from time to time think requisite and to advance education learning and research in the university in such other ways as may seem to them (the

Trustees) expedient but subject to clause three hereof. Clause three stated that the establishment and maintenance of the Society is the primary object of the Trust and only if there is a surplus may the other objectives be pursued.

Clause six allowed the Trustees to apply to the university for recognition of the Society as an Approved Foundation or for the grant to the Society of any other status in the university as may seem appropriate; it further allowed them to apply or concur in any application for the incorporation of the Society by Royal Charter, and to cause the Society to be incorporated as a Company under the Companies Acts. If either incorporation was to take place, the Trustees may transfer to the incorporated body the whole or part of the Trust Fund as they may think fit.

Clause seven was an enabling clause that allowed the Trustees to carry out the objects of the Trust by purchasing selling or developing land or property, by employing staff and providing fellowships or studentships etc. and by seeking further donations and endowments. Clauses eight and nine relate to investment procedures, specifically allowing Clare Hall to take shares in a pool of charitable Trust Funds (thus allowing the Clare Hall and Clare College to share an investment pool). The Trustees were required to keep accounts in a form acceptable to the university.

The internal administration of Clare Hall, unless varied by the Trustees, would be vested in the Governing Body which would consist of the President and all Fellows of the Society except Visiting Fellows and Honorary Fellows and would have power to delegate any of its functions and powers to any body constituted by regulations as specified in clause thirteen.

Regulations were to be of two types: (a) regulations which at the sole and absolute discretion of the Trustees shall be considered to touch or concern the financial administration or financial control of the Society or any disposal or dealing with the Trust Fund (in the deed, these were subsequently called "Regulations"); (b) all other regulations, which were to be called "Ordinances". The first regulations and ordinances were to be drawn up by the Trustees after consultation with the President-designate and fellows-designate of Clare Hall.

Clause sixteen allowed the Trustees to make changes in Regulations after consultation with the Governing Body (of Clare Hall) and allowed the Governing Body to make changes in the Ordinances after consultation with the Trustees. It also included the important provision, noted earlier, that allowed for the lifting of financial controls at the request of the Governing Body of Clare Hall after a period of fourteen years, or by mutual consent after a period of between seven and fourteen years. After the same period, if so requested by Clare Hall, the power to make changes in the Regulations and Ordinances governing the conduct of the Society would pass from Clare College to Clare Hall.

GOVERNING BODY AND COMMITTEES

After sealing the Trust Deed on 7 February 1966, the Master and Fellows of Clare College, meeting as Trustees, agreed to appoint Professor A. B. Pippard as President of Clare Hall, and to elect as fellows: nine (official) fellows, one professorial fellow, five research fellows, and three visiting fellows.

The provisional council held its final meeting on 8 February with the Master of Clare in the chair. They noted the sealing of the Trust Deed and the subsequent elections by the Trustees. After this the Master formally dissolved the provisional council.

After thanking the fellows of Clare College for their work on the provisional council, the President of Clare Hall invited the bursar (Cooper) to attend meetings of the governing body when financial matters were discussed, and Holister similarly for buildings. Kingsford, who had been Secretary of the provisional council, had agreed to continue to help during the development phase as Secretary of the governing body.

The Trust Deed included clauses providing for Regulations and Ordinances which would establish the rules under which the President and Fellows of Clare Hall should manage the society. Regulations were defined as those clauses that, in the view of the Trustees, concerned financial administration and control. Ordinances related to other clauses and it was not at all clear which was which. This may seem to imply draconian control by the Trustees; however, in practice there was evidently a more relaxed approach as is indicated by a note from Ashby in January 1969 saying that Clare Hall was asking for its Ordinances, which had yet to be approved by the Trustees, and adding that they were last heard of (by Ashby) when they were sent to the lawyers some two years earlier.

Meanwhile, the management of Clare Hall continued to be divided between the College and the Hall until the completion of the new buildings. With their completion in the summer of 1969, Clare Hall acquired its own staff, and for most purposes its management was independent of Clare College. The most important exception was that the investments committee of Clare College continued to manage the joint portfolio for the endowments of both College and Hall. However, there remained a further major change in the constitutional relationship between the College and the Hall, which led in 1984 to independence of Clare Hall and its recognition by the University as a fully established college. This change of status was achieved through an application for a Royal Charter.

ROYAL CHARTER, 1984

The Royal Charter for Clare Hall was approved by the Queen in Council on 12 September 1984 and the Royal Charter was subsequently sealed on 22 October.

The initiative for the change of status from Approved Foundation to a college with a Royal Charter came in 1981 from Sir Michael Stoker in his first year as the President of Clare Hall. He had been a fellow of Clare College from 1948 to 1958 and became an honorary fellow in 1976. On taking early retirement from his post as Director of the Imperial Cancer Research Laboratories, he had been elected a fellow of Clare Hall in 1978. Thus he was well placed to see the benefits of negotiating independence for Clare Hall whilst many of the fellows of Clare College who had taken part in the foundation were still active participants in the college.

There was no problem about gaining the support of the governing body of Clare Hall for this move and having gained approval in principle from Clare College a committee was formed to prepare proposals for the new Statutes and Ordinances. In 1983 the Master, Fellows and Scholars of Clare College petitioned the Queen for a Charter of Incorporation to Clare Hall and this was approved the following year. The grant of Charter began:

1. The first President and first fellows of Clare Hall and all such persons as may hereafter become members of the Body Corporate by the name and style of "The President and Fellows of Clare Hall in the University of Cambridge"

(hereinafter referred to as "the College") and by the same name shall have perpetual succession and a Common Seal with power to break, alter and make anew the said Seal from time to time at their will and by the same name shall and may sue and be sued in all Courts and before all Justices of Us, Our Heirs and Successors.

Clause 2 provided corporate rights to hold and manage property within the law.

3. The college is incorporated and shall be conducted with the following objects:
   (1) to advance education, learning and research in the University of Cambridge;
   (2) to provide for men and women who shall be members of the university a college wherein they may work for postgraduate degrees in the university or may carry out postgraduate or other special studies at Cambridge provided no member of the college and no candidate for membership thereof shall be subject to any test of a religious or social character;
   (3) to acquire and take over the properties and liabilities of the Approved Foundation now vested in the trustees;
   (4) to apply the moneys of the college including any money acquired or taken over as aforesaid to the objects of the college with power to invest as prescribed by the Statutes of the college;
   (5) to administer any trust or scheme for purposes connected with the objects of the college;
   (6) to do all such things as are incidental or conducive to the carrying out of the above objects.

Further clauses provided for the appointment of Sir Robert Megarry, Vice-Chancellor of the Supreme Court as the first Visitor to the College. His successors would be the Vice-Chancellors of the Supreme Court from time to time[13]. Another clause appointed as first President of the College, "Our trusty and well-beloved Sir Michael George Parke Stoker, Knight Commander of Our Most Excellent Order of the British Empire, Fellow of the Royal Society". Fellows of the Approved Foundation would be the first Fellows of the College. The Statutes of the College would apply to the first President and the first Fellows, and subsequent elections would be as prescribed in the Statutes.

The foregoing clauses were confirmed by the Queen on the twenty-second day of October in the thirty-third year of her Reign (22 October 1984).

---

[13] The Visitor may be called on to settle an internal dispute that cannot be resolved by the Governing Body.

The Statutes that were approved with the Royal Charter set out the constitution of the college and the procedures under which it is to function. Thus: there shall be a governing body, a council, a finance committee and such other committees and sub-committees as may be established and to whom authority may be delegated by authority of these statutes. The governing body would include all fellows (except visiting, emeritus and honorary fellows) and two graduate students.

The main group of permanent fellows, are under title A and called official fellows, usually holding faculty appointments in the university (or being a college officer), except professors who would be under title B, professorial fellows. Title C would be research fellows, usually appointed for three years. A fellow who had taken early retirement from a university or college post under which he or she had become a fellow in title A or B, could be elected under title D, supernumerary fellows. Fellows would retire at the end of the academic year in which they attained the age of sixty seven years. The President would be elected for a period of seven years and must be under the age of sixty three when elected.

The College Officers specified in the Statutes are: the vice-president, the bursar, the senior tutor and the tutors, the steward, the praelector, but the governing body is empowered to create other Offices that may qualify a member for election as an official fellow. The duties of each of the College Officers are outlined in general terms but include such other duties as shall be determined by the governing body.

Separate chapters of the statutes define the procedures and functions of the governing body and the committees. Further chapters define procedures for other categories of member of the college: visiting fellows, honorary fellows and emeritus fellows; senior members; and graduate students. Other chapters deal with discipline; the keeping of accounts powers of investment etc.; leave of absence; changes of statutes; the common seal; and questions of interpretation or validity of proceedings.

Chapter 11

LAND, BUILDINGS AND FINANCE

CLARE LAND IN WEST CAMBRIDGE

Although other items would have been considered, only one item was recorded in the minutes for the Clare College governing body meeting on 7 January 1963:

> The question of the disposal of a piece of land to the west of the University Library was discussed.

This land, owned by Clare, amounted to three quarters of an acre adjacent to Grange Road, and in the 1950s it was used as a tennis court by members of the college, additional to those at the (new) Clare sports field off Bentley Road. Earlier, this land had been part of a larger sports area including the Clare-King's cricket ground where the University Library now stands. The whole area had been taken over in 1914 during the Great War for a large temporary 'Eastern General Hospital'. Patients were brought to it by road from the railway sidings that had been constructed to the south of Cambridge station. In the housing shortage following the war, the wooden huts of the disused hospital were occupied by squatters until 1926–27, when they were displaced to allow the construction of the University Library[1].

By January 1963, it was evident that Clare might require building land reasonably close to the Memorial Court at some stage in the future. The fellows were therefore unwilling to give up our Grange Road tennis courts without some nearby land in exchange. The issue had been raised a year or so earlier by a request from the university to purchase the Clare land in order to obtain planning permission for building an extension to the University Library. Although, the university had no immediate intention

---

[1] Godwin, *Cambridge and Clare* (Cambridge 1985).

to build on the Clare land, and it was suggested that we might be able to continue to use it for tennis, its ownership by the university was essential to meet the planning regulations on the ratio between buildings and land areas. At a governing body meeting, the bursar was asked to take a tough line in his negotiations with the university authorities. It is interesting to note that, wearing different hats, both the bursar and the Master were on the relevant university committees.

The resolution of the problem was aided by the fortunate coincidence that the Vice-Chancellor at the time, the Rev. Boys-Smith was the Master of St. John's College, and had previously been bursar of his college. He therefore saw practical advantages to all parties of a triangular exchange[2]. Clare would sell the Grange Road land to the university, the university would sell the Divinity School (located directly opposite to the main gates of St. John's) to St. John's College, and the latter would sell to Clare the freehold of the land in Herschel Road on which Clare Hall now stands. At the time, there were three large houses on this land. There were long leases, nearing their end, for the land occupied by Elmside on the corner of Grange and Herschel Road, and for Huntley at 3 Herschel Road. However, Herschel House at 1 Herschel Road was owned by St. John's, and was divided into flats which were let on short leases, which could be terminated with six months notice[3]. The total area amounted to about three acres in all.

It was planned that St. John's would lease the Divinity School back to the university for a period of 25 years, during which time a new building would be provided for the Faculty of Divinity, eventually – it was thought – enabling St. John's to redevelop the site of the old building. Alas for these intentions – times changed! The optimism associated with rapid growth in education in the 1960s and general expectations of future national prosperity received a set-back in the 1970s with the oil crisis and

---

[2] Holister was at the meeting and has told me that it was Ashby who made the suggestion of the triangular exchange. Boys-Smith, since he was there in his role as Vice-Chancellor, said that he thought the university would be interested in seeking such a solution, but he added that he was uncertain how the Master of St. John's College (himself) might respond. Later, in the latter capacity, he gave his support to the proposal.

[3] The bursar of Clare (Cooper) had approached St. John's earlier about the Herschel Road land before the triangular deal was worked out. He had also found a property in Newnham that (subsidised by Clare) could be let at a nominal rent to one of the tenants of a flat in Herschel House.

198   *Land, buildings and finance*

the economic recession. The consequent reduction in capital grants to universities delayed the intended new building for the Faculty of Divinity beyond the 25 year period[4]. Further, the cultural environment changed, so that the old Divinity School acquired a preservation order and any future new development is likely to be severely constrained.

BUILDINGS REQUIRED: FIRST IDEAS

The initial ideas on the requirements for buildings were outlined in the proposal approved on 11 January 1964:

> In the first instance (the required buildings would be) not dissimilar to those already proposed for the Grange Road site, but with more emphasis on visitors' flats and on long term expansion possibilities, although for a major expansion – given sufficient money – a new site might be desirable. In the first instance the fellows of the Institute might lunch in Clare Small Hall or the Parlour and have no other meals provided. Even from a long term viewpoint I am doubtful whether there should be any emphasis on communal dining, but luncheon facilities should be provided at the Institute.

> 15 flats to be shared amongst families and bachelors in class B, C and D fellows, possibly also the Director should live on or near the site in a house provided.
> Dining Room, Common Room, Reading Room and 10 Studies.

The committee of three (Ashby, Northam and Eden) was given a general remit to work out the functions and purpose of the Body referred to in Dr Eden's paper, to recommend how the proposals might be implemented, and to report back to the governing body. I think we all took the view that the details in my paper were illustrative, rather than definitive, and we felt free to vary them as our ideas evolved.

When preparing the first paper for our committee, I was concerned about the need to make the new centre viable in academic terms.

> The Institute must develop an intellectual life of its own. In addition to acting as a centre for a larger community there must be facilities for advanced study and discussion within its walls. It must be the primary place of study for a significant fraction of the fellows, although others will work in university laboratories, libraries and departments.

---

[4] After 35 years, it seems likely that in 1998 a new building for the faculty of divinity will soon be under construction on the university's Sidgwick Avenue site.

With this in mind, I proposed that the number of studies be 20, additional to two administrative offices for the Director and a Secretary. I probably also discussed needs with Volker Heine since I included his earlier suggestion that there should be two dining rooms, one for academics and one for families.

The paper also suggested that the 5 existing flats in Herschel House be retained in addition to 12 flats to be included in the new building in the first stage of the development, and at a later stage – there would be a need to double the number of flats and studies; this might be done by purchasing a nearby site[5]. In 1964, we could be reasonably confident that, given the money and good intentions, there would be no problem about obtaining planning permission for new academic or residential buildings in West Cambridge.

At the first meeting of our committee we agreed to ask both Cooper and Holister to provide us with their estimates for the capital costs and running costs of the proposed first stage of development. Their estimates were to be based on more detailed specifications of the sizes of rooms and apartments, which were later included in our report to the governing body, and which set out the needs for accommodation:

7. *Buildings and accommodation.* We propose that the society should be housed in Herschel Road, and that an architect be appointed to prepare plans. We estimate that the maximum accommodation on the site already in our possession could include twenty flats (varying from single room plus bathroom and kitchen to flats with three bedrooms); twenty studies of different sizes from 100 sq. ft; and communal rooms as follows: reading room, common room, seminar room, dining room for fellows, dining room for family use, kitchen and offices. We think the working committee and the provisional council proposed in paragraph 10 should be left to decide the optimum amount of building to be done on the site in the first stage of development; if it were (for instance) thought advisable to start with 10 flats instead of 20, we believe the new society would nevertheless be viable. On the assumption that building costs will be about 120/- per sq. ft, we estimate that the capital cost for maximum development (22,000 square feet, with 20 flats) would be of the order of £132,000 (excluding fees and furniture). If fewer flats are built the capital cost (but also the income from rents) would be lower.

---

[5] In 1997 this early suggestion that the college might at a later stage purchase a nearby site to allow a significant development was fulfilled with the purchase of 11 Herschel Road.

8. *Annual cost.* This can be estimated only approximately. Our estimate is an annual total of about £17,000 (with 20 flats) or £15,500 (with 10 flats), which includes interest on capital spent on building and purchase of site, rates, office expenses, the cost of commons, and wages for cooking and service. It includes also a deduction for rents received from the flats.

Our report was approved by the governing body at their meeting on 6 March 1964, subject to some amendments relating to an acceptance of graduate students at an earlier date than we had indicated, if possible within about three years of the establishment of Clare Hall. The bursar reported a decision of the finance committee: that the governing body be advised that the provision of finance for the developments envisaged in the report ... would not prejudice other developments considered worthy by the college.

PROPERTIES TO BE ACQUIRED

When the committee of three reported to the governing body in March 1964, there had already been an agreement in principle about the triangular exchange of properties between Clare, St. John's and the University. Clare would be acquiring three houses and their gardens from St. John's: Elmside at 49 Grange Road, and two houses in Herschel Road. Elmside was occupied by Dr A. J. Berry on a 99 year lease expiring 25 Dec.1983. This house had originally been built, and occupied until his death in 1925, by Mr W. W. Rouse Ball, a fellow of Trinity College. Rouse Ball had been second Wrangler and first Smith's prizeman in 1874. He became a barrister and practised in London from 1876–80, also becoming a college lecturer in mathematics at Trinity in 1878 and later tutor in mathematics. He is best known as an historian of mathematics, and within the university for bequeathing an endowment to found two chairs, now known as the Rouse Ball Professorships in English law and in mathematics. Huntley at 3 Herschel Road was built in about 1897 for Mr W. G. Bell an assistant tutor and mathematics lecturer for non-collegiate students. In 1964 it was occupied by Dr Richard Keynes and owned on a 99 year lease expiring in 1996. A physiologist, Dr Keynes was a nephew of the economist Maynard Keynes and a great grandson of Charles Darwin. He was a fellow of Churchill College and later became Professor of Physiology in the university.

Properties to be acquired

Herschel House at 1 Herschel Road had been built in about 1890 for the Revd. John Lock, fellow, bursar and steward of Caius College. By 1964 it was owned by St. John's College and had been divided into five apartments occupied by tenants on six month tenancies. It was on this site that Clare College was planning to build Clare Hall. Initially, prior to the appointment of an architect, no decision was taken about whether to retain the house or pull it down.

Ashby returned to Cambridge in June 1964, after his leave of absence in the United States, and took over as chairman of the Clare Hall working committee at its 8th meeting on 12 June. Although the written approval for the transfers of land and property had not yet been received from the Ministry of Agriculture and Fisheries, there had been good progress on other aspects of planning for Clare Hall and a text of a public announcement had been approved by the committee.

The working committee held a joint meeting with the Clare fellowship committee on 15 June, at which there was agreement on the five first choices for 'fellows-elect' of Clare Hall. Each of these proposed candidates was approached personally by Ashby, who confirmed to the working committee on 22 June that they were all willing to be selected. The minutes of that meeting record:

It was agreed to recommend to the governing body that a general announcement (as drafted, with the addition of a statement that the names of the five initial fellows would shortly be announced) should be released as soon as the tenants of Herschel House had been informed by St. John's, i.e. in a week of two; and that, subject to acceptance by the five initial fellows, a second announcement of their election should be made shortly thereafter.

Ashby offered to approach the tenants of all the properties shortly before any public announcement was made. However, with his agreement, the first notification to each tenant came from the senior bursar of St. John's (Mr T. C. Thomas), followed a few days later by a letter from Ashby. He subsequently called on Dr Berry at Elmside and obtained an agreement in principle for Clare Hall to purchase the remaining lease of a strip of land at the bottom of his garden so as to extend the boundary of Herschel House to the East. He also obtained an agreement from Dr Keynes to negotiate on the sale of land that would extend the boundary to the west. There was no intention at that stage to build on this extra land, but its ownership by the college would allow more intensive building on the site of Herschel House.

The tenants of the five flats in Herschel House all replied expressing their concern at the prospect of having to move, though they were relieved to learn from Ashby that there would be some delay before it would be necessary for Clare to give them any statutory notice. This notice came about a year later in mid 1965, but Ashby's correspondence shows how he was personally concerned to avoid hardship for the tenants, and for more than one resident he made exceptional efforts to arrange for Clare or St. John's to provide alternative accommodation. Clare was able to take possession of all the flats in Herschel House by March 1966 just in time for the hoped-for start of building in April. However, there were other unforeseen causes of delay to which I shall return in a later section.

SCHEDULE OF REQUIREMENTS

In the absence of the Master on leave of absence in the United States during the Easter Term 1964, Professor Godwin was the chairman of the Clare Hall working committee. The selection of an architect was the first item discussed at the first meeting, held on 11 April 1964. Holister informed the committee that he did not wish to act as architect, and there was agreement that the best interests of the college would be served by his availability as a member of the committee. In addition to giving advice and assistance towards choosing an architect, Holister was asked in the second meeting on 6 May to compile a specification of the required building for consideration by the committee. His first draft of requirements and instructions to the architect was considered at the seventh meeting, held on 2 June. It followed the general scheme that had been proposed earlier by the committee of three, in discussion also with Holister, for flats of varying sizes, studies, a seminar room, common room, and dining rooms. Amendments of detail led to three more drafts, the final one being approved on 3 July in time for the visit of Ralph Erskine to discuss the possibility of him acting as the architect.

Holister's paper was entitled 'Schedule of Requirements and Instructions for the Architect.' It began with a general description of the proposed society:

Schedule of requirements

Clare College has decided to promote within the college a new development to be known as Clare Hall. The intention is that Clare Hall shall make a contribution towards meeting current Cambridge needs by providing a new graduate society for resident and visiting scholars. Its fellowship is designed to bring together four categories:

(i) scholars holding appointments in the university or in research institutions in Cambridge, whose subjects may not be in great demand for undergraduate teaching;
(ii) post-doctoral and other senior research workers;
(iii) visiting scholars in Cambridge on study-leave;
(iv) research fellows, elected from among more senior research students. When the new society has been established a body of research students who are not fellows will be added.

It is intended that fellowships of Clare Hall shall be open to men and women on equal terms.

The criterion for membership of this new society is to be a common interest in advanced research and scholarship. The college intends to offer facilities for fellows of Clare Hall to work individually without interruption, to work in groups and to meet one another informally and formally. It is also proposed to provide some residential facilities to enable some of the fellows to live on the site at a reasonable rent. It seems reasonable, therefore, that the buildings to be erected for Clare Hall should be arranged to provide for three main functions and also facilities for administration. The main functions that must be accommodated for are:

1. Academic
2. Social
3. Residential

The accommodation required is described under two stages. In the first stage provision should be made for a fellowship of 40, and, say, 20 research students. In the second stage these numbers might be doubled. It is not possible to prophesy exactly when this increase will occur, but it is reasonable to assume that it will be more than 10 years but less than 15 years from now.

The buildings described under Stage I are to be built initially and must be designed so that they may be conveniently extended or re-arranged in accordance with the requirements of the buildings described under Stage II.

The buildings must form a harmonious complex at both stages of development. The architect is expected to design Stage I bearing in mind the need for the future extensions although, at this stage, he will be expected to submit proposals for the initial development only.

Holister set out the requirements for stage I of the development in some detail. In outline, for academic accommodation these included 18 studies, a seminar room and a reading room. Administrative offices would be required for the President and a secretary. Social and dining facilities were to include a dining room / cafeteria for up to 80 persons, and kitchen facilities to provide up to 120 meals per day, mainly at mid-day. There should also be adequate circulation space for each facility, and lavatories, cloakrooms and cleaners' stores.

Residential accommodation was to be provided on the site for some of the fellows, some of whom would be married with families living on the site. Within the limitations of the site, sixteen flats were suggested, all with kitchen and bathroom: 2 with one large living room/bedroom, 2 with one large living room and one bedroom, 5 similar with two bedrooms, 4 larger flats with three bedrooms, one flat with larger rooms, 4 bedrooms and an additional WC / cloakroom, and a similar flat for the Warden' with more spacious rooms and 4 bedrooms. Finally, there would be a need for a guest unit with four bedrooms, shared bathroom and kitchenette facilities, and a small flat for a college caretaker.

The specification continued:

A laundry room providing communal facilities for the washing, drying and ironing of clothes is to be provided to remove these activities from the flats. One large store room is to be provided to serve all the flats and also a park for about six prams.

The flats are to be of a simple standard of finish but to have all facilities considered necessary today for modern living. For example it is essential that the kitchens are fully equipped with refrigerators, cookers and waste disposal units. As many bedrooms as possible should be designed to hold twin beds if required, so as to give maximum flexibility in use, but otherwise should be minimal in size, but provided with built-in wardrobes.

It is essential that whilst the flats are to be integrated harmoniously with the whole group of buildings, their presence must not constitute a nuisance to people working either in the seminar room or in their private study. To help ensure this a children's play area is to be provided adjacent to the flats but physically separated from the studies, seminar room and reading room.

Car parking space should initially be provided for at least 17 cars, including, if possible, two garages. In the second stage, the car parking space must be doubled.

Racks for 50 bicycles are to be provided.

The specification continued with a description of the site, and emphasised the need for the new buildings to be harmonious with the residential character of the neighbourhood. The basic costs of the proposed buildings were estimated to be less than £125,000, excluding interior furnishings, kitchen equipment and fees[6].

CHOICE OF ARCHITECT: RALPH ERSKINE

The selection of an architect was discussed at the first meeting of the Clare Hall working committee and Kingsford reported on a discussion with Sir Leslie Martin, Professor of Architecture, who had suggested some names for consideration. Other names were suggested by Holister, including Ralph Erskine – a British architect practising in Sweden, whom he had met during a public inquiry into the Cambridge City development plans. Holister was asked to obtain and circulate information about five possible architects or partnerships.

By the fifth meeting of the committee on 19 May, it was evident that Erskine was likely to be the favoured candidate, but a final decision would await photographs of his work. The photographs were considered on 12 June at a meeting chaired by Ashby following his return from sabbatical leave in the United States. It was agreed to recommend to the finance committee that Erskine be invited to visit Cambridge and meet with the committee, and a visit was arranged for 8 to 10 July 1964.

Erskine met with the working committee in the senior fellows' room on E staircase. He had already been briefed on our general aims – to form a community of scholars engaged in research and advanced studies, with buildings to include studies, common rooms and residential accommodation for some of the scholars and their families within the college grounds. His response concentrated on seeking our views on how the society would function in terms of the movement of members – the design should facilitate both informal encounters and the need for privacy, the need for common or private meals and for recreation, for studies, formal meetings or seminars, and for families and children.

There was immediate and unanimous support for the appointment of

---

[6] The costs were eventually more than twice this estimate. However, the total amount of the endowment from Clare College to Clare Hall (to cover the cost of the buildings and provide investment income) was in line with early estimates made by the bursar, Brian Cooper (private communication 1997).

16. Ralph Erskine, circa 1997.
Architect of Clare Hall 1964–69, 1983–85, Honorary Fellow 1997.

Ralph Erskine as the architect for the Clare Hall buildings. Later in his first visit, the five newly-chosen fellows-designate had an opportunity to meet Erskine, who startled them by asking for their views on how the new Society would function – by then the briefings that he had received from us considerably exceeded those that had been given to the new fellows.

The only problem that we foresaw from the choice of Erskine as architect was the fact that his practice was located in Sweden. This was resolved by the appointment of the Cambridge firm of architects Twist & Whitley as associates to provide local supervision of the building operations and otherwise look after local matters.

ERSKINE'S PLANS

In October 1964, the provisional council received from Ralph Erskine[7], seven sketches of alternative options for the development of the site to provide the required academic, social and residential accommodation. Unfortunately, we did not retain records of these alternatives and although I kept notes on my response to each of the options, it is not altogether clear what these options were. The options included several in which the existing Herschel House was retained and modified, with additional building. My notes indicate strong support for an option in which Herschel House was demolished. This option (number V) included terrace houses and court houses, and my notes commend the good separation of the academic area from the residential part and the good integration within each of the academic, social and residential parts.

A letter to Erskine from Holister dated 6 November 1964 notes that he will have received the comments of the fellows on his sketch plans, and asks for an early recommendation about the retention or demolition of Herschel House. Most of the fellows-designate of Clare Hall favoured its demolition when they were informed that there would be very little financial savings from its retention. Erskine visited the college again from Sunday 29 November until Wednesday 2 December. During this time he met with all members of the provisional council both formally and – in many cases – informally and individually. He also took an opportunity to visit the site of Herschel House on his own, having been assured that we had advised the tenants of the flats that a stranger would be wandering around their common garden.

A letter from Ashby to Erskine, written in the evening of 1 December, summarises the discussions that had been concluded on that day. This confirmed that we had decided on the demolition of Herschel House, and that we had agreed that sketch number V would be the basis for further drawings. On this basis we discussed moving the whole of the proposed new building eastwards, and we discussed the possible benefits of increasing the extent of two-storey buildings. The question of covered space for cars was considered, and Erskine advised that this could be

---

[7] I believe Erskine brought them with him in a brief visit on 16th October 1964, whilst in England for another job.

achieved by partially sinking the ground level, and partially raising the ground-floor level of the buildings on the Herschel Road front. It was noted that this would give a slope from north to south of the buildings, which would be an aesthetic advantage. We also had some discussion about the need to include a wine cellar and a launderette and arrangements for disposal of rubbish. Erskine's reply to Ashby's letter of 1 December agreed with the decision to demolish Herschel House and to the suggestions that we made for improvements in sketch number V.

Although we do not have any of Erskine's early sketches of building options, our archives include a rough copy that I made from Erskine's sketch number V, probably during the meeting on 1 December, which shows 10 terrace houses (presumably two-storey) and 4 court houses, and a common room, dining area, kitchen, and seminar room, library, and studies. The general layout has a close resemblance to the eventual layout of the buildings of Clare Hall – the terrace houses and court houses are separated by a walkway (family walk), and the latter are separated from the social and academic areas (by the scholars' walk). However, in this sketch the car-park is still above ground (suggesting that my sketch was made from Erskine's drawings at this meeting), and the terrace houses are to the east, adjacent to the Elmside garden, whilst the scholars' garden is to the west.

It was not until some time later that the planned layout was reversed so that the family houses and family garden were to the west of the site, with the studies and scholars' garden to the east. My recollection is that the change was made because the kitchen and dining room had been located to the south of the common room, with the studies on the north side, but this would have required vehicle access for kitchen deliveries from the rifle range road, on which we had no right of access since it belonged to Jesus College and we could not be certain of its long-term availability for use by Clare Hall. Changes to make kitchen access from Herschel Road, essentially by rotating the plans through 180 degrees, led to the present layout.

PROBLEMS GETTING STARTED

At one of the meetings with Erskine on 1 December 1964, I had sketched out an ideal timetable to construction of the proposed buildings assuming no delays. Ashby took my notes and formalised them in his letter to Erskine written in the evening of the same day. Noting that the assumption of no delays was unlikely, Ashby's timetable suggested that the buildings could be open for use by October 1967. Erskine's response, dated 16 December, gave a timetable for completion in February 1968. In his accompanying letter he indicated three possible ways in which the construction period might be shortened – the first (and most usual method) being 'wishful thinking'.

The preparation of plans during 1965 was complicated by continuing attempts to prevent the costs from rising above the level that Clare College could prudently finance, with suggestions for economies coming mainly from the quantity surveyors, Messrs Monk & Dunstone. On 24 June 1965, an outline application for the development costing approximately £250,000 was made to the Cambridge City Architect under the Town and Country Planning Acts.

However, on 27 July 1965 the Chancellor of the Exchequer in the Labour Government announced a building licensing system for all privately sponsored building projects costing over £100,000. A bill would be introduced in the Autumn to give effect to these new regulations which would be retrospective to the date of the Chancellor's announcement[8]. There were a number of exemptions, including educational buildings financed by the University Grants Committee, but these would not include Clare Hall, which was – in effect – privately financed.

Meanwhile, the provisional council had been considering the request from the President-elect of Clare Hall, Brian Pippard, for some increase in size of the President's house, so as to allow space for a small grand piano in the living room, to allow for up to ten in the dining room, and to provide an additional bedroom. These enlargements were agreed and sent to Erskine on 2 August 1965.

In September 1965, Ashby wrote directly to the Permanent Secretary at the Ministry of Public Works asking for advice on whether a building licence would be needed and, if so, how an application could be made – the reply was that the Ministry hoped to make an announcement 'very

---

[8] The government's objective was to hold back certain privately sponsored projects so that the construction industry would not become overloaded. The Bill would provide permanent administrative machinery ... to ensure that socially important work, such as housing, industrial building and work in development districts would get priority.

soon'. On 1 November, the Minister announced that he would consider applications for works to start which were urgent and in the public interest.

The application was made in the form of a letter dated 10 November from Ashby to the Ministry, giving an outline description of the proposed buildings and estimating their costs to be about £250,000 exclusive of land and fees. The reply was dated 21 January 1966, authorising the work provided it was commenced not earlier than April and not later than six months after that date. It would still be necessary to obtain local planning consents. On 26 May Ashby wrote to the Ministry to say that it might not be possible to complete all the drawings required for tenders so that work could begin before the final date. He was promptly informed that failure to meet the deadline would necessitate making a fresh application.

Various alternative procedures were considered at a meeting of Ashby, Pippard, Cooper and Holister with the architects and quantity surveyors in the Master's Lodge of Clare College on 18 August 1966. It was decided to consider the construction as a continuous two-stage process. Tenders would be invited on 23 September for the sub-structure (stage 1) and schedules of rates would be invited for the super-structure (stage 2). Using this procedure it would be possible to commence work before the end of October, within the period allowed by the licence. The timetable envisaged completing the sub-structure during February 1967, then starting the super-structure and completing it by October 1968.

COMPLETION, 1969

The contract for Clare Hall buildings was awarded to F. B. Thackray & Co., a building firm based in Huntingdon, and work commenced in October 1966. The construction was not helped by the wet Cambridge winters, but by the Spring of 1969 the buildings had been completed, and they were in use by June of that year. The furnishings were chosen by Erskine's daughter, working in collaboration with him.

Ralph Erskine has described the society and its needs on which his design was based in the following terms[9]

---

[9] Erskine in an article on Clare Hall in the *Architects' Journal Information Library*, 19 August 1970, pp. 409–424.

... a community of people who are elected to the college to further their self-chosen studies and who are selected according to capacity without regard to age, sex or origin – a group of scholars and their families ... It needed dwellings for families and dwellings for single people, work places for scholars, for house-wives (or house-husbands) and for children. It needed meeting places for mixed groups with many interests, and others for special groups with special interests, places for common or private meals and recreation, places for togetherness and others for privacy ...'

Erskine's aim was for buildings that would help achieve the social and scholarly objectives. He continued:

... the buildings are grouped around two main walkways – the family walk and the dwellings, and the scholars' walk with the studies, common room and bar. Beyond these, at each extremity of the site is a family garden and a scholars' garden. Breaking right through and across these groups is a cross-walkway ... (allowing) a varying degree of inter-relationship between scholastic work ... and recreation ... Within the dwellings are many choices of dwellings; there are nine 1-person bed-sitters, one 2-person bedsitter, two 3-person flats with a sleeping balcony, four terrace houses with three bedrooms, three court houses with four bedrooms and one court house with lounge, dining room, study, and four bedrooms. All the dwellings are equipped with full kitchen and cupboard space, and (are) fully furnished ...

The common room, bar and dining room are placed between the public space of the scholars' walk and the quiet seclusion of the scholars' garden, and are planned to give varying degrees of intimacy for relaxed or intensive conversation.

Ten studies, three rooms for the president and for secretaries, and a larger discussion room and a reading room are grouped around an enclosed court to form an enclave for concentration, for individual work or for intensive exchange.

The buildings were occupied during the summer of 1969, beginning in June. They were formally opened on 30 September by Lord Ashby, then acting in his capacity of Vice-Chancellor of the University, a position that he held for the two years 1967–69. The President of Clare Hall, Brian Pippard had by then moved into the President's house with his wife, Charlotte, and their three daughters. Although other colleges have Master's Lodges, it was unusual – though beneficial to the early residents of Clare Hall – to have a head of house who could available if the need arose to fix the drains or the electricity or the fire alarm during the early days of the new buildings. In spite of these unusual and unintended tasks, the Pippards recall that they enjoyed their time living in Clare Hall, which continued until the end of the first Presidency in September 1973.

CLARE COLLEGE INCOME AND EXPENDITURE

Like most Cambridge colleges, Clare reduced its holdings of government securities and invested mainly in equities in the 1950s, following a change of its Statutes that extended the scope for such investments. Some properties were retained but the total real estate was not increased – the growth of capital held by the college went mainly into equities. The success of this policy, begun in February 1953, became evident so rapidly that in March 1956 the college was able to start on a major programme for systematic renovation of the stonework and windows in the Old Court and the Chapel, which was to involve increasing annual expenditure over a seven year period. There was also extensive consideration of other college needs, initially concerned mainly with physical improvements to facilities, as outlined in chapter 4. These were managed by the bursar (Brian Cooper) with the assistance of the Chief Clerk (Mr Emery) until 1962, when the college appointed a domestic bursar (Darnton Holister) to take over the management of such activities. In addition, there were new buildings: the Thirkill Court extension of the Memorial Court, whose costs were mainly covered by donations from former Clare students, and new student accommodation in the Clare Colony in Chesterton Lane.

In November 1962, the bursar gave the governing body an outline of the college's income and expenditure over the previous twelve years. This review had been stimulated by the decision made in the previous month to explore the possibility of forming a new society, associated with Clare College but based on a new centre, as a means of increasing the number of fellows without changing the character of the existing fellowship. In 1950, before the change in investment policy, the net annual investment income of the college had been about £30,000, slightly larger than the total income of £27,000 from students' fees and charges[10]. By 1962, the investment

---

[10] In 1950 it was possible to build a house with four bedrooms in a good area of Cambridge for about £3,500. In a similar location a comparable house in 1997 would have a much smaller garden and would cost about £175,000 or 50 times as much. In the same period university salaries have increased about 20-fold, and the inflation index for the cost of living has increased about 15-fold.

income had increased to about £80,000, with about £42,000 from fees and charges. In the period from 1950 to 1962 the purchasing value of the pound fell by about 35 per cent, so the real increase in investment income was about 70 per cent, whilst the income from fees and charges barely kept pace with inflation[11].

The bursar's report also indicated the surplus of income less expenditure which was re-invested in each year[12]. The total surplus for the 13 year period amounted to £161,000, and in the same period the total benefactions received amounted to £169,000. In that period a total of £211,000 was spent on new building. The bursar's figures do not indicate the amount spent on improvements that resulted from the long list of items identified by the college's needs committee. For example, the original estimate for renovating the stonework in the Old Court was £28,000, to be spread over a period of seven years beginning in 1956, and I believe that this figure was exceeded by a considerable amount. However, by 1962 the end was in sight for the larger items in the extensive housekeeping programme, and the finance committee remained confident of future real growth in the college's investment income. Rationing had remained in effect until 1954 and economy and austerity were still virtues to be cherished in the decade of the 1950s. However, by the start of the 1960s the mood had changed and there was confidence in the prospect of growing national prosperity. Thus the Clare finance committee did not discourage the belief that the college could, from its own resources, finance a major development if it received sufficient support within the governing body. This could be additional to a modest increase in the fellowship to meet teaching needs.

EXPLAINING THE PROPOSAL

There were at least four versions of the draft for appeal for funds discussed by the 'committee of three' during January to March 1964. There was no further collaborative work on it while Ashby was away in America from mid-March to mid-June 1964. However, the report of the

---

[11] There was an overall increase in the number of students in the period so the fees and charges per student appear to have decreased (in real terms) during the period.

[12] This surplus came partly from the use of high yield gilts as an investment instrument, which were then associated with a sinking fund to compensate for inflation.

committee of three was clearly the basis for a detailed application[13] that Ashby sent to Ernest Brooks, President of the Old Dominion Foundation (now renamed the Andrew Mellon Foundation) on 25 May 1964. This formal application followed earlier discussions with Paul Mellon, a former student at Clare College, when Sir Eric and Lady Ashby visited him at his home in Virginia.

On his return to Cambridge, Ashby wrote to M. Cullen of the Ford Foundation on 19 June 1964, shortly before he (Cullen) visited Cambridge to meet with Ashby, Kingsford, Reddaway, Cooper, Holister, Eden, and Northam. Ashby's letter included a memorandum, which summarised his views and expectations for Clare Hall at that time.

... It is certain that if Cambridge is to remain one of the great universities of the world there must be a massive increase in its post-graduate population, not only of students working for Ph.D. degrees, but also of more senior research workers – post-doctoral and visiting scholars.

The libraries and laboratories needed by these senior research workers will be supplied by the university and financed by the University Grants Committee. But the university does not propose to supply those amenities, so valuable to senior research workers and visiting scholars, such as are offered by the institutes for advanced study in Princeton, Palo Alto, Washington (the Brookings Institution) and at Wesleyan University in Connecticut. A few Cambridge colleges (especially Churchill) offer hospitality to some senior visiting scholars, but without fresh developments the colleges will not be able to meet the future needs of Cambridge for centres where advanced scholars can live and work and exchange ideas.

Clare College has decided to make, from its own resources, a contribution to this need, by promoting within the college, a development to be known as Clare Hall. Clare Hall will be a graduate society – still legally part of the ancient foundation of Clare College

Ashby's memorandum outlined the proposed membership of Clare Hall: fellows holding permanent faculty or research posts in the university, research fellows, visiting fellows, and – at a later stage some research students working for Ph.D. Degrees. The prime purpose of the development was to establish in Cambridge a place which has the

---

[13] This application was followed up by discussions when Ashby visited Brooks in New York early in June 1964, following the receipt by Ashby of an Honorary Degree in Columbia University.

Explaining the proposal 215

function of a Centre for advanced scholars. He outlined the proposals for Clare Hall buildings, meanwhile temporary arrangements would be made for the society to begin operating from October 1964 in rooms loaned by Clare College.

After noting the support already provided by endowments from Clare College and from the Old Dominion Foundation, Ashby indicated that we would be looking for additional support sufficient to bring two visiting fellows to Clare Hall each year and also to provide some finance for special symposia.

17. Paul Mellon, KBE, D.Litt.
Benefactor and Honorary Fellow of Clare College and Clare Hall.

INITIAL ENDOWMENTS

The initial development and progress of Clare Hall was carried out within the institutional and financial framework of Clare College. This provided for the costs of commons of fellows-designate and fees for surveyors, architects and lawyers. In practice these costs were small in comparison with the uncosted benefits from services provided by members of Clare College and the University, particularly by Ashby and Cooper in Clare, and by the Registrary and other officials in the University.

The support from Clare College was formalised by the finance committee when the trust deed was completed in February 1966. The Trust Deed itself referred only to a nominal sum of £100, and the main gift was determined by a resolution of the finance committee. The Master and Fellows of Clare College as Trustees provided from their own property the land on which Clare Hall was to be built, and transferred the sum of £450,000 from their endowments for the use of Clare Hall, to pay for the buildings and to provide income for running costs.

The discussions of Ashby with Paul Mellon and Ernest Brooks in May and June 1964, led to a generous gift of $200,000 from the Old Dominion Foundation, which was to be used to assist in the costs of providing facilities in Cambridge for visiting fellows. This gift was later supplemented by an equal amount from the same foundation, which could be used for the general purposes of Clare Hall[14].

The application to the Ford Foundation led to a five-year grant totalling $175,000 which was used to provide financial support for visiting fellows. This enabled the college, jointly with departments in the university, to provide financial support for a number of visiting fellows who otherwise would not have been able to come to Cambridge, for example including visitors from Eastern Europe and from India[15].

---

[14] In 1970 after the receipt of the second Mellon grant, the college dividend income from the Old Dominion Fund is shown in the published accounts as £14,280. In 1996 it was £129,839 – a nine-fold increase, averaging nearly 9 per cent growth per annum, slightly above the average growth of the inflation index.

[15] Leszek Lukaszuk from Poland, Sukumari Bhattacharji, Kharma Kumar, Krishna Bharadwaj, and Devendra Kochhar from India.

Chapter 12

WHILE BUILDING CLARE HALL
1966 to 1969

THE START OF THE PRESIDENCY
OF BRIAN PIPPARD

Brian Pippard took the chair at the first meeting of the governing body of Clare Hall, held on 8 February 1966 immediately after the final meeting of the provisional council, which had been chaired by Eric Ashby. All nine official fellows and the one professorial fellow attended. At this time the total number of official and professorial fellows was limited to fifteen by the regulations associated with the trust deed. It was recognised that there should be restraint in the election of further fellows, but there was a need for the election of someone who would act as secretary to the governing body and as bursar. In the meantime, Kingsford would continue as secretary of the governing body, and Holister would attend meetings when the discussions concerned buildings.

Although the provisional council and earlier committees had put in place the main strands for the development of Clare Hall, the first President and the governing body were concerned with a variety of decisions that encompassed the full range of college activities: the drafting of regulations and ordinances, the selection and election of fellows, relations with the university and representation of Clare Hall on committees. On financial matters decisions were required on grants to research and visiting fellows, on the date for the end of the college's accounting year, on the college's liability to the university contribution[1], on the pay and allowances for the bursar when appointed, and expenses or

---

[1] After certain allowed deductions, all colleges paid a proportion of their income to the university. As an approved foundation, Clare Hall could ask for exemption for up to ten years and did so. The first contribution, paid ten years later for the year 1976–77 amounted to £6,343 or about eleven per cent of the college's endowment income in that year.

allowances to other members of the college. Although the President was able and willing to be involved at a detailed level in bursarial matters, and Kingsford would act as secretary of the governing body for a period, it was both necessary and urgent to identify and appoint a bursar for Clare Hall.

The bursar's financial duties would initially include liaison with the bursar of Clare College, since the accounts of Clare Hall were still being managed in the college bursary. Working with Holister, the bursar would also be expected to supervise the building programme and subsequent furnishing, and later would make arrangements for the provision of meals and for the engagement and supervision of staff, probably including a 'steward-housekeeper'. The bursar would also be expected to help find accommodation for visiting fellows who could not be accommodated in the Clare Hall flats. Such help over accommodation was at that time being provided on a voluntary basis by Mrs Gerda Cooper, the wife of the bursar of Clare College. There was also help from the Society of Visiting Scholars, which could put prospective visitors to the university in touch with academics and others in Cambridge who wanted to rent their houses or flats for a limited period.

Holister attended this first meeting and reported that a licence for a building costing £250,000 had been received, that demolition of Herschel House might start in May, and that it was hoped that detailed drawings would be ready so that tenders could be received by mid-September.

There was a resumed discussion on whether the spouses of fellows could compete for fellowships. Although individual names were not mentioned, most fellows were aware that one candidate under consideration was the wife of a fellow, but another – of recognised distinction – had assumed that such an application would be disallowed and had therefore not applied. There was concern that it would not be possible to ignore the fact that most spouses would be well known to other fellows, and it was thought that this would increase the difficulty of making an objective comparison with other candidates. However, it was thought that there would be a greater injustice if the spouse of a fellow was excluded for that reason, and therefore it was decided that they could be considered on their own merits on equal terms with other applicants. Although the social amenities of the Clare Hall buildings were open to the spouses of fellows, this should not affect any consideration of possible fellowships. Three new research fellows were elected: Miss Judith Martin, Dr Marie Singer, and Dr Ninon Leader.

Judith Martin had come to Cambridge from South Africa on a Commonwealth Scholarship in 1961, having taking a first degree in English and French. After obtaining a first class degree in English in Cambridge and a university scholarship, she studied for a year in France. At the time of her election, she was working towards a Ph.D. in medieval French and English romances of the twelfth to fourteenth centuries. Later, she married a fellow of Clare College, Dr (subsequently professor) Nigel Weiss, and she became a fellow and a director of studies in Robinson College, built in the 1970s across the road from Clare Hall.

Dr Marie Singer was already known internationally for her psychoanalytic studies of childhood and adolescence and had a practice in Cambridge for children and then for students. She had been born in the United States, where her grandfather had been a slave, and she grew up in a college in Mississippi founded by her parents. From Smith College and Boston University she came to London to train as a psychoanalyst and subsequently became a member of the teaching staff in the department of child psychiatry at the Middlesex Hospital. She was the widow of Burns Singer, poet, literary critic and marine zoologist, who died in 1964.

Dr Ninon Leader had come to Cambridge from Hungary in 1956, having taken an M.A. in the faculty of literature in Budapest. Initially in Cambridge as a refugee, she had supported herself by scrubbing floors in the old KP Restaurant whilst learning English until, in fairy-tale fashion, she was given a private scholarship to study for her Ph.D. at Girton College. From 1962 to 1965, like her husband Dr Elliot Leader, she had an appointment in the University of California, before returning with him to Cambridge. Her research on Hungarian classical ballads and their folklore was published by Cambridge University Press in 1967, and at the time of her election she was also preparing other books on Hungarian literature.

The endowment from the Mellon Foundation and the five-year grant from the Ford Foundation enabled the college to invite more visiting fellows to Cambridge and Clare Hall. These included Dr Leshek Lukaszuk, a theoretical physicist from Poland who would be working with Eden and Leader in the Cavendish Laboratory, and Mrs S. Bhattacharji from India, whose research would be on the background and analogues of the Sanskrit epics. She would be accompanied by her husband Professor Bhattacharya, both being on leave of absence from their faculty posts in Calcutta.

The first meeting of the governing body had noted that Miss A. M. Glauert (Mrs Franks) would be considered for a possible official fellowship at the next meeting. Audrey Glauert was indeed elected at the second meeting, held on 14 March 1966. She was Head of the department of electron microscopy at the Strangeways Research Laboratory, and her research was on the fine structure of bacteria and of cells in tissue and organ culture and on the molecular structure of biological membranes. Subsequently in 1970 she became a Cambridge Sc.D, and during 1970–72 she was President of the Royal Microscopical Society. She made many valuable contributions to the college, being honorary steward in the 1970s, honorary librarian in the 1980s and editor of the annual college newsletter for many years. On retirement in 1993 she became an emeritus fellow and continued to provide valuable help and advice in many areas of college life.

On 3 May 1966, Dr H. K. (Keith) Cameron was elected to an official fellowship, with the intention that he would become the secretary-bursar of Clare Hall. He had come to Cambridge in 1965 as a senior member of the control engineering group led by Professor John Coales of Clare Hall. He had studied in London, Munich and Vienna and took a Ph.D. in physical chemistry in 1930. His subsequent career was in industry with GEC, his final appointment being director of development to GEC (Engineering) during 1962–65. He was a distinguished authority on monumental brasses and some of his remarkable brass-rubbings were from time to time exhibited in Clare Hall making full use of the height of the roof. He remained a fellow until 1974 when he became an emeritus fellow.

In addition to Gumoski, Jones and Reed, mentioned earlier, visiting fellows resident during the summer of 1966 included: Luigi Radicati (theoretical physics) from Pisa, Toshiyuki Kitamori (control engineering) from Tokyo, Leshek Lukaszuk (theoretical physics) from Warsaw. Kitamori and Lukaszuk remained for part of the following academic year, and in October the following new visiting fellows were welcomed: Sukumari Bhattacharji (Sanskrit) from Calcutta, Dharma Kumar (economics) from Delhi, Frank Mitchell (geology) from Dublin, Uwe Radok (meteorology) from Melbourne, and Nur Yalman (anthropology) from Chicago.

In the Michaelmas Term two more research fellows were appointed: Dr Michael Yessik, a graduate from the United States, who held a NATO fellowship for work on crystallography in Dr Taylor's research group in the Cavendish Laboratory, and Dr Frances Young a graduate in classics from Girton College, who had recently completed two years research in the United States, and was working on the history of the early Christian Church.

MEALS

For more than seven centuries in Cambridge colleges, common meals have made an important contribution to social cohesion and to academic and cultural development of their members. Initially, members of Clare Hall took lunch with the fellows of Clare College at the high table in the college Hall. However, by October 1966 there were 26 fellows of Clare Hall, many of whom regularly took lunch in college and space at table was at a premium. Partly in anticipation of such a problem, the Small Hall of Clare had been recently redecorated, so Clare Hall lunch moved there, leaving the high table for fellows of the college. The fellows' combination room continued to be shared by both groups of fellows for coffee after lunch.

Meanwhile the fellows and their guests continued to have dinner on Tuesdays in the dining room of the Master's Lodge. However, numbers were limited to 18 so there was some concern during the Michaelmas Term of 1966 that it was no longer possible for all fellows to dine together. A sub-committee (Coales, Echlin, Glauert and Popperwell) was asked to examine the problem. When they reported in January 1967, there were 31 fellows. They recommended that the use of the dining room in the Lodge should continue so long as it was convenient for the Master, but that there should be two occasions in each term when fellows and their guests should dine together in a larger room, either in Trinity Old Kitchen or in Churchill College, or elsewhere. The governing body agreed to one or two such dinners each term, the first to be in Trinity Old Kitchen on Thursday 16 February 1967. The occasion was well attended, with the senior fellow (Will Taylor) taking the chair since the President had an unbreakable previous engagement elsewhere. It was on this occasion that Dr Taylor set a precedent by declining the Trinity butler's suggestion for a toast to the Queen ('I daren't set a precedent', he said).

In October 1967, the Master of Clare College, Sir Eric Ashby, became Vice-Chancellor of the University. In view of his new duties it was apparent that Clare Hall would not be able to continue its Tuesday dinners in the Master's Lodge. There was a preliminary change during the summer months, when dinners were held in the fellow's Parlour on E staircase of the Old Court, and from mid-September 1967 the Clare Hall dinners were held on Tuesdays in the new University Centre in Granta Place. They were well attended, both by fellows and their spouses, and beginning in February 1968, at each dinner two fellows of Clare College with their wives attended as guests of Clare Hall.

ADMINISTRATION

From the beginning it was expected that the President would preside, but the more detailed administration would be done by the bursar. Other fellows would be expected to assist and in due course there would be full-time appointments for staff. The Trustees had appointed Pippard as President until 1973, but the governing body had not itself considered the question of the length of tenure of the President, though it had been discussed earlier by the provisional council who had recommended a period of seven years. This was considered in May 1966 by a sub-committee, whose recommendation was accepted by the governing body, namely, that the wording of the relevant ordinance be amended to make it clear that at the end of a seven year period of tenure the President would not be eligible for re-election for a further period of office. It was also agreed that at the end of his or her tenure the governing body may invite the retiring President to become an official fellow, notwithstanding the regulation that limits the total number of official fellows.

The secretary/bursar was to be the key administrator. Cameron took over from Kingsford as secretary of the governing body at the meeting on 10 October 1966. Subsequently, he generally assisted the President in administrative matters, but only gradually took over full responsibility for bursarial duties. They were assisted or advised on all matters concerning the buildings by Holister. Financial matters continued to be managed mainly by the bursar of Clare College and his chief clerk until in 1969 the new buildings had been completed and paid for. However, Pippard and Cameron had the main responsibility with the governing body for ensuring that Clare Hall itself would be operating within its budget.

In January 1967 the governing body decided that a college council should be formed, as required by the regulations. This would consist of the President, the tutor, the bursar, the praelector, three elected fellows, and (later) two elected graduate students. Following a postal ballot, Taylor, Evans and Glauert were elected. The duties delegated to the council would include the impending negotiations on the second part of the building contract, action on graduate students, and financial provision for officers and staff. Graduate students, when admitted, would be able to join the fellows for lunch, but dinner would be difficult since we were then still limited by space in the Master's dining room.

BUILDINGS

On delegated authority from the governing body, the decision on which tender to accept for the Clare Hall buildings was made on 8 October 1966 by Pippard, Eden, Cameron, and Cooper (bursar of Clare College), in discussion with the local associate architect and the quantity surveyors. The first phase of construction work – for the foundations and basement – began on 17 October 1966. Before the second phase in the Spring of 1967 a

18. Foundations for the Clare Hall buildings, 1967.

19. *Elmside* from the garden.

number of economy measures were taken to keep the total cost within affordable limits[2]. The changes made included a reduction in the number of studies from 20 to 10, thus allowing all of them to be built on the ground floor.

In January 1967 the governing body was informed of the death of Mr Berry, who had occupied Elmside at 49 Grange Road, and that the house would become available for the use of Clare Hall in the near future. He had been most helpful in allowing part of his garden to be made available to Clare Hall so that the new buildings could extend right up to the eastern edge of the garden of Herschel House. The freehold for Elmside

---

[2] The total endowment capital for Clare Hall was fixed except for possible gains through growth in the stock market. Thus, excessive expenditure on the building could have reduced the income from the unspent endowment below the minimum level for operation of the college.

was already owned by Clare College under the earlier triangular transaction, and the bursar (Cooper) had prudently arranged for the college also to purchase from Berry the remainder of the lease under which the house had been built in the 1880s, whilst giving him a life-tenancy at a nominal rent.

Alterations were made in Elmside so as to accommodate 8 graduate students and provide a flat which would later provide accommodation for a housekeeper. The house came into use in October and two fellows and four graduate students took up residence. The labour of installing furniture in the right places and generally making Elmside habitable was carried out by volunteer fellows organised by Audrey Glauert who had temporarily taken on the responsibilities of honorary housekeeper – one of the first of her many contributions to Clare Hall. All members of the college and their spouses were invited to a meeting in Elmside on 9 November 1967 at which all fellows in order of seniority signed the Book of Fellows and confirmed their undertakings to conform to the statutes and ordinances of Clare Hall and generally to assist towards the success of the society. This ceremony was followed by a modest party at which sherry was served. The next official use of Elmside was for a meeting of the governing body on 11 January 1968, appropriately the fourth anniversary of the approval of the concept of Clare Hall by the governing body of Clare College.

In addition to the common rooms, which were used for meetings of the governing body and the council, one of the assets in Elmside was a large room, known as the Magic Room, that had been built to the south of the main house. It was unheated, uninsulated and very cold in winter. In the autumn of 1968, at the suggestion of Will Taylor, it was decided to renovate and improve the Magic Room so that it would be available for meetings or other functions, which it was suggested could include its rental for a long established painting class led by the notable Miss Vellacott, who was looking for a suitable venue. Its later uses included yoga classes, but eventually, following a donation from Obert Tanner, it was renovated again as the Ashby library.

The construction of the new buildings has been described in chapter 11. They were in use by the summer of 1969, and were formally opened by the Vice-Chancellor, Lord Ashby on 30 September.

20. Clare Hall Topping Out by the President, Brian Pippard, 1969.

FELLOWS AND ASSOCIATES

In May 1967 there were 37 fellows of Clare Hall, of whom 13 were official fellows, 12 were research fellows, and 12 were visiting fellows. One of the earlier research fellows, Tambiah, had been elected to an official fellowship when he became a lecturer in the Faculty of Archaeology and Anthropology. Later, his distinguished research on the anthropology of Thailand took him to a professorship at Harvard University.

In the spring of 1967 Clare Hall held its first competition for a stipendiary research fellowship which led to a short-list of two, both of whom we wished to elect. Happily, one of these – Malcolm Longair – was awarded an 1851 Exhibition, so we were able to economise sufficiently on his fellowship that we could also appoint David Buxton as a stipendiary research fellow. David Buxton had worked for the British Council for nearly 20 years, including a substantial period in Eastern Europe where he had become an authority on the architecture and history of wooden churches. He was also a splendid expert on etymology.

Dr Longair was a theoretical physicist working on astrophysics in the Cavendish Laboratory, and was in Moscow on leave of absence during 1968–69. Later he became a university lecturer in physics and an official fellow of Clare Hall before going to Edinburgh for a period of ten years as Professor of Astronomy and Astronomer Royal for Scotland. In 1990 he returned to Cambridge as Jacksonian Professor of Natural Philosophy in the Cavendish Laboratory, resuming his connection with Clare Hall by becoming a professorial fellow.

The visiting fellows in mid 1967 included the first husband and wife team in this category – Maurice and Trudy Goldhaber – both being physicists from Brookhaven National Laboratory on Long Island, New York. Maurice Goldhaber later became director of the laboratory, but much earlier – before the war, he had been a research fellow of Magdalene College. Academic gowns are not required in Clare Hall, but when asked to a formal dinner in Magdalene and inquiring of the college Porter whether a gown was necessary, Maurice was pleased to learn that his pre-war gown had been kept there for his use when required. He was not so lucky when he inquired whether Magdalene had a guest night when ladies could come as guests – he was told that indeed there was a ladies night but it had been earlier in the year. Trudy Goldhaber also was a distinguished nuclear physicist. It was perhaps not surprising that twenty-five years later their son Freddy Goldhaber, also a physicist, came with his young family to Clare Hall and was the first 'second-generation' visiting fellow.

Clare Hall has been fortunate in the number of visiting fellows who subsequently return as visitors, either making use of their life membership of the college to return to spend a second or third sabbatical leave in Cambridge, or calling in for a shorter visit – or sometimes coming for a few weeks in the summer. Some of the early visitors are in this group of frequent or regular visitors, including: Russell Ross (pathology) from the United States; Jim Livingston (theology) United States; and G. W. Rowley (Arctic studies) Canada. Donald Cross came as a visiting fellow on leave from his post as director of research in the architect's department of the Greater London Council. He subsequently took up permanent residence in Cambridge, working in the department of land economy except for a period when he held a post in the University of Manchester. He died in 1997 and bequeathed a major part of his estate to Clare Hall.

Until March 1969 all proposals for fellowships came directly to the governing body, where they were often discussed at length. In that month, resulting from a memorandum from a number of fellows, it was decided to form a fellowship committee which would be responsible for the preliminary processing and discussion of proposals for visiting fellows and research fellows. The names and details would be organised and brought to the governing body for decisions. Other fellowships would remain solely for consideration by the governing body. Under that procedure, three more official fellows were appointed in 1968: Betty Behrens, university lecturer in history and formerly a fellow of Newnham College, she became an emeritus fellow in 1972 and later made a substantial bequest to Clare Hall to fund a research fellowship; Michael Loewe[3], lecturer in Classical Chinese, who was vice-president of Clare Hall in 1989–90 before becoming an emeritus fellow; Nicolay Andreyev, lecturer in slavonic studies later becoming professor.

On 16 January 1969 the governing body were informed of a generous gift from Mr James Whitehead, a former graduate student at Clare College[4]. This gift was placed in Clare Hall's Whitehead Fund, which would provide an endowment income to help support visiting fellows.

In the Lent term of 1968, Professor Coales asked whether a new category of member, called an 'associate', could be established. The origin of his suggestion lay in the visitors to his control engineering research group, who were of less distinction (or younger) than visiting fellows, but with whom he was often working on a daily basis. His proposal was

---

[3] Like Carmen Blacker, during the war Loewe had worked in the code-breaking team at Bletchley. Later he worked in the Foreign Office for a period before becoming a lecturer in Cambridge.

[4] James Whitehead died in 1977 aged 89, *Clare Association Annual 1976–77*, obituary pp. 61–62.

accepted, though there was no restriction to ensure that associates were to be working closely with a fellow. The President put forward a suggestion from the Master of Clare College that the fellows of Clare College should all be elected associates. This was agreed with enthusiasm.

The proposal for creating this new class of member of Clare Hall, to be called associates, was accepted by the Trustees during the Easter Term. They did not set any limit on numbers, but Clare Hall itself decided that the numbers would normally be limited to about 15, with a maximum of 20 (not counting the fellows of Clare College in this total). Also in the Easter Term, it was decided to create another new class – that of guest scholar – for a limited number of visitors of the status of visiting fellow, but coming for only a short period. Later, it was generally accepted that exceptional distinction was required if a short-term visitor was to be given the status of guest scholar. The selection of (visiting) associates was delegated to the college council, but (in 1968–69) it was decided that anyone holding a university or research post in Cambridge would not be eligible for election as an associate.

During the period 1965–69, before Clare Hall had its own buildings, most of the visiting fellows and associates arranged their accommodation – usually with help from their local sponsors or host departments – with the aid of the Society for Visiting Scholars. This society had been established during the 1950s by Greta Burkill, the wife of my former tutor, Charles Burkill, who later became the Master of Peterhouse. As well as providing local information, advice on schools etc. and some social activities, the society assisted academic visitors to find family accommodation by putting them in touch with Cambridge academics going on leave of absence, or others wishing to rent furnished accommodation for a term or a year. After 1969, most of the visiting fellows and associates who could not be accommodated in Clare Hall apartments continued to be assisted by the Society for Visiting Scholars. It was particularly helpful to Clare Hall's visitors that Greta Burkill was succeeded as President of the Society for Visiting Scholars by Charlotte Pippard, who held this post from 1972 to 1982. Those visiting fellows to Clare Hall who had arranged to rent accommodation in Cambridge through correspondence with Lady Pippard were often surprised on arriving in the college to find her amongst the welcoming team in this different context.

GRADUATE STUDENTS

The governing body of Clare College had suggested in March 1964 that Clare Hall should seek to admit some graduate students within about three years of its foundation. In November 1966, Pippard and Glauert had discussions with the tutor of Clare College (Smiley) and Clare's tutor for advanced students (Heine) about the possibility of some joint arrangements for admitting graduate students to Clare Hall. It was suggested that the College might be able to give some help on student accommodation if the Hall wished to admit a few graduate students before any of its buildings were ready for occupation. In January the governing body of Clare Hall decided to make a tentative start on such admissions, initially planning to admit 6 to 10 students in October 1967. Terence Armstrong was appointed as tutor, initially for a period of one year, so as to give him an opportunity to assess the amount of work that would be involved – clearly, he did not wish it to have an adverse effect on his main work as an assistant director of research at the Scott Polar Research Institute.

Even before the arrival of graduate students, Clare Hall needed a Praelector to conduct to the degree ceremony any member of the college who has qualified for a university degree. These included some of the research fellows who graduated as Ph.Ds after their elections. Patrick Echlin was the first Praelector of the college, being appointed in 1966. Later Praelectors included Malcolm Longair, Marjorie Chibnall, Tony Harding and Murray Stewart.

In January 1968 an additional two graduate students were admitted, bringing the total to six. With the prospect of our own accommodation by the summer, Clare Hall was now included in the list of Cambridge colleges able to accept graduate students and it was planned to increase the numbers further in the academic year 1968–69. By October 1968 the total number of graduate students had increased to 18. Clare College helped Clare Hall by allowing graduate students and other members some use of the sporting facilities of the college's amalgamated (sports) clubs, particularly for tennis and squash. Some graduate students also played rugby for Clare College, though it was much later that enthusiasm for rowing developed in Clare Hall.

However, it was thought that Clare Hall would still have some spare capacity for serving meals. With this in mind it was agreed to give some help to Girton College for a limited period by allowing Girton graduates to take lunch in the new dining room when it became available. The numbers were expected to be less than 40, with less than half this number coming at any one time.

Chapter 13

CLARE HALL 1969 to 1980

SETTING UP HOUSE

During August 1969 Brian and Charlotte Pippard with their three daughters moved into the President's house at no. 1 Clare Hall. By the end of September, when the residents' list was prepared, fifteen of the flats and houses were occupied. The residents included two research fellows – Malcolm Longair and Barry Uscinski, four visiting fellows and six visiting associates with their families.

The new buildings were formally opened on 30 September 1969 by Sir Eric Ashby in the presence of the Chancellor, Lord Adrian. The speeches and the unveiling of the commemorative plaque, designed and made by Will Carter, were preceded by a buffet lunch for about 150 people, at which the talents of Francoise Mattock, the manageress, and Patrice, the chef, were displayed to an admiring public. This occasion confirmed the beginning of Clare Hall's reputation for excellent and varied food with a strong French flavour.

A suggestion to wear academic dress for the opening ceremony had been defeated by a vote but with prudence or courtesy the fellows had allowed the President to consult the Vice-Chancellor before a final decision was made. Ashby responded that since it was a university event as well as a college occasion, and since both the Chancellor and the Vice-Chancellor would be present, it would be both appropriate and desirable that academic dress should be worn. I believe that this was the last and only occasion that academic dress has been worn in Clare Hall, thus providing an opportunity for innovative change by our successors at some time in the future.

The national press had helped to bring to the public the unique character of Clare Hall as an academic community. At the time of the opening ceremony, there were about 40 adults and 16 children living in

21. Opening of the Clare Hall new buildings by the University Vice-Chancellor, Sir Eric Ashby, with the President of Clare Hall, Professor Brian Pippard (right), 30 September 1969.

the college grounds; the total strength was 46 fellows, 16 associates and 32 graduate students. Writing in the Clare Association Annual, only two months after the buildings had been occupied, Brian Pippard described how the 'family walk' echoed with the shouts of children, whilst only a few steps away in the 'scholars' walk' and the study court, something like a cloistered calm prevailed. He paid tribute to the architect Ralph Erskine's expert assessment of the problem of peaceful coexistence of families and scholars and was pleased to report that the society had got off to a triumphal start. He correctly forecast that in the years ahead Clare Hall would welcome a steady stream of distinguished scholars.

The early residents in Clare Hall assisted in identifying the numerous faults that appear to be inevitable in new buildings and they were asked to report these to the college office where a list would be kept. For example, Brian Pippard recalls one day at 4 a.m. when he had to silence the fire

22. Viewing the Clare Hall apartments, after the opening of the new buildings 30 September 1969, the University Chancellor, Lord Adrian (right), the Vice-Chancellor, Sir Eric Ashby (centre), and the President of Clare Hall, Professor Brian Pippard (left).

23. Children in Clare Hall Family Walk.

alarm with a pair of socks. Other duties that impinged on the President and his wife included opening up an apartment and making up the beds at 11 p.m. for a visiting family that had experienced the travel delays that were even more endemic then than now.

Not content with such duties Charlotte and Brian Pippard set high standards for their successors in their contribution to social activities in the college. Their presence at college guest nights always added to their quality and often to their gaiety. They had dinner parties and gatherings for meetings or music in the President's house, where much of the organisation was done by Charlotte. Other activities involved the whole Pippard family: the children's parties at Christmas and on Guy Fawkes night are good examples. The first Clare Hall Father Christmas was Paul Brantingham, a graduate student from the United States and living in college with his wife and child. Paul was a champion hammer thrower, and when handing out gifts to the smaller children and clad in a large red costume designed and made by Charlotte Pippard, he was a most

24. Entrance stairs to the Common Room in Clare Hall.

impressive Father Christmas, unmatched in physique by his successors in later years.

The Guy Fawkes party, followed an old English tradition which required the Guy to be burnt on a large bonfire. A splendid effigy of Guy Fawkes was prepared each year by the Pippard family with remarkable realism using clothes provided by Mr Stokes. Francoise Mattock suggested that a childrens' tea party should precede the lighting of the bonfire and the accompanying fireworks. Although not based on historical precedent, it was thought appropriate that Guy Fawkes should attend the tea party and be seated at the head of the table. Initially this arrangement was apparently enjoyed by all, but after its third year one of the mothers found that her children were distressed when their friend Guy, whom they had met at tea, was subsequently burnt at the stake. Thereafter, Guy Fawkes did not appear at the tea party, but the Pippard family memories do not reveal whether he was also absent from the bonfire.

MEALS

The duty of being regularly present at dinner and supper, and of behaving, while there, with the utmost quiet and decorum, was insisted on in all the (early) collegiate statutes in both universities. In the medieval college of Clare Hall it was required that all the fellows, scholars, and perendinants[1], should repair to the hall when the bell rang, and there to dine and sup together, because

> not only is it decent and orderly, but tends to the common advantage, that members of the same family should not take their food in hiding-places and corners, like wild beasts, but in some common dining room.[2]

In 1964, when Clare College founded the modern Clare Hall, it was accepted that attendance at common meals would be an important integrating factor in the new collegiate society. It was with this in mind that Ashby offered the use of the dining room in the Master's Lodge for a weekly Clare Hall dinner during the years 1964–67. It was at Ashby's suggestion that fellows' commons included a generous allowance for guests, in the expectation that meals would provide valuable opportunities for the exchange of ideas – and on occasion for the initiation of new research. With assistance from the Mellon Foundation grant, similar allowances were to be provided for visiting fellows.

In June 1969, Francoise Mattock was appointed as manageress, with responsibility both for the kitchen and for general housekeeping. She remained with the college until 1977, after which there were a series of short-term appointments and kitchen and housekeeping management were separated. In 1984 Daryl Pool was appointed as the chef/manager in charge of the kitchens and catering, having first come to Clare Hall as a chef in 1972. In 1997 Daryl himself, and Pat Jakes of the catering staff, completed twenty-five years with the college. Lunching and dining arrangements began in the new college buildings in Herschel Road on Friday 20 June 1969. The 'guest night', when there was waitress service at dinner, was changed from Tuesday to Wednesday, and in most terms

---

[1] Visitors (possibly paying guests) residing day-by-day, often with a limit of a two weeks on the total length of stay in college.
[2] Cited in Willis and Clark, *The architectural history of Cambridge,* vol. 3, p. 365 (Cambridge 1986).

25. Clare Hall dining room from Elmside garden.

there was a special dinner analogous to a feast in the older colleges, for example during February to commemorate the founding of the college. Unlike other colleges, Clare Hall did not have a May-week Ball, but instead had an "Event" which would change its format from year to year. Other special occasions included Christmas dinners for fellows, partners and guests, and Burns Night dinners at which bagpipes were played and Keith Cameron recited Burns' Ode to a Haggis.

With the arrival in the autumn of 1969 of families and children in the college flats, it became desirable to develop codes of practice, particularly in relation to meals. Notes for visiting fellows at this time made it clear that Clare Hall aimed to make welcome the whole family of each member of the society. Nevertheless (the notes continued), the prime purpose of the society is academic, and the design of buildings was intended to provide a separation between family activities and academic studies. Children should be discouraged from straying into Scholars' Walk. Further, care should be taken to prevent young children from obtruding into what should be an adult environment in the dining room. Children too young to

26. Clare Hall dining room.

play a part in general conversation should not be brought to the weekly dinners, but they would be welcome on supper nights, though it was suggested that families with small children might sit at a side table. Much later, a family night was introduced on a monthly basis, sometimes with the youngest children eating early and then watching a video whilst their parents and the older children had a later meal. The notes also suggested that husbands and wives should not sit together at table for Wednesday dinners as this would more quickly extend their own new friendships and would benefit the community.

Except for the conventions relating to children at meals, beginning with the earliest meals in Clare Hall, it became customary for each new arrival at lunch (for which there was no waitress service) to take the next free place at table and to introduce themselves to any neighbouring members whom they had not previously met. This social mixing was encouraged through the provision of soup at table in only two large tureens, from which members would help themselves and their neighbours. This

27. Daryl Pool, Chef-Manager (in 1997).

structured informality has continued to be a major factor in the welcome provided to new members and it has been an important element in securing the reputation of Clare Hall for its friendly and lively discussions at meals and after.

Before the formal opening of the new buildings, council had proposed a wine committee with Keith Cameron as its chairman. Both Patrick Echlin (fellows' steward) and Peter Dronke took an early interest in the selection of wines for use in the college. Meanwhile the wine steward of Clare College, Charles Chibnall, had thoughtfully begun to lay down additional wines to provide for some of the expected needs of Clare Hall. It was not long before there were regular gatherings of members for wine tasting, occasions which proved to be both popular and instructive.

MANAGEMENT AND THE COLLEGE STAFF

Much of the time in college council meetings during the spring of 1969 had been taken up by discussions on the new building and its furnishing. Until this time Keith Cameron had been termed the secretary-bursar, with most emphasis on his role as secretary of the governing body and the council. However, with the completion of the buildings and the appointment of staff, he began to have an increasingly important bursarial function as college manager. Mary Ogden was appointed as college secretary, doubling as secretary to the bursar (her main role) and secretary to the President (for his college activities only). Brian Routledge was appointed as the college clerk, responsible for maintaining the college accounts and working in Clare College until the Clare Hall buildings were completed. He also doubled as barman during the college's early years, and he continued to look after the accounts and was also in charge of the wine cellar until his retirement in 1994–5 after he had been with the college for twenty five years.

Mr Stokes was appointed as maintenance manager to look after the exterior of buildings and to service the boiler and other equipment, whilst Mrs Stokes became housekeeper for the Elmside accommodation. Mr and Mrs Stokes lived in the Elmside flat and also had the use of the Elmside Garage[3] – a cavernous space originally designed for horse-drawn carriages. After their retirement in 1978, Mr Fred Clark and Mrs Clark took over the responsibilities of head of maintenance and housekeeper for Elmside and continued to provide the willing and helpful service of their predecessors.

In the new residential building it had been found that the original laundry and playroom did not have a strong enough floor for the purpose of its planned use. It was therefore converted into a double guest suite, with bed-sitting room, shower and lavatory – and, if required, this flat could be used for letting. The intended hobby room in the basement was converted into a playroom, laundry room, and workshop[4].

In April 1970, the bursar expressed concern about the cost of central heating which had come to £1800 for December and January, and he suggested that it might be necessary to install double glazing to reduce heat losses. This possibility was discussed from time to time, particularly during

---

[3] Pippard recalls (1994) that the commitment of the garage to Mr Stokes' car was the primary reason for abandoning a plan to develop it for more general college purposes. Such a development took place many years later in 1993 with the McLean extension.

[4] The workshop was subsequently converted into a storeroom, and a new workshop was created near the cloakrooms in the main building.

the energy crises of the 1970s, but the probable savings did not provide a sufficient pay-back to justify the capital costs so no action was taken[5].

Keith Cameron resigned from the bursarship in January 1973, but continued as an official fellow. He was succeeded as bursar by Avril Yeo, formerly the acting bursar of New Hall and a mathematical graduate of Girton College. With her husband Peter Yeo, a botanist, she took up residence in one of the college apartments. Sadly, after less than two years as a clear-thinking and appreciated bursar, Avril Yeo died in October 1974. She was succeeded by Derek Adams, formerly in the education branch of the Royal Air Force specialising in international affairs and with the rank of Wing Commander. Adams was bursar and steward from 1975 to 1980 and with his wife Sheila lived in family walk, and together, they helped to maintain the informality that had become traditional in the social life of the college.

GOVERNING BODY

In 1973, the college celebrated the seventh anniversary of its foundation, and at the same time came to the end of its first presidential cycle as determined by the seven-year rule. Pippard retired from office in September 1973, and accepted an invitation to become a professorial fellow of the college, having resolutely declined invitations to fellowships elsewhere[6], and after a brief absence from the governing body as a courtesy to his successor he contributed fully to its activities. As the first President of Clare Hall his contribution to the successful mix of scholarship and informality, which is a hallmark of the college, was of crucial importance and greatly aided by the presence of his family in the college. In 1971, he had been appointed as Cavendish Professor and chairman of the department of physics and in 1975 he received a knighthood – providing an occasion for a celebratory dinner in Clare Hall.

---

[5] Erskine had included double glazing in his original designs, but this was changed in 1967 as an economy measure before construction, in response to earlier concerns about the cost of the buildings. New legislation in the 1990's on shared premises is expected to require extensive renovation of the older windows in the college during 1997–2000, and it is likely that this will provide an opportunity to introduce double glazing for most such windows.

[6] Except for an honorary fellowship at Clare College, which does not adversely affect his involvement with Clare Hall and provides an additional link between the Hall and the College.

That is not to say that there were never any disagreements amongst the fellows during this time. Not all fellows were happy with the informality, particularly if it was extended into meetings of the governing body, and unsuccessful attempts were made to introduce formal dinners when full academic dress would be worn. At the other extreme, there was nothing but admiration on the occasion when Marie Singer persuaded the President to take to the dance floor in hall after a special dinner – to perform with her a display of jive that I had not seen since the American invasion of England during the war.

As the fellowship increased with the election of new fellows, it was to be expected that new ideas for the structure of the membership and its procedures should develop. Governing body papers for the early years in the new buildings show a stream of proposals for new classes of member, countered by others to reduce or simplify the number of classes, or simply to change the titles of different classes to show parity of esteem. The number of associates increased and there was continuing pressure for the creation of more stipendiary research fellowships – there was only one in the early 1970s. There was a countervailing desire to balance the annual budget, which was in deficit through an unanticipated reduction in endowment income resulting from unexpectedly high inflation.

There was also disagreement about whether to build a series of study bedrooms along the south side of the Elmside garden, and the dispute over this ran in parallel with the election of the new President during the academic year 1972–73. The opposition did not dispute the need or the merits of the proposed buildings – the yearly increases in the number of graduate students had led to a total of nearly 50 students in 1972 – far in excess of the nine rooms available in Elmside. The capital cost of the proposed buildings would have had a significant effect on the endowment income[7] of the college and there were doubts whether this could be made up from rents and from other economies. Amongst these economies, in 1972 the fellows decided to forgo their entitlement to free dinners on the

---

[7] There were already signs of serious inflation in the British economy which meant that costs for running the college would increase more quickly than investment income. The counter-argument that building costs were rising even more quickly would have been relevant only if there was an adequate margin between college income and expenditure that allowed the release of capital for building. There was no such margin.

Wednesday guest nights[8], which had previously been included in their allowances. However, the opposition to any major capital expenditure on new buildings prevailed and the governing body decided as a temporary measure to allow the shared use by four graduate students of one of the court houses on family walk and later for a short period two of the houses.

THE PRESIDENCY OF ROBERT HONEYCOMBE 1973 to 1980

Professor Robert Honeycombe, Goldsmiths' Professor and Head of the Department of Metallurgy and Fellow of Trinity Hall since 1966, was elected as the second President of Clare Hall in 1973. He had originally come to Cambridge from the University of Melbourne in 1948, firstly as an ICI research fellow and later as the Royal Society's Armourers and Braziers research fellow. In 1951 he moved to Sheffield University as a senior lecturer, becoming Professor of Physical Metallurgy in 1955. After moving back to Cambridge in 1966, Robert Honeycombe's wife June became a principal research scientist in The Welding Institute (TWI), and during his presidency of Clare Hall they lived in college Monday to Friday, hosting numerous receptions in the President's house and continuing the social informality that had become traditional during the presidency of Brian Pippard.

The Honeycombe presidency proved to be a period of consolidation, during which earlier innovations became customs and welcoming informality became traditional. The pace of change was moderated, though this was not entirely a voluntary choice by the college. The financial concerns that had worried fellows two years earlier became more serious in the years following the world oil crisis of October 1973, which heralded a long period of high inflation and low economic growth in the UK. In real terms (i.e. net of inflation) between 1970 and 1976 there was a 40 per cent decrease in the endowment income of the college[9], of which 20 per cent was in the year to 1975, a year in which inflation of the retail price index reached 24 per cent.

---

[8] The decision to forgo the allowance of free dinners was made originally to help the possibility of having a second stipendiary research fellow, but the cost savings were also an element in the discussion about the proposed new building.

[9] The endowment income was provided from a share in the joint investment portfolio of Clare College and Clare Hall.

28. Robert Honeycombe, President 1973–80, with June Honeycombe.

In May 1974, the President suggested that a small committee be set up to review the long term aims and needs of the college[10] and report to the governing body from time to time. Our first recommendation was that proposals for new official fellows be considered only once a year and that they be scrutinised by an special sub-committee, later called the official fellowship committee, before consideration by the governing body. We hoped that this would lead to more measured assessment of the need to elect official fellows who would contribute to the social, intellectual and management activities of the college, including some who would be

[10] Honeycombe (chairman), Eden, Popperwell, Lapidge and Fenn.

prepared to become tutors for a period. This objective was sometimes in conflict with the desire of fellows to elect those with the greatest academic distinction or potential.

However, the early discussions of the President's committee on long-term aims were dominated by the short-term problem of the expected deficit in the college's annual accounts. We recommended that a monthly establishment charge be introduced for visiting fellows and associates, which was approved and commenced in the year 1975–76. Although it was introduced in response to a financial crisis, the establishment charge was subsequently retained as a contribution towards meeting 'overheads', including the costs of college staff who provide an ongoing service to all members, the cost of utilities and equipment, and the maintenance of buildings and their improvement. There is a corresponding element of support for overheads from the fees paid by the graduate students to the college. Although there was general acceptance of the principle of increasing charges to members in line with inflation, the levels of inflation were not always fully anticipated and the financial position remained difficult. Measures were taken to reduce expenditure, both through reducing the totals for grants-in-aid to visiting fellows and through postponing a plan to increase the number of stipendiary fellowships so that one could be elected each year.

There were discussions about the possibility of fund-raising more actively, but it was argued that the college should first put in place a programme for future development to which such fund-raising might be directed. However, there were some individual initiatives, notably one from Ronald Popperwell, lecturer in Norwegian, who arranged support from Hambro's Bank for a fellowship for a visiting scholar from Norway. There was also a personal contribution from Brian Pippard who was a long-term adviser to the Encyclopaedia Britannica and arranged for the fees for this advice to be paid to Clare Hall. The governing body decided that these annual gifts would be used towards a capital endowment to be called the Pippard Fund whose income would be used as a source of grants to graduate students in the college[11].

---

[11] Initially the governing body decided that the fund be used for grants to visiting fellows, but this was changed two years later to provide help to graduate students.

In 1979–80 inflation rose again nearly to 20 % in one year, and the college council found it necessary to make an interim increase in charges in April 1980. Earlier in the year, the President had asked me to chair a meeting of council in his absence, and we had decided once again to advise that the college could not afford to appoint a new stipendiary research fellow in 1980. In reporting this to the governing body, I took the opportunity to suggest that the President and the President-elect be asked to review the arrangements for financial decisions which had until then been the responsibility of the council. The subsequent review by Honeycombe and Stoker led to the creation of the finance committee which would in future be responsible to the governing body for managing the financial affairs of the college.

When Clare Hall was founded in 1966, the Trust Deed allowed it the option of seeking independence after 14 years. In 1978 there were preliminary discussions on this option and a committee[12] was appointed in June of that year to examine the advantages and disadvantages of independence. Any decision to become independent would require several years to achieve this end, so it was thought best to wait until the election of the new President when the procedures could be carried through during one presidency. Other events and developments that took place during Honeycombe's presidency are described in later sections and include: in 1976 the celebration of the tenth anniversary of the founding of Clare Hall, in 1978 the purchase of the neighbouring house at 3 Herschel Road to provide more rooms for graduate students, and during 1977–78 the establishment of the annual Tanner Lectures.

Robert Honeycombe retired from the presidency in September 1980, but he continued to take an active part in the university as head of department and in the college as a professorial fellow until 1988 and then as an emeritus fellow. He also retained his links with Trinity Hall where he had been elected to an honorary fellowship in 1975. He was the Prime Warden of the Goldsmiths Company in 1986–87 and the Treasurer of the Royal Society from 1986 to 1992, and he was knighted in 1990.

---

[12] Honeycombe (chairman), Adams, Cullen, Eden, Pippard.

FELLOWS

In January 1975 the college elected Lord Ashby as its first honorary fellow. We were fortunate that, on his retirement later that year from the mastership of Clare College, Ashby regarded Clare Hall as his normal college home, competing for his attention only with the House of Lords. He was regularly seen at lunch, sometimes with Helen, Lady Ashby, and was always ready to engage in discussions with old and new friends. On more than one occasion a fellow of the college was invited to contribute ideas or research support for a speech by Ashby in the House of Lords, though such input was usually translated to a form more suited to their lordships.

On 11 February 1976, Clare Hall celebrated the tenth anniversary of its foundation with an anniversary dinner. Attended by 165 people[13], the guests included the Clare College members of the Provisional Council, who had been involved in the foundation, with their wives, the architect Ralph Erskine, and his local representative Kenneth Twist, who had supervised the construction. Lord Ashby spoke engagingly and generously about the founding of Clare Hall, and later the college newsletter included an edited version of the talk[14]. Ashby began with characteristic modesty:

There is a belief among some members of Clare Hall who are not familiar with its origins that I am the Founding Father. This is flattering but embarrassing – embarrassing because it is wrong. I cannot disclaim some responsibility, but if there are to be allegations of paternity, I plead guilty only to paternity-by-association. So I welcome this opportunity to put the record straight.

The story I have to tell is not a mere chronicle. It has for me fascinating implications. It demonstrates how an idea, if it is not codified and allowed to 'set' too soon, has a life and development of its own, and for a time its creators should just watch and let it grow. It demonstrates how the timing for the moment of transition from talk to action is critical ...

Ashby then reviewed the historical background of university development that has been described in some detail in earlier chapters and the

---

[13] The seating plan for 165 was made possible by tables in the bar and the common room as well as the dining room, and Ashby's talk was relayed by loud-speakers to the assembled throng.

[14] Ashby's talk was printed in the *Clare Hall Newsletter 1974–75* and again in the 1983–84 Newsletter, a special number celebrating the Royal Charter. It is included in this book as Appendix 1. See also chapters 6 and 10.

initiatives in Cambridge and Clare College that led to the founding of Clare Hall. He referred to the proposal for a Clare Institute for Advanced Study, which he received in January 1964 as the seminal document[15] that marked the moment of transition of idea into action. "This was", he said, "the moment of conception (of Clare Hall)". He continued by describing the crucial contribution to the successful outcome from many members of the College and the University.

In 1976 on the tenth anniversary of the founding of Clare Hall there were 23 official fellows, 5 emeritus fellows comprising former official fellows who had passed the retirement age of 67 years, and there were about 12 research fellows, most of them non-stipendiary[16]. The first of the emeritus fellows were Will Taylor (crystallography) and Betty Behrens (history), then in 1974 they were joined by John Coales (control engineering), who had been the first professorial fellow of the college, and Keith Cameron on his retirement from the bursarship. Although emeritus fellows were not members of the governing body, it soon became apparent that they could make an important contribution to the well-being of the college, since their new-found freedom from teaching and departmental duties allowed them to be more frequently in the college than their younger colleagues. They both strengthen the social environment for visiting fellows and provide continuity in the relationship with the increasing numbers of visitors who come to Clare Hall on academic leave for a second or third time.

Some of the early research fellows of Clare Hall were appointed by the governing body on an ad hoc basis, usually initiated by a fellow who drew attention to an exceptional opportunity that often derived from the absence of any rules on age or seniority that were normal in other colleges. This procedure led to the election of several whose distinction was already recognised internationally, including Jeyaraj Tambiah, an assistant lecturer in anthropology – soon to become a lecturer (and an official fellow) and later a professor at Harvard; Polly Hill (Mrs Humphreys), who became the university's Smuts Reader in Commonwealth Studies in

---

[15] The proposal is printed in appendix 2. See also chapters 6 and 7.
[16] A total of nineteen research fellows were elected between the foundation of Clare Hall and 1969, but some of these had left by September 1969, and one had been elected an official fellow.

1973 and was elected to an official fellowship in that year; and Ronald Lewcock a historian of architecture from South Africa, who was elected an official fellow in 1976 and was later appointed to the Aga Khan professorship in Harvard and MIT. In the 1970's, following the creation of a fellowship committee, the election procedure for research fellows became more formal and generally was based on an annual competition. The disappearance of ad hoc decisions had the effect of encouraging the election of less established scholars as research fellows, although the absence of an age limit remained and this continued to differentiate Clare Hall from most other colleges through allowing the election of more mature scholars to fellowships.

From the early 1970's, there would be an annual discussion about the size and composition of the governing body, and this would normally lead to a target number of 20 for the research fellows at any time. The discussion was complicated by a desire by some to renew research fellowships for a second period of three years, which implied that a lower number of new elections would be necessary if we were to keep total numbers within the target figure. When the college received its Royal Charter in 1984 it was necessary to prepare new statutes and ordinances. In order to avoid the sometimes-acrimonious annual discussions on allowed numbers, a constraint was built into the statutes that limited the numbers of research fellows to a maximum of twenty one unless there was a special resolution supported by at least two-thirds of the membership of the governing body.

Unlike the early non-stipendiary elections, the stipendiary research fellowship competition was always conducted on a formal basis. The first such fellow, Malcolm Longair, became an official fellow and praelector, and in 1975 married Deborah Howard, Leverhulme fellow in fine arts and a research fellow of the college. This was not the first marriage arising from the foundation of Clare Hall, for in 1968 Judith Martin of Clare Hall married Nigel Weiss of Clare College, thus setting the relationship of the two colleges on the best possible footing. Earlier husband and wife partnerships as fellows of Clare Hall included Peter and Ursula Dronke, and Elliott and Ninon Leader.

VISITING FELLOWS, ASSOCIATES, AND LIFE MEMBERS

In October 1969 when the new buildings were first occupied, there were 11 visiting fellows, and 16 visiting associates. The associates were a new class of member, introduced in 1968 so as to include younger visiting members, whose career had not yet reached the level of distinction that was expected for visiting fellows. There was an initial requirement that such visiting associates should be involved in research of particular interest to a fellow on the governing body though this was not enforced for long. The title, *associate* was also introduced for directors of studies appointed to provide guidance to graduate students in subjects such as law, education or medicine in which there were no official fellows.

In the period 1965–69 there were 41 visiting fellows, of whom 18 came from the USA, 5 from India, 4 from universities in the UK, 3 from Australia, 2 each from Canada, Czechoslovakia and Poland, and 1 each from Eire, Hungary, Italy, Japan and Nigeria. The fields of study ranged widely, the most frequent being theoretical physics (8), economics (4), control engineering (4) and anthropology (3). To some extent, in these early years the dominant subjects represented the interests of the permanent fellows, but this correlation disappeared in later years when applications became more influenced by the increasing awareness of Clare Hall amongst academic communities around the world.

The college has been fortunate in the distinction of its visiting fellows and a future college history could be built around their role and influence in the world academic scene. Anthony Low was a visiting fellow in 1972, en route from Sussex to Australia, later becoming Vice-Chancellor of the Australian National University, and in 1987 President of Clare Hall. In 1972 also, Michael Ashby (the son of Lord and Lady Ashby) was a visiting fellow, and in 1973 he returned from a professorship at Harvard to take up a Cambridge chair in engineering and a professorial fellowship in Clare Hall. He was soon to become chairman of the fellowship committee and to contribute to musical activities in the college. Frank Rhodes, distinguished geologist and President of Cornell University, came first as a visiting fellow in 1981 and later as a visiting life member. Jim Freedman, Dean of Law in the University of Pennsylvania was a visiting fellow in 1976–77, and later became President of Dartmouth.

In 1976, the visiting fellows also included Michael Stoker, then the Director of the Imperial Cancer Research Laboratories and a future President of Clare Hall, and Witold Rodzinski from the University of Warsaw. Rodzinski's early career had included a period as a bomber pilot in Corsica at the base immortalised in Joseph Heller's novel *Catch – 22*, which Rodzinski always maintained was a faithful description of life in the base. Later, after a period in academic life, he became Polish Ambassador in London, after which he became Ambassador in Beijing. This was during the Cultural Revolution, a particularly tense and dangerous period for embassy staff from which he returned with relief to Warsaw University to work on his distinguished volumes on the history of China, partly researched and written whilst in Clare Hall.

Dr Ivor Giaever, who had been amongst the first resident visiting fellows resident in the Clare Hall apartments, was awarded a Nobel Prize for physics in 1973. Miss Morna Hooker, who was a visiting fellow in 1974, was elected to the Lady Margaret Professorship of Divinity, succeeding the Revd.C.F.D. Moule of Clare College, who was amongst the fellows who founded Clare Hall. In 1977/78 one of the visiting fellows, Joseph Brodsky, was invited to Clare Hall as the Poet in Residence. He had been born in Leningrad in 1940 and was already one of the most distinguished poets in Russia when he was forced into exile in 1972. He moved to the United States and through English translations of his poetry he acquired a world-wide reputation. In 1987 he was awarded the Nobel Prize for literature.

The link with our alma mater and trustee was further strengthened by the establishment of the principle that a Clare College fellow may take sabbatical leave across the river in Clare Hall: thus Richard West of Clare College had the rights and privileges of visiting fellowship in 1974, a visit happily repeated in later years when he had become professor of botany in the university. His first visit set a precedent that later developed so that in almost every year Clare Hall would include a fellow of Clare College on sabbatical leave.

By 1975 there were 14 visiting fellows and 35 visiting associates. There were also 4 visiting scholars – who were required to be at least comparable in distinction with visiting fellows, but in Cambridge for only a short period. For a visiting fellowship, the minimum duration has normally been three months – with a preference for more. In addition, there were 20 *other associates* a title then being used for former fellows or visiting fellows still living in Cambridge. Some signs of stability in numbers of visitors were beginning to show by 1980, when there were 21 visiting fellows and 22 visiting associates. In that year there were 58 *other associates*[17] – a class that was expected to continue to grow as former members of the college took other appointments in Cambridge – in the university, in other colleges or in industry and commerce.

GRADUATE STUDENTS

From its conception in January 1964 it was intended that Clare Hall would develop its own group of graduate students distinct from those in Clare College. It was originally expected that the numbers of graduate students would be very limited during the early years whilst members were the guests of the fellows of Clare College. However, in response to the wishes of the founders that graduate students be admitted as soon as possible, the first 6 students were admitted in 1967. When the new buildings were occupied in June 1969 there were 17, but an additional 16 graduate students joined in October of that year, bringing the total to 33. By October 1971 the number had increased to 58, and the official total remained near that level until in the late 1970s it was decided to increase the target number to 70. The official total is given by the number paying college fees, but if a student researching for a Ph.D. takes longer than the statutory period of three years, the college does not normally charge further fees, even though the student may remain in Cambridge and continue to use the facilities of the college. These 'time-expired' students also continue to pay the lower 'student prices' for meals taken in college. Their numbers were initially small, but by 1980 there was a total of nearly 90 graduate students, of whom about 15 had completed three years of residence towards a Ph.D.

Terence Armstrong was the first tutor for the college's graduate students, with responsibility for admissions and for allocating accommodation in college as well as giving help in other respects. Armstrong became senior tutor in 1972 when Leslie Barnett became a

---

[17] In 1986, when former visiting fellows and associates were made *life members* of the college, the *other associates* were retitled as resident life members, or visiting life members.

tutor and she succeeded Armstrong as senior tutor in 1975, continuing in this post until 1988 when she became an emeritus fellow. From 1975 other tutors also took a share of the responsibilities for admitting and advising the graduate students.

In 1972, with a total of 59 graduate students in Clare Hall, about half were from universities in the U.K. There were 5 from the U.S.A., 3 each from Australia and Italy, and 1 or 2 each from Belgium, Brazil, Canada, Ceylon (now Sri Lanka), the Netherlands, New Zealand, Poland, Portugal, Rhodesia (now Zimbabwe), and Uruguay. Their fields of study ranged over 28 different subjects, and the numbers of men and women were nearly equal.

The world-wide student unrest in the second half of the 1960s and the early 1970s had relatively little impact in Cambridge University and no direct impact on Clare Hall. However, indirectly Clare Hall briefly attracted public attention when the college accepted Rudi Dutschke as a research student in the Spring of 1970. Dutschke had been a sociology student in the Free University of West Berlin and became leader of the Socialist Students Federation in demonstrations to express opposition to the German government. Although Dutschke was opposed to physical violence, such violence often followed from the street demonstrations. In April 1968, he was shot in the head by a would-be assassin, and subsequently in December of that year he was admitted to Britain for medical treatment. In August of 1970, Dutschke took up residence in a college apartment with his wife and two children, and whilst in Clare Hall he was seeking permission to stay in the UK as a student. His application received support from faculty and students in Cambridge and in Clare Hall, but was refused by the Home Secretary in a highly publicised case whose procedures attracted heavy criticism[18]. He left Clare Hall in February 1971 after a well-attended "being-thrown-out party" at which members of Clare Hall seemed unusually orthodox in comparison with the intellectual and sartorial variety of other guests. Dutschke moved to Aarhus in Denmark where he became an assistant tutor at the university and he died there in an accident 8 years later at the age of 39.

---

[18] This brief note is based on the oral history of Rudi Dutschke's stay in Clare Hall, edited by Henry Ryan, a visiting fellow of Clare Hall in 1996.

As well as contributing to scholarly work and social events in the college, representatives of the graduate students increasingly participated in management through representation on the college council and on some of the committees. Their numbers were initially too small for full participation as a college in sporting activities, but some members rowed in Clare College boats. In 1972 a Clare Hall student, Leslie Jenkins, was awarded a Golf Blue as a member of the university's team in the match against Oxford. The level of enthusiasm for sports fluctuated, and in 1979–80 teams were fielded in rowing (briefly), volley-ball, squash, table tennis, and cricket. In that year, the cricket team was considerably strengthened by the recruitment of a former visiting fellow, Geoff Harcourt, on his second visit to Clare Hall from Australia. Harcourt remained in Cambridge as a lecturer in the faculty of economics, becoming also a fellow of Jesus College but continuing to be seen regularly in Clare Hall.

The shortage of affordable accommodation for graduate students in college continued to be a problem throughout the 1970's for the students

29. *Keyneside*, renamed *Leslie Barnett House* in 1996.

and for the tutors. Two of the family houses became shared graduate residences for a period, and in 1976/7 a house with ten student rooms were borrowed from Robinson College, newly founded across Herschel Road from Clare Hall. The mismatch between available college accommodation and numbers of students was exacerbated during this period by the creditable desire within the college to increase the numbers of students in response to the wish of many university departments to expand their graduate teaching and research. In the mid-1970s there were serious problems from inflation and forward projections of college finances were singularly difficult so there was no opportunity to spend our way out of the problem.

However, in 1978 the college was able to begin negotiations to purchase the remainder of the lease of no. 3 Herschel Road from our neighbour Professor Richard Keynes – subject to an arrangement under which Keynes was able to build a smaller house on the far garden. In 1980 the house was converted for use by nine of our graduate students, and with the approval of Prof. and Mrs Keynes, it became known as *Keyneside*. The land acquired with this transaction was landscaped and planted with the aid of a gift from Mr Tom Usher, a regular visitor to the college. The name *Keyneside* was used until 1996 when postal confusion with our neighbours led to its renaming as *Leslie Barnett House*, honouring Leslie Barnett, who was tutor and then senior tutor for 19 years and on retirement became an emeritus fellow.

CLARE HALL TALKS, CONCERTS AND EXHIBITIONS[19]

With the prospect of our own buildings and a meeting room, a lectures committee had been formed early in 1969. There were three Clare Hall talks during the Michaelmas term on Thursday evenings after supper. They were all illustrated by slides and intended to be comprehensible to people working in different fields from the speakers. These were: Malcolm Longair on physics recently done in Russia, Carmen Blacker on Japan

---

[19] The earlier records of these events have been gleaned from file notes in the college archives. The *Clare Hall Newsletter* began in 1972/73, and is the main source of later information of most organised social activities in the college, ranging from scholarly talks to parties and croquet.

and Japanese studies, and David Buxton on Ethiopia and Ethiopian studies.

Later talks were equally varied: wooden churches in Poland, Kibbutz in Israel, the Japanese home, ancient Nigerian bronzes, alchemy in ancient China, antique silver, the Universe, tourism in Sri Lanka, modern Chinese history, the coming age of energy conservation, South African rock paintings, clarinets – old and new. Other cultural activities included whisky tasting with a musical accompaniment, poetry readings, films, and (less frequently) original drama in the style of Shakespeare. There were also occasional seminars of specialist groups, in botany, in history, and in other areas, though it was not until the 1980s that these became regular events. Thus the meeting room was not in use on every evening for college activities and for a period in the 1970s about fifty members of the Cambridge Flower (arranging) Club, at that time chaired by Elsie Eden, met once a month in Clare Hall until the increased numbers attending enforced a move to a larger hall in Newnham College.

From 1969, concerts were a regular feature of Clare Hall life though their frequency varied from year to year. Amongst the fellows who were also performers were Michael Ashby, Malcolm Longair, Ronald Popperwell, Brian Pippard, and Nick Shackleton. Musical talent amongst visiting fellows and their partners was as impressive as it was welcomed.

Stimulated by some generous gifts from departing visiting fellows, it was decided that further desirable furnishings could be afforded. These included a Bechstein grand piano that was purchased for the college by Drs Longair and Popperwell for £305 and installed in the Studio in Elmside. Also using these gifts, the college purchased garden furniture which had originally been included in Erskine's plans, but had been struck out during the earlier period of financial concern about the cost of the buildings. In 1976, as a mark of their relation with Robert Honeycombe, the Goldsmiths' Company made a gift to the college of a specially designed silver coffee pot and sugar basin.

The courtyard, where dramatic waterfalls can be seen during rainstorms, has periodically been a home for ducks – though discouraged by successive bursars. The surrounding corridor was soon found to be an excellent location for art exhibitions, and over the years Clare Hall has made a valuable contribution to the display of pictures by new or established artists, much appreciated by members of the college. These

30. Signing the Trust Deed for the Tanner Lectures Foundation, July 1979, in the President's House at Clare Hall:
(a) (above) Obert Tanner with Audrey Glauert,
(b) (below) Eric Ashby, with Audrey Glauert.

exhibitions have also enabled the college to acquire an interesting and varied collection of paintings some of which are displayed in the public rooms and some are on loan in members rooms or apartments.

THE TANNER LECTURES

The Tanner Lectures on Human Values[20] were formally founded at Clare Hall on 1 July 1978 with the signing of a Trust Deed. The purpose of the lectures is to advance scholarly and scientific learning in the field of human values, and the intention is that they should be wide-ranging in appeal and choice of topic, that they should be international and intercultural, transcending ethnic and national origins as well as religious and ideological distinctions. Permanent Tanner Lectureships, with lectures given annually, were established at six universities: Clare Hall for Cambridge University, Harvard University, Brasenose College for Oxford University, Stanford University, University of Michigan, University of Utah. Each year Lectureships may be granted to not more than four additional universities for one year only.

The Lectures are funded by an endowment set up by Obert C. Tanner, Professor Emeritus of Philosophy at the University of Utah, and his wife Grace A. Tanner, and are directed by a Board of Trustees advised by a Commission. The founding Trustees, meeting in Clare Hall in 1978, included Obert Tanner himself and Lord Ashby. This planning meeting was also attended by members of the Commission: Derek Bok, President of Harvard, Robben W. Fleming, President of the University of Michigan, and Richard Lyman, President of Stanford University. The gathering was hosted in Clare Hall by the President, Robert Honeycombe with his wife June, and the formalities for the signing of the Trust Deed by Obert Tanner and Lord Ashby were presided over by Audrey Glauert JP.

The chairman of the Trustees at their inaugural meeting was David Gardner, President of the University of Utah. A year later, in 1979, we were very pleased to welcome him as a visiting fellow of Clare Hall accompanied by his wife Libby and their daughters[21]. The Gardner family

---

[20] Tanner Lectures, *The Tanner Lectures on Human Values*, Eds. S. M. McMurrin (Cambridge, and Utah, University Presses), annual from 1980, vols. 1– .

[21] See also chapter 14 which describes the presentation to Clare Hall in 1997 of the Libby Gardner memorial fountain.

was resident in the college during their visit and, as with most children of visiting fellows, their daughters attended local schools.

The first Tanner lecture in Clare Hall was given in 1978 by Conor Cruise O'Brien, the editor of the Observer, who lectured on *Morality, Politics and the Press*. The following year, Raymond Aron lectured on *Arms Control and Peace Research*, and a format was established for two or three lectures, a reception in the college, followed by a seminar-discussion with several invited participants. This format has been continued successfully each year and the Tanner lectures have become a distinguished event in the annual calendar of Clare Hall and the University of Cambridge. Later Tanner lecturers included Steven Gould, from Harvard on *the Challenges of Neo-Darwinism*, Amartya Sen from Oxford on *the Standard of Living*, Louis Blom-Cooper on *the Penalty of Imprisonment*, and Dr Gro Brundtland, Prime Minister of Norway on *Environmental Challenges*. The lectures and lecturers are listed in appendix 8.

Chapter 14

CLARE HALL 1980 to 1998

THE PRESIDENCY OF MICHAEL STOKER
1980 to 1987

In 1980, Sir Michael Stoker was elected as the third President of Clare Hall and with his wife Veronica he took up residence in the college. They maintained the traditional informality and the welcome given to new members, and each academic year they aimed to invite all the fellows and their partners to dine with them in the President's house. This entailed a very full programme of dinner parties and, like Charlotte Pippard earlier, Veronica always prepared and cooked the meals herself.

Michael Stoker had returned to Cambridge in 1947 after war service in the Royal Army Medical Corps, and he held lectureships in pathology and was a fellow, assistant tutor and director of studies in medicine at Clare College until 1958 when he became the professor of virology in Glasgow University. He was the Director of the Imperial Cancer Research Fund Laboratories from 1968–79, and was a visiting fellow of Clare Hall in 1976, the year in which he became the Foreign Secretary of the Royal Society. In 1979 he returned to academic work in Cambridge and an official fellowship in Clare Hall, and he was knighted in 1980 shortly before becoming president of the college.

In 1981, after consultation with former visiting fellows and donors, Michael Stoker established the President's Fund for expenditure at the discretion of the President to enhance life in the college, and in 1982 the Foundation Fund to provide a visiting fellowship for someone from a developing country or Eastern Europe. It was at his suggestion that Obert Tanner made generous gifts for the Ashby Room and the Ashby lectures, both of which are described later. In 1986 he encouraged the governing body to decide that all former fellows and associates of the college would

31. Michael Stoker, President 1980–87, with Veronica Stoker.

become Life Members. Thus, there are now just two categories of former member: Life Members and Graduate Members – the former graduate students or alumni of the college. Another early initiative by the President was to set in progress the procedures for Clare Hall to become an independent college in the university. This had been previously discussed in 1978, but after preliminary inquiries it was decided then to await the next presidency.

When Clare Hall was founded in 1966, our Trustees had accepted that the passage of time would require a loosening of the initial ties. It transpired that these ties amounted mainly to friendly encouragement and

Clare Hall was left remarkably free to manage its own affairs. However, the trust deed allowed the option after fourteen years for Clare Hall to seek full independence, subject to the approval of Clare College.

As an Approved Foundation since 1966, Clare Hall functioned in most respects like an independent college, though Clare College continued as its trustee. There were some advantages in this arrangement since it was relatively easy to amend the regulations under which Clare Hall operated; in addition there was a valuable benefit from the skilful management of the joint investment portfolio by the investments committee of Clare College[1]. However, it was thought that negotiations for legal independence would be assisted by the presence on the governing body of Clare College of many of those fellows who had taken the original decision sixteen years earlier to found Clare Hall. There was an additional advantage that the President and three of the fellows[2] of Clare Hall had earlier been fellows of Clare College. After extensive discussion in Clare Hall and with the Trustees, in November 1981 it was decided to seek incorporation by Royal Charter so that Clare Hall would become an established college recognised as such by the University.

Although the formal application would be made by the Trustees on behalf of Clare Hall, it was first necessary to draft our charter and statutes, all of which would eventually have to be approved by Clare College, by the University, and by the Privy Council. This process was to take nearly two years. The task of preparing the statutes was largely delegated to a committee, which was fortunate to have Marjorie Chibnall as the principal scribe – as a distinguished medieval historian she could appreciate and interpret the medieval subtleties of college statutes, which were mostly first drafted in the Middle Ages. However, the eventual outcome was the work of many fellows, and Geoffrey Cass, fellow of the college and chief executive of the University Press, played a significant role in removing inconsistencies that seem to be endemic in most college statutes if sufficiently analysed. This problem is recognised by a clause in the statutes ensuring that any doubts about interpretation can be resolved by the President's ruling, subject *in extremis* to an appeal to the Visitor.

---

[1] Although Clare Hall had representation on the investment committee, its name had not been changed and it continued to follow the policies that had operated successfully since 1953 (see chapters 4 and 11).

[2] Pippard, Eden and Harding.

The choice of a Visitor, to whom disputes in the governing body may be referred for a final ruling, was one of the more interesting decisions that had to be made. The outcome was the result of a suggestion from Michael Stenton, one of the research fellows, and we were fortunate in obtaining the Vice-Chancellor of the Supreme Court of England and Wales, Sir Robert Megarry, as our first Visitor. He and his wife soon became welcome visitors to the college and a source of informal and wise advice. The grant of charter stated that the successors to the first Visitor shall be the Vice-Chancellors of the Supreme Court from time to time.

Clare Hall's graduate students devoted a considerable amount of time to discussions on proposed statutes, and their contribution was particularly valuable at a time when Cambridge was adjusting to the idea that students should have a role in institutional government. Their chairman during this period was Roderick McDowell, who also led the Clare Hall graduates in their organisation of the Third World Cultural Forum in January 1982 at the University Centre, opened by the Vice-Chancellor, which attracted over 4,000 visitors. For Clare Hall, it was decided that in the new statutes, the two representatives on the governing body elected by the graduate students would have full voting rights on all matters except on certain items of reserved business.

On 12 September 1984, the Queen in Council approved our Petition for a Royal Charter, which was subsequently sealed on 22 October. Concurrently the Council of the Senate announced that the statutes of the University had been amended to record the fact that Clare Hall was no longer an Approved Foundation but a College in the University of Cambridge.

In the ordinary life of the college, the changes when an approved foundation becomes a college would be hardly noticeable except perhaps that the conduct of affairs may be more exact as a result of the thought that had been given to precision in the college statutes. In Clare Hall the discussions in preparing statutes had also resulted in a wider appreciation amongst the fellows of the value of defined procedures of government in an institution that was increasing in both size and complexity.

The Royal Charter was collected by Terence Armstrong, then Vice-President of the college, in a modest ceremony[3] at the Home Office, which acts in such matters on behalf of the Queen: The porter at the Home

---

[3] Described in more detail in the *Clare Hall Newsletter 1983–84*.

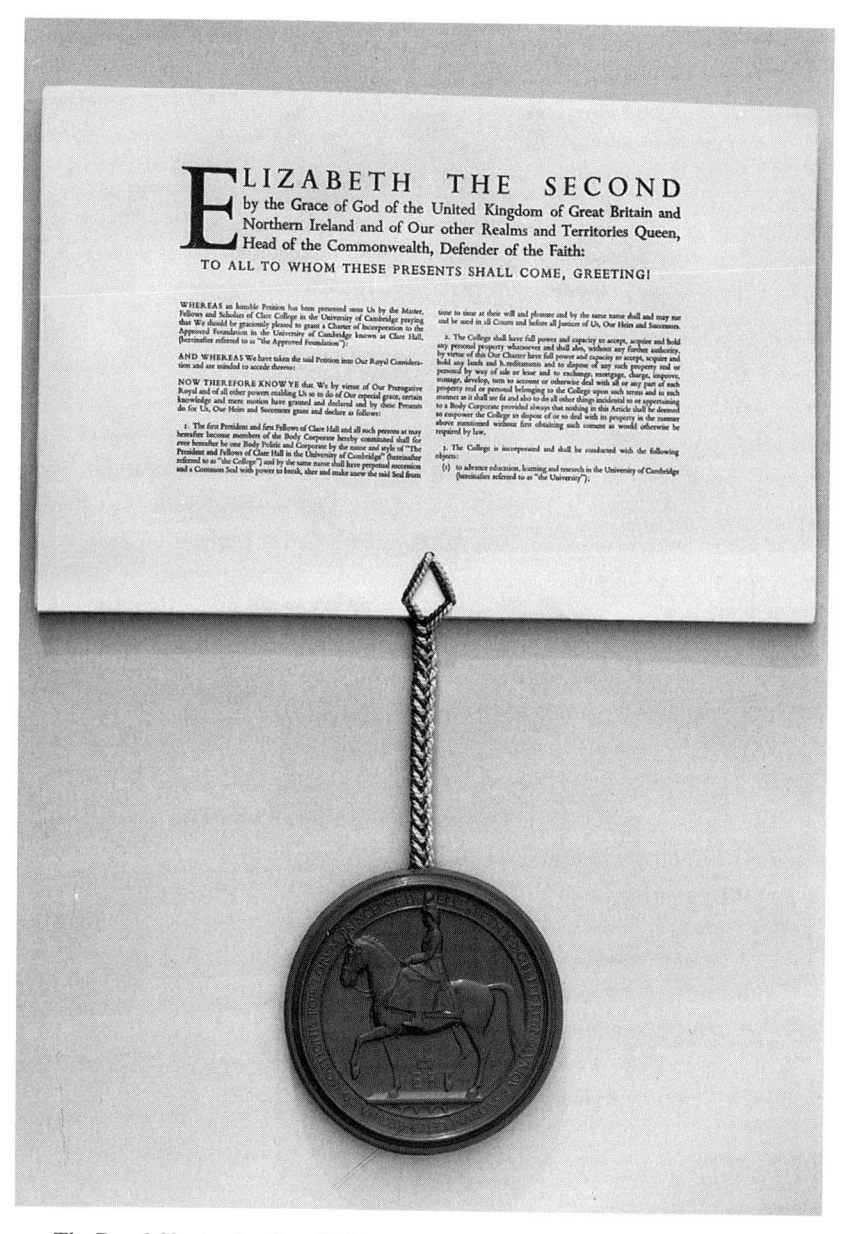

32. The Royal Charter for Clare Hall, 1984.

Office, told him to take a seat for a few minutes, just inside the main entrance. Armstrong's account continues,

"Quite soon a young lady emerged from the throng of passers-by, clutching a big, flat box, none too securely wrapped round with plastic cord. "Mr Armstrong is it?", she said, "Here you are then. I hope the string holds". In thirty seconds I was out in the street carrying my trophy, and reflecting on how many man-hours of academic and civil service time had led up to this, perhaps in a way rather British culmination. After all, what more is there to say about the issue now? It was all written down, on vellum probably, and spoken words would have been superfluous..."

On 5 November the fellows of Clare Hall were invited by the fellows of Clare College to a reception in the Master's Lodge, where the Acting Master, Timothy Smiley, on behalf of our former Trustees, received and handed back our Royal Charter to the President, Michael Stoker, thus formally granting our independence. On 15 December, Clare Hall held a reception to which were invited all members of the college including the staff, the fellows of Clare, the Vice-Chancellor and all heads of colleges. Clare Hall held a foundation dinner on 19 December, where the guests included Sir Robert and Lady Megarry, Lord and Lady Ashby, and Professor and Mrs John Northam.

In celebration of the Royal Charter, a former visiting fellow, George C. Smith II who is now a life member, offered to pay for a drawing or painting of the President. Michael Stoker said he would prefer that the gift be used for a drawing of three members of the college who had played a role in the foundation and development of Clare Hall. The outcome was a *conversation piece*, drawn by Bob Tulloch and showing Eric Ashby, Brian Pippard and Richard Eden. For many years it has been located in the common room, equidistant between the bar and the dining room. More recently it has been joined by individual drawings of Robert Honeycombe, Michael Stoker and Anthony Low.

When the college petitioned for the Charter, the governing body decided to seek a Grant of Arms from the Heralds of the College of Arms[4]. On the

---

[4] The reader may be astonished to learn that there was significant opposition in the governing body to the idea of Clare Hall acquiring something so traditional as a coat of arms and there were even grumbles about the cost. This opposition almost entirely disappeared when Geoffrey Cass, with his great experience of charities and their funding, explained that a coat of arms provided a symbolic recognition of the distinction of a charity and such recognition would be valuable in its own right and also for future fund-raising.

33. *Conversation Piece* in Clare Hall: Brian Pippard (left), Richard Eden (centre), and Eric Ashby (right). Drawing by Bob Tulloch, 1984.

day of incorporation of Clare Hall as an independent college this was approved by the College of Heralds and granted in Letters Patent from the Earl Marshall:

Chevronny Or and Gules; on a Chief Sable
five Gouttes, three and two, Argent.

The design is based on the arms of Clare College indicating that Clare Hall's own foundation comes in part from a share of the original endowment made by Lady Clare in 1336. Red chevrons derive from the arms of the Clare family, and the silver tears from the border around Clare College's Coat of Arms.

NEW BUILDINGS

For several years prior to 1980, it had been recognised in the college that there was a pressing need for more accommodation for graduate students, and this need became more urgent with the increase in student numbers. The target figure of 70 fee-paying students was supplemented by about 25 students who had completed the three years of residence required for a Ph.D. but were still living in Cambridge whilst completing their dissertations. Accommodation in the town was becoming increasingly expensive following the inflation of the 1970's and the consequent explosion in the price of houses.

However the financial position of the college was not sufficiently strong to allow a major building programme on the college site or the purchase of houses. Although by 1980 the college's investment income had nearly recovered from the low values of the mid 1970's, the need for more graduate accommodation was competing with a desire for more stipendiary research fellowships. Fortunately, it was at this time that the university decided to change its policy on the uses of the college contributions to the university, which – after certain allowed deductions – amounted to about 20 per cent of each college's endowment income. In future these would be paid into a *Colleges' Fund* from which grants would be made to supplement the corporate capital of the less well-endowed colleges.

Clare Hall was amongst the first of the colleges to receive a substantial grant from the Colleges' Fund in the early 1980s, amounting to £580,000 over two years. With the prospect of new building, an outline plan was prepared for the full development of the college site. This contemplated building a small conference suite adjacent to the dining room on the north side of the Elmside garden, which could include a new entrance to the college providing an elevator to enable access by wheelchair. Between the conference suite and Elmside there could be a new residential wing for graduate students. On the south side of the garden the outline plan indicated three more residential units that would permit most of the trees to be retained, thus completing an attractive courtyard for the eastern part of the college. To the west of the main buildings, the plan indicated a new residential wing adjacent to Herschel Road between the existing apartments and the Leslie Barnett Building (then called Keyneside).

Although the suggestions for building in the Elmside garden had considerable support because of the new facilities and meeting rooms that could be provided, they encountered strong opposition, particularly from some research fellows for whom the Victorian garden was an important part of the college. This opposition and the urgent need for new graduate student accommodation led to the decision to build a new residential wing

34. The *Michael Stoker Building* and the Clare Hall Apartments (architect Ralph Erskine).

to the west of the apartments. Ralph Erskine, the original architect of the buildings of Clare Hall, accepted the President's invitation for him to design the new building, and led to a continuity of style with the earlier apartments. The landscaping of the garden adjacent to the new building was later carried out with the aid of a gift from Obert Tanner.

The oversight for much of the planning for the new building and its subsequent construction was provided by the bursar, Dr Tony Harding, who had succeeded Adams in 1980. Harding had taken early retirement from a senior management position in Imperial Chemical Industries in 1979 and returned to live in Cambridge after an absence of 25 years. In the early 1950s he had been a fellow and assistant tutor in Clare College. Whilst bursar, he was also steward and showed great skill in choosing wines to lay down, having had a new wine cellar constructed for that purpose. He retired as bursar in 1985 but continued as a fellow until 1986 in order to supervise construction of the new building, appropriately named as the *Michael Stoker Building*. Harding was succeeded as bursar by John Garrod, who had previously been bursar of Van Mildert's College in Durham University after an earlier career in education in Nigeria.

Sir Michael Stoker retired from the presidency in 1987 and became an emeritus fellow. As a parting gift, he presented the Graduate Student Body with a punt, which they named *The Sir Michael Stoker*. Except when building a house in Spain, Michael and Veronica continued to be seen frequently in Clare Hall, where their presence was always appreciated by their many friends in the college.

THE PRESIDENCY OF ANTHONY LOW 1987 to 1994

Professor Anthony Low, Smuts Professor of the History of the British Commonwealth since 1983, became President of Clare Hall in 1987. He had studied in Oxford and took a doctorate there before joining the faculty at Makerere College, Uganda in 1951. In 1959 he became a research fellow at the Australian National University (ANU) in Canberra, and in 1964 he was the founding Dean of the School of African and Asian Studies in the University of Sussex and was Professor of History there from 1964–72. After a year in Cambridge as Smuts Fellow in 1972–73, when he was a visiting fellow of Clare Hall, he returned to Canberra as Professor of History, and was Vice-Chancellor of ANU during 1975–82. In 1987 Anthony Low succeeded Lord Ashby as the Cambridge Trustee for the Tanner Lectures Foundation.

During his presidency of Clare Hall from 1987 to 1994, Anthony Low and his wife, Belle, lived in college except for a sabbatical term in 1989, and they both continued the Clare Hall tradition of providing a social focus and giving a warm welcome to visiting fellows and their families and to graduate students.

In 1987, the college had accommodation on site for 35 graduate students, sufficient in that year to provide single rooms for most new students. The total of fee-paying students at that time was about 80, and there were about 30 more students still working on their dissertations for the degree of Ph.D. but were no longer fee-paying, having completed the required three years of residence. With 35 graduate students living in college, and their ex officio representation on college committees, there was a valued increase in their participation in college activities and

35. Anthony Low, President 1987–94, with Belle Low.

events. However, there was also pressure from the university for colleges to accept more graduate students in order to allow departments to increase their graduate teaching, particularly for the newly established one-year courses for Master's degrees. With the needs of the university in mind, the governing body decided to increase the number of graduate students from 80 to 100, even though this would exacerbate the tutors' problem in helping students to find accommodation. Since many of the graduate students in Clare Hall come from overseas, there was an urgent need to arrange additional accommodation.

It was hoped to solve this problem in the short-term through renting student rooms in Westminster College, a theological college at the end of Queens Road. This provided a partial solution – at least for a period – but it turned out that our students were less tolerant of the austere nature of the rooms than the earlier theological students of Westminster College and the option was not popular. At the same time, other colleges had also decided to expand their intake of graduate students, so Clare Hall did not receive a sufficient number of applicants wanting to study for a Ph.D. to reach the new target figure. Consequently to make up numbers the tutors accepted a larger number of one-year students studying for the newly created courses for a Master's degree. This resulted in a disproportionate increase in the number of new students each year, taking the total beyond the level that could be provided with rooms either on the college site or in Westminster College. As an emergency measure, the bursar arranged also for the college to rent a large furnished house in Chaucer Road, nearly two miles from the college. It was an expensive solution as students on one-year courses often required rooms for only nine months in the year, and the house was not very popular in comparison with college rooms.

Unfortunately, the alternative of providing student rooms through purchasing houses to provide college-owned student lodgings was not helped by the financial conditions at the time. Prices of houses were exceptionally high in the 1980s and the fall in the stock market in the autumn of 1987 had discouraged the use of further corporate capital in order to build or buy property. At that time it was normal for college-owned rooms to be rented to students at about two-thirds of the market rent and, taking into account also the requirement for repayment via a sinking fund, the purchase of property for rental to students would have led to a reduction in college income. However, the main reason for postponing a decision to buy or build was that there appeared to be a possibility of purchasing land for building nearly adjacent to the college on the other side of the rifle range footpath – a possibility that, following an extremely protracted public enquiry, disappeared in 1991 when the land to the west of the rugby ground was once again confirmed as a permanently green area. Subsequent developments are described later in this chapter.

In the Easter Term of 1989, Anthony Low asked me to be Acting President whilst he was on leave of absence in Australia. It was a

36. (a) (above left) Leslie Barnett, Senior Tutor 1972–88, Emeritus Fellow 1988,
(b) (above right) Marjorie Chibnall, Fellow 1971–83, Emeritus Fellow 1983,
(c) (below left) Geoffrey Bailey, Senior Tutor, 1989–96,
(d) (below right) Hugh Whittaker, Senior Tutor 1996– .

rewarding experience[5], which gave my wife and I an opportunity to appreciate both the privileges and the work involved when entertaining in the President's House. In that term also, there was a potential crisis in the tutorial arrangements when Hugh Williamson, who had succeeded Leslie Barnett as senior tutor, and Philip Duffus, who was the second tutor, were offered professorships in Oxford and Bristol, respectively. We took the unusual step of writing to every tenured lecturer, not already a fellow of a college, and were pleasantly suprised at the degree of interest. Anthony Low returned in June in time to agree our selection of Geoff Bailey as senior tutor and Jim Russell as the second tutor. In the same month, Anthony and Belle Low hosted a full meeting of the Tanner Trustees, including Obert and Grace Tanner themselves, the first in Cambridge since its foundation eleven years earlier.

Soon after the beginning of his presidency in 1987, Anthony Low had begun discussions with St. John's College about the possibility of new accommodation for Clare Hall visitors in a proposed housing development on the old Nursery Site of St. John's opposite to Churchill College. After considerable delay due to local planning regulations, this initiative by St. John's came to fruition late in September 1993, when Clare Hall rented and then furnished and sublet 12 apartments in Benian's Court, a new block of apartments and town houses. The installation of furniture was completed just in time for occupancy by newly arriving visiting fellows and their partners or families at the beginning of October, thus increasing to 33 the number of apartments owned or managed by Clare Hall.

In 1990, the college received a generous legacy from the late Bill McLean, who had been a visiting fellow in the early years of the college. On the initiative of the President, this legacy was used to convert the old coach house at the southern end of Elmside into an annex with six studies for the use of graduate students or fellows. The resulting McLean studies, designed by Nicholas Ray Associates, were completed in 1994 and provide a pleasing balance to the Ashby room.

---

[5] And well-timed, since I retired at the end of September 1989, becoming an emeritus fellow and returning again to the Institute for Advanced Study in Princeton for a semester. As an emeritus fellow, my role in college affairs was small until November 1992, when the Bursar, John Garrod became seriously ill. At the request of the President, I helped with administration until after the death of John Garrod, continuing until Edward Jarron was appointed Bursar in January 1996.

Lord Ashby died in the autumn of 1992. As the Master of Clare College he had played a crucial role in the founding of Clare Hall, always persuasive but also ready to adopt new ideas. Following the unanimous approval of the Clare Hall project by the governing body in January 1964, he gave it his unstinted support. The endowment funds from Clare College were a collective decision of the finance committee but it was Ashby's initiatives and personal involvement that led to the major endowment from the Old Dominion Foundation and the funding of an initial programme of visiting fellowships by the Ford Foundation. It was his willingness to adapt to circumstances that allowed the transition of the idea of Clare Hall as a centre for advanced study in Clare College to an approved foundation with the same objectives – and eventually to an independent college. His support for Clare Hall continued into his retirement and for many years Eric Ashby was the only honorary fellow of Clare Hall, regularly to be seen at lunch and often accompanied by Helen, Lady Ashby.

In 1984 Mr Obert Tanner made a donation to the college in honour of Lord Ashby for his help in setting up the Tanner lectures. This gift was used to convert the 'magic room' at the southern end of Elmside into the handsome Ashby Room, providing a work-place for a number of members of the college adjacent to the student accommodation in Elmside. The landscaping of the approach to the Ashby Room was aided by gifts from a number of former visiting fellows[6]. In recognition of his help to scholarship in the college, Obert Tanner was elected as the second honorary fellow of Clare Hall in 1986. Through the Tanner lectures and many other gifts he continued to help the college until his death in 1994.

During the presidency of Anthony Low, in 1992 the governing body elected two more honorary fellows – Brian Pippard and Richard Eden. Early in the presidency of his successor, Gillian Beer, two more honorary fellows were elected: Ralph Erskine, the architect for Clare Hall, and the distinguished philanthropist Paul Mellon, benefactor of Clare College and of Clare Hall.

---

[6] Bill Craig, Bill McClean, and others.

BOOKS, LECTURES, STUDY GROUPS, CONCERTS, AND ART

The creation of the Ashby room provided the honorary librarian, Audrey Glauert, with an opportunity to reorganise the collection of books – mainly donated by members of the college. Any member of the college who is the author or co-author of a book is invited to give a signed copy to the college. These members' books were placed in the Ashby room together with some key reference books – mostly purchased from members' donations. Travel books, guides and books for general reading and novels remained in the reading room, which continued to provide a small selection of newspapers and periodicals.

In 1983 in addition to the Tanner Lectures which Clare Hall organised and hosted as a contribution to scholarship in the University, the college was able to initiate its own series of lectures – the annual Ashby lectures, which also received financial support from the Obert Tanner foundation. The Tanner lecturer's visit was usually limited to the time required for the lectures, seminars and discussions, but it was intended that the Ashby lecturer would normally live in the Clare Hall community for a period of a month or more. In 1983 the Ashby lecturer was Paul Berg, a Nobel Lauriate from Stanford, whose work on gene splicing and his concern about the possible consequences had led in the 1970s to a national response in the UK through a study by a committee chaired by Lord Ashby. In 1986, the veteran Australian poet, Alec Hope, spoke on narrative verse and read three examples of his own work, drawing many members of the English faculty in addition to members of Clare Hall. The next Ashby lecturer was a visiting fellow from Canada, David Baguley who lectured on naturalism in fiction and was resident in the college for the Lent term of 1987.

Like the Tanner lectures the Ashby lectures provide an important event in the annual calendar of the college. Meanwhile, the more informal and more frequent Clare Hall talks continued to be given by members of the college for a general audience of members – in 1986/87 for example, titles included: enjoying Cambridge, an historian's visit to China, life on dark volcanoes, some small harvest for a biblical scholar. The final talk of that academic year was appropriately by Michael Stoker in the last year of his presidency and described some of his work on cancer research.

37. The Gamelin Band in Clare Hall dining room, May 1995.

In addition to these general talks, regular meetings of more specialised seminar or discussion groups became normal features in the Clare Hall calendar. The cell biology and history groups were well-established by 1982, both drawing members from Clare Hall and elsewhere in the university. Others have included a literature group, an interdisciplinary group, and more recently a women's group – the latter meeting once a week at lunchtime during 1995–98. Most groups depend on individual members of the college for their organisation, so their nature and character changes as some go into remission for a period.

The quaternary discussion group QDG, has a long history in Cambridge with membership drawn from the departments of earth sciences, geography, plant sciences, archaeology, and zoology. It has distinguished guest speakers and has a tradition of meeting in the college of the Director of the Godwin Institute which serves as its focus. Thus it has met regularly in Clare Hall since 1988 when Nick Shackleton became the Director. It was particularly appropriate that he was awarded the Crafoord Prize in 1995 by the Swedish Royal Academy of Sciences for his pioneering contributions to the understanding of climatic change in the Quaternary period. This distinguished prize was presented to him by the King of Sweden.

A notable feature of music in Clare Hall is its diversity – a result of its dependence on the musical talent and interests of the changing membership. 1983–84, the year of the Royal Charter, was an *annus mirabilis*: the college had four professional musicians/musicologists in residence. This led to a remarkable series of events, including: an evening of Japanese traditional chamber music in a format mixing performance and explanation by David Hughes, a wind quintet with Nick Shackleton using one of his huge collection of clarinets, a Sunday afternoon medieval dance recital, with audience participation, by the Capriol Society with Gunnel Clark, Greek folk dance music for summer bacchanalia and Scots folk music for Burns night. International variety is evident in most years. Concerts in the year 1994–95 began with a lecture-recital on the clavichord by Chilean-born Ruby Reid Thompson, who was later to become the college archivist, and concluded with a concert of Balinese music by the Gamelin band Kembangkirang.

The art exhibitions that had begun in the 1970s, had become a regular feature of the college by the 1980s, though – as always – dependent on finding a wise and enthusiastic coordinator or chairman of the art committee. The traditional gift to the college by each exhibiting artist of one of the pictures on display has led to a valued collection of paintings or drawings that is used to enhance the public rooms and the residential rooms in the college. Exhibits seen in the college included sculptures by Roydon Rabinowitch, a life member, some of which were subsequently on display in the Fitzwilliam Museum.

THE LONGAIR REVIEW

In the autumn of 1992, at the suggestion of the President, Anthony Low, the governing body asked a small group of fellows[7], chaired by Malcolm Longair, to undertake a review of the future of the college. Their report noted that the urgency of the review was caused by the decision of the university to increase the numbers of graduate students, a decision that

---

[7] Stefan Collini, Chris Hope, Barbara Knowles, Malcolm Longair (chairman).

The Longair review

38. (a) (above left) Malcolm Longair, Fellow 1967–80, 1991–, Vice-President 1994–, (b) (above right) Nick Shackleton, Fellow 1974–.

had the support of departments and faculties. This had led to requests to colleges to increase their intake of graduate students, to which some colleges were responding positively. However, for Clare Hall, a decision to increase the numbers of graduate students would have numerous consequences academically, socially and domestically. The report argued that any decision on this issue should be taken in the context of generally agreed policy guidelines. The objectives of the review were therefore to identify a set of policy options for future development of the college. It would also seek to identify factors that should be taken into account when setting priorities, including financial constraints and the feasibility of extending existing accommodation.

From replies to a questionnaire that they had circulated, the review committee concluded that there was a strong conviction amongst members of Clare Hall that it is a valuable and highly distinctive institution and that it should remain so. It was clear that most members of the college supported the aims of the founders, namely :

* to provide some facilities for advanced study and residence, and to establish a society of fellows primarily engaged in advanced study in Cambridge;
* to bring together an international community of visiting scholars, of Cambridge University lecturers and professors, and members of the university primarily engaged on research.

There was also support for the guidelines indicated by the founders including:

* The Institute must develop an intellectual life of its own. In addition to acting as a centre for a larger community there must be facilities for advanced study and discussion within its walls. It must be the primary place of study for a significant fraction of the fellows, although others will work in university laboratories, libraries and departments.

The committee found that the greatest area of disagreement concerned the graduate students – how well or poorly they were integrated into the college, whether they should have separate facilities, and whether the college should significantly expand the numbers of students. The main policy options identified by the review committee concerned the composition of the college. Its evolution is summarised in table 14.1.

The review committee identified six possible options for development, in each case indicating the building requirements and financial implications. These can be considered in two groups, though some would not be feasible without a very large new endowment.

1. *Slow evolution* retaining the one class society that has characterised Clare Hall in its first thirty years. Sub-options considered by the review committee were: (a) a reduction in the numbers of students, perhaps by admitting only students taking a Ph.D., (b) no significant change in numbers, (c) a small increase in the numbers of students.
2. *Provide separate facilities for graduate students.* Sub-options included:

    (a) steady-state in which the numbers of graduate students does not change, (b) a gradual increase in the numbers of students, (c) a rapid increase in the numbers of graduate students.

However, before future options for other development could be considered there was a prior need for new graduate student accommodation. This need had arisen because earlier policies had allowed an increased intake of graduate students before either the buildings or the associated finance

Table 14.1 *Composition of the College*

	1969	1980	1990	1998
The Visitor			1	1
The President	1	1	1	1
Honorary Fellows		1	2	4
Official Fellows[a]	17	21	26	28
Research Fellows	17	21	14	21
Emeritus Fellows		7	12	13
Visiting Fellows[b]	11	21	40	43
Visiting Associates[c]	16	22	4	6
Graduate Students[d]	33	70	95	96
Total	95	164	195	213
Additional Visitors[e]	–	10–15	10–20	10–30
Additional Students[f]	–	15–25	12–25	12–25

[a] Official Fellows includes Professorial and Supernumerary Fellows
[b] The total number of Visiting Fellows in the period 1966–69, when Clare Hall was based in Clare College, was 41. Later, during the 1980s and 1990s, the total number in each year was about 80, with an average length of stay about 7 months (see appendix 7 for further details).
[c] The class of Visiting Associate was abolished in 1986, but re-emerged a year later to accommodate a small number of visitors whose research is closely associated with a fellow of Clare Hall. There was a compensating increase in the total number of Visiting Fellows.
[d] Graduate Students include only those who are paying fees. Those not paying fees are listed as Additional Students.
[e] Additional Visitors are generally former Visiting Fellows, now Life Members, in Cambridge on study leave. The numbers vary considerably during a year, usually rising to a peak of more than 25 during the summer.
[f] Additional Students are those Graduate Students no longer paying fees, usually having completed the three years of residence in Cambridge required for a Ph.D., but who have not yet submitted their dissertations.

were available to provide them with college-owned accommodation. In 1993 the number of fee-paying graduate students was 100, of whom only 38 were housed in college. The proportion of students housed was one of the lowest figures for any Cambridge college, and since these statistics are published annually in the university's publicity literature the senior tutor advised the Longair committee that this would adversely influence future applications. This adverse effect was already evident through difficulty in admitting sufficient students who would be studying for a Ph.D. over a three-year period. In these circumstances more one-year students studying for Master's degrees were being admitted, thus increasing the problem of providing college accommodation for all first-year students.

Following the report of the Longair committee, a buildings committee chaired by the President was formed to examine options for a longer term solution to the problem of student accommodation. From the Spring of 1994, the President-elect, Gillian Beer, was invited to attend meetings of this committee, though no final decisions were to be reached until she had taken up office later that year.

THE PRESIDENCY OF GILLIAN BEER 1994 –

Professor Gillian Beer, the King Edward VII Professor of English, became President of Clare Hall in October 1994. A graduate of Oxford University, she taught at the University of London and after her marriage, for a short time, at Liverpool University before coming to Cambridge in 1964 when her husband John became a lecturer and subsequently a professor in the English Faculty. A year after arriving in Cambridge she became a research fellow at Girton College where she remained a fellow until moving to Clare Hall, serving as Vice-Mistress from 1983–87. In the English Faculty she was successively an assistant lecturer, lecturer, reader and British Academy research reader, and then professor, before her appointment in 1994 to the King Edward VII chair – the most senior professorship of English.

May 1996 saw the inauguration of an annual Clare Hall publication party, where Clare Hall fellows, life members, graduate students, and friends, gathered to view a selection of the books and articles written by members of the college and published during the past year. In that year and again in 1997, about sixty members of the college donated books, which they had authored, co-authored or edited, to the college library. In addition to taking an interest in books by members, in 1997 the President had the formidable task of reading 100 or-so novels as the Chair of the judges for the Booker Prize. More to her surprise, in that year the Clare Hall Boat Club gave the name *Gillian Beer* to the first boat to be owned by the club. Thus encouraged, in their second season in the May week races they moved up from the 6th to the 5th division.

Other cultural activities continued to flourish. Almost from its

39. Gillian Beer, President 1994– .

foundation, Clare Hall had spontaneously acquired the Cambridge tradition that formal dinners are often accompanied by music. In 1995/96 and again the following year the culinary menu was augmented in a variety of ways – Gothic Voices performed Anglo-Norman songs in celebration of Marjorie Chibnall's 80th birthday, the Venezuelan guitarist Eduardo Gonzalez played contemporary works during a South American evening, an Italian evening was enhanced by the tenor David Wickham giving a tour of Italian operatic highlights, and the Dr Jazz trio played throughout a summer garden party.

40. Clare Hall Novice Crew of the *Gillian Beer* Boat at Clare College Boat House, November 1997. (From left to right, all are graduate students unless otherwise noted) Claudia Vasquez (Chile, partner), Felipe Menanteau (Chile), Garrett Green, (USA, visiting fellow), Denis Low (Malaysia), Catherine Hayles, coxwain (Australia), Andrew Sellwood (UK), Lars P. Mikkelsen (Denmark, visiting fellow), Gerald Deshais, coach (France), Christoph Schlegel (Germany), Joerg Tuske (Germany).

In October 1994 during the first month of Gillian Beer's presidency, the college began to implement the recommendations of the buildings committee. After a further review by the finance committee, the governing body agreed that the college would release from its endowment a substantial capital sum for the purchase of student housing off-site, and it was also decided to proceed with the first stage of a new graduate building on the college site. The need for these developments had been recognised for some time, but they would not have been possible without beneficial improvements in the college's finances during the presidency of Anthony Low. The grants to Clare Hall from the Colleges' Fund that had provided the Michael Stoker Building had continued for a number of years, and by 1994 their total amounted to an increase of nearly 40 per cent in the endowment funds of the college. With earlier endowments these were invested in the joint portfolio managed by the Clare College Investments Committee. The general improvement in the Stock Market during the decade to 1994 was reflected in the growth of the endowment income from these investments. Additionally, there had been a substantial fall in real terms in prices of houses and in building costs, though in Cambridge the market rents for furnished property had not decreased to the same extent. These various factors were all favourable to disinvestment from Clare Hall's corporate capital for re-investment in property that could be rented to students or visiting fellows.

The use by a college of its corporate capital to purchase property or to build is permitted provided it is repaid over a stated period of years not exceeding 50 years. Yearly repayments must be indexed to inflation based on the retail prices index. This index does not fully reflect annual increases in college costs because wages and some other costs rise faster than averaged retail prices, but when account is taken of the rental income from the new properties the sinking fund repayment rule is considered to be sufficiently prudent financially. In situations where a college has an adequate margin of income over expenditure, it may not be necessary to limit expenditure to buildings that can provide rental income – thus corporate capital may be used to enhance college facilities, such as the provision of more studies or of meeting rooms, provided that sinking fund payments are made.

As a first step in the new developments, two houses were purchased in Newnham village, about one mile from the college and providing accommodation for 10 graduate students. The buildings committee, which had been formed in 1994 was asked to commission plans for building in the college grounds to the south-west of the visiting fellows' apartments, and submit them for planning approval by the city council. During much of this period, the bursar John Garrod was seriously ill,

41. (a) (above left) Geoffrey Cass, Fellow 1979–, (b) (above right) Edward Jarron, Fellow and Bursar 1996– .

though with support from the staff he continued in office until his death in November 1995. The domestic bursar, Diana Smith, acted as the secretary of the buildings committee in addition to her work in managing the housing for visiting fellows[8].

In January 1996, Edward Jarron was appointed bursar in succession to John Garrod. He was formerly an Air Commodore in the Royal Air Force with NATO in Brussels, and his earlier appointments included: Station Commander of the RAF Training College at Cranwell, RAF Director of Flying Training, and a period with the British Embassy in Moscow. His international experience was very appropriate in the multinational community of Clare Hall, and his management skills were soon evident in the exceptional developments in the college described in the following paragraphs.

The student housing in Elmside and in Leslie Barnett House required

---

[8] In December 1993, when John Garrod became seriously ill, my first recommendation was that the college appoint a part-time domestic bursar to manage the increasingly complex arrangements for housing visiting fellows. Diana Smith was appointed to this post in January 1994.

major renovation to meet new standards for dwellings in multiple occupancy, and lesser renovation was also required for the Michael Stoker building. This was carried out during 1995–6 and, on its completion, work commenced on the construction of a graduate student building on the south side of the west garden. The architects, Nicholas Ray Associates, retained the classical Clare Hall style in this building which includes 15 bed-sitting rooms with shared dining and kitchen areas, and three student apartments In addition, the college purchased two more houses in Barton Road, located about a mile from the college. This brought to 80 the total number of student rooms owned by the college, and it was hoped that this would be sufficient to meet the needs of most Clare Hall students.

New legislation on financial management required that Clare College and Clare Hall should either set up a new legal entity to manage the joint investment portfolio or split the portfolio so that each college would take responsibility for its own share. The latter option was chosen and a Clare Hall investments committee was formed in the summer of 1996. Chaired by the President, Gillian Beer, the committee involved some members of the finance committee and was supported by three advisers[9]. After the long and successful management by Clare College it was tempting to suppose that a similar system of direct management might be possible. However, it was thought that the technical information and procedures for financial management had become much more sophisticated since the earlier successes of Clare College. After examining various alternatives it was decided to invite Lazards' Fund Management to manage the investment portfolio on behalf of Clare Hall, following policy guidelines that were established in discussions between the committee and representatives of Lazards.

In September 1996, we learnt that the former family home of Lord and Lady Rothschild at 11 Herschel Road would be coming on the market. This large and attractive house is situated at the end of Herschel Road – only a short walk from the college. It was purchased by Clare Hall in January 1997 creating new opportunities for development that could not have been foreseen when the college had reviewed its development

---

[9] Dr Chris Johnson, formerly Senior Bursar of St John's, Prof Richard Eden, Honorary Fellow of Clare Hall, and Mr Niven Duncan who had great experience in investments and financial management both in London and internationally.

strategy three years earlier. At the request of the President, the Longair Committee was reconvened in late 1996 with the objective of studying options for the future of the college in the light of these new developments[10].

Their report began by summarising the priorities determined after their earlier report, notably: more accommodation for graduate students, more academic studies and meeting rooms and the enhancement of academic aspects of college life. Recent purchases and new college buildings had provided enough college-owned rooms for 80 per cent of the fee-paying graduate students. Thus the provision of graduate housing would remain satisfactory provided the college maintained its policy of limiting the growth in numbers to the facilities available. Following the committee's recommendations, the house at 11 Herschel Road was converted during the summer to provide nine flats, primarily for visiting fellows, a double guest room and three studies. The suite of three larger rooms would be public rooms for use by members of the college, and were equipped with facilities for lectures and meetings of study groups or committees, and may also be used for social and cultural events including occasional small dinners.

In October 1997 the governing body decided that the property at 11 Herschel Road should be called *Clare Hall West Court*. Subsequently, in January 1998 they decided that the three public rooms – the meeting room, the dining room, and the study – would be called the *Richard Eden Rooms*.

Soon after the purchase of Clare Hall West Court, some fellows had noticed that the swimming pool and sauna adjacent to the property were not part of the purchase, and concern was expressed about the competing desires to refurbish the derelict tennis court or to use the land for a future college building. Both concerns were resolved by the purchase during the summer of the swimming pool and some adjacent land that could be used for a new tennis court.

On 26 September 1997, the new graduate accommodation in the college was formally opened by the Pro-Vice-Chancellor and named as the *Brian*

---

[10] The members of the new Review Committee were Prof. Malcolm Longair (chair), Dr Stefan Collini (vice-chair), Mr Edward Jarron (bursar), Dr Hugh Whittaker (senior tutor), Dr Terri Apter, Dr Rosemary Luff, Dr John Carman, Dr Claire Chandler, Mr Darrin Lee Long, and Ms Carol McDavid, the last two being graduate students.

The presidency of Gillian Beer 1994–

42. Gathering at Clare Hall on 26 September 1997: (a) (above) Charlotte and Brian Pippard with Michael Stoker (centre), Tony Harding is on the right of the picture, Gillian Beer and Nicholas Ray are in the background between, and partly hidden by, Pippard and Harding. (b) (below) John Northam with Elsie Eden.

43. The *Libby Gardner Memorial Fountain*, David Gardner (left), Gillian Beer, and Nathan David (sculptor, right).

Pippard Building. On the same day a memorial fountain adjacent to this building was dedicated by David Gardner in memory of his first wife, Libby, who had accompanied him in 1979–80 when he was a visiting fellow of Clare Hall[11]. It was also a day of celebration, with lunch for nearly 200 members of Clare Hall and guests in a large marquee in part of the garden of West Court. Guests included fellows of Clare College who had a key role in the founding of Clare Hall: present were: John and Rachel Northam, Brian Reddaway, Brian and Gerda Cooper, and Don Holister. The spacious grounds of West Court and their potential for the future development of Clare Hall led some to speak of the occasion as almost a second founding of the college. The day concluded with a feast in the college with the Vice-Chancellor, the Pippards and the Gardner family as guests of honour.

[11] See the section on the Tanner Lectures in chapter 13.

44. Brian and Charlotte Pippard, with the Pro-Vice-Chancellor David Harrison, at the opening of the *Brian Pippard Building*, September 1997 (architects: Nicholas Ray Associates).

The importance of adequate finance to meet new needs and opportunities was underlined by the ability of Clare Hall to purchase and develop West Court. There is a high priority for fund-raising so that the college can meet currently identified needs and future opportunities. Earlier chapters have shown how the college's funds were provided in the past, and they have illustrated the achievements that have been made possible as a result of such benefactions. The structure of Clare Hall's funds is outlined in appendix 9. For *endowment funds* the capital is invested and only the income can be spent. Depending on the fund, this expenditure may be for general college purposes or for specific purposes, for example to help with the support of visiting fellows or of graduate students. Endowment funds are suitable for gifts where the benefactor wants to provide capital from which the resulting investment income can be used in perpetuity for college purposes. The Old Dominion Fund is an example of such a benefaction. Other endowment funds provide income

45. Clare Hall West Court from the garden.

that can be used to provide grants for students, for research or visiting fellows, for music in the college, and for the college archives.

In addition to the endowment funds, the college has a number of other funds, which in this context I shall call *general funds*; these are directed to specific needs and are managed on a cash-flow basis rather than on the use of income from invested capital. The five-year grant from the Ford Foundation to support visiting fellowships was in this category. Another example is the *President's Fund*, for which the income from gifts is used at the discretion of the President for expenditure to enhance life in the college. Past uses have included grants to students, the purchase of books for the Library, improvements of gardens, the purchase of pictures, and grants towards communal activities.

A new *general fund* was set up in 1996 to help with expenditure on new developments in the college. This is called the *New Buildings and Facilities Fund* and it is intended to be one of the main vehicles for future fund-raising activities to help with major capital expenditure. Income to this fund in its first year was used to help with the extensive refurbishment

The presidency of Gillian Beer 1994– 293

46. The Terrace at Clare Hall West Court, 26 September 1997.

of graduate housing. Further plans include help towards the purchase and renovation of a swimming pool adjacent to West Court and the construction of a tennis court. Other major building developments to which fund-raising is likely to be directed include additional accommodation for graduate students and visiting fellows in the grounds of West Court. Plans for these developments were prepared by Nicholas Ray Associates and early in 1998 they were submitted to the local authority for planning permission.

Both of the review committees chaired by Longair had also given a high priority to enhancing academic activities within the college, a view that had been endorsed by the governing body. This would require endowments to fund additional fellowships and studentships and funds specifically directed to the provision of additional studies and work stations. Ideally, they might be grouped around discussion rooms in a new college building and would create new opportunities for study groups in areas where formal or informal collaboration is of special value. Past experience of initiatives in Clare Hall shows that the academic direction

47. The *Richard Eden Rooms* in Clare Hall West Court.

of such groups could come from resident fellows in Cambridge or from life members or visiting fellows from universities elsewhere.

The scholarly programme for editing the letters of Charles Darwin is a good example of such a study group, though only partly based in Clare Hall. Led by Fred Burkhardt[12], life member and former visiting fellow of Clare Hall, the group has met in Cambridge each summer for the past twenty years, with help from facilities provided by the University Library, by Clare Hall, and by Robinson College, and with financial support from a number of Foundations. The resulting series of volumes[13], published by the Cambridge University Press, is a valuable contribution to scholarship in the history of science.

---

[12] From 1 September 1997, the Darwin project has been directed by Professor Duncan Porter, who is also a life member of Clare Hall and a former visiting fellow. Fred Burkhardt continues as the General Editior of the series of published volumes.

[13] *The Correspondence of Charles Darwin*, eds. F. Burkhardt, S. Smith et al., Vol.1 (1985) to Vol.10 (1997), continuing, Cambridge University Press.

MEANWHILE IN CLARE COLLEGE 1966 to 1998

On 14 February 1966 a study group was set up[14]

to consider as widely as it sees proper the implications of admitting women members to Clare College and to report, without recommendations, back to the Governing Body.

The study group reported in November 1968 and, after a lengthy period of discussion, in May 1970, the governing body of Clare College repealed the statute which read,

No woman shall be admitted a member of the College either on the Foundation or otherwise.

A change of statutes required a majority of two-thirds of those present and voting at a governing body meeting. This was achieved in two successive meetings and in the following year the first women fellows were elected: Dr Lucy King and Mrs Alison Sinclair. In 1972 Clare admitted 30 women undergraduates, and was one of the first three of the undergraduate colleges in Cambridge to become co-residential[15]. By 1997, 48 per cent of the total of 440 undergraduates in Clare were women, the highest proportion of women in any former men's college.

In 1958 when Ashby was appointed Master there were 32 fellows in Clare College. By 1964 when the decision was made to found Clare Hall the number had increased to 47. Twelve years later there were 55 fellows, and in 1993 there were 85 of whom only 10 were women fellows – reflecting the scarcity of women holding academic posts in the university, though numbers should increase as more women take up academic careers.

Ashby was Vice-Chancellor from 1967 to 1969. During that time he steered the University towards the establishment of its own medical school at Addenbrooke's Hospital. He also ably encouraged the faculties to involve students in discussions of university affairs, an approach which enabled Cambridge to avoid most of the potential fall-out from the world-wide student unrest that was endemic at that time. From 1971 to 1973 he was chairman of the Royal Commission on environmental pollution, and

---

[14] See Ashby in the *Clare Association Annual, 1986–87*.
[15] Clare, Churchill, and King's.

in 1973 he was made a life peer. On his retirement in 1975 Lord Ashby was elected to an honorary fellowship in Clare Hall, and he and Lady Ashby moved from the Master's Lodge to a house in Newnham, conveniently close to Clare Hall.

John Northam left Clare in 1972 to become Professor of Drama in Bristol University, but after taking early retirement he returned to Clare in 1987 where his fellowship and teaching role in English and Drama were renewed. He was followed as Senior Tutor of Clare College by Timothy Smiley (1966–69), Charles Feinstein (1969–78), Kenneth Riley (1978–97) and Simon Franklin (1997–).

In 1978 Brian Cooper retired after nearly twenty years as the bursar of Clare College, but he then became a life fellow and continued on a number of university committees. As described in earlier chapters, his support for the founding of Clare Hall was an important factor for its success and his purchase of St. Regis in Chesterton Road in 1964 came at a most opportune time. As the existing tenancies ended, these flats became available for graduate students. In the 1990s a block of offices on the same site was also purchased and converted to graduate accommodation. In the old court of the college, a middle common room had been provided in the early 1960s, and as the numbers increased from 47 in 1964 to 140 in 1996 the MCR became a significant centre for activities in the college.

Brian Reddaway retired from his university professorship in 1980 but continued to teach economics, and as a life fellow he remained a key member of the Clare investments committee, working with the bursar Brian Smale-Adams looking after the joint portfolio of Clare College and Clare Hall until in 1996 their shares in the portfolio were separated.

Ashby's successor as Master of Clare College was Robin Matthews, a distinguished economist and at that time chairman of the Social Sciences Research Council, a body responsible for distributing all research and postgraduate funding in the social sciences. He remained Master for 18 years, becoming also a professor[16] in the faculty of economics in 1980. His time as Master saw extensive building and modernisation, for which Don Holister as buildings bursar made a major contribution. The Clare site in Chesterton Lane, now called the Colony, was extended to a frontage on Castle Hill, providing more undergraduate rooms that made it the largest

---

[16] Professor of Political Economy, the chair from which Brian Reddaway had just retired.

of the three residential groupings of undergraduates in the college. In Memorial Court there was a major addition to the college with the building of the Forbes-Mellon Library in a central position, which created a second court named after Lord Ashby.

In 1993, Bob Hepple became Master of Clare College. He was born in South Africa, where he graduated in law and lectured for a period, before his active opposition to the apartheid regime led in 1963 to his detention without trial. On provisional release he escaped into Bechuanaland (now Botswana) and took refuge in Britain. From 1964 to 1966 he was a graduate in Clare, and in 1968 he became a fellow on his appointment as a lecturer in law in the university. Thus, in that year he met with the fellows of Clare Hall when they were still guests of Clare College.

Bob Hepple left Cambridge in 1976 for a succession of professorial appointments and five years as a full-time chairman of industrial tribunals before returning to Clare as Master in 1993. Two years later he was appointed to a professorship in the faculty of law. In the meantime the college continued its building activities by initiating an extensive renovation programme in Memorial Court, and made changes in the way in which responsibilities for teaching, advising and administration are shared between tutors, directors of study, and other college officers. More recently the College launched a major development campaign directed at raising funds for a variety of purposes, including scholarships, bursaries and student hardship, and possibly new buildings.

In 1993–94 Clare College was at the centre of one of the most remarkable developments in mathematics in this century when Andrew Wiles established a proof of Fermat's last theorem. The theorem was first stated without proof by Fermat more than 350 years ago. It states that the equation

$$a^n + b^n = c^n, \quad \text{where } n \text{ is an integer,}$$

has no solution in non-zero integers n, a, b, and c, if n is greater than or equal to 3.

Wiles came to Clare as a graduate student in 1974, and later became a research fellow in Clare before leaving for Princeton[17]. He announced the

---

[17] He had also been at school in Cambridge when his father Maurice Wiles was Dean of Clare College.

first version of his proof in a series of lectures at the Newton Institute in Cambridge in June 1993, but after some months study this version was found to be incomplete. Wiles completed the proof in the autumn of 1994 using a new formulation in which he made use of help from Richard Taylor, formerly his research student, and then on leave from his fellowship in Clare where he was director of studies in mathematics[18]. The importance of Fermat's theorem lies not in the theorem itself but in the widespread theoretical developments in mathematics that have come from attempts to prove it. This tradition was maintained in the remarkable range of mathematical theory that was eventually brought to bear on the problem by Andrew Wiles in providing the final proof of the theorem.

[18] Like Andrew Wiles, Richard Taylor is now a professor in Princeton. Coincidentally, his father, John Taylor, was one of my research students when I was director of studies in mathematics at Clare in the early 1950s, and he later became a professor of theoretical physics in Cambridge.(RJE)

Appendix 1

ASHBY'S TALK ON THE FOUNDING OF CLARE HALL

The address[1] given by Lord Ashby on 11 February 1976: the tenth anniversary of the founding of Clare Hall.

There is a belief among some members of Clare Hall who are not familiar with its origins that I am the Founding Father. This is flattering but embarrassing – embarrassing because it is wrong. I cannot entirely disclaim some responsibility, but if there are to be allegations of paternity, I plead guilty only to paternity-by-association. So I welcome the opportunity to put the record straight.

The story I have to tell is not a mere chronicle. It has for me fascinating implications. It demonstrates how an idea, if it is not codified and allowed to 'set' too soon, has a life and development of its own, and for a time its creators should just watch it and let it grow. It demonstrates how the timing for the moment of transition from talk to action is critical. And (though this may seem irrelevant) the story I shall tell has a parallel in the disengagement of Britain from her colonies in Africa (a matter which was engaging a lot of my time in the 1960s).

THE HISTORICAL BACKGROUND

It is essential first to put the story into the context of a much broader development: the changing balance between the University and its Colleges over the last 150 years. In the early 19th century the Colleges were supreme in Cambridge. The University was little more than an examining and certifying body, controlled by a hegemony of the Colleges. Two royal

---

[1] Edited by Lord Ashby immediately after his talk at the Foundation Dinner in Clare Hall. This version was reprinted in the *Clare Hall Newsletter 1983–84*.

commissions (in 1852 and 1876) began to restore the balance. By an act of 1877 the Colleges were obliged to pay a tax towards the upkeep of the University which, by 1960 (when the story starts), was over £120,000 a year. A further royal commission in 1922 opened the way for support for the University from the University Grants Committee (UGC). There followed a phase of rapid development of the University: new buildings (including the library and laboratories), an expansion of teaching and technical staff, and a reassertion of the University's ancient influence vis-à-vis the Colleges. University Teaching Officers (UTOs), for instance, looked to the University and not to the Colleges for their main source of income: a change which has proceeded much further in Cambridge than it has up to this day in Oxford.

All these developments created strains between the Colleges and the University. Owing to its massive income from the UGC and its massive grants for research, the University was outgrowing its traditional relationship with the Colleges. The three most sensitive points were: (a) a big increase in the number and the percentage of UTOs who were not Fellows of Colleges; (b) a big increase in the number of research students, for whom the Colleges made scant provision; (c) an increase in the number of senior visiting scholars to Cambridge, for whom most Colleges made no provision at all.

The following Table (compiled from data in the Cambridge University Reporter, xcii, No. 28, 13.3.1962) illustrates these points.

	1929–30	1961–62
UTOs	372	946
UTOs without Fellowships	109	433
Percentage of UTOs without Fellowships	29	45
Research students (approximately)	204	916
Visiting scholars (assigned laboratory space) i.e. in science etc. alone	?	144

The need to do something about these impending strains was realised as early as 1945. In that year a committee was appointed to consider the foundation of a Graduate College – and in 1947 a syndicate was appointed to consider the foundation of a club for non-Fellows and research students. Both these bodies presented reports which were discussed, criticised, and (with that genius Cambridge has for putting a problem in the way of every solution) shelved *sine die*.

THE BRIDGES REPORT

By 1960 these discontents had reached a level which prompted the University to make another attempt to alleviate them. A syndicate was appointed in June 1960 "to report on any ways in which they think the relations between the University and the Colleges could be improved...". (Note the frank use of the word "improved"). It was an unusual step to include on the syndicate four 'outsiders': Lord Bridges (recently retired from being Britain's top civil servant), two vice-chancellors of other universities (Durham and Glasgow), and the Master of University College, Oxford. Among the 'insiders' were three heads of Colleges, some dyed-in-the-wool College men, and some senior UTOs without Fellowships.

At the very earliest meeting there was evidence of the smouldering resentment which some UTOs felt towards Colleges. Pressure was brought to bear on the chairman (Bridges) to extract from the Colleges particulars about their finances which in the published accounts are cleverly concealed from all except bursars. To have done this would have been to alienate the considerable amount of goodwill which some Colleges had towards the whole operation; and I recollect the wise reply which Bridges gave when feelings became a little overheated at one discussion. "Mr X", he said, "do you know the Spanish proverb: 'God made eyelids as well as eyes'?"

The syndicate worked very hard, with meetings almost once a week. A rough draft was ready by the end of the Michaelmas Term 1961. Bridges and I (for I was vice-chairman) spent most of the Christmas vacation rewriting it. It was agreed unanimously and presented to the University on 13 March 1962. The recommendations relevant to my story were: (a) The building of a University Centre particularly for research students and non-Fellows, but also to be the University's centre for its own hospitality and for visiting scholars. (b) A proposal that Colleges could, if they were prepared to co-operate, absorb all UTOs appointed to the retiring age and assistant directors of research (ADRs) of more than 5 years' standing, without the necessity to create more Colleges (though discussions about one new College were already under way). The syndicate did not propose specifically that new Colleges should be created. It published a Table which set out the present number of Fellows in each College, together with the quota of new Fellows each College would need to absorb the 'qualified' UTOs. There were, of course, many other recommendations, but they are not germane to my story.

At first it looked as though the Bridges report would share the fate of the reports of 1945 and 1947. Public discussion of its recommendations was punctuated with that exasperating remark: "I am far from convinced" (which means "I don't understand this. I don't intend to try to understand it. And I shall vote against it"). Some Colleges took umbrage at the proposal that they might absorb more Fellows. ("Impossible for my College", said one speaker, "for our high table cannot hold more than twenty".)

However, this time the inertia had been overcome. Despite the public censure of the report, Colleges quietly got to work in private to decide what contribution they might make. It was in this atmosphere that Clare began sustained discussions on action to be taken in consequence of the Bridges report. We had a flying start because I was myself closely associated with the report and Bridges stayed in Clare Lodge and dined in Hall regularly during the sittings of the syndicate.

The quota of qualified UTOs which each College was asked to absorb was calculated on the student-numbers in each College. Clare (in 1960) had 38 Fellows, and its notional extra quota was 11, making a total of 49. The College willingly agreed to go up to about 50, and in fact we elected 10 additional Fellows during 1960–62. So we had already fulfilled that part of the Bridges' recommendations.

THE CONCEPTION OF CLARE HALL

The Bridges report was discussed through the Easter term of 1962. When we reassembled for the Michaelmas term a committee turned to the question of provision for more research students, together with the possibility of creating more opportunities for Fellowships if it could be done without exceeding 50 in Clare itself (which we thought was the limit above which we would lose cohesion in the society). We conceived the bright idea of a student village for married and single research students, with (perhaps) some additional Fellows (who would be bye-fellows of the College – though we did not know what that meant). We had some land

and some money which could be used for this village. It was to have married quarters, a crêche, a laundry, perhaps a shop, a café, and (one Fellow suggested) a resident midwife. It was an attractive idea and we played with it – and variations of it – in ten committee meetings during that academic year 1962–63. Until on 14 June 1963, the idea fell sick and died.

On that day I held a wine and cheese party in the Lodge and asked all the Clare research students to come, to discuss how they would like to live. (We had at the back of our minds a variant of Leckhampton, which Corpus had built for research students). It was a surprising and decisive meeting. The student from Australia or America wanted to live in the austere 18th century environment of Old Court, innocent of plumbing and other amenities. The Clare graduate, after three years in the College, could not get away fast enough to a room or a flat in Panton Street where he could live in freedom unmolested by tutors and the like. It seemed pretty clear that the customers were not as keen on our village as we were.

But the search for ways in which Clare could contribute to the University's needs went on, and I noticed that in my engagement book the meetings were now called "Satellite Committee", a significant clue which I would like you to bear in mind. There now emerged a difference of opinion among the Fellows of Clare. Some wanted the main effort to go into the provision for research students; others believed that this could be done inside Clare, and wanted the main effort to be provision for visiting scholars and for Fellowships for UTOs in the subjects for which Colleges have no teaching needs. The problem was how to provide for an increased Fellowship without swamping Clare itself, making its Governing Body so unwieldy that the intimacy which we valued so much would be lost.

Discussions of this sort, if they go on too long, get stale; the idea ceases to grow; the arguments go round in circles; opposition to action rises steeply. After a lot of experience one can sense when this critical point is approaching. By the Michaelmas term in 1963, I felt that the time had come to turn talk into action. On 1 November 1963, there is a note in my engagement book: "walk with John Northam" (who was Senior Tutor of Clare). We went out on the Coton footpath, and we both concluded that the College must soon be brought to jump the fence. The question we had to decide was which fence to jump[2]. By the end of that walk we came to the view that we ought to devise a specific scheme which would (a) increase Fellowships without increasing the size of Clare Governing Body; (b) provide for visiting scholars in some unspecified way; and that we should ask the College to deal separately with the still unresolved problem of research students. All this was not, of course, decided on the Coton footpath. It represented a point of view which Richard Eden (now a Fellow of Clare Hall but at that time a Fellow of Clare College) had suggested as a way to mediate between the various proposals under discussion; and we turned to him for help.

Through November and December 1963 John Northam and I had almost weekly working lunches in the Lodge to draft something to put to the Governing Body in January. But it was Richard Eden who broke the deadlock. He was not happy about our draft. He took it to Harwell in early January (where he was consulting for the Atomic Energy Research Establishment) and (so he tells me) he wrote an alternative draft between 5.15 and 7.00 p.m. on 4 January 1964 and gave it to me just in time to be considered by the Governing Body on 11 January.

THE FOUNDING FATHER

This seminal document, dated 9 January 1964, marks the moment of transition of idea into action. Eden's paper was entitled: *Proposal for an Institute for Advanced Study having special relationship with Clare College*. If you are looking for a moment of conception and for identification of paternity, this was the moment and Richard Eden was the man.

The paper proposed an Institute for UTOs not primarily in teaching subjects, visiting scholars, post-doctoral students without research

---

[2] See chapter 6 for a more detailed account of the related discussions. Lord Ashby read an early draft of my account of the founding of Clare Hall, much of which is based on documents and annotations on them that were not available to Lord Ashby when he gave his talk in 1976. After reading my account, he told me that his preference was for documentary evidence over personal memories, and he explained that his shortened version involved some 'poetic licence', necessitated by the brevity of his talk. His talk shows that his high regard and close collaboration with Northam was unaffected by the disagreements to which I refer in chapters 5, 6 and 10. They were, however, important facets of the evolution of the proposals for Clare Hall. (RJE)

fellowships, and (later on) research students. It was to be governed by a council comprising the Master of Clare as Chairman, 4 Clare Fellows, 8 members of the Institute, and the Institute's Director. The estimate for capital cost was £120,000.

On 11 January 1964 the Clare Governing Body discussed this document, approved it in principle, and appointed the Master, Dr Northam and Dr Eden to work out the details. There was still some opposition, in favour of putting the effort into provision for research students. We solved this problem by a simple device (though it is not always practicable), namely, when in doubt about which of two things to do, do both. At that same meeting it was resolved that the College Needs Committee should meet to consider provision for research students in the College; and later on that month, thanks to the imaginative initiative of the Bursar, the College bought a whole block of flats in Chesterton Road (St. Regis) which has become in some ways the student village we had talked about back in 1962.

Events now began to move quickly. Ten days after the Governing Body meeting Richard Eden produced a draft which set out the aims of the Institute in a form which I could use as a basis for getting money from foundations to help finance the venture. His memo was entitled *The Clare Institute* and its statement of aims was precisely what Clare Hall has become. Listen to this:

... to establish a society of Fellows primarily engaged on advanced study ...
... to bring together an international community of Visiting Scholars, of Cambridge University Lecturers and Professors ...

John Northam, Richard Eden and I met on 3, 10, 15, 17 and 22 February and reported to the Governing Body on 6 March 1964, just eight weeks after the approval in principle of the idea. Our paper was entitled *Proposed Extension to Clare College*. It embodied all Eden's ideas, and provided for a gradual build-up of research students as well. But pause for a moment to reflect on the title: an *extension* to Clare College; still governed by a council with the Master in the chair. Here was the assumption that there would be a permanent and indestructible umbilical cord attaching the Institute to Clare College. How reminiscent of the constitutions of the governing councils of Nigeria and Ghana before independence! And animated by a similar paternalistic goodwill.

On 6 March 1964, the Governing Body approved this paper with very few amendments. The working party was enlarged to include the Bursar (Brian Cooper), Domestic Bursar (Don Holister), Brian Reddaway and Bill Kingsford, and empowered to propose the names of five foundation Fellows for the new Institute (just what Fellowship would involve was still to be worked out, except that they would not be members of the Clare Governing Body) and to co-opt them, when they had been elected by the Governing Body, to form a provisional Council.

The infant had begun to grow in the womb.

GESTATION AND BIRTH

At this stage, in anticipation of the birth, the care of the unborn infant fell to a team of midwives (all male, for even 12 years ago Clare anticipated what has since become the Sex Discrimination Act). They were Bill Kingsford, who acted as secretary to the working party, Brian Cooper, who secured the site, Don Holister, who sought an architect, and Harry Godwin, who took the chair for its first seven meetings, while I went to America to seek (among other things) an endowment to finance the first visiting Fellowships.

In addition to the midwives there was a consultant obstetrician: John Northam. Under Harry Godwin the working party made a vigorous start. At its first meeting Bill Kingsford produced a list of architects and Don Holister undertook to make enquiries about some of them, and Colin Turpin was asked to draft a first attempt at a constitution. By May the working party had assembled a list of 32 names from which to choose (with the co-operation of the Clare Fellowship Committee) the people who should be approached as the five foundation Fellows.

June 1964 was a decisive month. First, we heard that the Old Dominion Foundation would endow Clare Hall with $200,000. Second, we got authority to approach the people we wanted as the five foundation Fellows. The decision to approach them was made at a meeting on 15 June. My engagement book for 16 June records that I got on my bike and made the following visits on that day: Armstrong 11.15, Hesse 12.45, David 3.30, Taylor 4.30, Dronke 6.00. I had to be very careful at these visits, for we still did not know what the status of the satellite would be, nor the standing of its Fellows; and we were still assuming that the umbilical cord would persist long after birth. So it is a testimony to the courage of those five people that they all consented to accept nomination. Thereupon the working party dissolved and the Provisional Council (still under the chairmanship of the Master of Clare) met for the first time on 22 July 1964. Meanwhile Ralph Erskine made his first visit to us (8–11 July) to discuss the building, and we had to make a painful (and at the time very controversial) decision, whether to pull down Herschel House, which stood on the site (and was occupied by tenants who were, not surprisingly, reluctant to leave) or to use the house as the nucleus of the new building. In the event it was decided to pull down the house, which stood where the President's flat and the kitchen are now. The acquisition of the site is a separate story, which I can only touch upon here. Briefly, it happened this way. Clare owned the land between the University Library and Grange Road. Planning permission to extend the Library would not be given unless this land was left permanently open. Therefore the University needed to acquire it from Clare. Clare agreed to sell it to the University provided a roughly equivalent piece of land could be bought by Clare in that neighbourhood. St John's College owned the land in Herschel Road on which Clare Hall stands. It was this piece of land which – in a complicated triangular transaction – Clare College acquired in exchange for the land the College sold to the University to make possible the extension to the University Library; and the College then donated the land to Clare Hall.

But the new society developed vigorously without waiting for a roof over its head. The Fellows were given full dining and lunching rights in the College and from October 1964 they met for dinner every Tuesday night in the dining room of the Master's Lodge and kept that up until I became Vice-Chancellor in 1967, and regretfully had to decant Clare Hall (as it had then become) to meet in the University Centre. Visiting scholars were elected and began to turn up. Mrs Cooper very generously consented to act as lodgings officer to find places for them to live. The Society (I used to think after those Tuesday dinners) was like nothing so much as a lively government-in-exile for some foreign state.

It was during this Michaelmas term 1964 that we began to realise that the idea of Clare Hall was growing beyond our first comprehension of it. It dawned on us that there was no satisfactory future for Clare Hall simply as an extension of Clare College. The umbilical cord would have to be cut, and the sooner the better. But there were two difficulties to be overcome first. One was financial. We were assuming at that time that Clare would give Clare Hall an annual subvention (as in fact Darwin College was to get from the three colleges sponsoring it); and annual subventions are inseparable from control – any decision to increase expenditure would need to have the consent of the paymaster. The other difficulty was to know what status Clare Hall would have if it were not simply an extension of Clare, as (for example) Leckhampton is simply an extension of Corpus. To have status in its own right, Clare Hall would have to be recognised by the University as an Approved Foundation, ultimately leading to full collegiate status. Before the end of the term we had decided that the Trust Deed for Clare Hall must be drawn up in such a way that we could apply to the University for its recognition as an Approved Foundation, a status which is almost indistinguishable from complete collegiate autonomy.

There remained the problem of finance. Clare had given to Clare Hall its last remaining piece of land in Cambridge suitable for collegiate building and it had agreed to underwrite the cost of putting up the building (architects' sketches were going the rounds of the Fellows at Christmas 1964); so it was understandable that the College was hesitant about relinquishing some form of control. Besides, there was a strong desire to create a new sort of intercollegiate association; not simply to finance a new College (as Trinity, John's and Caius were jointly doing) and then to abandon any association with it. We had in mind a perpetual "family relationship" with reciprocal rights for the Fellows of the two societies, facilities for exchange of Fellows between the two societies, and so on.

It was not until May 1965 that the financial problem was solved. Credit for the solution goes to two assistant midwives: Brian Cooper as Bursar and Brian Reddaway. Finance committees notoriously strain at gnats and swallow camels, but I have never seen a finance committee swallowing a camel at such speed as this one did, on 24 May. No haggling about the size of an annual subvention; simply the decision to transfer £450,000 of Clare's endowments, to be used by Clare Hall at its own discretion for the building and for an initial endowment[3]. This heroic decision (I can call it that without immodesty, for although I was in the chair I took no initiative in the proposal) cleared the way for the last stages of the story.

Two further steps remained to be taken. The first was to elect a President of the new society. On 15 June the Provisional Council decided to ask Brian Pippard whether he would allow his name to go forward. I approached him armed with a battery of arguments as to why he should consent, and a battery of rejoinders to any objections he might be likely to raise against consenting. In the event none of these armaments was necessary. To our delight he accepted, with what I am sure was unfeigned pleasure, and with only one condition: that the President's drawing room should be large enough to hold a grand piano.

So we began the academic year 1965–66 with one remaining step to be taken by Clare before the actual achievement, namely to secure the recognition of Clare Hall as an Approved Foundation. Our application had been referred to a committee of the Council of the Senate. It was too much to expect any University Committee to agree a proposal without quibbling. Sure enough, the quibble came. The committee were apprehensive lest Clare, even though the umbilical cord was going to be cut, would nevertheless keep the infant in leading strings indefinitely. Would it not be better, the committee said, to have more than one College as trustee? At what stage, the committee asked, did Clare have it in mind to withdraw all control? Is there not a danger that in Clare's enthusiasm for a lasting association between the two societies the mother College might keep the daughter College in a state of permanent suzerainty? This catalogue of misgivings was delivered to me in November; it was essential to meet the objections before the term ended. I remember sitting down

---

[3] Brian Cooper, bursar of Clare informs me that there was concern about how much money should be spent on the building. It looked like being between £200,000 and £250,000, and likely to be added to in the expensive way of making changes during building. He (Cooper) did not want to be involved in such decisions, so the gift of a lump sum would put the onus on the President and fellows-designate of Clare Hall. He thought that an adequate income stream could be provided by an additional endowment approximately equal to the cost of the building. He also thought the benefit to Clare College of avoiding a major expansion of the fellowship fully justified a gift to Clare Hall totalling up to £500,000. Having this view prior to the meeting of the finance committee, he had no difficulty in "swallowing the camel". Cooper's recollection also is that Brian Reddaway was influenced by the feeling that inflation being inevitable it was a good policy to spend now if there was a good project. (RJE)

and typing a 2500-word letter to the Council of the Senate, trying to meet all their apprehensions with appropriate reassurances. It was at that stage that I suggested the formula which appears in the Trust Deed, and to which the Governing Body of Clare Hall will soon, doubtless, be giving attention. Would the University be satisfied (I asked) if at any time after 7 years and in any case not beyond 14 years from the sealing of the Deed, the Trust expires[4] and there remains no formal link between Clare College and Clare Hall? This did satisfy the University. On 6 December 1965 the Council of the Senate passed the application on to the Regent House recommending approval. The Governing Body of Clare approved and sealed the Deed on 7 February, having been assured that the status of an Approved Foundation would be granted. On the next day, 8 February, the Provisional Council of Clare Hall met in the Lodge. The Master reported that the labour pains were over. The Governing Body had, after approving the Trust Deed, agreed formally to the election of the first President and 18 Fellows (including 9 'official' Fellows, one professorial Fellow, 5 research Fellows and 3 visiting Fellows). This was followed by item 4 on the minutes which reads: "The Master formally dissolved the Provisional Council". Clare Hall was "liberated".

---

[4] Ashby's recollection was wrong, in fact he was more cautious: the Trust Deed would not expire, since this would have placed Clare Hall in a legal vacuum, but there would be a change in the degree of control by the Trustees, and Clare Hall could request them to initiate a move towards independence. Ashby wrote a memo to this effect in 1982 to the President of Clare Hall (Stoker) giving a corrected account of the evolution of the Trust Deed. More detail is given in chapter 10. (RJE)

Appendix 2

PROPOSAL FOR A CLARE INSTITUTE FOR ADVANCED STUDY

The proposal from Dr R. J. Eden dated 9 January 1964 for the governing body meeting on 11 January

Proposal for an Institute for Advanced Study having Special Relations with Clare College

1 NEEDS

There is an increasing need in Cambridge for an expanded fellowship to include people in the following classes: (a) University Lecturers not in primary teaching subjects, (b) Visiting Scholars, (c) Research PhDs not financed by Colleges. There is an increasing need for means of bringing research students into a wider community of Scholars than in Departments.

2 PURPOSES

An Institute for Advanced Study should provide facilities for a Society of Fellows in the following main categories:-

(a) University Lecturers etc. to form a semi-permanent nucleus for the Society, since the other fellows are all temporary.
(b) Visiting Fellows selected from scholars on study-leave from overseas and (in increasing numbers) from other Universities in the UK.
(c) Research Fellows selected from (i) post-doctoral research workers on temporary appointments in departments (e.g. Applied Economics, Medical Research Council, Engineering etc.) and (ii) Research Students holding DSIR or other awards.

In addition there should be

(d) Associate Fellows, who are Fellows of Colleges e.g. some members of Clare College.

All the above Fellows to be non-stipendiary. In addition there could be Research Students in the Society but this might well come as the second stage or stage 1B of the development. First the Society should be set up as a single class society.

3 PROPOSALS

First Stage of Development

(1) *The Institute to consist of Fellows in the following Classes:-*

A. Fellows (men and women) holding University Appointments but not holding College Fellowships. About 15, commons provided but no stipend. In general permanent unless the Fellow moves to a College Fellowship.
B. Visiting Fellows. About 15, commons provided, and accommodation for renting to some of them and families but no stipend. Funds to be sought to provide some grants-in-aid and some free accommodation but neither is essential in the first instance.
C. Research Fellows. About 10, commons provided. No stipend from the Institute. These to be selected from amongst the post-doctoral research men and women in the University financed for example by DSIR Fellowships or Research Contracts. Tenure normally 3 years but limited to duration of their University Research Appointment. Funds should be sought to provide Stipends for Arts Research Fellowships in this category. Accommodation for rent to some of them.
D. Junior Research Fellows. About 10, commons provided and accommodation for renting to some of them (and families where relevant). No stipend. These Fellows to be selected from research students with about one year's research completed and to be of 1 or 2 years tenure or to the end of their research grant whichever is less.
E. Associate Fellows. About 10, partial commons provided. To be selected from Fellows of Colleges particularly associated with class B

Appendix 2 313

– the Visiting Fellows, tenure 3 years not renewable without a lapse of 3 years. These would normally include some Clare Fellows.

(2) *The Institute to be governed by a Council consisting of:-*

A. Chairman, the Master of Clare College.
B. 4 Fellows of Clare College, including the Bursar.
C. 4 Fellows of the Institute in class A.
D. 4 Associate Fellows of the Institute (in class E).
E. The Director of the Institute.

The Council to be responsible for the selection of all Fellows of the Institute, and the Director to be responsible for administration. In the first instance the Finances etc. could be looked after by the Bursar of Clare College (there would later need to be a Bursar – both Director and Bursar to be part-time appointments and be ex officio Fellows in class A). The reason for a Council of this type is that Fellows in class A will not in general be sufficiently representative of Faculties to be competent to select and nominate Fellows in other classes all of which are temporary.

(3) *Buildings Required*

In the first instance not dissimilar to those already proposed for the Grange Road site, but with more emphasis on visitors' flats and on long term expansion possibilities although for a major expansion given sufficient money a new site might be desirable. In the first instance the Fellows of the Institute might lunch in Clare Small Hall or the Parlour and have no other meals provided. Even from a long term viewpoint I am doubtful whether there should be any emphasis on communal dining, but luncheon facilities should be provided at the Institute.

15 flats to be shared amongst families and bachelors in class B, C and D Fellows, possibly also the Director should live on or near the site in a house provided.

Dining Room, Common Room, Reading Room and 10 Studies.

(4) *Finance*

A. Buildings £120,000 capital, subsequently maintained by rents on flats.
B. Commons for 50 Fellows: £3,000 p.a.

C. Salaries for Administration, Secretaries and Contingencies: £5,000 p.a.
D. Grants for Visitors and Research Fellows should be obtainable from outside sources which might well contribute also towards (B) and (C). The seeking of funds would be a major task which both the Chairman of the Council and the Director must be willing to undertake if Stage 2 of the Development is to go ahead. Stage 1 requires only finance noted in (A), (B) and (C) above which should be within the capacity of the College.

Second Stage of Development

There are two alternatives at the second stage. Either the Institute could be extended to include Research Students, or it could be expanded without change of character. Whichever course is adopted will need more financing and it would presumably depend on whether other more satisfactory arrangements had been made for Clare Research Students.

Expansion towards its maximum viable size of about 150 Fellows. This is crucially dependent on finance. If sufficient funds can be obtained:

(1) The Fellowship Categories could increase to give (A) 30 Permanent Fellows, (B) 60 Visiting Fellows, and (C) (D) 40 Research Fellows, (E) 20 Associate Fellows. This would require another £200,000 for buildings and an extension of the site.
(2) Grants-in-aid for Visitors, so that the Institute could itself invite Visitors for periods of a few months to a year, particularly from countries or places where finance is not readily available for study-leave. It would probably be quite easy to get £20,000 pa for this but one could easily use £100,000 pa. One would hope to include visitors from outside the University World.

R. J. Eden, 9th January, 1964.

Appendix 3

FELLOWS OF CLARE COLLEGE, JANUARY 1964

PRESENT AT THE MEETING ON 11 JANUARY 1964

In order of Seniority; date of (initial) election, and appointment.

Sir Eric Ashby, 1958, Master
Prof H. Godwin, 1925, Professor of Botany
Prof R. S. Hutton, 1936, Emeritus Professor of Metallurgy
Dr E. N. Willmer, 1936, Reader in Histology
Mr W. B. Reddaway, 1938, Reader and Director Department of Applied Economics

Dr A. C. Chibnall, 1943, formerly Professor of Biochemistry
Prof Sir John F. Baker, 1943, Professor of Mechanical Sciences
Prof the Revd. Canon C. F. D. Moule, 1944, Lady Margaret Professor of Divinity
Mr B. Cooper, 1944, Bursar and Financial Tutor, Lecturer in Engineering
Prof A. B. Pippard, 1947, Librarian, Plummer Professor of Physics
Mr R. J. L. Kingsford, 1949, Secretary to the Syndics Cambridge University Press 1948–63

Dr J. R. Northam, 1950, Senior Tutor, Lecturer in English
Prof J. D. Boyd, (1935) 1951, Professor of Anatomy
Dr A. H. McDonald, 1951, Lecturer in Ancient History
Dr R. G. West, 1954, Lecturer in Botany
Mr D. Forbes, (1947) 1951, Praelector, Lecturer in History
Mr C. W. Parkin, 1955, Forbes Librarian, Assistant Lecturer in History
Dr T. J. Smiley, 1955, Assistant Tutor, Lecturer in Moral Sciences
Dr K. Lipstein, 1956, Reader in Conflict of Laws
Dr C. B. Reese, 1956, Lecturer in Organic and Inorganic Chemistry
Dr R. J. Eden, (1951) 1957, Stokes Lecturer in Applied Mathematics

Dr I. S. Laurie, 1959, Assistant Tutor, Assistant Lecturer in French
Rev M. F. Wiles, 1959, Dean, Lecturer in Divinity
Dr W. W. Black, 1960, Assistant Tutor, Lecturer in Geology
Mr R. L. Fortescue, 1960, Lecturer in Engineering
Dr V. Heine, 1960, Lecturer in Physics
Dr D. Lynden-Bell, 1960, Assistant Lecturer in Applied Mathematics

Dr M. G. Bown, 1961, Lecturer in Mineralogy and Petrology
Mr C. C. Turpin, 1961, Registrar for Admissions, Lecturer in Law
Dr K. F. Riley, 1961, Demonstrator in Physics
Mr B. Hartley, 1962, Research Fellow in Mathematics
Dr R. S. Schofield, 1962, Research Fellow in History
Mr F. D. Holister, 1962, Domestic Bursar, Lecturer in Land Economy
Dr R. L. Tapp, 1962, Demonstrator in Physiology
Dr J. P. Chilton, 1963, Lecturer in Metallurgy
Mr J. H. Dickson, 1963, Research Fellow in Botany, Assistant in Quaternary Research

OTHER FELLOWS WHO WERE NOT PRESENT AT THE MEETING ON 11 JANUARY 1964

(but those marked * were present at the GB meeting on 6 March 1964 when the recommendations on Clare Hall from the *Committee of Three* were approved, some of the others were on leave)

Sir Henry Thirkill, 1910, Master 1939–58
Mr W. J. Harrison, (1907) 1913, Bursar 1926–49
Prof O. T. Jones, 1930, Emeritus Professor of Geology.
Prof R. S. Hutton, 1936, Emeritus Professor of Metallurgy

Mr J. S. L. Gilmour, 1951, Director of the Botanic Garden
Mr K. W. Wedderburn, 1952, Lecturer in Law
Dr G. Elton, 1954, Reader in Tudor Studies
Dr G. H. Wright, 1958, Assistant Tutor, Lecturer in Anatomy
*Dr A. Korner, 1960, Assistant Tutor, Lecturer in Biochemistry
*Mr P. A. Roubiczek, 1961, Assistant Lecturer in German
*Mr J. M. Newton, 1961, Assistant Lecturer in English
Dr N. M. Temperley, 1963, Assistant Lecturer in Music
*Dr C. H. Feinstein, 1963, Assistant Lecturer in Economic History

Appendix 4

THE COMMITTEE OF THREE

Eric Ashby, 1904–1992. Married to Helen, Lady Ashby.
Knight 1956, Baron 1973 (Life Peer).
Master of Clare College 1958–75.
Graduated in Botany at Imperial College, London University.
Academic appointments in London, Bristol, Sidney (Australia), Manchester.
Science Counsellor at Australian Legation, Moscow 1945–46.
Vice-Chancellor Queen's University Belfast 1950–59, Chancellor 1970–83.
Member University Grants Committee 1959–67, and member/chairman other committees.
Vice-Chancellor Cambridge University 1967–69.
Chairman Royal Commission on Environmental Pollution 1970–73.
Life Fellow of Clare College 1975.
Honorary Fellow of Clare Hall 1975.

Richard Eden, Married to Elsie Eden.
Scholar in Mathematics, Peterhouse, Cambridge, 1940–42, bye-Fellow 1949.
War service in REME, Airborne Forces, in Europe and India, 1942–46.
Smith's Prize in Mathematics 1949, bye-Fellow Peterhouse 1949, Stokes Student Pembroke 1950.
Royal Society's Smithson Research Fellow 1952–55. Senior Lecturer in Physics, Manchester 1955–57.
Cambridge University: Lecturer in Mathematics 1957–64, Reader in Theoretical Physics 1964–82, Professor of Energy Studies 1982–89, Emeritus Professor 1989.
Fellow of Clare College 1951–55, 1957–66. Fellow of Clare Hall, 1966–89, Vice-President 1987–89, Emeritus Fellow 1989, Honorary Fellow 1992.

Richard Eden (continued)
OBE 1978. Chairman Caminus Energy 1985–91. Non-executive Director Eastern Electricity 1985–92.
Member Princeton Institute for Advanced Study, 1954, 1959, 1973,1989.
Visiting appointments, various dates 1954–89, in USA, Canada, Switzerland, France, Italy, Germany.

John Northam, married to Rachel Northam.
Major scholar in Classics, Clare College 1941–42, read English 1946–48.
Charles Oldham Shakespeare Scholarship, Cambridge University 1947.
War service 1942–46 in RAF Intelligence, learnt modern Greek, served in S.E.Asia!
Fellow of Clare College 1950–72, 1987–, Assistant Tutor 1954–57, Senior Tutor 1957–66.
Cambridge University Faculty of English 1951–72.
Bristol University, Professor of Drama 1972–87. Member of Norwegian Academy 1974.
University of Baroda, India, Tagore Visiting Professor 1980.
Medal of the Order of St.Olaf, awarded 1983 by the King of Norway.
Member of newly founded Centre for Advanced Study at Norwegian Academy, Oslo 1992–94.
Visiting Fellow Clare Hall 1981, Life Member.

Appendix 5

CLARE HALL WORKING COMMITTEE, AND THE PROVISIONAL COUNCIL

CLARE HALL WORKING COMMITTEE

The committee was set up by the governing body of Clare College on 6 March 1964.
It held 10 meetings between 11 April and 22 June 1964.

Prof H. Godwin (Acting Master) was chairman of the first seven meetings.
Sir Eric Ashby (Master) was chairman of the last three meetings.
The following fellows of Clare College were members of the committee:
Mr B. Cooper
Dr R. J. Eden
Mr F. D. Holister
Mr R. J. L. Kingsford (honorary secretary)
Dr J. R. Northam
Mr W. B. Reddaway

Mr C. C. Turpin attended meetings which discussed changes in college statutes.
Dr W. W. Black, Dr K. Lipstein, Prof C. F. D. Moule attended meetings to select the initial five fellows-designate of Clare Hall.

CLARE HALL PROVISIONAL COUNCIL

The Provisional Council consisted of the Fellows of Clare College who were members of the Clare Hall Working Committee together with the first five Fellows-designate of Clare Hall, elected at a special meeting of the Governing Body on 25 June 1964.

Appendix 5

The first meeting of the Provisional Council was held on 22 July 1964. The Council remained in being until 8 February 1966, the day after Clare Hall became an Approved Foundation. On that day, 8 February, the Governing Body of Clare Hall held its first meeting.

The Provisional Council's members from Clare College were:
Sir Eric Ashby (Master of Clare College, Chairman)
Mr B. Cooper
Dr R. J. Eden[1]
Mr F. D. Holister
Mr R. J. L. Kingsford (honorary secretary)
Dr J. R. Northam
Mr W. B. Reddaway

The Council's members from the fellows-designate of Clare Hall were:
Dr T. E. Armstrong
Mr R. W. David
Dr E. P. M. Dronke
Miss M. B. Hesse (until January 1965)
Dr W. A. Taylor
Prof A. B. Pippard (President-designate, from June 1965)

[1] Also a fellow-designate of Clare Hall from November 1964, but remaining a fellow of Clare College until Clare Hall became an Approved Foundation on 7 February 1966.

Appendix 6

PRESIDENTS OF CLARE HALL

1966–73, Brian Pippard, married to Charlotte, Lady Pippard.
Knight 1975. Cavendish Professor of Physics 1971–82.
Clare College, 1938–41, Fellow 1947–66, Honorary Fellow 1973.
Research on radar, 1941–45. Stokes Student Pembroke College 1945–46.
Demonstrator, Lecturer, Reader, then Professor of Physics in the Cavendish Laboratory, 1946–71.
Visiting Professor University of Chicago 1955–56.
Fellow of Clare Hall 1973–87, Emeritus Fellow 1987, Honorary Fellow 1992.

1973–80, Robert Honeycombe, married to June, Lady Honeycombe.
Knight 1990. Goldsmiths' Professor of Metallurgy 1966–84
Graduate of the University of Melbourne, research in Australia, 1941–47.
Research Fellowships in the Cavendish Laboratory 1948–51.
Senior Lecturer then Professor of Physical Metallurgy, Sheffield University 1951–66.
Fellow of Trinity Hall 1966–73, Honorary Fellow 1975.
Fellow of Clare Hall 1980–88, Emeritus Fellow 1988.
Member of the Court of the Goldsmiths Company since 1977, Prime Warden 1986–87.
Treasurer of the Royal Society 1986–92.

1980–87, Michael Stoker, married to Veronica, Lady Stoker.
Knight 1980. Foreign Secretary of the Royal Society 1976–81.
Sidney Sussex College, Cambridge 1937–40, Honorary Fellow 1981.
St. Thomas' Hospital, 1940–42. War service in RAMC in India.
Demonstrator then lecturer in pathology, Cambridge 1947–58.
Fellow of Clare College 1948–58, Honorary Fellow 1976.
Professor of Virology, Glasgow University 1958–68.

1980–87, Michael Stoker (continued)
Director of the Imperial Cancer Research Fund Laboratories 1968–79.
Visiting Fellow of Clare Hall 1976, Fellow 1978–80, Emeritus Fellow 1987.

1987–94, Anthony Low, married to Belle, Mrs Belle Low.
Smuts Professor of the History of the British Commonwealth 1983–94.
Oxford 1944–51. Senior lecturer, Makerere, Uganda 1951–58.
Australian National University (ANU) 1959–64. University of Sussex 1964–72
Visiting Fellow Clare Hall 1971–72, Emeritus Fellow 1994.
Professor of History ANU 1973–83, Vice-Chancellor ANU, 1975–82.
Fellow of Churchill College 1983–87.

1994– , Gillian Beer, married to John Beer, Emeritus Professor of English Literature.
King Edward VII Professor of English Literature 1994– ...
Graduate of St. Anne's College, Oxford University.
Taught at University of London, then after her marriage, for a short time, at Liverpool University.
Fellow of Girton College 1965–94, Vice-Mistress 1983–87.
Cambridge Faculty of English 1966, Assistant Lecturer, Lecturer, then Reader and British Academy Research Reader.
Professor of English 1989–94.
Guest lecturer in Tel-Aviv, Harvard, M.I.T. and elsewhere.
Trustee of the British Museum. Chairman of the Booker Prize Committee 1997.

Appendix 7

CLARE HALL NUMBERS IN SELECTED YEARS

COMPOSITION OF THE COLLEGE

Average numbers	1969	1980	1990	1998
The Visitor			1	1
The President	1	1	1	1
Honorary Fellows		1	2	4
Official Fellows[a]	17	21	26	28
Research Fellows	17	21	14	21
Emeritus Fellows		7	12	13
Visiting Fellows[b]	11	21	40	43
Visiting Associates[c]	16	22	4	6
Graduate Students[d]	33	70	95	96
Total	95	164	195	213
Additional Visitors[e]		10–15	10–20	10–30
Additional Students[f]		15–25	12–25	12–25
Additional Senior Members[g]		33	105	105
Additional Graduate Members[h]	22	42	30	30

[a] Official Fellows includes Professorial and Supernumerary Fellows.

[b] The number of Visiting Fellows is an average over the year.

[c] The class of Visiting Associate was abolished in 1986, but there was a compensating increase in the total number of Visiting Fellows. At the same time all former fellows and associates were made life members of Clare Hall. The class of Visiting Associate re-emerged a year later to accommodate a small number of visitors whose research is closely associated with a fellow of Clare Hall.

[d] Graduate Students include only those who are paying fees. Those not paying fees are listed as Additional Students (see footnote below).

[e] Additional Visitors are generally former Visiting Fellows, now Life Members, in Cambridge on study leave. The numbers vary considerably during a year, usually rising to a peak of more than 25 during the summer. They form a very active part of the college community, often living in college apartments.

[f] Additional Students are those Graduate Students no longer paying fees, usually because they have completed the three years of residence in Cambridge required for a Ph.D. but have not yet submitted their dissertations.

[g] Additional Senior Members include former Fellows who are resident in Cambridge. In 1998 these included four former Official Fellows and 40 former Research Fellows, many having appointments in the University and some being Fellows of other colleges, and 61 Life Members (former Visiting Fellows) and spouses of deceased Fellows.

[h] Additional Graduate Members are former graduate students resident in the Cambridge area.

Appendix 7

VISITING FELLOWS' COUNTRIES OF ORIGIN AND AREAS OF STUDY

1965–68 The total number of visiting fellows in this period was 41.

Countries of origin
USA 18, India 5, UK 4, Australia 3, Canada 2, Czechoslovakia 2, Poland 2, Eire 1, Hungary 1, Italy 1, Japan 1, Nigeria 1.

Fields of study
physical sciences 12, social sciences 10, biosciences 7, humanities 6, engineering 6.

1996/97 The total number of visiting fellows during the year[1] to September 1997 was 86, with an average length of stay of about 7 months.

Countries of origin
USA 27, Australia 8, Japan 9, Italy 7, UK 7,
Canada 4, New Zealand 4, Poland 3, Finland 2, Mexico 2, Israel 1, Denmark 1, Eire 1, France 1, India 1, Korea 1, Namibia 1, Norway 1, South Africa 1, Sweden 1, Switzerland 1, Taiwan 1, Ukraine 1.

Fields of study
mathematics 4, physical sciences 7, history of science 2, environmental sciences 2, engineering and management 2, English literature and linguistics 15, other literature and linguistics 4, history 10, philosophy 6, classics 4, religious studies 3, music 1.
law and law history 11, economics 6, politics 4, psychology 2.
archaeology and anthropology 3.

---

[1] This total includes about 20 arriving in September, thus resident for only one month in the academic year to 30 September. The total number of visiting fellows is limited to about 40 at any one time.

GRADUATE STUDENTS:
NUMBERS AND COUNTRIES OF ORIGIN

1997–98   The number of graduate students in residence in the Michaelmas Term was 119, of whom 74 were studying for a Ph.D, and 43 were on one-year courses (M.Phil.etc.), 61 of the graduate students were male and 58 were female.

Of the total (119), 96 were fee-paying, the others being in their fourth year or more.[2]

The number of new graduate students starting in October 1997 was 45, of whom 11 were beginning a Ph.D course of 3 or more years, and 27 were on short term courses, including M.Phil., some of these 27 may later register for a Ph.D. course (possibly backdated to the start of their Cambridge research).

Regional origins (including 40 countries)
UK 27, Other European countries 33, Asia and Middle East 25, North America 15, West Indies and Central and South America 9, Australia 6, Africa 4.

Fields of study: these cover all faculties of the University.

---

[2] The 23 non-fee-paying students are those who have completed their required period of residence, for example three years for Ph.D. students, but are still working on their dissertations. About half of these students are expected to have completed during the year, thus their end-year number is likely to be about 12.

Appendix 8

THE TANNER LECTURES[1]

1978/79	*Morality, Politics and the Press.* Dr Connor Cruise O'Brien, Editor of the Observer.
1979/80	*Arms Control and Peace Research.* Raymond Aron, Professor, College de France and Ecole Pratique des Hautes Etudes, Paris.
1980/81	*The Arts as a Source of Truth.* John A. Passmore, Professor, Australian National University.
1981/82	*A Voluntary Society.* Dr Kingman Brewster, President of Yale University, and formerly US Ambassador in London.
1982/83	*Haydn and Eighteenth Century Patronage in Austria and Hungary.* H. C. Robbins Landon, Professor of Music, Cardiff University.
1983/84	*Challenges of Neo-Darwinism.* Steven Gould, palaeontologist and evolutionary biologist, Professor, Harvard University.
1984/85	*The Standard of Living.* Amartya Sen, Professor of Political Economy, Oxford University.
1985/86	*Architecture: Modernist and Post-modernist.* Aldo van Eyck, Architect, Netherlands.
1986/87	*Technology, Bureaucracy and Healing.* Dr Roger Bulger, Professor, University of Texas.

[1] Clare Hall acts as the host in Cambridge for the Tanner Lectures on Human Values which were established by the Obert. C. Tanner Trust of the University of Utah (see chapter 13).

1987/88	*The Penalty of Imprisonment* Louis Blom-Cooper, QC, London, formerly Chairman of the Howard League for Penal Reform.
1988/89	*Islam in European Thought: The Nineteenth Century and After.* Dr Albert Hourani, Oxford.
1989/90	*Interpretation and Over-interpretation: World, History, Texts.* Umberto Eco, Writer and Professor, University of Bologna.
1990/91	*Environmental Challenges of the 1990s: our responsibilities towards future generations.* Dr Gro Brundtland, Prime Minister of Norway.
1991/92	*On Doing Science in the Modern World.* Dr David Baltimore, President of Rockefeller University.
1992/93	*The Sources of Normativity.* Christine Korsgaard, Professor of Philosophy, Harvard University.
1993/94	*Problems of Christianization in Rome and the Post-Roman West.* Peter Brown, Professor of History, Princeton University.
1994/95	*The Large, the Small and the Human Mind.* Sir Roger Penrose, Professor of Mathematics, Oxford University.
1995/96	*The History of Jazz.* Gunther Schuller, Jazz historian, performer, arranger and editor.
1996/97	*Evolution of Mind and Language (Monkey communication).* Dorothy Cheney, primatologist and Professor, University of Pennsylvania.
1997/98	*The Idol of Stability.* Stephen Toulmin, Professor, University of Southern California, (formerly at Oxford University).

Appendix 9

CLARE HALL FUNDS[1]

(A) ENDOWMENT FUNDS

Endowment funds are derived from gifts that have been invested to provide income to the college. The capital in endowment funds may not be used for ordinary college expenditure. Exceptionally, the college may borrow from corporate capital for certain projects such as the construction of a college building; in such cases the loan must be repaid over a specified period of years by means of a sinking fund (indexed to inflation). The college's investment policy is to maintain or increase the real value of the income from all the endowment funds and normally to reinvest unspent income.

Corporate Capital and General Capital
The general endowment of the college is held in two funds, corporate capital and general capital. They are derived mainly from the early gifts from Clare College supplemented by reinvestment of the unspent margin that prudent Bursars aim to maintain each year, and supplemented also during the 1980s and 1990s by grants from the University's Colleges' Fund. Together, in 1996/7 these two funds provided about 60 per cent of the total endowment income of the college. The income from either of the funds can be used for any collegiate purpose.

Old Dominion Fund
The Old Dominion Foundation made an initial grant to Clare Hall to provide support for Visiting Fellows and Research Fellows. This was followed by a similar grant a few years later for general endowment of the college. These two grants are held in the same fund, which has increased in real terms and in 1996/97 it provided nearly 24 per cent of the college's endowment income.

[1] Further details about the funds may be obtained from the Bursar.

Other endowment funds have been set up with donations or legacies from members of the college. The income from them adds up to nearly 16 per cent of the total endowment income. These funds are:

Foundation Fund
This fund was established through donations from members of the college to help rising scholars either from a developing country or from an East European country. Any unspent income may be used to make smaller grants to Visiting Fellows with financial difficulties or special needs.

Whitehead Fund (fund now closed)
For grants to Visiting Fellows.

Betty Behrens Fund (fund now closed)
For a Research Fellowship relating to aspects of social/individual development.

Pippard Fund
For grants to Graduate Students.

Leslie Barnett Fund
For grants to Graduate Students.

Will Taylor Fund
For music in Clare Hall.

Ashby Fund
For music in Clare Hall.

Eden Fund
For the archives of Clare Hall.

Building Fund
This is a reserve fund held for the maintenance of college buildings and it is usual to make transfers into the fund on an annual basis. It is intended that income from the fund will provide for normal maintenance, but – for this fund only – the capital may be used for the maintenance or renovation of college buildings if an exceptional need arises. There are also reserve funds for maintenance of equipment in the kitchens and elsewhere but these are 'general' funds with the balances carried forward each year.

(B) GENERAL FUNDS

Donations to *general funds* are used as required, and they are not designed to build up capital for investment except in relation to designated capital projects, for example for new buildings. End of year balances are carried forward for later use. These funds include:

President's Fund

This fund was set up in response to regular and occasional gifts that are received from life members and from departing visiting fellows. It provides a convenient method of combining such gifts in a fund that can be used at the discretion of the President to enhance life in the College. Past uses have included grants to graduate students, purchases of books for the Library, improvements of gardens, the purchase of pictures, and grants towards communal activities.

New Buildings and Facilities Fund

This is a new fund set up in 1996 to help with new developments in the College and it will be one of the main vehicles for future fund-raising activities. Income during its first year was used to help with the extensive refurbishment of graduate housing during 1996/97. Further plans include help towards the purchase and renovation of a swimming pool adjacent to Clare Hall West Court and the construction of a tennis court. Other major developments to which fund-raising is likely to be directed include building additional accommodation in the grounds of West Court, and additional studies, either there or in the grounds of the College.

Other General Funds for Visiting Fellows and Scholars

The grant from the Ford Foundation has been described in chapter 11. It commenced in 1964 and continued until 1969, enabling Clare Hall to make grants towards the expenses of Visiting Fellows during this period. Since 1969 there have been a number of fellowships or scholarships that have been supported in part by funds received (usually for limited periods) on an annual basis. Some have been associated with particular countries or subjects and they have included Carlsberg Fellowships, Hambros Fellowships, Usher Fellowships, Wasilewski Scholarships, East European Scholarships, and Spalding Fellowships.

Appendix 10

PLANS OF CLARE HALL MAIN COLLEGE AND WEST COURT

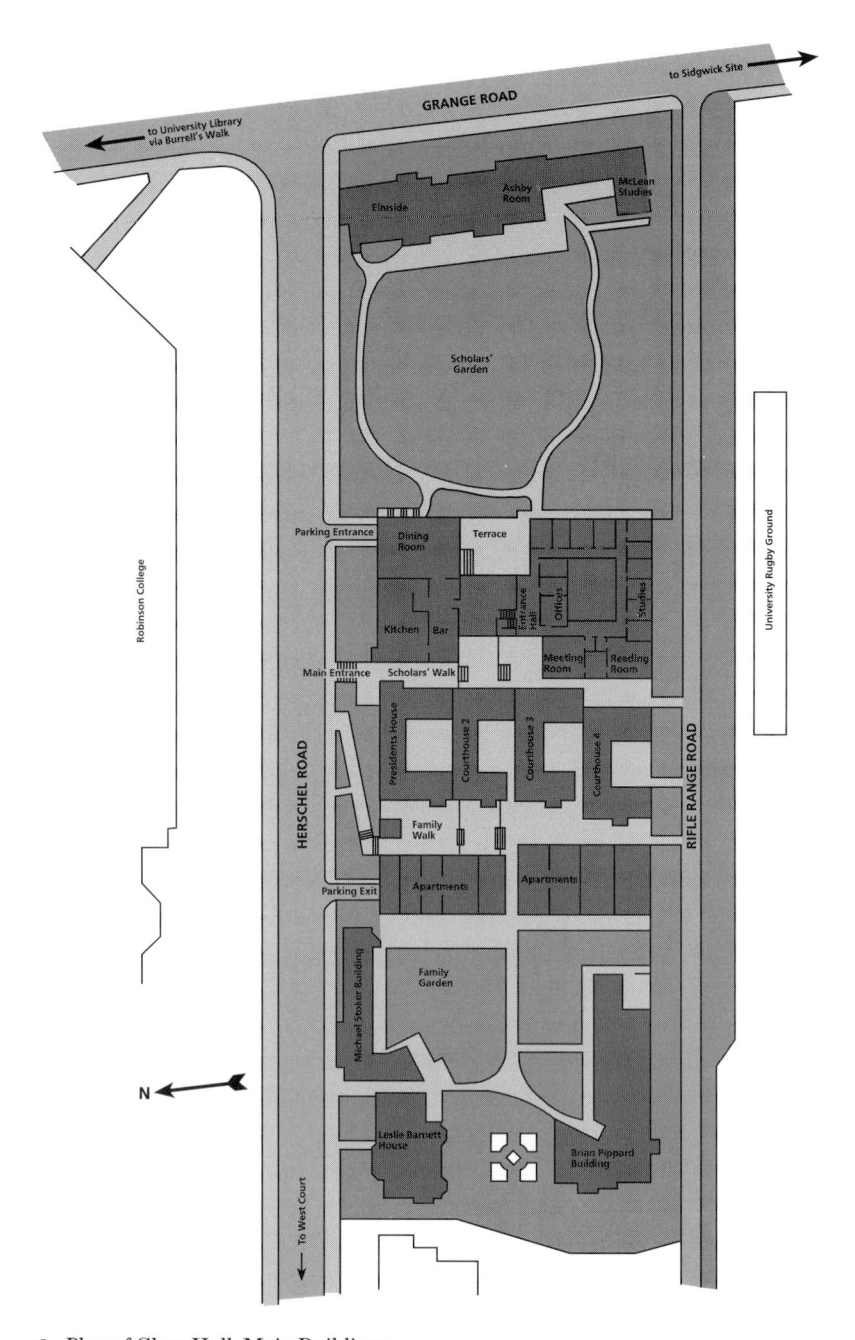

332   *Appendix 10*

48. Plan of Clare Hall, Main Buildings.

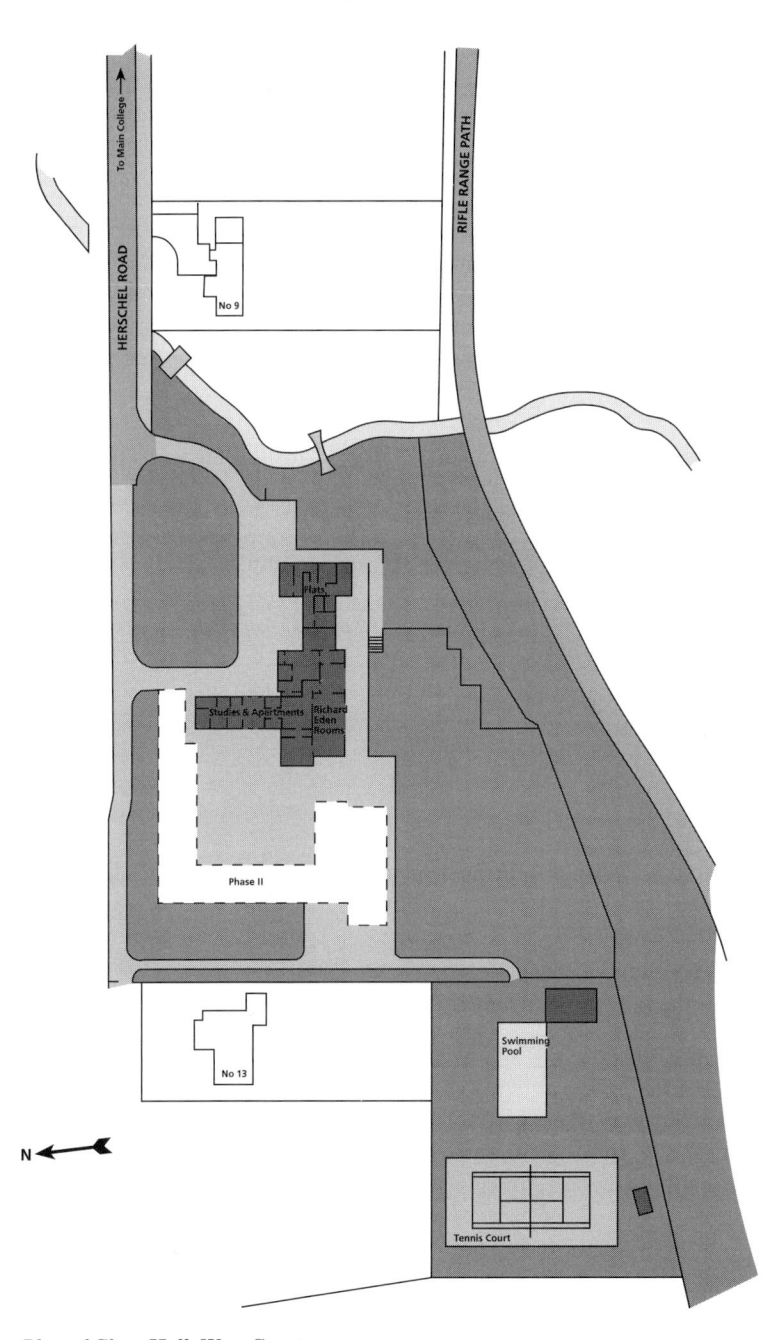

Appendix 10 333

49. Plan of Clare Hall, West Court.

BIBLIOGRAPHICAL REFERENCES

Alumni Cantabrigienses, part 2, 1752–1900, edited by J. and J. A. Venn (Cambridge 1922–1954).

Anderson, C. *Grants to Students*, Command 1051 (HMSO 1960).

Ashby, Eric, *The Founding of Clare Hall*, talk in 1976 on the tenth anniversary of the founding (Clare Hall Newsletters, 1975–76 and 1983–84, reprinted as appendix 1).

Ashby, Eric, *However did women get into Clare?* Article in the Clare Association Annual, 1986–87.

Bridges Report, *Cambridge University Reporter 1961–62*, pp. 1073–1151 (13 March 1962).

Bridges Report, responses to, *Cambridge University Reporter 1961–62*, pp. 1714–54 (memoranda and comments), and pp. 1840–54 (discussion).

Brooke, C. N. L. *A History of the University of Cambridge, vol IV, 1870–1990* (Cambridge 1993).

Brooke, C. N. L. *A History of Gonville and Caius College* (Woodbridge 1985).

Brooke, C. N. L. *The churches of medieval Cambridge*, in *History, Society and the Churches: Essays in Honour of Owen Chadwick*, ed. D.Beales & G.Best (Cambridge 1985).

Brooke, Highfield and Swaan, *Oxford and Cambridge*, pp. 55–56, (Cambridge 1988).

Cambridge Historical Register 1910 , ed. J.R.Tanner (Cambridge 1917, reprinted 1984), in full: *The Historical Register of the University of Cambridge.*

Cambridge University General Board: *Report on the Development of the University* (Cambridge University Reporter 1955–6, p. 411 et seq.).

Carey, Hugh, *Mansfield Forbes and his Cambridge* (Cambridge 1984).

Carswell, J. *Government and the Universities in Britain, 1960–1980,* (Cambridge 1985).

Chibnall, A. C. *Richard de Badew and the University of Cambridge 1315–1340,* (Cambridge 1963).

Bibliographical references

Darwin, Charles, *The Correspondence of Charles Darwin*, eds. F. Burkhardt et al. Vol.1 (1985) to Vol.10 (1997), and continuing (Cambridge).

Eden, R. J. *Proposal for a Clare Instititute for Advanced Study*, 11 Jan. 1964 (Clare College archives, reprinted as appendix 2).

Erskine, Ralph, Article on Clare Hall in *The Architects' Journal Information Library*, 19 August 1970.

Forbes, Mansfield, *Clare College 1326–1926*, 2 vols. (Cambridge 1928, 1930).

Godwin, H. *Cambridge and Clare*, (Cambridge 1985).

Grave, W. W. *Fitzwilliam College, 1869–1969* (Cambridge 1983).

Hackett, M. B. *The original statutes of Cambridge University: the text and its history* (Cambridge 1970).

Harrison, W. J. *Clare College*, in *The Victoria History of Cambridgeshire, vol.III*, ed. J. P. C. Roach, pp. 340–346 (London 1959)

Harrison, W. J. *Life in Clare Hall, Cambridge 1658–1713* (Heffers 1958).

Leader, D. R. *A History of the University of Cambridge, vol.I, The University to 1546*, (Cambridge 1988).

Leedham-Green, E. *A Concise History of the University of Cambridge* (Cambridge 1996).

Rubin, M. *Charity and Community in Medieval Cambridge* (Cambridge 1987).

Robbins, *Report of the Committee on Higher Education* (chaired by Lord Robbins), Cmnd. 2154 (HMSO 1963).

Searby, P. *History of the University of Cambridge, vol.III, 1750–1870*, (Cambridge 1997).

Tanner Lectures, *The Tanner Lectures on Human Values*, ed. S. M. McMurrin, annual from 1980, vols. 1– ... (Cambridge, and Utah University Press).

Wardale, J. R. *Clare College*, p. 202 (Robinson, London 1899).

Walker, T. A. *Peterhouse*, chapter I (Heffer 1935).

Willis R. and Clark J. W. *The Architectural history of the University of Cambridge, vol.3*, (Cambridge 1986).

Willis, R. and Clark, J. W. *The Architectural history of the University of Cambridge, vol.I*, (Cambridge 1988).

Winstanley, D. A. *The University of Cambridge in the Eighteenth Century*, (Cambridge 1958).

INDEX

Clare College or 'Clare' refers to the ancient foundation, called Clare Hall until 1856.
Clare Hall refers to the modern college founded by Clare College in 1966.
University of Cambridge Institutions are listed under Cambridge University.
Colleges in the University are listed under Cambridge Colleges, except for Clare College and Clare Hall, which have separate listings.

Abbreviations:
CLC Clare College; CLH Clare Hall;
FCLC Fellow of Clare College;
FCLH Fellow, and VFCLH Visiting Fellow, of Clare Hall.

Adams, Derek, FCLH, Bursar of Clare Hall, 242, 269
Anderson, Sir Colin, 41
Andrew Mellon Foundation, formerly Old Dominion Foundation, 147
Andreyev, Nicolay, FCLH, 228
Apter, Terri, FCLH, 288
Armstrong, Iris, CLH, 172
Armstrong, Terence, FCLH, 154, 156, 159; Royal Charter for CLH 264, 266; Senior Tutor, 230, 253; plate, 155
ASHBY, ERIC, approach to Fellows-designate of CLH, 154; Ashby Fund, 329; Ashby Lectures, 261, 276; Ashby Room, 261, 274; Bridges Syndicate, 45, 46, 79; Clare extension, 90–2; Clare extension paper "A", 114–5; CLH buildings, 207–11; CLH constitution, 101–3; CLH opening, 232; Committee of Three, 135–48; concern about bye-Fellows, 181–3; death of, 275; draft appeal, 138; election as Master of Clare, 70–2; Fellowship policies, 81; Ford Foundation, 214, 216; future of Colleges, 113–4; Herschel House tenants, 201; Honorary Fellow of Clare Hall, 248; lecture on Founding of Clare Hall, 248, 299–310; Master of Clare, 77, 90, 125, 132–3, 175–87, 295; Royal Charter celebration, 266; student village idea, 98; Vice-Chancellor, 221, 225, 295; visit to USA, 149, 201; welcome to proposal for Clare Institute 120; which fence to jump, 109–16; plates, 73, 233, 234, 258, 267
Ashby, Eric and Helen Ashby, visit to Mr and Mrs Paul Mellon, 147, 214
Ashby, Helen, 171, 248
Ashby, Michael, FCLH 251; Music in CLH 257
Atkinson, Edward, Master of Clare, 25

Bailey, Geoff, FCLH, Senior Tutor, 273–4; plate, 273
Baker, Sir John, FCLC, 132
Bannister, Jean, VFCLH, 160, 165
Barnett, Leslie Barnett House, 256
Barnett, Leslie, FCLH, Senior Tutor, 253; plate 273
Battle of Jutland, Gilbert West CLC, 30
BEER, GILLIAN, President of Clare Hall, 275, 282–94, 322; plates, 283, 290
Beer, John, Emeritus Professor of English, 282
Behrens, Betty, FCLH, 228; Betty Behrens Fund, 329
Benian's Court, 274
Berg, Paul, VFCLH, Ashby Lecturer and Nobel Lauriate, 276
Berkeley, California, 121

Index

Berry, Dr A. J., 200, 224
Bhattacharji, S., VFCLH, 219
Bishop of Ely, Hugh de Balsham, 7
Black, Bill, FCLC, Acting Senior Tutor, 90, 93, 99, 152
Blacker, Carmen, FCLH, 163; plate, 164
Bloomington, Indiana, 121
Bodmer, Walter, FCLC, 36
Booker Prize Chair, Gillian Beer, 282
Boys-Smith, Revd. J., Master of St. John's, 89; Vice-Chancellor, 89, 197
Bradfield, Dr John, Bursar of Trinity, 59; founding of Darwin College, 59
Brantingham, Paul, CLH Father Christmas, 236
Brian Pippard Building, 289–90
Bridges Syndicate, 45–59; Report discussed in Clare, 75
Brodski, Joseph, VFCLH, Nobel Lauriate, 252
Brooke, Christopher, 110, 334
Building Fund, CLH, 329
Burkhardt, Fred, VFCLH, Darwin Letters 294
Burkill, Charles, Master of Peterhouse, 123
Burkill, Greta, Society for Visiting Scholars, 123, 229
Burns' Night in CLH, 238
Buxton, David, FCLH, 227
bye-Fellowships problem, 181–7

Cambridge, Hospital of St. John, 8; medieval charters 5
CAMBRIDGE COLLEGES, Churchill, 20, 123; constitution of, 175; Corpus, 10, 59, 84; Darwin, 3, 59; Fitzwilliam, 16; foundings, 7–10; Girton, 20, 231; Gonville Hall, 10; Jesus, 11; King's, 11; Lucy Cavendish, 20; New Hall, 20; Newnham, 20; Pembroke, 10; Peterhouse, 7–9, 39, 123; Queens', 11; relation to University, 4; role of Masters, 175–6; St. Catharine's, 11; St. John's, 11, 16, 197; statutes, 175; Trinity, 11, 16; Trinity Hall, 10; University (now Wolfson), 58, 172
Cambridge Flower Club, 257
CAMBRIDGE UNIVERSITY, admissions, 2; affiliated students, 15; Approved Foundations, 186; beginnings, 5; Board of Graduate Studies, 4; Caput, 12; Cavendish Laboratory, 15, 17, 87, 120; Colleges Fund, 268; Divinity School, 197–8; Faculty numbers, 46; General Board 1955 Report, 42–5; government finance, 16–7; graduate colleges, 3, 21; graduate student admissions, 4; graduate student numbers, 54; Graduate Students, 52; honours degrees, 29; Library, 17, 89, 196, 294; post second world war 39; Regent House, 190; Registrary, 159, 189; relation to colleges, 3, 4; religious tests abolished, 15; Rouse Ball Professorships, 200; Royal Commission of 1922, 46; Royal Commissions, 14–5; Schools Quadrangle, 11; Smith's Prizes, 29, 34, 200, 317; statutes, 11; Tripos reform, 15; Women's Colleges, 20; women's status, 19
Cameron, Keith, FCLH, Bursar of Clare Hall, 220, 222, 238, 249; plate, 164
Carman, John, FCLH, 288
Carter, Will, 232
Cass, Geoffrey, 263, plate, 286
Cavendish Professor (first), Clerk Maxwell, 25
Chadwick, Prof H. M., FCLC, 33
Chandler, Claire, FCLH, 288
Chaudri, Sachin, VFCLH, 165
Chibnall, Charles, FCLC, 240
Chibnall, Marjorie, FCLH, 240, 283; Praelector, 230; plate, 273
Clare Association Annual, 233
Clare Centre for Advanced Study (proposal and discussion), 125–145; 311–14
CLARE COLLEGE, admissions policies, 74; Bridges Report discussed, 79; building at the Colony, 66; Butts Close dispute, 26; bye-Fellowships problem, 181–7; Centre for Advanced Study, 125–45; Chapel Crypt, options for use, 79; Chesterton Lane site, 78–9, 86–7, 91; Clare avenue, 75; Clare Fellows 1964, 315–6; Clare Colony, 212, 296; classes of Fellow, 179; CLH Working Committee, 149–59; Committee of Three, 135–48; election of Fellows, 76; endowment for Clare Hall, 138–40, 147; entrance examinations, 116; extension, 86–108; Extension Committee, 90, 99; extension proposals, 109–121, 143–5; Fellows' Garden, 74; Fellows on leave at CLH, 252; Fellowship Committee, 76, 80; fellowship policies, 67–9, 76, 82;

Index

Finance Committee, 62, 146, 213; finances, 212–3; financial policy, 26, 31, 60, 62; founding of Clare, 9; Governing Body, 33, 67–9, 73, 109, 125–34, 145–7, 156, 190, 197; Governing Body members, 33, 315; graduate centre proposal, 83, 84; Graduate Students, 79, 98, 126, 134; Grange Road land, 89, 200; ideas for a new society, 83–4; Institute for Advanced Study proposal, 118, 125–34, 311–4; investment policy, 60, 212; Investments Committee, 62; land, 28; management, 176; Masters, 22, 25–9, 295–7; Mastership election, 70–2; Mathematics, 29, 36, 297; Memorial Court attics, 93; name change, 10; Needs Committee 64, 78; Queen's Road site, 78; Senior Tutor, 109, 296; silver seal, *frontispiece*, 10; statutes, 10, 31, 295; student admissions, 109; student numbers, 27; students' bar, 75; Thirkill Court, 212; Trust Deed for CLH, 173–4; Trust Fund for CLH, 189; Visiting Fellows, 76, 111; women as dinner guests, 84–5, 171; women Fellows, 295; women undergraduates, 295; working lunches, 110, 135–48; plates, 13, 14, 27, 32

CLARE COLLEGE 1966-98; admission of women, 295; Ashby as Vice-Chancellor, 295; Cooper, Brian, 296; Feinstein, Charles, 296; Fermat's last theorem, 297; Forbes-Mellon Library, 297; Hepple, Bob, 297; Holister, Don, 296; Matthews, Robin, 296; Northam, John, 296; numbers of Fellows, 295; Reddaway, Brian, 296; Riley, Kenneth, 296; Smale-Adams, Brian, 296; Smiley, Timothy, 296; The Colony, 296; Wiles, Andrew, 297–8

CLARE HALL, accommodation, 200, 232, 274, 285–90; administration initially, 222; announcement of proposed founding, 158; Approved Foundation, 161, 167, 173, 187, 189–90; Architect, 150–1, 205; Ashby Lectures, 276; Associates, invention of, 228; buildings, 207–11, 256, 270, 274, 288, 290; Bursars, 218, 222, 242, 269, 286; CLH Talks, 257, 276; children, 232, (plate) 235, 238–9; choice of name, 142, 144; classes of Fellow, 195; Coat of Arms, 266–7; College Officers, 195; committees set up by statute, 195; composition and numbers, 281; concerts, 257, 278; constitution, 175–87, 190–3, 263; constitutional problems, 161; Conversation Piece (plate), 267; date of foundation, 190; development forecast, 148; development policy, 278–82, 288; dinners in Clare Master's Lodge, 160; discussion groups, 277; election of Fellows (procedures), 245; Elmside in use, 225; Emeritus Fellows, 249; endowments, 216, 268; endowment funds, 328; estimated costs, 200; Events, 238; Exhibitions, 257; Feasts, 237–8; Fellows-designate, 154–6, 160, 163–5; Fellows' numbers, 226; Finance Committee, 247; first President, 168–70; Foundation Dinner, 266; Funds, 291–2, 328–30; gifts, 278; Governing Body, 191, 224, 242; Graduate housing, 243, 247, 256, 267–72, 284–90; Graduate Members, 262; Graduate Student Body, 264; Graduate Students, 144, 148, 230, 253, 264, 281; Grants from Colleges' Fund, 268; Honorary Fellows, 248, 275; Housing Officer, 218, 276; Instructions to Architect, 203–4; Investments Committee, 287; land exchange, 197; Librarian, 276; Life Members, 262; Longair review, 278–82, 288; meals, 160, 171, 221; Memorial Fountain, 290; music, 257, 278; name Clare Hall suggested, 132; numbers, 323–5; official foundation, 190; Ordinances, 191; Other Associates, 253; planning application, 209–10; Praelectors, 230; President instead of Warden, 160, 167; President's Fund, 261; Presidents' short cvs., 321; Provisional Council, 159–173, 179, 319; Regulations, 191; relation to Clare College, 141, 163; Research Fellows, 249; Royal Charter, 193, 250, 264; Seminar Groups, 277; site plans, 332–3; sketch plans, 208; Sports, 255; Spouses of Fellows as guests, 171; Statutes, 193; Statutes & Ordinances, 250; Stipendiary Research Fellow, 250; student housing, 255–6, 270, 272, 284–8; Tanner Lectures, 247, 326; Tenth Anniversary, 248; Trust Deed for Clare Hall, 190–2; Trust Fund from Clare College, 189; Tutors, 230, 253; Visiting Associates, 253; Visiting

CLARE HALL (cont.)
  Fellows, 160, 165, 251; Visitor to the College, 194, 266; Wednesday guest nights, 237; Wine, 240; Women Fellows-designate, 160
CLARE HALL BUILDINGS, completion, 210–1; housing for graduate students, 243, 247, 256, 267–72, 284–90; opening by Ashby, 211; problems getting started, 208; requirements, 137; tender accepted, 223; West Court, 288–90; plates, 223–4, 226, 233–6, 238–9, 255, 269, 277, 289, 292–4
Clare, Lady Elizabeth of, 9–10
Clare–King's playing field, 28
Coales, John, FCLH, 163–4, 220, 228, 249; plate, 164
Coates, John, FCLH, 165
Cockroft, Sir John, Master of Churchill, 123
Code-breaking, Bletchley, 18
Cohen, Bernard, VFCLH, 160, 165
Committee of Three, 317–8; appointed, 133; buildings for CLH, 198; meetings and report, 135–48
COOPER, BRIAN, FCLC, Bursar of Clare, 37, 296; bye-Fellowships problem, 183–6; Clare Hall, 131, 149, 180, 192, 199, 223; CLC Investment Committee, 62; CLH Working Committee and Provisional Council, 149–174; Engineering in Clare, 76, 176; Extension Committee, 90, 93, 98; purchase of St. Regis, 108; Regent House discussions, 58, 79–80, 107; plate, 61
Cooper, Brian with Gerda Cooper, Cambridge Mayor and Mayoress, plate, 61
Cooper, Gerda, CLH accommodation, 218
Craafoord Prize, Nick Shackleton, 277
Cullen, M., Ford Foundation, 214

Darwin, Charles, Darwin Letters, 294
Daryl Pool, Chef-Manager, CLH, plate, 240
David, Dick, FCLH, 154; plate, 155
Dronke, Peter, FCLH, 156, 160, 240, 250; plate, 155
Dronke, Ursula, FCLH, 250
Duke of Devonshire, William Cavendish, 15, 25
Dutschke, Rudi, 254

Eastern General Hospital, 30, 196

Echlin, Patrick, FCLH, 166, 240; Praelector, 230; University Proctor, 166; plate, 164
Eden, Elsie, Cambridge Flower Club, 257; wives as guests in Clare Hall, 171; plates, 122, 289
EDEN, RICHARD, FCLC, Cambridge post-war, 38; Clare Extension, 88, 94, 107; Clare Hall buildings required, 198; Clare Hall Provisional Council, 149; Clare Institute proposal, 119, 126–8, 176, 311–14; collaborative research, 121; Committee of Three, 135–48; elected Fellow-designate of CLH, 163; forecast for growth of CLH, 148; Harwell, 116–7; Institute facilities required, 137, Institute paper no. 2, 135–8; Mathematics at Clare, 36, 70; Princeton and USA visits, 121; role in election of Ashby, 71–2; Visiting Fellowships proposed at Clare, 76–7; working lunches with Ashby and Northam, 111, 135–48; plates, 120, 122, 267
EDEN, RICHARD, FCLH, Acting President, 273–4; Eden Fund, CLH, 329; Honorary Fellow 275; Investments Committee, 287; Richard Eden Rooms, 288, (plate) 294
Elmside, 197, 224, 241
Elmside garden, 243
Elton, Geoffrey, FCLC, 90
Emeritus Fellows of Clare Hall, 249
Enclosures Act, 27
ERSKINE, RALPH, Architect for Clare Hall, 151–2, 205–11, 233, 248, 269; Honorary Fellow of CLH, 275; writing about Clare Hall, 211; plate, 206
Evans, Stanley, FCLH, 166, 223

Fawkes, Guy, 236
Feinstein, Charles, Senior Tutor of Clare, 76, 296
Forbes, Mansfield, FCLC, 28, 33
Ford Foundation, 147, 214, 216, 219
Foundation Fund, CLH, 329
Franciscans in Cambridge, 6
Francoise Mattock, Manageress Clare Hall, 232
Franklin, Simon, Senior Tutor of Clare, 296
Freedman, James, VFCLC, 251
Funds, CLH, 328

Gamelin Band Kembangkirang, plate, 277

Gardner, David, VFCLH, 259, Memorial Fountain, 290; plate, 290
Gardner, Libby, 259; Memorial Fountain, 290
Garland, J. W. VFCLH, 165
Garrod, John, FCLH, Bursar of Clare Hall, 270, 285–6
Giaever, Ivor, VFCLH, Nobel Lauriate, 252
Gillian Beer Boat, plate, 284
Glauert, Audrey, FCLH, 219–20, 223; Honorary Librarian, 276; Tanner Lectures Trust Deed, 258–9; plates, 258
GODWIN, HARRY, FCLC, 28, 42, 128; Acting Master, 73, 149; CLH Provisional Council, 149; CLH Working Committee, 202; suggests name "Clare Hall", 132; plate, 151
Goldhaber, Freddy, VFCLH, 227
Goldhaber, Maurice, VFCLH, 227
Goldhaber, Trudy, VFCLH, 227
Goldsmiths' Company, 257
Graduate College, early suggestions, 42
Graduate Students in Cambridge University, admission, 2, 4, 15; numbers, 54
Graduate Students in CLC and CLH, see under Clare College, and Clare Hall
Grange Road, 128

Hambros Fellowship, 246
Harding, Tony, FCLC, 37
Harding, Tony, FCLH, Bursar of Clare Hall, 269; Praelector, 230
Harrison, W. J., FCLC, Bursar of Clare, 29–36, 60; plate, 35
Harwell, UKAEA, 116
Heine, Volker, FCLC, 76, 121, 199, 230; Clare Extension, 86–97
Heisenberg, Werner, 22, 77
Hele, Dr, Vice-Chancellor, 42, 45
Hepple, Bob, FCLC, 297; Master of Clare, 297
Herschel House, 197, 200–2, 207
Herschel Road, 197, 199, 287; land in, 89, 101
Hesse, Mary, Fellow-designate of CLH, 156, 160, 181–2; resignation, 172
Hill, Polly, FCLH, 166, 149
Holister, Darnton, FCLC, 143, 176, 192, 290, 296; Buildings for CLH, 199, 202, 218; Clare Extension Report, 101; CLH Provisional Council, 149; plate, 151
Honeycombe, June, 244, 259

HONEYCOMBE, ROBERT, President of Clare Hall, 244–7, 257, 321; Tanner Lectures Trust, 259; plate 245
Honeycombe, Robert and June, plate, 245
Hope, Chris, FCLH, 278
Hughes, David, FCLH, music in CLH, 278
Huntley, 3 Herschel Road, 197, 200

Jakes, Pat, CLH, 237
Jarron, Edward, FCLH, Bursar of Clare Hall, 286–8; plate, 286
Jones, J. B., VFCLH, 165

Keynes, Richard, 200, 256
Keyneside (now Leslie Barnett House), 256; plate, 255
King Edward I, 9
King Henry III, 7, 9
King John, 5
Kingsford, R. J. L., FCLC, 146, 179; Secretary of Clare Hall Working Committee and Provisional Council, 149–74; plate, 151
Kirk-Greene, A. H. M., VFCLH, 77

Laurie, Ian, FCLC, 96
Lazards' Fund Management, 287
Leader, Elliott, FCLH, 166, 250
Leader, Ninon, FCLH, 219, 250
Leckhampton, 59, 84
Leslie Barnett Fund, CLH, 329
Leslie Barnett House, 256
Lewcock, Ronald, FCLH, 250
Lipstein, Kurt, FCLC, 152
Lock, Revd. John, 201
Loewe, Michael, FCLH, 228
Long, Darren Lee, CLH Review Committee, 288
Longair, Malcolm, FCLH, 227, 232; Longair Review Committee, 278–82, 288; Music in CLH, 257; Praelector, 230; Vice-President of Clare Hall, 288; plate, 279
LOW, ANTHONY, President of Clare Hall, 270–5, 321; Benian's Court, 274; Longair Review, 278; McLean Studies, 274; VFCLH, 251; plate, 271
Low, Anthony and Belle, plate, 271
Low, Belle, 270
Luff, Rosemary, FCLH, Review Committee, 288
Lukaszuk, Leshek, VFCLH, 219
Lynden-Bell, FCLC, 36

Marshall, Walter, 117
Martin, Judith, FCLH, 219, 250
Mattock, Francoise, Manageress Clare Hall, 237
Maxwell, Clerk, Cavendish Professor, 25
McCrum, Michael, Bridges Report, 59; founding of Leckhampton, 59
McDavid, Carol, CLH, Review Committee, 288
McDonald, Alec, FCLC, 76, 90
McDowell, Roderick, CLH, 264
McLean Studies, 274
Medieval Universities, 6
Megarry, Sir Robert, The Visitor to Clare Hall, 194, 266
Mellon Foundation, 219
Mellon, Andrew, Old Dominion Foundation, 214
Mellon, Paul, Benefactor, 147, 214–5; Honorary Fellow of Clare, 75; of Clare Hall, 275; plate, 215
Michael Stoker Building, 270; plate 269
Ministry of Agriculture and Fisheries, 201
Mollison, William, Master of Clare, 31–3
Monk and Dunstone, Quantity Surveyors for CLH buildings, 209
Mott, Sir Nevill, Cavendish Professor, 87
Moule, Revd. C. F. D., FCLH, 35, 76, 90, 152
Murray, Sir Keith, 40

New Buildings and Facilities Fund, CLH, 330
Nicholas Ray Associates, Architects for Brian Pippard Building, 274
Nobel Prizes, 36, 252
NORTHAM, JOHN, FCLC, 37, 76, 128–31; bye-Fellowships problem, 183–5; Clare extension paper "B", 102–5, 115; CLH Provisional Council, 149–174; Committee of Three, 135–48; intervention on extension proposal, 99–100; Senior Tutor of Clare, 109, 176, 296; plates, 99, 289
Northam, John and Rachel, 290

Ogden, Mary, 241
Old Dominion Foundation, 147, 216
Old Dominion Fund, CLH, 328
Oxford Colleges, Merton, 8
Oxford University, 5, 7

Parkin, Charles, FCLC, 90
Pat Jakes, CLH, 237

PIPPARD, BRIAN, FCLC, 22, 37, 76–7, 132; Clare extension, 87–91
PIPPARD, BRIAN, CLH, Brian Pippard Building, 290; Music in CLH, 257; Pippard family in the President's House, 211, 232; Pippard Fund, CLH, 329; President-designate of Clare Hall, 170; President of Clare Hall, 190, 192, 209, 217, 223, 230, 232, 235, 321; plates, 226, 233, 234, 267, 289, 291
Pippard, Brian and Charlotte, plates, 289, 291
Pippard, Charlotte, 170, 211, 232, 235; Society for Visiting Scholars, 229
Pool, Daryl, Chef/Manager Clare Hall, plate, 240
Popperwell, Ronald, FCLH, 246, 257; Music in Clare Hall, 166
Porter, Duncan, VFCLH, Darwin Letters, 294
President's Fund, CLH, 330
Priestley, Raymond, FCLC, 33
Princeton Institute for Advanced Study, 123, 133, 172

Quaternary Discussion Group, 277
Queen Elizabeth I, 11
Queen Elizabeth II, 193–4, 265

Rabinovitch, Roydon, VFCLH, Sculptor, 278
Rankin, Robert, FCLC, Mathematics at Clare, 36
Rattenbury, R. M. University Registrary, 187, 189
REDDAWAY, BRIAN, FCLC, 34, 71, 75–6, 290; Clare Hall, 131; CLH Working Committee and Provisional Council, 149–174; Economics in Clare, 76; Extension Committee, 90, 93, 95, 101; Fellowship Committee Report, 80; Investment Committee, 62, 296; plate, 63
Reese, Colin, FCLC, 75
Regent House, bye-Fellows not members, 181; Society for Women Members, 20, 57; University discussions, 44, 56
Reid Thompson, Ruby, Archivist and Music in Clare Hall, 278
Religious Houses in Cambridge, 5
Research Fellows in CLH, procedures for election, 250
Rhodes, Frank, VFCLH, 251

Index

Richard de Badew, 9
Richard Eden Rooms, 288; plate, 294
Riley, Kenneth, FCLC, Senior Tutor of Clare, 76, 296
Rodzinski, Witold, VFCLH, 252
Rothschild's Cambridge House (now CLH West Court), 287
Rouse Ball, W. W., Elmside, 200
Routledge, Brian, CLH College Clerk, 241
Royal Charter for Clare Hall, see under Clare Hall
Rutherford, Lord, Cavendish Professor, 15

Searle, Dr G. F. C. , 25
Sellers, W., VFCLH, 165
Shackleton, Nick, FCLH, Crafoord Prize, 277; Music in Clare Hall, 257; plate, 279
Singer, Marie, FCLH, 219
Site plans of Clare Hall, 332-3
Smale-Adams, Brian, Bursar of Clare, 296
Smiley, Timothy, FCLC, 36; Acting Master of Clare, 266; Senior Tutor, 230, 296
Smith, Diana, CLH Domestic Bursar, 286
Society for Visiting Scholars, 123, 229
Society for Women Members of the Regent House, 20, 57
St. Regis, purchase by Clare, 108, 179; extension, 296
Stenton, Michael, FCLH, 266
Stewart, Murray, FCLH, Praelector, 230
STOKER, MICHAEL, FCLC, 37; medical studies in Clare, 69
STOKER, MICHAEL, President of Clare Hall, 261-70; Michael Stoker Building, 269-70; Sir Michael Stoker Punt, 270; VFCLH, 252; plate, 262
Stoker, Michael and Veronica, plate, 262
Stoker, Veronica, 261
Stokes, Mr and Mrs, 241
Students, fees 16; numbers in University, 12, 16

Tambiah, Jeyaraj, FCLH, 125, 226, 249
Tanner Lectures, 259, 326
Tanner, Obert, Ashby Lectures founded, 276; Ashby Room, 275; Honorary Fellow of Clare Hall, 275; Tanner Lectures Trust Deed, 259; plate, 258
Tapp, Roger, FCLC, 93, 96
Taylor, Harold, FCLC, University Secretary-General, 42, University Treasurer, 36, 62
Taylor, Will, FCLH, 154, 160, 221, 249; Will Taylor Fund, 229; plate, 155
Telfer, Revd. W., FCLC, Dean of Clare, 24; plate, 35
Thackray, & Sons, Builders of Clare Hall, 210
Thirkill, Henry, Master of Clare, 22-4, 40, 42, 62, 67, 70, 73; plates 23, 35
Thomas, Trevor, 186-7, 201
Thomson, J. J., Cavendish Professor, 25
Todd, Professor Lord, 44
Turpin, Colin, FCLC, 156, 178, 186; bye-Fellowships problem, 181-6; plate, 151
Twist and Whitley, Associate Architects for Clare Hall, 206
Twist, Kenneth, 248

UK Atomic Energy Authority, 117
Undergraduates, admissions, 2
United States, academic visits, 39
University Graduate Centre, 55
University expansion, 40, 42
University Grants Committee (UGC), 40
University Hall (original name of Clare), 9
Uscinski, Barry, FCLH, 232
Usher, Tom, 256
UTO, University Teaching Officer, 42, 52, 56

Vellacott, Miss, 225
Visiting Fellows, family accommodation, 137; proposal for, 119, 123, 126

Wardale, J. R., Tutor of Clare, 33
Watson, James, CLC Nobel Lauriate, 36
Webb, William, Master of Clare, 26
Wedderburn, K. W., FCLC, Clare Extension, 86, 90; graduates in CLH, 145
Weiss, Nigel, FCLC, 250
West Cambridge, 88, 197, 200
West Court, Clare Hall, 288; plates, 292-4
West, Gilbert, Battle of Jutland, 30
West, Richard, FCLC, 30, 75
Westminster College, 272
Wheeler, John, Clare Visiting Fellow, 77
Whitehead, James, CLC, 228; Whitehead Fund, CLH, 329
Whittaker, Hugh, FCLH, Senior Tutor, 288; plate, 273
Wiles, Andrew, FCLC, Fermat's last theorem, 297-8
Will Taylor Fund, CLH, 329

Willmer, Nevill, FCLC, Clare Fellows' Garden, 74
Wilson, G. H. A., Master of Clare, 31, 34–5; University Treasurer, 34
Wilson, Meridith, Guest Scholar CLC, 147
Wolfson Foundation, gift for University Graduate Centre, 58
World War (1914–18), 16, 30

World War (1939–45), 34
Wright, Gordon, FCLC, Clare Extension, 93; Medical Studies at Clare, 69

Yeo, Avril, Bursar of Clare Hall, 242
Young, F. G., Bridges Syndicate, 45, 59; Master of Darwin College, 59